THE GUINNESS
WORLD
DATA BOOK

GUINNESS PUBLISHING

Editors: Clive Carpenter and Tina Persaud
Systems support: Kathy Milligan
Layout: Robert and Rhoda Burns
Cover Design: Amanda Ward
Artwork, maps and diagrams: Eddie Botchway, Rhoda and
Robert Burns, Peter Harper
Contributors: David Bradshaw, University of Bournemouth;
Richard Brown, University of Sussex; Dr Stephen Burman,
University of Sussex; Dr David Dyker, University of Sussex; Dr
John Pimlott, The Royal Military Academy Sandhurst; Francis
Toase, The Royal Military Academy Sandhurst; Dr John
Walton, University College of Wales Aberystwyth, Dr Andrew
Williams, University of Kent

2nd Edition
First published 1993
Reprint 10 9 8 7 6 5 4 3 2 1 0

© Guinness Publishing Ltd., 1993

Published in Great Britain by Guinness Publishing Ltd.,
33 London Road, Enfield, Middlesex

Colour origination by Bright Arts (HK) Ltd., Hong Kong
Printed and bound in Portugal by Printer Portuguesa

'Guinness' is a registered trademark of Guinness
Publishing Ltd.

British Library Cataloguing in Publication Data
The Guinness World Data Book
1. World Statistics
910.21

ISBN 085112-709-6

CONTENTS

THE PHYSICAL WORLD

THE POLITICAL WORLD

THE ECONOMIC WORLD

COUNTRIES OF THE WORLD

THE PHYSICAL WORLD

THE EARTH

Earth is the only planet in the solar system that is known to support life. Its atmosphere consists mainly of nitrogen (78%) and oxygen (21%). Over two-thirds of its surface is covered in water which has an average depth of 3900 m (12 900 ft). The land rises above the oceans to an average height of 880 m (2800 ft).

DIMENSIONS

The Earth is not a true sphere but an ellipsoid. Its equatorial diameter is 12 756·274 km (7 926·381 mi) and its polar diameter is 12 713·505 km (7 899·806 mi).

The Earth's equatorial circumference is 40 075·02 km (24 901·46 mi), and its polar meridianal circumference is 40 007·86 km (24 859·73 mi). The volume of the Earth is 1 083 207 000 000 km³ (259 875 300 000 cubic mi).

MASS AND DENSITY

The Earth, including its atmosphere, has a mass of 5·974 × 10²¹ tonnes (5 879 000 000 000 000 000 000 tons) – the average density is 5·515 times that of water.

STRUCTURE

Moving outwards from the Earth, man has been to the Moon, landed spacecraft on planets, and sent space probes to the outermost reaches of the Solar System. But in the opposite direction the story is very different. Man's direct access to the Earth's interior is limited to the depth of the deepest mine, which is less than 4 km (2.5 mi). The Russians spent most of the 1980s drilling a hole in the crust to a target depth of 15 km (9.3 mi), but in doing so they penetrated no more than the upper 0.24% of the Earth.

Unable to visit the Earth's deep interior or place instruments within it, scientists must explore in more subtle ways. One method is to measure natural phenomena – the magnetic and gravitational fields are the chief examples – at the Earth's surface and interpret the observations in terms of the planet's internal properties. A second approach is to study the Earth with non-material probes, the most important of which are the seismic waves emitted by earthquakes. As seismic waves pass through the Earth, they undergo sudden changes in direction and velocity at certain depths. These depths mark the major boundaries, or *discontinuities*, that divide the Earth into crust, mantle and core.

THE CRUST   The outermost layer of the Earth, the crust, accounts for only about 0.6% of the planet's volume. The average thickness of the *oceanic crust* is 5–9 km (3–5½ mi) and varies comparatively little throughout the world. By contrast, the *continental crust*

has the much higher average thickness of 30–40 km (18½–25 mi) and varies much more. Beneath the central valley of California, for example, the crust is only about 20 km (12½ mi) thick, but beneath parts of major mountain ranges it can exceed 80 km (50 mi).

The rocks that form the continental crust are varied, including volcanic lava flows, huge blocks of granite, and sediments laid down in shallow water when parts of the continents were inundated by the sea. Despite the diversity of materials, the average composition is roughly that of the rock granite.

The oceanic crust is much more uniform in composition and, apart from a thin covering of sediment, consists largely of the rock basalt, possibly underlain by the rock gabbro. Oxygen apart, the most common elements in the oceanic crust are again silicon and aluminium, but there is markedly more magnesium than in the upper continental crust. The composition of the lower crust, which cannot be sampled directly, is uncertain, but the predominant rock is probably gabbro.

THE MANTLE   Under the crust is the mantle, with a total diameter of 2900 km (1800 mi). It accounts for about 82% of the Earth's volume. The sharp boundary between the crust and the mantle is called the *Mohorovičić discontinuity* (or *Moho* for short) after the Yugoslav seismologist Andrija Mohorovičić who discovered it in 1909.

The mantle is in two parts. The outer rigid layer – together with the crust – forms the *lithosphere*. The inner semi-molten layer known as the *asthenosphere* is the source of volcanic *magma* (molten rock). The solid region of the mantle below the asthenosphere is called the *mesophere*. The mantle ranges in temperature from 1300 °C under the crust to 5000 °C in semi-molten parts.

The mantle is thought to consist largely of peridotite, a rock that contains high proportions of the elements iron, silicon and magnesium, in addition to oxygen. The mantle is inaccessible, but evidence of its composition comes from rocks that originated there.

THE CORE   The Earth's iron-rich core is also in two parts. The liquid *outer core* extends down to a depth of about 5155 km (3200 mi) and has a diameter of 2000 km (1242 mi). The *inner core* – which is solid – has a diameter of 1370 km (850 mi). The core extends from the base of the mantle to the Earth's centre and accounts for about 17% of the Earth's volume. The discontinuity between the mantle and core is called the *core-mantle boundary* or, sometimes, the *Gutenberg discontinuity*, after the German-American seismologist Beno Gutenberg.

The main constituent of the core is iron, although measurements of the Earth's rate of rotation show that the density must be slightly lower than that of pure iron. The core must therefore contain a small proportion (5–20%) of some lighter element.

THE CONTINENTS

The Earth's land surface comprises seven continents, each with their attendant islands. Europe, Africa and Asia, though politically distinct, physically form one land mass known as Afro-Eurasia which covers 57.2 per cent of the Earth's land mass. Central America (which includes Mexico) is often included in North America (Canada, the USA and Greenland), with South America regarded as a separate continent. Europe includes all of Russia west of the Ural Mountains. Oceania embraces Australasia (Australia and New Zealand) and the non-Asian Pacific islands. The seventh continent is Antarctica.

ASIA *Area:* 44 614 000 km^2 (17 226 000 sq mi).
Greatest extremity north to south: 6435 km (4000 mi).
Greatest extremity east to west: 7560 km (4700 mi).

Russia, which straddles the divide between Asia and Europe, does not recognize a dividing line between the two continents. However, a boundary running along the eastern foot of the Ural Mountains and following the boundary of Kazakhstan to the Caspian Sea is generally recognized internationally. The boundary between Asia and Europe in the Caucasus is disputed – some authorities recognize the crest of the Caucasus Mountains between the Caspian and Black Seas as the dividing line, while others prefer a boundary following the valley of the River Manych to the estuary of the River Don. In the East, the boundary between Asia and Oceania is also disputed. Western New Guinea – Irian Jaya – is politically part of Indonesia but is generally regarded as part of Oceania rather than part of Asia. The rest of Indonesia, the Philippines and Japan are regarded as part of Asia.

AFRICA *Area:* 30 216 000 km^2 (11 667 000 sq mi).
Greatest extremity north to south: 7080 km (4400 mi).
Greatest extremity east to west: 6035 km (3750 mi).

The boundary between Africa and Asia is usually regarded as being the Suez Canal rather than the political boundary between Egypt and Israel.

NORTH AMERICA *Area:* 24 230 000 km^2 (9 355 000 sq mi).
Greatest extremity north to south: 7885 km (5000 mi).
Greatest extremity east to west: 6035 km (3750 mi).

North America includes Central America (up to the Panama–Colombia border) as well as Greenland, and the Caribbean islands of the Greater Antilles, the Leeward and Windward Islands. Hawaii (politically part of the USA) is often included as part of North America although it is physically part of Oceania.

SOUTH AMERICA *Area:* 17 814 000 km^2 (6 878 000 sq mi).
Greatest extremity north to south: 7240 km (4500 mi).
Greatest extremity east to west: 5150 km (3200 mi).

South America includes the Caribbean islands of Trinidad and Tobago, the Venezuelan Lesser Antilles, and Aruba, Bonaire and Curaçao. The northern boundary of the continent is usually taken to be the political frontier between Panama and Colombia, rather than the Panama Canal. (Until the 20th century, what is now Panama was considered to be part of South America.)

ANTARCTICA *Area:* 14 245 000 km^2 (5 500 000 sq mi).
Greatest extremity: 4340 km (2700 km).

Antarctica includes a relatively small number of attendant islands.

EUROPE *Area*: 10 505 000 km^2 (4 056 000 sq mi).
Greatest extremity north to south: 2900 km (1800 mi).
Greatest extremity east to west: 4000 km (2500 mi).

Europe excludes Asiatic Turkey, thus dividing the city of Istanbul between two continents. (The boundary between Europe and Asia is described above – see Asia.) The islands of Madeira, the Azores and the Canary Islands – although strictly attendant islands to Africa – are almost always included in Europe.

OCEANIA *Area*: 8 503 000 km^2 (3 283 000 sq mi).
Greatest extremity* north to south: 3000 km (1870 mi).
Greatest extremity* east to west: 3700 km (2300 mi).

Oceania comprises Australia, New Zealand and the entire island of New Guinea as well as the Melanesian, Micronesian and Polynesian islands. Hawaii – although physically part of Oceania – is often included in North America because it is politically part of the USA.
* Australia.

CONTINENTAL DRIFT

There is ever-increasing evidence that the Earth's land surface once comprised a single primaeval land mass, now called Pangaea, and that this split during the Upper Cretaceous period (100 000 000 to 65 000 000 years ago) into two super-continents, the northern one called Laurasia and the southern one Gondwanaland.

Throughout almost the whole of human history, most people have imagined the continents to be fixed in their present positions and the ocean floors to be the oldest and most primitive parts of the Earth. In the space of a few years during the early 1960s, however, both of these assumptions were overthrown in an intellectual revolution. It suddenly became possible to prove that the continents are drifting across the Earth's surface, that the ocean floors are spreading, and that none of the oceanic crust is more than about 200 million years old – less than 5% of the age of the Earth (4600 million years).

The Earth's *lithosphere* – the rigid layer that comprises the crust and the uppermost mantle – is divided into 15 *plates* of various sizes. The plates 'float' on the partially molten layer – the *athenosphere* – below, and it is because they are floating that they have the freedom to move horizontally. A few of the plates (for example, the Pacific) are almost completely oceanic, but most include both oceanic and continental lithosphere. There are no completely continental plates. The plate boundaries are the most tectonically active parts of the Earth – they are where most mountain building, earthquakes and volcanoes occur.

The Continents

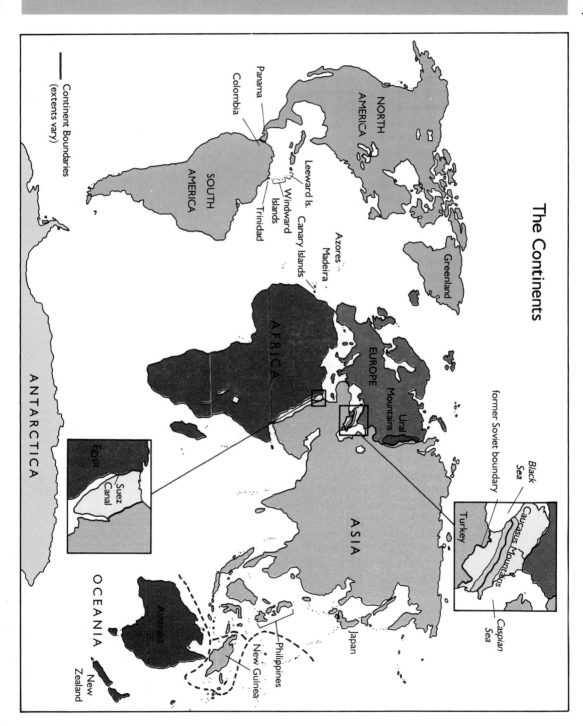

NORTH AMERICA

SOUTH AMERICA

Panama

Colombia

Leeward Is.

Windward Islands

Trinidad

Canary Islands

Azores
Madeira

Greenland

AFRICA

EUROPE

Ural Mountains

former Soviet boundary

Black Sea

Caucasus Mountains

Turkey

Caspian Sea

ASIA

ANTARCTICA

OCEANIA

Australia

New Zealand

New Guinea

Philippines

Japan

Egypt

Suez Canal

—— Continent Boundaries
(extents vary)

OCEANS AND SEAS

The oceans cover a greater area of the Earth than does the land – 71% of the Earth's surface. The three major oceans are the Pacific, Atlantic and Indian Oceans. The Pacific is the largest ocean, and covers more than a third of the surface of the Earth. The Arctic is not always regarded as an ocean. It is smaller than the other three and is covered almost entirely by ice. The International Hydrographic Bureau recognizes 20 principal seas, all smaller than the four oceans. The depth of the oceans is very small compared with their area. The deepest part of the oceans – the Mariana Trench in the Western Pacific – is only about 11 022 m (36 160 ft) deep. However this is greater than the height of the highest mountain on land, Mount Everest, which is 8863 m (29 078 ft) high.

SEAS

Principal seas	Average area (km²)	Average area (miles²)	depth (m)	depth (ft)
1. South China*	2 974 600	1 148 500	1200	4000
2. Caribbean Sea	2 753 000	1 063 000	2400	8000
3. Mediterranean Sea	2 503 000	966 750	1485	4875
4. Bering Sea	2 268 180	875 750	1400	4700
5. Gulf of Mexico	1 542 985	595 750	1500	5000
6. Sea of Okhotsk	1 527 570	589 800	840	2750
7. East China Sea	1 249 150	482 300	180	600
8. Hudson Bay	1 232 300	475 800	120	400
9. Sea of Japan	1 007 500	389 000	1370	4500
10. Andaman Sea	797 700	308 000	865	2850
11. North Sea	575 300	222 125	90	300
12. Black Sea	461 980	178 375	1100	3600
13. Red Sea	437 700	169 000	490	1610
14. Baltic Sea	422 160	163 000	55	190
15. Persian Gulf†	238 790	92 200	24	80
16. Gulf of St Lawrence	237 760	91 800	120	400
17. Gulf of California	162 000	62 530	810	2660
18. English Channel	89 900	34 700	54	177
19. Irish Sea	88 550	34 200	60	197
20. Bass Strait	75 000	28 950	70	230

* The Malayan Sea, which embraces the South China Sea and the Straits of Malacca (8 142 000 km²/3 144 000 miles²), is not now an entity accepted by the International Hydrographic Bureau. † Also referred to as the Arabian Gulf or, popularly, 'the Gulf'.

DEEP-SEA TRENCHES

Length (km)	Length (miles)	Name	Deepest point	Depth (m)	Depth (ft)
2250	1400	Mariana Trench,* W Pacific	Challenger Deep†	11 022	36 160
2575	1600	Tonga-Kermadec Trench,‡ S Pacific	Vityaz 11 (Tonga)	10 882	35 702
2250	1400	Kuril-Kamchatka Trench,* W Pacific		10 542	34 587
1325	825	Philippine Trench, W Pacific	Galathea Deep	10 497	34 439
		Idzu-Bonin Trench (sometimes included in the Japan Trench, see below)		9 810	32 196
800	500	Puerto Rico Trench, W Atlantic	Milwaukee Deep	9 220	30 249
320 +	200 +	New Hebrides Trench, S Pacific	North Trench	9 165	30 080
640	400	Solomon or New Britain Trench, S Pacific		9 140	29 988
560	350	Yap Trench,* W Pacific		8 527	27 976
1600	1000	Japan Trench,* W Pacific		8 412	27 591

* The Mariana, Kuril-Kamchatka, Yap and Japan Trenches are sometimes regarded as a single 7400 km (4600 mile) long system. † In March 1959 the USSR research ship Vityaz claimed 11 022 m (36 198 ft), using echo-sounding only. ‡ Kermadec Trench is sometimes considered to be a separate feature. Depth 10 047 m (32 974 ft).

Oceans and Seas of the World

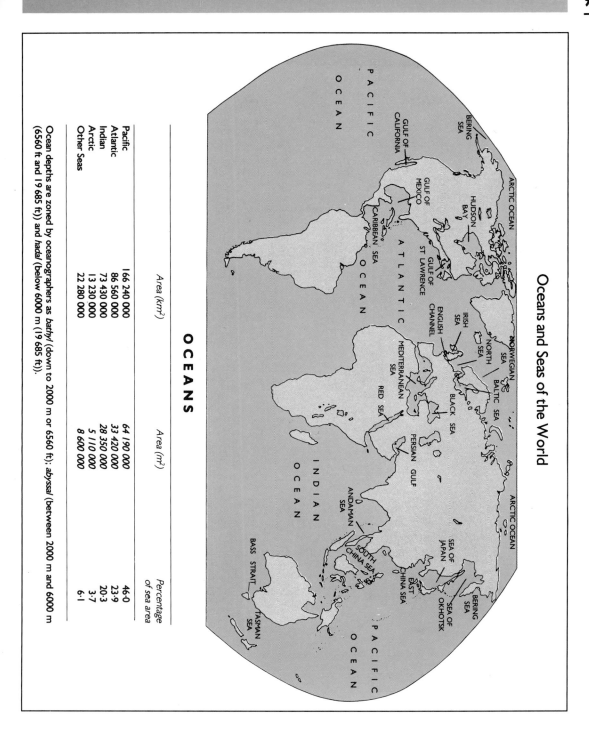

OCEANS

	Area (km²)	Area (m²)	Percentage of sea area
Pacific	166 240 000	64 190 000	46·0
Atlantic	86 560 000	33 420 000	23·9
Indian	73 430 000	28 350 000	20·3
Arctic	13 230 000	5 110 000	3·7
Other Seas	22 280 000	8 600 000	6·1

Ocean depths are zoned by oceanographers as *bathyl* (down to 2000 m or 6560 ft); *abyssal* (between 2000 m and 6000 m (6560 ft and 19 685 ft)) and *hadal* (below 6000 m (19 685 ft)).

The World's Largest Islands

1. Greenland
Area: 2 175 600 km²
(840 000 sq mi)
Location:
Arctic Ocean
Status: an internally self-governing
part of the Kingdom of Denmark.

2. New Guinea
Area: 821 030 km²
(317 000 sq mi)
Location:
western Pacific

Status: divided between
Indonesia and
Papua New Guinea

3. Borneo
Area: 744 366 km²
(287 400 sq mi)
Location:
Indian Ocean

Status: divided between
Indonesia, Malaysia
and Brunei

4. Madagascar
Area: 587 041 km²
(226 658 sq mi)
Location:
Indian Ocean
Status: republic

5. Baffin Island
Area: 476 068 km²
(183 810 sq mi)
Location:
Arctic Ocean
Status: part of Nunavut
Territory, Canada

**6. Sumatra
(Sumatera)**
Area: 473 607 km²
(182 860 sq mi)
Location:
Indian Ocean
Status: part of
Indonesia

7. Honshu
Area: 230 448 km²
(88 976 sq mi)
Location:
NW Pacific
Status: part of Japan

ISLANDS

An island is a body of land, smaller than a continent, that is completely surrounded by water. Islands occur in rivers, lakes, and the seas and oceans. They range in size from very small mud and sand islands of only a few square metres, to Greenland, which has an area of 2 175 600 km² (840 000 sq mi). (Note that Australia is normally considered to be a continent rather than an island.)

Islands, especially those in seas and oceans, have a range of origins. Islands can develop through constructional processes. They may also be formed by erosional processes that cause an area of land to become separated from the mainland. Rising sea levels can also lead to the development of islands, by drowning low-lying areas of land and separating higher areas from the main land mass.

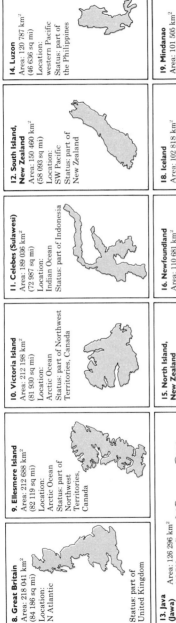

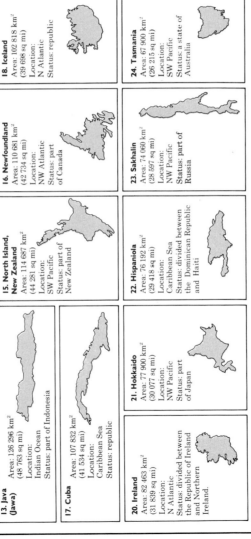

8. Great Britain
Area: 218 041 km² (84 186 sq mi)
Location: N Atlantic
Status: part of United Kingdom

9. Ellesmere Island
Area: 212 688 km² (82 119 sq mi)
Location: Arctic Ocean
Status: part of Northwest Territories, Canada

10. Victoria Island
Area: 212 198 km² (81 930 sq mi)
Location: Arctic Ocean
Status: part of Northwest Territories, Canada

11. Celebes (Sulawesi)
Area: 189 036 km² (72 987 sq mi)
Location: Indian Ocean
Status: part of Indonesia

12. South Island, New Zealand
Area: 150 460 km² (58 093 sq mi)
Location: SW Pacific
Status: part of New Zealand

13. Java (Jawa)
Area: 126 296 km² (48 763 sq mi)
Location: Indian Ocean
Status: part of Indonesia

14. Luzon
Area: 120 787 km² (46 636 sq mi)
Location: western Pacific
Status: part of the Philippines

15. North Island, New Zealand
Area: 114 687 km² (44 281 sq mi)
Location: SW Pacific
Status: part of New Zealand

16. Newfoundland
Area: 110 681 km² (42 734 sq mi)
Location: NW Atlantic
Status: part of Canada

17. Cuba
Area: 107 832 km² (41 534 sq mi)
Location: Caribbean Sea
Status: republic

18. Iceland
Area: 102 818 km² (39 698 sq mi)
Location: N Atlantic
Status: republic

19. Mindanao
Area: 101 505 km² (39 191 sq mi)
Location: western Pacific
Status: part of the Philippines

20. Ireland
Area: 82 463 km² (31 839 sq mi)
Location: N Atlantic
Status: divided between the Republic of Ireland and Northern Ireland.

21. Hokkaido
Area: 77 900 km² (30 077 sq mi)
Location: NW Pacific
Status: part of Japan

22. Hispaniola
Area: 76 192 km² (29 418 sq mi)
Location: Caribbean Sea
Status: divided between the Dominican Republic and Haiti

23. Sakhalin
Area: 74 060 km² (28 597 sq mi)
Location: NW Pacific
Status: part of Russia

24. Tasmania
Area: 67 900 km² (26 215 sq mi)
Location: SW Pacific
Status: a state of Australia

25. Sri Lanka
Area: 65 600 km² (25 332 sq mi)
Location: Indian Ocean
Status: republic

Volcanic islands When volcanic activity occurs beneath the oceans, it can lead to the growth of islands. This is often closely linked to the movement of the Earth's crustal plates, with island-building (e.g. Iceland) occurring at plate margins. Volcanic islands (e.g. Hawaii) can also form far from any plate boundary.

Island archipelagos The collision of crustal plates at margins can generate significant volcanic activity. If this occurs at the edge of a land mass it can cause mountain building, but when the collision zone lies beneath an ocean, island development can result. Islands that are born in this way do not occur singly, but in chains or archipelagos ('arcs') that parallel the plate boundary. This is well illustrated on the western side of the Pacific Ocean.

Coral islands Coral islands and reefs are an important component of warm tropical and subtropical oceans and seas. They are formed from the skeletons of the group of primitive marine organisms known as corals. Coral islands develop where coral grows up towards the ocean surface from shallow submarine platforms.

MOUNTAINS

The Earth's largest mountain ranges today – the Alps, Himalaya, Rockies and Andes – are all relatively young, resulting from plate collisions in the last 25 million years or so. Much older ranges include the Scottish Highlands, the Scandinavian mountains and the Appalachians in the USA, which are all around 300–400 million years old. The deeply eroded remnants of even older ranges – up to 3000 million years old – occur in many parts of Africa and Australia.

Folded mountains The world's largest and most complex continental mountain ranges are the result of the collision of tectonic plates. Mountains formed directly by plate collisions are known as *fold mountains*, because they are conspicuously folded, faulted and otherwise deformed by the huge collision pressures. In some cases the collision is between landmasses. Thus India is pressing into the rest of Asia to form the Himalaya, and Africa is being forced into Europe, producing the Alps.

Fault-block mountains In *fault-block mountains* a central block of the Earth's crust has sunk and the adjacent blocks have been forced upwards. Mountains of this type define the Basin and Range Province of the western USA and form the Sierra Nevada of California.

Upwarped mountains In *upwarped mountains*, on the other hand, a central block has been forced upwards. Examples are the Black Hills of Dakota and the Adirondacks of New York.

Volcanic mountains Spectacular mountains may also be built by volcanic action. Mauna Loa in Hawaii for example, is, at 10 203 m (33 476 ft), the world's highest mountain if measured from the Pacific Ocean floor, although less than half is above sea level. Intense volcanism also occurs where oceanic and continental plates collide. The Andes, for example, owe not a little of their mass to volcanic activity.

WORLD'S GREATEST MOUNTAIN RANGES

Length (km/miles)	Name	Culminating Peak	Height (m/ft)
7200 (4500)	Andes	Aconcagua (Argentina)	6960 (22 834)
4800 (3000)	Rocky Mountains	Mt Elbert (USA)	4400 (14 433)
3800 (2400)	Himalaya–Karakoram–Hindu Kush	Mt Everest (China/Nepal)	8863 (29 078)
3600 (2250)	Great Dividing Range	Kosciusko (Australia)	2230 (7316)
3500 (2200)	Trans-Antarctic Mts	Mt Vinson	5140 (16 863)
3000 (1900)	Brazilian Atlantic Coast Range	Pico de Bandeira (Brazil)	2890 (9 482)
2900 (1800)	West Sumatran–Javan Range	Kerintji (Indonesia)	3805 (12 484)
2650 (1650)*	Aleutian Range	Shishaldin (USA)	2861 (9 387)
2250 (1400)	Tien Shan	Pik Pobeda (Kyrgyzstan/China)	7439 (24 406)
2000 (1250)	Central New Guinea Range	Ngga Pulu or Jayakusumu† (Indonesia)	5030 (16 503)
2000 (1250)	Altai Mountains	Gora Belukha (Russia)	4505 (14 783)
2010 (1250)	Ural Mountains	Gora Narodnaya (Russia)	1894 (6 214)
1930 (1200)	Kamchatka Mountains**	Klyuchevskaya Sopka (Russia)	4850 (15 910)
1930 (1200)	Atlas Mountains	Jebel Toubkal (Morocco)	4165 (13 665)
1610 (1000)	Verkhoyansk Mountains	Gora Mas Khaya (Russia)	2959 (9 708)
1610 (1000)	Western Ghats	Anai Madi (India)	2694 (8 841)
1530 (950)	Sierra Madre Oriental	Citlaltépetl (Mexico)	5610 (18 405)
1530 (950)	Zagros Mountains	Zard Kuh (Iran)	4547 (14 921)
1530 (950)	Scandinavian Range	Galdhopiggen (Norway)	2469 (8 098)
1450 (900)	Ethiopian Highlands	Ras Dashen (Ethiopia)	4620 (15 158)
1450 (900)	Sierra Madre Occidental	Nevado de Colima (Mexico)	4265 (13 993)
1370 (850)	Malagasy Range	Tsaratanana (Madagascar)	2885 (9 465)
1290 (800)	Drakensberg	Thabana Ntlenyana (Lesotho)	3482 (11 425)
1290 (800)	Chersky Range	Gora Pobeda (Russia)	3147 (10 325)
1200 (750)	Caucasus	Elbrus, West Peak (Georgia/Russia)	5642 (18 510)
1130 (700)	Alaska Range	Mt McKinley, South Peak (USA)	6194 (20 320)
1130 (700)	Assam–Burma Range	Hkakabo Razi (Myanmar (Burma))	5881 (19 296)
1130 (700)	Cascade Range	Mt Rainier (USA)	4392 (14 410)
1130 (700)	Central Borneo Range	Kinabalu (Malaysia)	4101 (13 455)
1130 (700)	Apennines	Corno Grande (Italy)	2931 (9 617)
1130 (700)	Appalachians	Mt Mitchell (USA)	2037 (6 684)
1050 (650)	Alps	Mt Blanc (France)	4807 (15 771)

* Continuous mainland length (excluding islands) 720 km (*450 miles*). ** Comprises the Sredinny and Koryak Mountains. † Formerly known as Carstensz Pyramid.

Mountains and mountain ranges are largely formed by the interaction of mountain-building processes (orogeny) and the subsequent erosional processes that tend to destroy them. The distribution of the world's major mountain ranges generally follows those belts of the Earth's land-masses where earthquakes and volcanoes are common.

These phenomena are in turn caused by the collision of the moving plates that make up the Earth's lithosphere. Such collisions often result in the margin of one plate being forced upwards, and this process has resulted in the formation of many mountain ranges - although other processes may also play a part in mountain building.

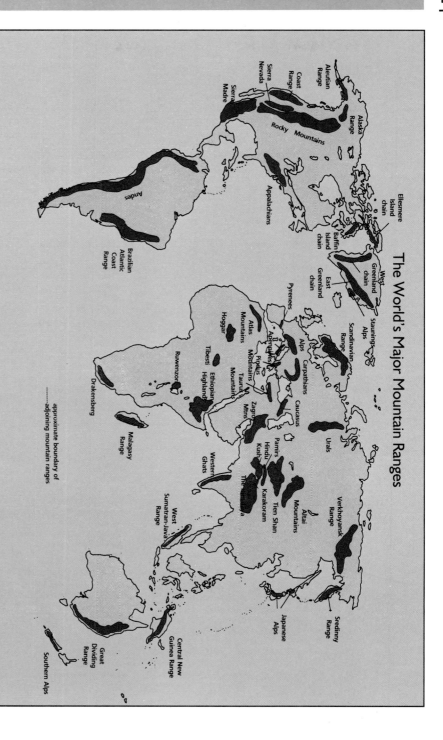

The World's Major Mountain Ranges

approximate boundary of
------- adjoining mountain ranges

WORLD'S HIGHEST MOUNTAINS

Key to Ranges: H = Himalaya K = Karakoram. Subsidiary peaks or tops in the same mountain massif are italicized.

Mountain	Height (m)	Height (ft)	Range	Date of First Ascent (if any)
1. Mount Everest	8863	29 078	H	29 May 1953
Everest South Summit	*8750*	*28 707*	*H*	*26 May 1953*
2. K2 (Chogori)	8610	28 250	K	31 July 1954
3. Kangchenjunga	8598	28 208	H	25 May 1955
Yalung Kang (Kangchenjunga West)	*8502*	*27 894*	*H*	*14 May 1973*
Kangchenjunga South Peak	*8488*	*27 848*	*H*	*19 May 1978*
Kangchenjunga Middle Peak	*8475*	*27 806*	*H*	*22 May 1978*
4. Lhotse	8511	27 923	H	18 May 1956
Subsidiary Peak	*8410*	*27 591*	*H*	*unclimbed*
Lhotse Shar	*8383*	*27 504*	*H*	*12 May 1970*
5. Makalu I	8481	27 824	H	15 May 1955
Makalu South-East	*8010*	*26 280*	*H*	*unclimbed*
6. Dhaulagiri I	8167	26 795	H	13 May 1960
7. Manaslu I (Kutang I)	8156	26 760	H	9 May 1956
8. Cho Oyu	8153	26 750	H	19 Oct 1954
9. Nanga Parbat (Diamir)	8124	26 660	H	3 July 1953
10. Annapurna I	8091	26 546	H	3 June 1950
Annapurna East	*8010*	*26 280*	*H*	*29 Apr 1974*
11. Gasherbrum I (Hidden Peak)	8068	26 470	K	5 July 1958
12. Broad Peak I	8047	26 400	K	9 June 1957
Broad Peak Middle	*8016*	*26 300*	*K*	*28 July 1975*
Broad Peak Central	*8000*	*26 246*	*K*	*28 July 1975*
13. Shisham Pangma (Gosainthan)	8046	26 398	H	2 May 1964
14. Gasherbrum II	8034	26 360	K	7 July 1956

HIGHEST MOUNTAINS IN EACH CONTINENT

AFRICA   The highest mountain in Africa is Kilimanjaro in Tanzania. Its highest summit is Uhuru Point (also called Kibo) at 5894 m (19 340 ft). The second highest African mountain is Mt Kenya (in Kenya) at 5199 m (17 058 ft).

ANTARCTICA   The highest mountain surveyed in Antarctica is Mt Vinson (in that part of Antarctica claimed by Chile). It reaches 5140 m (16 863 ft) high.

ASIA   The highest mountains in the world are in the Himalaya–Karakorum range in Asia – see above.

EUROPE   The highest mountain in Alpine Europe is Mont Blanc, whose summit in France reaches 4807 m (15 771 ft). A major subsidiary peak in the same massif, Mont Blanc de Courmayeur (on the French-Italian border), reaches 4748 m (15 577 ft). The second highest mountain in Alpine Europe, Monte Rosa (Switzerland) reaches 4634 m (15 203 ft) in its main peak, the Dufourspitze. One of the two traditional geographical boundaries of Europe (see p. 6) runs along the spine of the Caucasus Mountains, which include 15 mountains and three subsidiary peaks higher than Mont Blanc. The highest mountain in Caucasia is the West Peak of Elbrus in Karbardino-Balkaria (Russia) at 5642 m (18 510 ft).

NORTH AMERICA   The highest mountain in North and Central America is the South Peak of Mt McKinley (in Alaska, USA), which reaches 6194 m (20 320 ft). The second highest mountain in the continent is Mt Logan (in Yukon Territory, Canada), which reaches 5951 m (19 524 ft). The continent contains 10 other mountains in excess of 5000 m (16 404 ft).

OCEANIA   The highest mountain in Oceania is Ngga Pulu or Jayakusumu (formerly known as Carstensz Pyramid) in West Irian (New Guinea), Indonesia. It reaches 5030 m (16 503 ft). The continent contains six other mountains in excess of 4500 m (14 764 ft), all in New Guinea.

SOUTH AMERICA   The Andes contain 14 mountains in excess of 6500 m (21 315 ft). The highest is Aconcagua in Argentina at 6960 m (22 834 ft). Aconcagua is the highest mountain in the world outside the great ranges of Central Asia. Ojos de Salado – on the Argentine-Chilean border – is the continent's second highest mountain at 6895 m (22 588 ft).

VOLCANOES

A volcano is a mountain, often conical in shape, which has been built up above an opening in the Earth's crust during violent and spectacular events called *eruptions*. When these occur, molten rock, or *magma*, wells up from deep below ground and is thrown out through the opening, frequently with other rock debris. In the most violent volcanic eruptions, tremendous explosions inside the volcano hurl large rocks, cinders and great clouds of ash, steam and gas high into the sky from the opening, or *crater*, at the top. Streams of molten rock known as *lava*, and sometimes boiling mud, pour down the surrounding slopes destroying everything in their path.

Volcanoes are like gigantic safety valves that release the tremendous pressures that build up inside the Earth. Molten magma in the mantle is forced upward under pressure through any breaks it can find in the surface rocks. As it rises, gases dissolved in it are released by the fall in pressure, and the magma shoots out of the volcano in explosive eruptions. Volcanoes are found where the Earth's crust is weakest, especially along the edges of the crustal plates and most notably in the 'Ring of Fire' around the Pacific Ocean plate.

Although above 800 volcanoes have been recorded as active in historic times, 500 to 350 million years ago there were very violent periods of volcanic activity. Many thousands of volcanoes erupted constantly, and many mountain ranges today consist of the remains of long dead volcanoes. Even now, thousands of volcanoes may be erupting unseen beneath the oceans. Many volcanoes soar to great heights amid the Earth's major mountain ranges. The highest is Aconcagua, a snow-clad peak 6960 m (22 834 ft) high in the Andes of Argentina.

Because Aconcagua no longer erupts, it is said to be *extinct*. Other volcanoes that have been quiet for a very long time but may erupt again are described as *dormant*. Volcanoes that are known to have erupted in historic times are referred to as *active*, and these are always dangerous. The highest volcano regarded as active is Ojos del Salado, which rises to a height of 6895 m (22 588 ft) on the frontier between Chile and Argentina. The mountain has recently produced vents emitting hot gases and steam known as *fumaroles*. In modern times, scientists have been able to observe and record the dramatic birth and growth of new volcanoes. A famous example is Paricutín, in Mexico, which began as a plume of smoke in a farmer's field in 1943 and by 1952 had grown more than 430 m (1400 ft). Another appeared 20 years later, when the volcanic island of Surtsey emerged from the sea off southern Iceland amid loud explosions and billowing clouds of ash and steam. The new island now occupies 2.5 km² (1 sq mi).

MAJOR VOLCANOES

Name	Height (m)	Height (ft)	Range or location	Country	Date of last notified eruption
in Africa					
Mt Cameroun	4069	13 353	isolated mountain	Cameroon	1986
Nyiragongo	3470	11 385	Virunga	Zaïre	1982
in Antarctica					
Erebus	3795	12 450	Ross Island	Antarctica	1990
in Asia					
Klyuchevsk Volcano	4850	15 913	Khrebet Mountains	Turkmenistan	1974
Fujiyama	3776	12 388	Kanto	Japan	steams
Rindjani	3726	12 224	Lombok	Indonesia	1966
in Europe					
Pico de Teide	3716	12 192	Tenerife, Canary Is	Spain	1909
Mt Etna	3311	10 855	Sicily	Italy	1987
in North America					
Orizaba	5610	18 405	Altiplano de Mexico	Mexico	1687
Popocatépetl	5451	17 887	Altiplano de Mexico	Mexico	1920–steams
Mt Rainier	4396	14 410	Cascade Range	USA	1882
in Oceania					
Mauna Loa	4170	13 680	Hawaii	USA	1978
in South America					
Ojos del Salado	6895	22 588	Andes	Argentina/Chile	1981–steams
Llullaillaco	6723	22 057	Andes	Chile	1877
San Pedro	6199	20 325	Andes	Chile	1960

ICE

It has been estimated that over a tenth of the Earth's land surface – 15 600 000 km² (6 020 000 sq mi) – is permanently covered with ice. Ice is in fact the world's biggest reservoir of fresh water, with over three quarters of the global total contained in ice sheets, ice caps and glaciers. These range in size from the huge Antarctic and Greenland ice sheets, to the small glaciers found in high-latitude and high-altitude mountain ranges. Ice bodies develop where winter snowfall is able to accumulate and persist through the summer. Over time this snow is compressed into an ice body, and such ice bodies may grow to blanket the landscape as an *ice sheet* or *ice cap*. Alternatively, the ice body may grow to form a mass that flows down a slope – a *glacier* – often cutting a valley and eroding rock material that is eventually deposited at a lower altitude as the ice melts.

THE FORMATION OF ICE BODIES Ice bodies develop mainly through the accumulation of snow, or sometimes by the freezing of rain as it hits an ice surface. Obviously, not all the snow that falls is turned into ice – during the northern-hemisphere winter over half the world's land surface and up to one third of the surfaces of the oceans may be blanketed by snow and ice. Most of this snow and ice is only temporary, as the Sun's warmth and energy are able to melt the cover during warm winter days or as winter passes into spring and summer. In some places, however, the summer warmth is unable to melt all the snowfall of the previous winter. This may be because summer temperatures are low, or summer is very short, or because winter snowfall is very high. Where this occurs, snow lies all year round and becomes

covered by the snow of the next winter. As this process continues from year to year, the snow that is buried becomes compressed and transformed into *glacier ice*.

Latitude and altitude both determine where permanent snow can accumulate. The level that separates permanent snow cover from places where the snow melts in the summer is called the *snowline* or *firnline*. The snowline increases in altitude towards the Equator: in polar regions it lies at sea level, in Norway at 1200–1500 m (4000–5000 ft) above sea level, and in the Alps at about 2700 m (9000 ft). Permanent snow and ice can even occur in the tropics close to the equator: in East Africa, for example, the snowline lies at about 4900 m (16 000 ft), so that glaciers are found on Mount Kenya, Kilimanjaro, and the Ruwenzori Mountains.

GLACIERS AND THE LANDSCAPE Glacier ice is a very powerful erosional agent, smoothing rock surfaces and cutting deep valleys. *Fjords* (for example, along the coasts of Norway and Alaska) are U-shaped glacial valleys that become submerged by the sea after the melting of the ice that produced them. A sliding glacier erodes by *plucking* blocks of rock from its bed and by *abrading* rock surfaces, i.e. breaking off small particles and rock fragments. The rock that is eroded is transported by the ice and deposited as the glacier travels down slope and melts. Glacial deposits can form distinct landforms such as *moraines* (ridges) and *drumlins* (small hills), or they may simply be deposited as *glacial till*, a blanket of sediment covering the landscape.

ICE AGES Ice ages, more correctly called glacial periods, have been a major phenomenon of the last 2 million years. Geological evidence, however, demonstrates that glacial periods have affected the Earth periodically over 2300 million years. It is not known why the Earth's atmosphere and surface changes substantially, although it is thought that the triggers needed to cause major ice ages relate to cyclic changes in the pattern and character of the Earth's orbit around the Sun.

It is thought that there have been between 15 and 22 glacials during the last 2 million years – they become harder to determine further back in time. At its height the most recent glacial period saw Canada and Scandinavia covered by great ice sheets, ice caps centered on Highland Scotland, Snowdonia, the English Lake District and the Alps, with outlet and valley glaciers extending out over the neighbouring lowlands. Sea level was much lower than today owing to colder temperatures and the retention of large amounts of water in the ice sheets. Consequently the North Sea was dry, although it was covered by ice extending east and south from Scandinavia.

RECENT GLACIAL PERIODS The last six glacial periods (identified from ocean core evidence) have been dated as follows:

	began	*ended*
1.	72 000 years ago	10 000 years ago
2.	188 000 years ago	128 000 years ago
3.	280 000 years ago	244 000 years ago
4.	347 000 years ago	334 000 years ago
5.	475 000 years ago	421 000 years ago
6.	650 000 years ago	579 000 years ago

GLACIATED AREAS OF THE WORLD

It is estimated that 15 600 000 km² (6 020 000 miles²) or about 10·4 per cent of the world's land surface is permanently covered with ice.

	km²	miles²
South polar regions	12 588 000	5 250 000
Antarctic icesheet	*12 535 000*	*4 839 000*
other Antarctic glaciers	*53 000*	*20 500*
North polar regions	2 070 000	799 000
Greenland ice sheet	*1 726 000*	*66 640 095*
other Greenland glaciers	*76 200*	*29 400*
Canadian archipelago	*153 200*	*59 100*
Svalbard (Spitsbergen)	*58 000*	*22 400*
other Arctic islands	*55 700*	*21 500*
Asia	115 800	44 400
Alaska/Rockies	76 900	29 700
South America	26 500	10 200
Iceland	12 170	4 699
Alpine Europe	9 280	3 580
New Zealand	1015	391
Africa	12	5

DESERTS

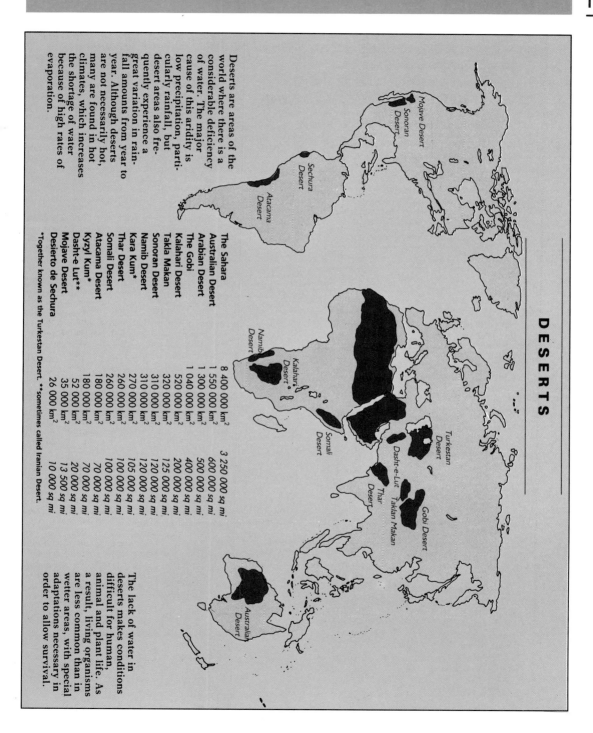

Deserts are areas of the world where there is a considerable deficiency of water. The major cause of this aridity is low precipitation, particularly rainfall, but desert areas also frequently experience a great variation in rainfall amounts from year to year. Although deserts are not necessarily hot, many are found in hot climates, which increases the shortage of water because of high rates of evaporation.

The Sahara	8 400 000 km²	3 250 000 sq mi
Australian Desert	1 550 000 km²	600 000 sq mi
Arabian Desert	1 300 000 km²	500 000 sq mi
The Gobi	1 040 000 km²	400 000 sq mi
Kalahari Desert	520 000 km²	200 000 sq mi
Takla Makan	320 000 km²	125 000 sq mi
Sonoran Desert	310 000 km²	120 000 sq mi
Namib Desert	310 000 km²	120 000 sq mi
Kara Kum*	270 000 km²	105 000 sq mi
Thar Desert	260 000 km²	100 000 sq mi
Somali Desert	260 000 km²	100 000 sq mi
Atacama Desert	180 000 km²	70 000 sq mi
Kyzyl Kum*	180 000 km²	70 000 sq mi
Dasht-e Lut**	52 000 km²	20 000 sq mi
Mojave Desert	35 000 km²	13 500 sq mi
Desierto de Sechura	26 000 km²	10 000 sq mi

*Together known as the Turkestan Desert. **sometimes called Iranian Desert.

The lack of water in deserts makes conditions difficult for human, animal and plant life. As a result, living organisms are less common than in wetter areas, with special adaptations necessary in order to allow survival.

RIVERS AND LAKES

Rivers and lakes are the most important bodies of surface water on land masses. A river is a freshwater body confined in a channel which flows down a slope into another river, a lake or the sea, or sometimes into an inland desert. Rivers may receive their water from several sources, but all of these are indirectly or directly related to *precipitation* – a collective term for the fall of moisture onto the Earth's surface from the atmosphere. Rain falling on the ground may immediately run down slopes as *overland flow*, becoming concentrated and eventually forming a stream. This tends to occur when the ground surface is *impermeable* (i.e. water cannot pass through it). It may also occur when the ground is saturated with water, or when rainfall is very heavy.

Often, however, rivers receive their water from *springs*. This is because rainfall will commonly soak into the ground, to accumulate in the soil or to pass into permeable and porous rocks as *groundwater*. In *permeable* rock, water can pass right through the rock itself, whereas in *porous* rock there are holes and fissures through which water can pass. Springs occur where the top of the aquifer – a layer of rock containing water – intersects with the ground surface. Groundwater is important as a source for rivers in that it can supply water even when precipitation is not occurring, thereby maintaining river flow. A third source of water for rivers is the melting of snow or ice. This is particularly important in high-latitude and mountainous areas.

Rivers occur in all the world's major environments, even in polar areas and deserts. In temperate areas, such as Western Europe, northeastern USA and New Zealand, and in the wet tropics, enough precipitation tends to fall, fairly evenly throughout the year, to replenish groundwater constantly and therefore to allow rivers to flow all year round. These *perennial rivers* do, however, experience seasonal and day-to-day variations in the volume of water they carry (the *flow regime*), owing to seasonal fluctuations and additional inputs from individual storms. Some rivers may only flow seasonally, particularly in environments with Mediterranean-type climates, which have a very distinct wet, winter season and a dry summer. Rivers in glaciated areas may also have very seasonal flow regimes. *Glacial meltwater streams*, which receive their water directly from glaciers, usually only flow during the few months in the summer when the ice melts. In dry desert climates, rivers may not flow for years on end, because of the infrequency of desert storms, and then only for a few days, or even hours. However, when storms do occur these *ephemeral rivers* may flow at great rates, because desert rainfall is often very heavy.

Only some very short rivers are able to flow from a source to the sea without either being joined by others or becoming a *tributary* of a large river. Most rivers therefore form part of a *drainage network*, occupying a *drainage basin*. In fact, the whole of the Earth's land surface can be divided up into drainage basins, and these basins are separated by areas of relatively high ground called *watersheds*. Some drainage basins occupy only a few square kilometres, but others are enormous – the largest, the Amazon Basin, covers over 7 million sq km (2.7 million sq mi).

MAJOR WATERFALLS BY HEIGHT

Name	Total Drop (m)	Total Drop (ft)	River	Location
Angel (highest fall – 2648 ft/807 m)	979	3212	Carrao, tributary of Caroni	Venezuela
Tugela (5 falls) (highest fall – 410 m/1350 ft)	947	3110	Tugela	Natal, S. Africa
Utigård (highest fall – 600 m/1970 ft)	800	2625	Jostedal Glacier	Nesdale, Norway
Mongefossen	774	2540	Monge	Mongebekk, Norway
Yosemite (Upper Yosemite – 435 m/1430 ft; Cascades in middle section – 205 m/675 ft; Lower Yosemite – 97 m/320 ft)	739	2425	Yosemite Creek, tributary of Merced	Yosemite Valley, Yosemite National Park, Cal., USA
Østre Mardøla Foss (highest fall – 296 m/974 ft)	656	2154	Mardals	Eikisdal, W. Norway
Tyssestrengane (highest fall – 289 m/948 ft)	646	2120	Tysso	Hardanger, Norway
Kukenaam (or Cuquenán)	610	2000	Arabopó, tributary of Caroni	Venezuela
Sutherland (highest fall – 248 m/815 ft)	580	1904	Arthur	nr. Milford Sound, Otago, S. Island, New Zealand

The World's Largest Lakes

1. Caspian Sea
(Russia, Kazakhstan,
Turkmenistan, Azerbaijan
and Iran)
Area: 371 800 km²
(143 550 sq mi)
Length: 1225 km
(760 mi)

2. Superior
(Canada and USA)
Area: 82 350 km²
(31 800 sq mi)
Length: 560 km
(350 mi)

3. Victoria Nyanza
(Uganda, Tanzania
and Kenya)
Area: 69 500 km²
(26 828 sq mi)
Length: 360 km
(225 mi)

4. Huron
(Canada and USA)
Area: 59 600 km²
(23 010 sq mi)
Length: 330 km
(206 mi)

5. Michigan
(USA)
Area: 58 000 km²
(22 400 sq mi)
Length: 494 km
(307 mi)

6. Aral Sea
(Aral'skoye More)
(Uzbekistan and Kazakhstan)
Area: 40 000 km²
(15 444 sq mi)
Length: 350 km
(217 mi)

7. Tanganyika
(Zaire, Tanzania,
Malawi and
Mozambique)
Area: 32 900 km²
(12 700 sq mi)
Length: 725 km
(450 km)

8. Great Bear
(Canada)
Area: 31 800 km²
(12 275 sq mi)
Length: 373 km
(232 mi)

9. Baikal
(Ozero Baykal)
(Russia)
Area: 30 500 km²
(11 780 sq mi)
Length: 620 km
(385 mi)

10. Malawi
(Malawi, Tanzania
and Mozambique)
Area: 29 600 km²
(11 430 sq mi)
Length: 580 km
(360 mi)

11. Great Slave
(Canada)
Area: 28 500 km²
(10 980 sq mi)
Length: 480 km
(298 mi)

12. Erie
(Canada and USA)
Area: 25 700 km²
(9 900 sq mi)
Length: 387 km
(241 mi)

13. Winnipeg
(Canada)
Area: 24 500 km²
(9464 sq mi)
Length: 428 km
(266 mi)

14. Ontario
(Canada and USA)
Area: 19 500 km²
(7520 sq mi)
Length: 310 km
(193 mi)

15. Ladoga
(Ozero Ladozhskoye)
(Russia)
Area: 17 700 km²
(6835 sq mi)
Length: 193 km
(120 mi)

16. Balkhash
(Kazakhstan)
Area: 17 400 km²
(6720 sq mi)
Length: 482 km
(300 sq mi)

17. Onega
(Ozero Onezhskoye)
(Russia)
Area: 9600 km²
(3710 sq mi)
Length: 233 m
(145 ft)

18. Titicaca
(Lago Titicaca)
Bolivia and Peru)
Area: 8300 km²
(3200 sq mi)
Length: 209 km
(130 mi)

19. Nicaragua
(Lago Nicaragua)
(Nicaragua)
Area: 8270 km²
(3190 sq mi)
Length: 160 km
(100 mi)

20. Athabasca
(Canada)
Area: 8100 km²
(3120 sq mi)
Length: 334 km
(208 mi)

Chad (Lac Tchad)
(Nigeria, Chad, and
Cameroon)
Area: varies
from 10 000 km²
to 26 000 km²
(4 000 and 10 000 sq mi)

Eyre
maximum extent
(Australia)
Area: varies from
0 km² and 8800 km²
(3430 sq mi)

A lake is an inland body of water occupying a depression in the Earth's surface. Usually, lakes receive water from rivers, but sometimes only directly from springs. Lakes normally lose water into an outlet or river, but some, called *closed lakes*, have no outlet and lose water only by evaporation – for example, Lake Eyre in Australia and Great Salt Lake in Utah, USA. Lakes can occur along the course of a river, where it flows into a depression. Such depressions can be *erosional*, formed by glaciers or wind, or *depositional*, formed, for example, by a landslide blocking the course of a river. Lakes may also be *structural*, formed by earth movements, for example, in rift valleys.

WORLD'S GREATEST RIVERS

Length (km)	(miles)	Name of Watercourse	Source	Basin Area (km²)	(miles²)	Mean Discharge Rate (m³/s)	(ft³/s)
1 6670	4145	Nile (Bahr-el-Nil)–White Nile (Bahr el Jabel)–Albert Nile–Victoria Nile–Victoria Nyanza–Kagera–Luvironza	Burundi: Luvironza branch of the Kagera, a feeder of the Victoria Nyanza	3 350 000	1 293 000	3120	110 000
2 6448	4007	Amazon (Amazonas)	Peru: Lago Villafro, head of the Apurimac branch of the Ucayali, which joins the Marañon forming the Amazon	7 050 000	2 722 000	180 000	6 350 000
3 6300	3915	Yangtze (Chang Jiang)	Western China, Kunlun Shan Mts (as Tuotuo and Tongtian)	1 960 000	756 000	21 800	770 000
4 6020	3741	Mississippi–Missouri–Jefferson–Beaverhead–Red	Beaverhead County, southern Montana, USA	3 224 000	1 245 000	18 400	650 000
5 5540	3442	Yenisey–Angara–Selenga	Mongolia: Ideriin branch of Selenga (Selenge)	2 580 000	996 000	19 000	670 000
6 5464	3395	Huang He (Yellow River)	China: W of Bayan, Qinghai Province	979 000	378 000	2 800 to 22 650	100 000 to 800 000
7 5409	3361	Ob'–Irtysh	Mongolia: as Kara (Black) Irtysh	2 978 000	1 150 000	15 600	550 000
8 4880	3032	Rió de la Plata–Paraná	Brazil: as Paranáiba. Flows	4 145 000	1 600 000	27 500	970 000
9 4700	2920	Zaïre (Congo)	Zambia–Zaïre border, as Lualaba	3 400 000	1 314 000	41 000	1 450 000
10 4400	2734	Lena–Kirenga	Russia: hinterland of W central shores of Ozero Baykal as Kirenga	2 490 000	960 000	16 300	575 000
11 4350	2702	Mekong (Me Nam Kong)	Central Tibet (as Lants'ang), slopes of Dza-Nag-Lung-Mong	987 000	381 000	11 000	388 000
12 4345	2700	'Amur–Argun' (Heilongjiang)	Northern China in Khingan Ranges (as 'Argun')	2 038 000	787 000	12 400	438 000
13 4241	2635	Mackenzie–Peace	Tatlatui Lake, Skeena Mts, Rockies, British Columbia, Canada (as River Finlay)	1 841 000	711 000	11 300	400 000
14 4184	2600	Niger	Guinea: Loma Mts near Sierra Leone border	1 890 000	730 000	11 750	415 000
15 3750	2330	Murray–Darling	Queensland, Australia: as the Condamine, a tributary of the Culgoa, a tributary the Balonne-Darling	1 059 000	408 000	400	14 000

The World's Longest Rivers and their Basins

——— approximate boundary of adjoining river basins

The following rivers are also over 3100 km long:

Zambezi 3540 km (2300 mi). Flows from northwest Zambia into Angola, back into Zambia, and forms the boundary between Zambia and Zimbabwe before crossing Mozambique to the Indian Ocean.

Volga 3530 km (2193 mi). Flows from the Valdai Hills near Moscow, south and east to the Caspian Sea.

Madeira-Mamoré-Grande 3380 km (2100 mi). Rises as the Beni in Bolivia and flows north and east to join the Amazon in Brazil.

Jurua 3283 km (2040 mi). Rises in Peru and flows east and north to join the Amazon.

Purus 3211 km (1995 mi). Rises in Peru as the Alto Purus and flows north and east to join the Amazon.

Yukon-Teslin 3185 km (1979 mi). Rises in northwest British Columbia as the Teslin and flows north through the Yukon and Alaska to the Bering Sea.

St Lawrence 3130 km (1945 mi). Rises as the St Louis River, Minnesota (USA) and flows east through the Great Lakes to the North Atlantic.

CLIMATOLOGY

VEGETATION ZONES

Climate is a major factor in determining the type and number of plants (and to a lesser extent animals) that can live in an area. Three main terrestrial ecosystems can be recognized: deserts, grasslands and forests. Precipitation is the element that determines which vegetation type will occur in an area. If the annual precipitation is less than 250 mm (10 in) then deserts usually occur. Grasslands can be found when precipitation is between 250 and 750 mm (10 and 30 in) per annum, while areas that receive more than 750 mm (30 in) rainfall a year are usually covered by forests.

The average temperature and the nature of the seasons in a region are important in that they can determine the type of desert, grassland or forest. Wherever the monthly average temperature exceeds 21 °C (70 °F) then hot deserts, savannah grasslands or tropical forests occur.

In the middle latitudes, the winter temperatures are low enough (one month or more below 5 °C/41 °F) to cause vegetation to become dormant. In autumn, growth stops, leaves are often shed and the plant survives the unfavourable winter months in a resting or dormant phase. In spring, when temperatures rise, new growth begins. In high latitudes, the winter conditions are such that between four and six months are dark and average temperature falls well below 0 °C (32 °F). The evergreen conifers can survive these conditions but growth is very slow and confined to the short, cool summers. In the highest latitudes, trees disappear and only small low-growing plants can survive the low temperatures.

CLIMATIC ZONES

Climate is merely average weather, and climatic patterns are complicated but logical results of meteorological and geographical factors. Temperature roughly follows the bands of latitude, warm near the Equator, cold in Polar regions, and often modified because of cloud cover created by the physical processes of the atmosphere. Low pressure generally breeds clouds and precipitation; high pressure areas have little or no cloud. There are four major pressure belts around the world.

Tropical low pressure, an area between 10° N and S of the Equator, where there is frequent and regular rain mainly from convection clouds. The large equatorial forests lie within this band.

Subtropical high pressure, an area approximately 10–40° N and S, where there is little cloud or rain. High pressure extends across to the interior of continents in middle latitudes during the winter, but retreats into smaller cells over the relatively cold oceans during summer. The major hot deserts of the world lie within this subtropical belt.

Mid-latitude low pressure, an area of mainly low pressure in the mid latitudes 40–70° N or S, where there

is frequent but irregular rain from depressions and convection clouds, interspersed with occasional spells of high pressure. The interiors of continents in this zone are very cold in winter (when there is high pressure) but hot in summer with some rain (low pressure). Regions bordering the oceans have a more equable climate, with much less fluctuation in temperature.

Polar high pressure, belts of mainly high pressure between the poles and 70° N and S, because the air is too cold to contain much water vapour.

The middle latitudes are called *temperate*, having cool summers and mild winters in maritime climates, and hot summers with cold winters in continental climates. There is very little change in temperature in equatorial regions because of season, but a great difference between winter and summer temperatures in polar regions.

The climatological statistics given in the table opposite enable you to confirm the differences in climate due to physical factors of geography and topography.

Rainfall increases when air is forced over high ground. Compare the precipitation figures of Bergen – which lies in the path of westerly moist air masses – and Stockholm in the rain shadow to the east of the Scandinavian Mountains.

Rainfall increases with proximity to the most frequent paths of depressions (areas of low pressure). Compare the precipitation totals of Dublin, often close to depression centres, with those of London which is usually more remote from centres of low pressure.

Rainfall is often markedly seasonal, when monsoon winds blow off cool sea on to warm land in summer, as at Darwin, Australia. Monsoon rain is particularly heavy over India and Pakistan when accentuated by the summer low pressure area over the Thar desert. Rainfall may also be seasonal because of the shift of the subtropical high-pressure belt. Beijing (Peking), China, for instance, has little rain in winter, but plenty in summer; Madrid, Spain, has little rain in summer, but experiences appreciably more in winter.

CLIMATIC EXTREMES

Hottest place On an annual mean basis with readings taken from 1960 to 1966, the temperature at Dallol, in Ethiopia, was 34 °C (94 °F).

Coldest place Polus Nedostupnosti (Pole of Cold), Antarctica, (78 °S, 96 °E), is the coldest place in the world, with an extrapolated annual mean temerprature of – 58 °C (– 72 °F).

Driest place The annual mean rainfall on the Pacific coast of Chile between Arica and Antofagasta is less than 0.1 mm (0.004 in).

Wettest place By average annual rainfall, the wettest place in the world is Mawsynram, in Meghalaya State, India, with 11 873 mm (468 in) per annum.

Windiest place The windiest place in the world is Commonwealth Bay, George V Coast, Antarctica, where gales reach 320 km/h (200 mph).

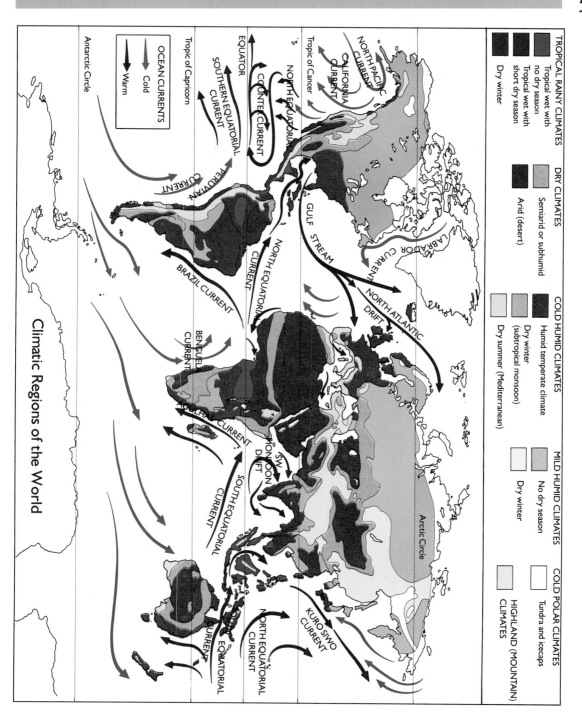

Climatic Regions of the World

OCEAN CURRENTS

Warm
Cold

TROPICAL RAINY CLIMATES

Tropical wet with no dry season
Tropical wet with short dry season
Dry winter

DRY CLIMATES

Semiarid or subhumid
Arid (desert)

COLD HUMID CLIMATES

Humid temperate climate
Dry winter (subtropical monsoon)
Dry summer (Mediterranean)

MILD HUMID CLIMATES

No dry season
Dry winter

COLD POLAR CLIMATES

Tundra and icecaps

HIGHLAND (MOUNTAIN) CLIMATES

Antarctic Circle
Tropic of Capricorn
EQUATOR
Tropic of Cancer
Arctic Circle

NORTH PACIFIC CURRENT
CALIFORNIA CURRENT
NORTH EQUATORIAL CURRENT
COUNTER CURRENT
SOUTHERN EQUATORIAL CURRENT
PERUVIAN CURRENT
BRAZIL CURRENT
NORTH EQUATORIAL CURRENT
GULF STREAM
NORTH ATLANTIC DRIFT
LABRADOR CURRENT
BENGUELA CURRENT
AGULHAS CURRENT
SW MONSOON DRIFT
SOUTH EQUATORIAL CURRENT
EQUATORIAL CURRENT
NORTH EQUATORIAL CURRENT
KURO-SIWO CURRENT

AVERAGE RAINFALL IN SELECTED CITIES
(to the nearest 5 mm)

	J	F	M	A	M	J	J	A	S	O	N	D
Adelaide, Australia	20	20	25	45	70	80	70	65	50	45	30	25
Athens, Greece	45	35	40	25	15	5	5	5	15	15	55	65
Beijing, China	5	5	5	15	30	75	250	125	60	10	10	5
Bergen, Norway	190	145	140	110	100	115	140	180	235	245	205	195
Berlin, Germany	30	30	40	40	60	70	80	70	50	40	40	40
Bombay, India	5	0	5	5	15	520	710	440	300	90	20	0
Budapest, Hungary	40	40	35	45	60	75	60	55	40	40	65	50
Caracas, Venezuela	25	10	15	40	70	100	110	110	105	100	85	45
Casablanca, Morocco	65	55	55	40	20	5	0	0	5	40	60	85
Dakar, Senegal	0	0	0	0	0	15	90	250	160	50	5	5
Darwin, Australia	385	310	250	95	15	5	<5	5	15	50	120	240
Douala, Cameroon	20	65	145	180	205	150	55	75	200	300	125	120
Jeddah, Saudi Arabia	30	0	0	0	0	0	0	0	0	0	40	10
London, UK	40	30	40	40	45	50	40	50	55	45	55	50
Manaos, Brazil	235	230	245	215	180	90	55	35	50	105	140	195
Manila, Philippines	20	10	20	35	115	235	440	405	365	170	130	80
Montreal, Canada	25	15	35	65	65	80	90	90	90	75	60	35
Moscow, Russia	40	35	30	50	55	75	75	75	50	70	45	40
Nairobi, Kenya	50	110	75	210	130	50	20	25	25	50	150	90
New York, USA	85	80	105	90	90	85	95	130	100	8	90	85
Rome, Italy	80	75	75	50	35	20	5	35	75	85	125	110
Tehran, Iran	40	25	30	25	15	0	5	0	0	5	25	25
Yakutsk, Russia	30	5	10	15	30	55	45	65	40	35	15	5

AVERAGE TEMPERATURES IN SELECTED CITIES (°C)

	J	F	M	A	M	J	J	A	S	O	N	D
Adelaide, Australia	23	23	21	18	14	12	11	12	14	17	19	22
Athens, Greece	9	10	12	15	20	25	27	26	23	18	14	11
Beijing (Peking), China	−5	−4	4	15	27	31	31	30	26	20	10	−5
Bergen, Norway	1	1	3	6	10	13	14	14	12	9	4	2
Berlin, Germany	−1	1	4	8	13	17	18	17	14	8	4	1
Bombay, India	24	25	27	28	31	29	28	28	27	28	27	26
Budapest, Hungary	−1	2	6	12	16	20	21	21	17	11	6	2
Caracas, Venezuela	18	18	19	20	21	21	20	20	21	20	19	18
Casablanca, Morocco	12	13	15	16	18	20	22	23	22	19	16	13
Dakar, Senegal	21	20	21	22	23	26	27	27	27	27	26	23
Darwin, Australia	28	28	29	29	28	26	25	26	28	29	30	29
Douala, Cameroon	24	25	24	24	24	23	22	22	23	23	22	24
Jeddah, Saudi Arabia	23	25	27	29	30	32	33	31	30	28	27	25
London, UK	5	6	7	10	13	16	18	18	16	13	9	6
Manaos, Brazil	27	27	27	27	27	27	27	28	28	28	28	26
Manila, Philippines	25	26	27	28	28	28	27	27	27	27	26	25
Montreal, Canada	−10	−9	−3	6	13	18	21	20	15	9	2	−7
Moscow, Russia	−9	−9	−4	4	12	17	18	17	11	4	−3	−8
Nairobi, Kenya	18	18	19	18	17	16	15	16	17	19	18	17
New York, USA	0	0	5	11	16	22	25	24	20	15	8	2
Rome, Italy	8	9	11	14	17	22	24	24	21	17	13	9
Tehran, Iran	4	4	8	15	20	27	29	28	25	18	10	7
Yakutsk, Russia	−43	−37	−23	−9	5	15	19	16	6	−9	−29	−41

THE POLITICAL WORLD

THE UNITED NATIONS

'A general international organization . . . for the maintenance of international peace and security' was encapsulated in Clause 4 of the proposals of the Four-Nation Conference of Foreign Ministers signed in Moscow on 30 October 1943 by Anthony Eden, (for the UK), Cordell Hull (USA), Vyacheslav Skryabin Molotov (USSR) and Foo Ping-sheung (China).

Proposals to found such an organization were agreed between the four powers at Dumbarton Oaks, Washington DC, USA between 21 August and 7 October 1944. On the final day of the United Nations Conference at San Francisco (beginning on 25 April 1945) delegates of the 50 participating countries signed the United Nations Charter, which came into force on 24 October 1945. The first United Nations General Assembly had 51 members – the 50 original signatories plus Poland, which signed the Charter on 15 October 1945.

There are 181 members of the United Nations. The following sovereign states are not members of the UN:

Andorra, China (Republic of – Taiwan), Kiribati, Monaco, Nauru, Switzerland, Tonga, Tuvalu, and the Vatican City (the Holy See). However, Switzerland and the Vatican City have observer status at the UN, with the right to be present at sessions of the General Assembly but without the privilege of being able to participate.

MEMBERS OF THE UNITED NATIONS

Original members: (October 1945)
Argentina, Australia, Belgium, Bolivia, Brazil, Belarus[1], Canada, Chile, China[2], Colombia, Costa Rica, Cuba, Czechoslovakia[3], Denmark, the Dominican Republic, Ecuador, Egypt, El Salvador, Ethiopia, France, Greece, Guatemala, Haiti, Honduras, India[4], Iran, Iraq, Lebanon, Liberia, Luxembourg, Mexico, the Netherlands, New Zealand, Nicaragua, Norway, Panama, Paraguay, Peru, the Philippines, Poland, Saudi Arabia, South Africa, Syria, Turkey, Ukraine[1], USSR[5], UK, USA, Uruguay, Venezuela and Yugoslavia (suspended 1992).

[1] Belarus and Ukraine became independent countries in 1991. Despite their status as Union republics of the USSR before 1991 they had separate memmbership of the UN. Belarus was elected as Byelorussia.
[2] From 1945 until 1971 the seat for China at the UN was occupied by the Republic of China (Taiwan). In 1971 the UN withdrew recognition of the Republic of China in favour of the People's Republic of China.
[3] Since 1993 this seat has been held by the Czech Republic.
[4] Although India did not gain independence until 1947, an Indian delegation signed the UN Charter in 1945.
[5] Since 1992 this seat has been held by Russia.

Members elected in 1946: Afghanistan, Iceland, Sweden, Thailand.
Members elected in 1947: Pakistan, Yemen. (From 1962 Yemen was officially known as the Yemen Arab Republic and popularly known as North Yemen. In 1990 North Yemen merged with the People's Democratic Republic of Yemen – popularly known as South Yemen – which had been a UN member since 1967.)
Member elected in 1948: Burma (since 1989 officially known as Myanmar).
Member elected in 1949: Israel.
Member elected in 1950: Indonesia.
Members elected in 1955: Albania, Austria, Bulgaria, Cambodia, Finland, Hungary, Ireland, Italy, Jordan, Laos, Libya, Nepal, Portugal, Romania, Spain, Sri Lanka[1].
[1] Elected as Ceylon
Members elected in 1956: Japan, Morocco, Sudan, Tunisia.
Members elected in 1957: Ghana, Malaysia (elected as Malaya).
Member elected in 1958: Guinea.
Members elected in 1960 Benin[1], Burkina Faso[2], Cameroon, Central African Republic, Chad, Congo, Cyprus, Gabon, Ivory Coast, Madagascar, Mali, Niger, Nigeria, Senegal, Somalia, Togo, Zaïre[3].
[1] Elected as Dahomey.
[2] Elected as Upper Volta.
[3] Elected as the Republic of the Congo.
Members elected in 1961: Mauritania, Mongolia, Sierra Leone, Tanzania[1].
[1] Tanganyika and Zanzibar – a UN member since 1963 – merged to form Tanzania in 1964.
Members elected in 1962: Algeria, Burundi, Jamaica, Rwanda, Trinidad and Tobago, Uganda.
Members elected in 1963: Kenya, Kuwait.
Members elected in 1964: Malawi, Malta, Zambia.
Members elected in 1965: The Gambia, the Maldives, Singapore.
Members elected in 1966: Barbados, Botswana, Guyana, Lesotho.
Members elected in 1968: Equatorial Guinea, Mauritius, Swaziland.
Member elected in 1970: Fiji.
Members elected in 1971: Bahrain, Bhutan, Oman, Qatar, United Arab Emirates.
Members elected in 1973: The Bahamas, Germany[1].
[1] From 1973 to 1990 both the German Democratic Republic – East Germany – and the Federal Republic of Germany – West Germany – were members of the UN.
Members elected in 1974: Bangladesh, Grenada, Guinea-Bissau.
Members elected in 1975: Cape Verde, the Comoros,

Mozambique, São Tomé e Principe, Papua New Guinea, Suriname.

Members elected in 1976: Angola, Seychelles, Western Samoa.

Members elected in 1977: Djibouti, Vietnam.

Members elected in 1978: Dominica, Solomon Islands.

Member elected in 1979: St Lucia.

Members elected in 1980: St Vincent and the Grenadines, Zimbabwe.

Members elected in 1981: Antigua and Barbuda, Belize, Vanuatu.

Member elected in 1983: St Christopher and Nevis.

Member elected in 1984: Brunei.

Members elected in 1990: Liechtenstein, Namibia.

Members elected in 1991: Estonia, Korea (People's Democratic Republic – North Korea), Korea (Republic of – South Korea), Latvia, Lithuania, Marshall Islands, Micronesia.

Members elected in 1992: Armenia, Azerbaijan, Bosnia-Herzegovina, Croatia, Georgia, Kazakhstan, Kyrgyzstan, Moldova, San Marino, Slovenia, Tajikistan, Turkmenistan, Uzbekistan.

Member elected in 1993: Slovakia.

THE ORGANIZATION OF THE UN

The UN has six principal organs (see below). All are based in New York, with the exception of the International Court of Justice, which is based in The Hague (Netherlands).

THE GENERAL ASSEMBLY The Assembly is composed of all member states and can discuss anything within the scope of the Charter. Each member state has up to five delegates but only one vote. The annual session of the General Assembly begins on the third Tuesday of September. The Charter also has provision for special sessions. A President is elected by the General Assembly each September for a single term.

Decisions of the General Assembly are made by a qualified majority of those present (two thirds) on 'important' questions, and by a simple majority on other issues.

THE SECURITY COUNCIL The Charter of the UN identifies the Security Council as the main organ for maintaining international peace and security. It has 5 permanent members – China, France, Russia (from 1945 to 1991 this seat was held by the USSR), the UK and the USA (the 'great powers' at the end of World War II) – and 10 other members who are elected by the General Assembly for a term of two years. (From 1945 to 1971, China was represented by the Republic of China – Taiwan. Since 1971, China has been represented by the People's Republic of China.)

Decisions of the Security Council are reached by a majority vote of at least 9 of the 15 members. However, any one of the permanent members of the Security Council can exercise its right of veto.

THE ECONOMIC AND SOCIAL COUNCIL The Economic and Social Council acts as a coordinating

Key to abbreviated countries

A:	AUSTRIA	CZ: CZECH REPUBLIC	PORT: PORTUGAL
ARM:	ARMENIA	GAB: GABON	ROM: ROMANIA
AZER:	AZERBAIJAN	GAM: GAMBIA	SEN: SENEGAL
B:	BOSNIA-HERZEGOVINA	GEO: GEORGIA	SIE: SIERRA LEONE
BELA:	BELARUS	GUIN: GUINEA	SLO: SLOVENIA
BOTS:	BOTSWANA	H: HUNGARY	SWITZ: SWITZERLAND
BUL:	BULGARIA	LIB: LIBERIA	TUR: TURKMENISTAN
BUR:	BURKINA FASO	LUX: LUXEMBOURG	UKR: UKRAINE
COT:	COTE D'IVOIRE	NETH: NETHERLANDS	Y: YUGOSLAVIA
CR:	CROATIA	POL: POLAND	ZIM: ZIMBABWE

COUNTRIES OF THE WORLD

A country may variously be described as an area that is distinguished by its people, its geography or its culture, or as a land that enjoys political autonomy, more usually referred to as 'sovereignty'. In theory, a sovereign state exercises unrestricted power over its own destiny. However, in some ways the concept of sovereignty is of limited value in the closing years of the 20th century. It could be argued that there is no such thing as a truly independent state. The overwhelming majority of sovereign states are members of various economic and military alliances. Most states have come to recognize that the demands of security and trade bring agreed limits upon the freedom of action of individual countries. Countries rely upon their neighbours and other states, at least economically, and are therefore restricted in their independence. Some states have considerable restrictions to their independence. Monaco, for example, is obliged by treaty to act 'in complete conformity' with French interests and has a French civil servant as its head of government. Andorra has experienced difficulties in obtaining international recognition owing to perceived limitations on its sovereignty. There is, however, a distinctive and intangible characteristic by which we may recognize a country.

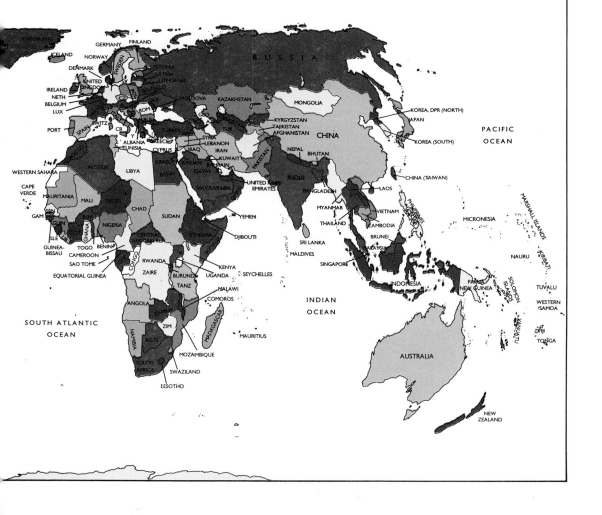

body for the numerous specialized agencies created by the UN. The Council – which has 54 members elected for a term of three years – aims to promote international cooperation in the economic, social and related fields.

THE TRUSTEESHIP COUNCIL The Trusteeship Council has effectively been wound up as all of the territories – mostly former German and Japanese colonies – placed under its supervision have achieved independence, except for Belau (Palau).

THE INTERNATIONAL COURT OF JUSTICE The International Court of Justice (the 'World Court') is available to offer legal rulings on any case brought before it by UN members. (All member states plus Switzerland are parties to the Statute of the Court.) In the event of a party failing to adhere to a judgement of the Court, the other party may have recourse to the Security Council.

The World Court comprises 15 judges elected by the Security Council and the General Assembly for a term of nine years.

THE SECRETARIAT The Secretariat performs the role of a civil service for the UN. Its head is the Secretary General, who combines the tasks of chief administrative officer of the organization with that of international mediator.

Secretary-General: Boutros Boutros Ghali (Egypt), since 1992.

SPECIALIZED AGENCIES OF THE UN

GATT (General Agreement on Tariffs and Trade)
Aim: to lay down a common code of practice in international trade. **Headquarters:** Geneva, Switzerland.

IAEA (International Atomic Energy Agency)
Aim: to encourage the use of atomic energy for peaceful means. **Headquarters:** Vienna, Austria.

ICAO (International Civil Aviation Organization)
Aim: to encourage safety measures and coordinate facilities for international flight. **Headquarters:** Montreal, Canada.

IDA (International Development Organization)
Aim: to assist less developed countries by providing credits on special terms. **Headquarters:** an affiliate of the World Bank, see below.

IFAD (International Fund for Agricultural Development)
Aim: to generate grants or loans to increase food production in developing countries. **Headquarters:** Rome, Italy.

IFC (International Finance Corporation)
Aim: to promote the flow of private capital internationally and to stimulate the capital markets. **Headquarters:** an affiliate of the World Bank, see below.

ILO (International Labour Organization)
Aim: to establish international labour standards and to improve social and economic well-being. **Headquarters:** Geneva, Switzerland.

IMF (International Monetary Fund)
Aim: to promote international monetary cooperation. **Headquarters:** Washington DC, USA

IMO (International Maritime Organization)
Aim: to coordinate safety at sea. **Headquarters:** London, UK.

ITU (International Telecommunications Union)
Aim: to allocate telecommunications frequencies and to standardize telecommunication procedures. **Headquarters:** Geneva, Switzerland.

UNESCO (UN Educational, Scientific and Cultural Organization)
Aim: to stimulate popular education and the spread of culture. **Headquarters:** Paris, France.

UNIDO (UN Industrial Development Organization)
Aim: to promote industrialization in developing countries. **Headquarters:** Vienna, Austria.

UPU (Universal Postal Union)
Aim: to unite members in a single postal territory. **Headquarters:** Berne, Switzerland.

WHO (World Health Organization)
Aim: to promote the attainment by all peoples of the highest possible standards of health. **Headquarters:** Geneva, Switzerland.

WIPO (World Intellectual Property Organization)
Aim: to promote protection of intellectual property (inventions, copyright, etc.). **Headquarters:** Geneva, Switzerland.

WMO (World Meteorological Organization)
Aim: to standardize meteorological observations and apply the information to the greatest international benefit, for shipping, agriculture, etc. **Headquarters:** Geneva, Switzerland.

WORLD BANK (International Bank for Reconstruction and Development)
Aim: to encourage development through capital investment (in particular, investment in poorer member nations). **Headquarters:** Washington DC, USA.

SUBSIDIARY ORGANS OF THE UN

Subsidiary organs of the UN include:

UNHCR (United Nations High Commissioner for Refugees)
Aim: to provide international protection for refugees. **Headquarters:** Geneva, Switzerland.

UNICEF (United Nations International Children's Emergency Fund)
Aim: to meet the needs of children, particularly those in developing countries. **Headquarters:** New York, USA.

UNRWA (United Nations Relief and Works Agency)
Aim: to provide relief and welfare services for Palestinian refugees. **Headquarters:** Vienna, Austria.

EUROPEAN ORGANIZATIONS

THE EUROPEAN COMMUNITY

In 1950 the governments of Belgium, France, the Federal Republic of Germany, Italy, Luxembourg and the Netherlands began negotiations to integrate their interests in specific fields. The result was the Treaty of Paris (1951) under which the European Coal and Steel Community was created. Attempts to establish a community concerned with cooperation in foreign affairs and defence proved abortive, but in 1957 the European Economic Community (the EEC) and the European Atomic Energy Community (Euratom) – with memberships identical to the European Coal and Steel Community – came into being under the terms of the Treaty of Rome.

The three Communities were distinct entities until 1967, when they merged their executives and decision-making bodies into a single European Community (the EC). The Community has been enlarged through the accession of Denmark, Greece, Ireland, Portugal, Spain and the UK.

EC plans for economic and monetary union have been discussed, and there has been increased coordination in foreign policies and research and development. Since 1975 the EC has had its own revenue independent of national contributions.

The Single European Market In 1992 the EC achieved a Single European Market in which all duties, tariffs and quotas have been removed on trade between member states and many obstacles to the free movement of people, money and goods have been abolished within the Community.

EC INSTITUTIONS

The Commission of the European Community consists of 17 members appointed by their national governments for a term of four years. The Commissioners elect from their number a President and six Vice Presidents. The Commission – which acts independently of national governments – makes proposals to the Council of Ministers and executes the decisions of the Council.
Composition of the European Commission: Belgium is represented by 1 Commissioner, Denmark 1, France 2, Germany 2, Greece 1, Ireland 1, Italy 2, Luxembourg 1, Netherlands 1, Portugal 1, Spain 2, UK 2.
President: Jacques Delors (France)

The Council of Ministers is the main decision-making body of the EC. The Council consists of the foreign ministers of each of the member states. Specialist councils – for example, of the 12 ministers of agriculture – also meet, while heads of government meet three times a year as the **European Council**.

Ministers represent national interests. The decisions of the Council are normally unanimous although there is provision for majority voting in certain areas. The Presidency of the Council of Ministers rotates, with each member state taking the chair for a period of six months (see the table below).

The European Parliament consists of 567 members directly elected for five years by universal adult suffrage according to the local practice of each member state. Members (MEPs) have the right to be consulted on legislative proposals submitted by the Council of Ministers or the Commission and the power to reject or amend the budget of the EC. The Parliament meets in Strasbourg (France), its committees meet in Brussels (Belgium), and its Secretariat is based in Luxembourg. *Composition of the European Parliament*: Belgium returns 25 MEPs, Denmark 16, France 87, Germany 99, Greece 25, Ireland 15, Italy 87, Luxembourg 6, Netherlands 31, Portugal 25, Spain 64, UK 87.

The European Court of Justice consists of 13 judges and six advocates-general appointed for six years by the governments of member states acting in concert. At least one representative is appointed from each member state. The Court is responsible for deciding upon the legality of the decisions of the Council of Ministers and the Commission and for adjudicating between states in the event of disputes.

Candidates for EC membership Austria, Finland, Norway and Sweden are expected to begin negotiations for membership in 1993. Turkey, Cyprus, Malta and Switzerland are also applicants. The Czech Republic, Hungary, Poland and Slovakia have indicated that EC membership is a long-term aim.

MEMBERS OF THE EC

	Date of accession	Next period as President of the Council of Ministers
Belgium	1950	Jul–Dec 93
Denmark	1973	Jan–Jun 93
France	1950	Jan–Jun 95
Germany	1950	Jul–Dec 94
Greece	1981	Jan–Jun 94
Ireland	1973	Jul–Dec 96
Italy	1950	Jan–Jun 96
Luxembourg	1950	Jul–Dec 97
The Netherlands	1950	Jan–Jun 97
Portugal	1986	Jul–Dec 98
Spain	1986	Jul–Dec 95
United Kingdom	1973	Jan–Jun 98

CONFERENCE ON SECURITY AND COOPERATION IN EUROPE (CSCE)

The CSCE was established in 1975 under the Final Act of a security conference held in Helsinki, Finland. The aims of CSCE were formulated in the Charter of Paris, which was signed by the 34 member nations on 21 November 1990. Members affirmed a 'commitment to settle disputes by peaceful means' and a 'common

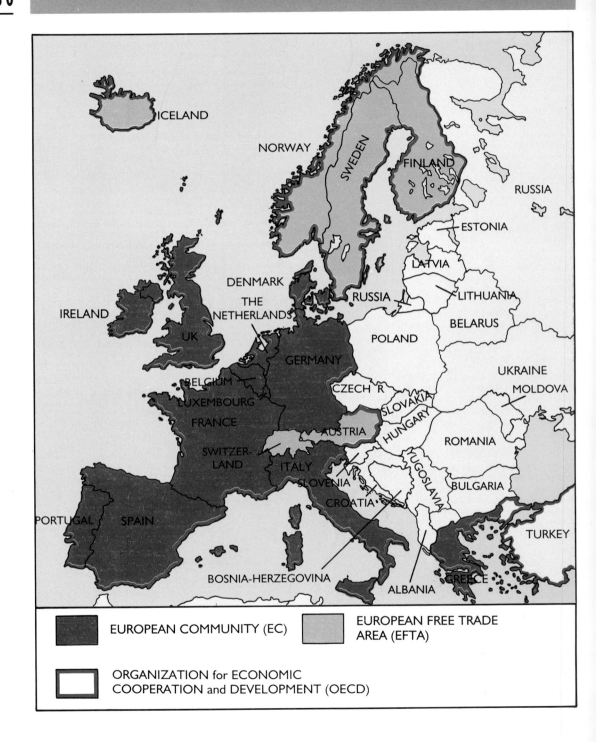

ICELAND

NORWAY

SWEDEN

FINLAND

RUSSIA

ESTONIA

LATVIA

DENMARK

THE
NETHERLANDS

RUSSIA

LITHUANIA

IRELAND

UK

BELARUS

POLAND

GERMANY

BELGIUM

CZECH R

UKRAINE

MOLDOVA

LUXEMBOURG

FRANCE

SLOVAKIA

HUNGARY

AUSTRIA

SWITZER-
LAND

ITALY

SLOVENIA

YUGOSLAVIA

ROMANIA

BULGARIA

CROATIA

PORTUGAL

SPAIN

TURKEY

BOSNIA-HERZEGOVINA

ALBANIA

GREECE

EUROPEAN COMMUNITY (EC)

EUROPEAN FREE TRADE
AREA (EFTA)

ORGANIZATION for ECONOMIC
COOPERATION and DEVELOPMENT (OECD)

adherence to democratic values and to human rights and fundamental freedoms'.

The Charter – which was described as formally ending the Cold War – envisaged a CSCE parliamentary assembly with members of parliament drawn from all 34 states. It was agreed that CSCE foreign ministers should meet at least once a year. The Charter established the following CSCE institutions:

CSCE Secretariat A small secretariat has been established in Prague, the Czech Republic.

CSCE Conflict Prevention Centre The Centre has been charged with reducing the risk of conflict in Europe. It is based in Vienna, Austria.

CSCE Office of Free Elections The Office was established to monitor the conduct of elections throughout Europe. It is based in Warsaw, Poland.

Membership: Albania, Armenia, Austria, Azerbaijan, Belarus, Belgium, Bosnia-Herzegovina, Bulgaria, Canada, Croatia, Cyprus, Czech Republic, Denmark, Estonia, Finland, France, Georgia, Germany, Greece, Hungary, Iceland, Ireland, Italy, Kazakhstan, Kyrgyzstan, Latvia, Liechtenstein, Lithuania, Luxembourg, Malta, Moldova, Monaco, Netherlands, Norway, Poland, Portugal, Romania, San Marino, Slovakia, Slovenia, Spain, Sweden, Switzerland, Tajikistan, Turkey, Turkmenistan, Ukraine, UK, USA, Russia, Uzbekistan, Vatican City and Yugoslavia (suspended 1992).

CEFTA

The Central European Free Trade Agreement was signed in December 1992 by Poland, the Czech Republic, Slovakia and Hungary. Under the terms of the agreement member states intend to set up a free trade area between them by the year 2001 (see p. 43).

COUNCIL OF EUROPE

The Council of Europe was founded in 1949. It aims to achieve a greater unity between its members to safeguard their common European heritage and to facilitate their economic and social progress. Membership is restricted to European democracies, that is those states which 'accept the principles of the rule of law and of the enjoyment by all persons within their jurisdiction of human rights and fundamental freedoms'.

The Council of Ministers, consisting of the foreign minister of each member state, meets twice each year. Agreements by the Council members are either formalized as European Conventions or recommendations to individual governments. The Parliamentary Assembly of the Council meets three times a year to debate reports on social, economic, political and other matters. The Council has achieved some 140 conventions and other agreements, including the European Convention for the Protection of Human Rights in 1950.

Headquarters: Strasbourg, France.

Membership: Austria (which joined the Council in 1956) has 6 Assembly members, Belgium (1949) 7, Bulgaria (1992) 12, Cyprus (1961) 3, Czech Republic (joined as Czechoslovakia in 1991) 7, Denmark (1949) 5, Finland (1989) 5, France (1949) 18, Germany (1951) 18, Greece (1949; withdrew 1969–74) 7, Hungary (1990) 6, Iceland (1950) 3, Ireland (1949) 4, Italy (1949) 18, Liechtenstein (1978) 2, Luxembourg (1949) 3, Malta (1965) 3, Netherlands (1949) 7, Norway (1949) 5, Poland (1992) 12, Portugal (1976) 7, San Marino (1988) 2, Spain (1977) 12, Sweden (1949) 6, Switzerland (1963) 6, Turkey (1949) 12, UK (1949) 18.

Albania and Slovenia have associate member status.

EUROPEAN ECONOMIC AREA

EEA is an open market area agreed between EC and EFTA nations. It was originally scheduled to come into existence in 1992, but Swiss rejection of participation has postponed its establishment until 1993.

EUROPEAN FREE TRADE ASSOCIATION

The European Free Trade Association (EFTA) aims to achieve free trade in industrial goods between member states, to help create a single West European market and to encourage an expansion in world trade. The first aim was met in December 1966 when nearly all internal tariffs on industrial goods were abolished. Considerable progress was made towards the second aim in April 1984 when trade agreements with the EC abolished tariffs on industrial goods between EFTA and EC countries. The EC and EFTA are creating a single European trading area (see European Economic Area, above), which would not, however, replace either of the two existing trade groupings, although most EFTA members have applied or are considering an application to join the EC.

EFTA was founded in 1960 with Austria, Denmark, Norway, Portugal, Sweden, Switzerland and the UK as original members. Iceland joined EFTA in 1970. Denmark and the UK withdrew from EFTA in 1972 and Portugal withdrew in 1986 to become members of the EC. Finland, an associate member of EFTA since 1961, became a full member in 1986. Liechtenstein, formerly an associate member, became a full member of EFTA in 1991.

Each full member state maintains a permanent delegation in Geneva, the heads of which meet once a fortnight. Ministers of EFTA governments meet twice a year.

Headquarters: Geneva, Switzerland.

Current membership: Austria, Finland, Iceland, Liechtenstein, Norway, Sweden and Switzerland.

WEST EUROPEAN UNION

The WEU was founded 1948 with the original intention of collaborating 'in economic, social and cultural matters and for collective self-defence'. These functions have been gradually transferred to the EC, the Council of Europe and NATO. However, in 1984 the WEU was reactivated to improve military cooperation between members and to strengthen NATO.

Headquarters: London, UK.

Membership: Belgium, France, Germany, Italy, Luxembourg, Netherlands, Portugal, Spain, UK.

Denmark, Greece, Ireland and Turkey are associate or observer members.

WORLD ORGANIZATIONS

THE COMMONWEALTH

The Commonwealth may be said to have its foundations in the 1926 Imperial Conference, which defined the position of the dominions of the British Empire as 'freely associated...members of the British Commonwealth of Nations'. The modern Commonwealth dates from 1949 when India became a republic but remained a member of the British Commonwealth recognizing 'the King as the symbol of the free association of...independent member nations'. The majority of Commonwealth members are republics and some have their own sovereign, but all recognize the British sovereign as Head of the Commonwealth.

The Commonwealth is an informal grouping of the UK and the majority of its former dependencies. It has no written constitution. It aims to encourage international, scientific and technical, educational and economic cooperation between members.

Commonwealth heads of government meet every two years, and other ministers meet at irregular intervals. The Commonwealth Secretariat was established in 1965 as the main agency for multilateral communications between the governments of members.

Secretary General: Chief Emeka Anyaoku (Nigeria).

Headquarters: London, UK.

Membership: Antigua and Barbuda, Australia, Bahamas, Bangladesh, Barbados, Belize, Botswana, Brunei, Canada, Cyprus, Dominica, The Gambia, Ghana, Grenada, Guyana, India, Jamaica, Kenya, Kiribati, Lesotho, Malawi, Malaysia, Maldives, Malta, Mauritius, Namibia, Nauru (special member), New Zealand, Nigeria, Pakistan, Papua New Guinea, St Christopher and Nevis, St Lucia, St Vincent and the Grenadines, Seychelles, Sierra Leone, Singapore, Solomon Islands, Sri Lanka, Swaziland, Tanzania, Tonga, Trinidad and Tobago, Tuvalu (special member), Uganda, UK, Vanuatu, Western Samoa, Zambia, and Zimbabwe. (Special members do not participate in ministerial meetings.)

'GROUP OF SEVEN' (G7)

G7 is an informal grouping of the leading Western economic powers. Since 1975 the heads of government of these states have met for regular summits concerning major economic, monetary and political problems.

Membership: Canada, France, Germany, Japan, Italy, UK, and USA. The EC has observer status.

INTERNATIONAL CRIMINAL POLICE ORGANIZATION

INTERPOL was established in 1923 as the International Criminal Police Commission and was restructured and renamed in 1956. It aims to promote mutual assistance between criminal police authorities. The policy-making body of the Organization is the General Assembly which meets annually.

Headquarters: Lyon, France.

Membership: 155 member states.

INTERNATIONAL ENERGY AGENCY

IEA, an autonomous agency of OECD (see below), was founded in 1974. It aims to improve energy supplies and to develop alternative sources of energy.

Headquarters: Paris, France.

Membership: OECD members except Finland, France and Iceland.

INTERNATIONAL RED CROSS AND RED CRESCENT

The International Red Cross and Red Crescent movement is a neutral organization founded to negotiate between warring parties, to protect casualties of armed conflict, to develop the activities of individual societies, to protect prisoners of war (through the terms of the *Geneva Convention*) and to coordinate relief for the victims of natural and other disasters. The Conference of the International Red Cross and Red Crescent meets every four years.

Headquarters: Geneva, Switzerland.

Membership: the Red Cross or Red Crescent Societies of over 160 countries.

NON-ALIGNED MOVEMENT

The nonaligned movement is not a formal organization but a conference that usually meets every three years. The aims of the movement are to promote world peace, to reject the system of world power blocs and to help bring about a more even distribution of the world's wealth. Over 100 countries attended the last two conferences of the non-aligned movement, membership of which varies from one conference to another.

ORGANIZATION OF THE PETROLEUM EXPORTING COUNTRIES

OPEC was founded in Baghdad, Iraq, in 1960. It aims to coordinate the petroleum-producing and exporting policies of its member states.

Headquarters: Vienna, Austria.

Membership: Algeria, Gabon, Indonesia, Iran, Iraq, Kuwait, Libya, Nigeria, Qatar, Saudi Arabia, United Arab Emirates, and Venezuela.

ORGANIZATION FOR ECONOMIC COOPERATION AND DEVELOPMENT

OECD was founded on 30 September 1961 to replace the Organization for European Economic Cooperation which had been established in connection with the Marshall Aid Plan in 1948. It aims to encourage economic and social welfare in member states and to stimulate aid to developing countries.

Headquarters: Paris, France.

Membership: Australia, Austria, Belgium, Canada, Denmark, France, Finland, Germany, Greece, Iceland, Ireland, Italy, Japan, Luxembourg, the Netherlands, New Zealand, Norway, Portugal, Spain, Sweden, Switzerland, Turkey, UK, USA, Yugoslavia (observer; suspended 1992).

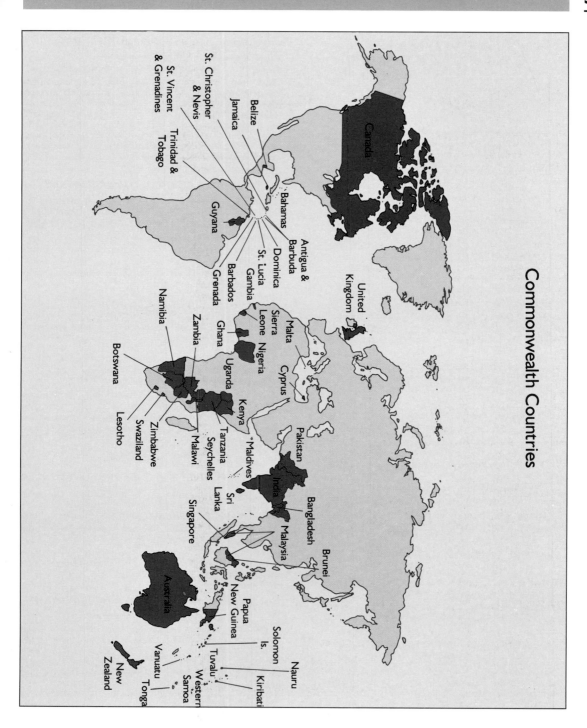

Commonwealth Countries

Canada

United Kingdom

St. Vincent & Grenadines

St. Christopher & Nevis

Jamaica

Belize

Trinidad & Tobago

Guyana

Bahamas

Antigua & Barbuda

Dominica

St. Lucia

Barbados

Grenada

Gambia

Namibia

Zambia

Ghana

Sierra Leone

Nigeria

Malta

Cyprus

Uganda

Kenya

Botswana

Lesotho

Swaziland

Zimbabwe

Malawi

Tanzania

Seychelles

Maldives

Pakistan

Sri Lanka

Singapore

India

Bangladesh

Malaysia

Brunei

Australia

Papua New Guinea

Solomon Is.

Nauru

Vanuatu

Tuvalu

Kiribati

Western Samoa

Tonga

New Zealand

REGIONAL ORGANIZATIONS

ANDEAN PACT

The Andean Pact was established in 1992 to create a free-trade area – with a common external tariff – in northern and eastern South America.

Headquarters: Lima, Peru.

Members: Bolivia, Colombia, Ecuador, Peru, Venezuela.

LATIN AMERICAN INTEGRATION ASSOCIATION

ALADI (Asociación Latinoamericana de Integración) was established on 31 December 1980 as a replacement for the Latin American Free Trade Area, which was formed in 1961. It aims to encourage trade and to remove tariffs between member states.

Headquarters: Montevideo, Uruguay.

Secretary General: Jorge Luis Ordonez (Colombia).

Members: Argentina, Bolivia, Brazil, Chile, Colombia, Ecuador, Mexico, Paraguay, Peru, Uruguay, and Venezuela.

Costa Rica, Cuba, Dominican Republic, El Salvador, Guatemala, Honduras, Italy, Nicaragua, Panama, Portugal and Spain have observer membership.

ASSOCIATION OF SOUTH EAST ASIAN NATIONS

ASEAN was founded in Bangkok, Thailand in 1967. It aims to accelerate the economic, social and cultural development of member states, to maintain stability in South East Asia, and to encourage cooperation between members.

Headquarters: Djakarta, Indonesia.

Secretary General: Rusli Noor (Indonesia).

Members: Brunei, Indonesia, Malaysia, Philippines, Singapore, and Thailand.

BLACK SEA ECONOMIC COOPERATION ZONE

Founded in 1992, the Black Sea Economic Cooperation Zone aims to promote trade and economic cooperation between member states and to control pollution.

Members: Armenia, Azerbaijan, Bulgaria, Georgia, Moldova, Romania, Russia, Turkey, Ukraine.

CARIBBEAN COMMUNITY AND COMMON MARKET

CARICOM was founded 1973 at Chaguaramas, Trinidad. The aims of the Caribbean Community are to promote cooperation in cultural, educational, health, scientific and technological matters, and to co-ordinate foreign policy. The associated Caribbean Common Market aims to promote economic cooperation.

Headquarters: Georgetown, Guyana.

Secretary General: Roderick Rainford (Jamaica).

Members: Antigua and Barbuda, Bahamas (Community only), Barbados, Belize, Dominica, Dominican Republic, Grenada, Guyana, Haiti, Jamaica, St Christopher and Nevis, St Lucia, St Vincent and the Grenadines, Trinidad and Tobago. Suriname and Venezuela are associate members. Non-sovereign territories in membership: Montserrat, British Virgin Islands, Turks and Caicos Islands.

CENTRAL AMERICAN COMMON MARKET

CACM was founded in 1960 but lapsed in 1969. The organization was revived (1992–93) and is scheduled to establish a free-trade area in Central America by 1994.

Headquarters: Guatemala City, Guatemala.

Secretary General: Rafael Rodriguez Loucel (Guatemala).

Members: Costa Rica, El Salvador, Guatemala, Honduras, and Nicaragua.

COLOMBO PLAN

The Colombo Plan for Cooperative Economic and Social Development in Asia and the Pacific was founded in 1950 to promote economic and social development within the region and to encourage training programmes, capital aid and technical cooperation.

Headquarters: Colombo, Sri Lanka.

Members: Afghanistan, Australia, Bangladesh, Bhutan, Cambodia, Canada, Fiji, India, Indonesia, Iran, Japan, Korea (South), Laos, Malaysia, Maldives, Myanmar (Burma), Nepal, New Zealand, Pakistan, Papua New Guinea, Philippines, Singapore, Sri Lanka, Thailand, UK, and USA

COMMONWEALTH OF INDEPENDENT STATES

Following the dissolution of the USSR in December 1991, most of the former Soviet republics formed the CIS. It maintains some elements of the economic, military and political coordination that existed within the former USSR. Azerbaijan withdrew in 1992.

Members: Armenia, Belarus, Kazakhstan, Kyrgyzstan, Moldova, Russia, Tajikistan, Turkmenistan, Ukraine, Uzbekistan.

COOPERATION COUNCIL FOR THE ARAB STATES OF THE GULF

The Council was established in 1981 to promote economic, cultural and social cooperation between the Arab states of the Gulf. It has since also taken on a security role, notably during the Second Gulf War (January to February 1991). In March 1991 member states concluded economic and defence agreements with Egypt and Syria, although the latter two states are not members of the Council.

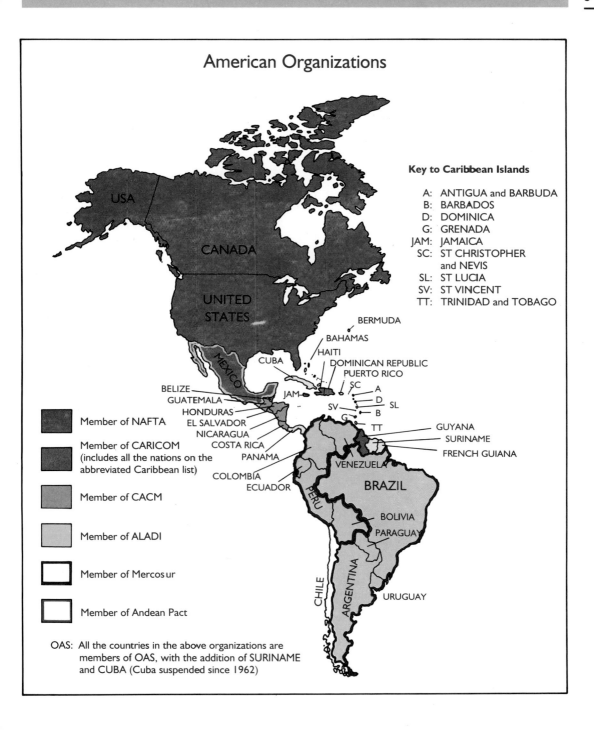

American Organizations

Key to Caribbean Islands

A:	ANTIGUA and BARBUDA
B:	BARBADOS
D:	DOMINICA
G:	GRENADA
JAM:	JAMAICA
SC:	ST CHRISTOPHER and NEVIS
SL:	ST LUCIA
SV:	ST VINCENT
TT:	TRINIDAD and TOBAGO

Member of NAFTA

Member of CARICOM (includes all the nations on the abbreviated Caribbean list)

Member of CACM

Member of ALADI

Member of Mercosur

Member of Andean Pact

OAS: All the countries in the above organizations are members of OAS, with the addition of SURINAME and CUBA (Cuba suspended since 1962)

Headquarters: Riyadh, Saudi Arabia.
Members: Bahrain, Kuwait, Oman, Qatar, Saudi Arabia, UAE.

ECONOMIC COMMUNITY OF WEST AFRICAN STATES

ECOWAS was founded in Lagos, Nigeria, in May 1975. It aims to promote trade and cooperation between member states and to increase self-reliance within West Africa. An ECOWAS force intervened in an attempt to stop the civil war in Liberia in 1990. The Assembly of heads of state and heads of government meets once a year and is chaired by each country in turn.
Headquarters: Abuja, Nigeria.
Members: Benin, Burkina Faso, Cape Verde, The Gambia, Ghana, Guinea, Guinea-Bissau, Ivory Coast, Liberia, Mali, Mauritania, Niger, Nigeria, Senegal, Sierra Leone, and Togo.

ECONOMIC COOPERATION ORGANIZATION

The ECO was founded in 1965 to promote trade in southwest Asia. The organization lapsed but was revived and expanded in 1992 to aid the development of Central Asia.
Members: Azerbaijan, Iran, Kyrgyzstan, Pakistan, Tajikistan, Turkmenistan, Turkey, Uzbekistan.

LEAGUE OF ARAB STATES

The League of Arab States, which is popularly known as the *Arab League*, was founded in Cairo, Egypt, on 22 March 1945. It aims to protect the independence and sovereignty of member states, to strengthen ties between them, and to encourage coordination of their social, economic, political, cultural and legal policies. The League comprises a Council (on which each state has one vote), special committees, over 20 specialized agencies and a Secretariat.
Headquarters: Cairo, Egypt.
Secretary General: Dr Ahmad al-Meguid (Egypt).
Members: Algeria, Bahrain, Djibouti, Egypt, Iraq, Jordan, Kuwait, Lebanon, Libya, Mauritania, Morocco, Oman, Palestine Liberaton Organization, Qatar, Saudi Arabia, Somalia, Sudan, Syria, Tunisia, United Arab Emirates, and Yemen.

MERCOSUR

Originating in a free-trade pact between Argentina and Brazil in 1988, Mercosur is scheduled to become a free market in goods, services and labour in 1994.
Members: Argentina, Brazil, Paraguay, Uruguay.

NORTH AMERICAN FREE TRADE AGREEMENT

NAFTA was founded in 1992 to eliminate tariffs, quotas and import licences between member states.
Members: Canada, Mexico, USA.

ORGANIZATION OF AFRICAN UNITY

The OAU was founded on 25 May 1963 in Addis Ababa, Ethiopia. It aims to promote African unity and collaboration in economic, social, cultural, political, defence, scientific, health and other matters, and to eliminate colonialism and apartheid from Africa. The Assembly of heads of state and heads of government meets annually and is presided over by a chairman elected for a one year term by the Assembly. The main administrative body is the Secretariat.
Headquarters: Addis Ababa, Ethiopia.
Secretary General: Salim Ahmed Salim (Tanzania).
Members: Algeria, Angola, Benin, Botswana, Burkina Faso, Burundi, Cameroon, Cape Verde, Central African Republic, Chad, Comoros, Congo, Djibouti, Egypt, Equatorial Guinea, Ethiopia, Gabon, The Gambia, Ghana, Guinea, Guinea-Bissau, Ivory Coast, Kenya, Lesotho, Liberia, Libya, Madagascar, Malawi, Mali, Mauritania, Mauritius, Mozambique, Namibia, Niger, Nigeria, Rwanda, São Tomé e Principe, Senegal, Seychelles, Sierra Leone, Somalia, Sudan, Swaziland, Tanzania, Togo, Tunisia, Uganda, Zaïre, Zambia, and Zimbabwe. In 1982 the Sahrawi Arab Democratic Republic (Western Sahara) was admitted to membership; Morocco, which claims the Western Sahara, withdrew from the OAU in protest.

ORGANIZATION OF ARAB PETROLEUM EXPORTING COUNTRIES

OAPEC was founded in 1968 to encourage cooperation in economic activities, to ensure the flow of oil to consumer markets, and to promote a favourable climate for the investment of capital and expertise. The oil ministers of member countries form the Ministerial Council, which meets twice a year. The General Secretariat is the executive organ of OAPEC.
Headquarters: Cairo, Egypt.
Members: Algeria, Bahrain, Egypt, Iraq, Kuwait, Libya, Qatar, Saudi Arabia, Syria, and the United Arab Emirates.

ORGANIZATION OF AMERICAN STATES

OAS was founded in Bogota, Colombia in 1948 as a successor to the International Union of American Republics (later the Pan American Union) founded 1890. Its aims are to maintain the independence and territorial integrity of member states, to achieve peace and justice on the continent, and to encourage collaboration and inter-American solidarity.
Headquarters: Washington DC, USA
Secretary General: João Clemente Baena Soares (Brazil).
Members: Antigua and Barbuda, Argentina, Bahamas, Barbados, Belize, Bolivia, Brazil, Canada, Chile, Colombia, Costa Rica, Cuba (suspended since 1962), Dominica, Dominican Republic, Ecuador, El Salvador, Grenada, Guatemala, Guyana, Haiti, Honduras, Jamaica, Mexico, Nicaragua, Panama, Paraguay, Peru, St Christopher and Nevis, St Lucia, St Vincent and the Grenadines,

Suriname, Trinidad and Tobago, USA, Uruguay, and Venezuela.

ORGANIZATION OF THE ISLAMIC CONFERENCE

OIC was established in Rabat, Morocco, in May 1971 to promote Islamic solidarity, to consolidate economic, social and cultural cooperation between member states, and to safeguard the Holy Places of Islam and the independence of Muslim peoples.

Headquarters: Jeddah, Saudi Arabia.

Members: Afghanistan, Algeria, Bahrain, Bangladesh, Benin, Brunei, Burkina Faso, Cameroon, Chad, Comoros, Djibouti, Egypt, Gabon, The Gambia, Guinea, Guinea-Bissau, Indonesia, Iran, Iraq, Jordan, Kuwait, Lebanon, Libya, Malaysia, Maldives, Mali, Mauritania, Morocco, Niger, Oman, Pakistan, Palestine Liberation Organization, Qatar, Saudi Arabia, Senegal, Sierra Leone, Somalia, Sudan, Syria, Tunisia, Turkey, Uganda, UAE, and Yemen. Mozambique is an associate member.

SOUTH ASIAN ASSOCIATION FOR ECONOMIC CO-OPERATION

SAARC was founded in December 1985. It aims to encourage trade and economic development in South Asia.

Headquarters: Delhi, India.

Members: Bangladesh, Bhutan, India, Maldives, Nepal, Pakistan, and Sri Lanka.

SOUTHERN AFRICAN DEVELOPMENT COORDINATION CONFERENCE

SADCC was founded in Arusha, Tanzania, in July 1979. It aims to harmonize the development plans of member states and reduce their dependence on South Africa. An annual summit meeting is held.

Headquarters: Gaborone, Botswana.

Members: Angola, Botswana, Lesotho, Malawi, Mozambique, Namibia, Swaziland, Tanzania, Zambia, and Zimbabwe.

SOUTH PACIFIC FORUM

The Forum was founded in 1971 in Wellington, New Zealand. It has no formal constitution but exists to further cooperation in a wide range of issues of mutual interest. The membership and the organization of the Forum is common with the South Pacific Bureau for Economic Co-operation (SPEC), established in 1973 to encourage trade, economic and transport matters.

Headquarters: Suva, Fiji.

Secretary General: Ieremia Tabai (Kiribati).

Members: Australia, Cook Islands (a self-governing New Zealand territory), Fiji, Kiribati, Marshall Islands, Micronesia, Nauru, New Zealand, Niue (a self-governing New Zealand territory), Papua New Guinea, Solomon Islands, Tonga, Tuvalu, Vanuatu, and Western Samoa.

DEFENCE

The existence of nuclear weapons of proven capability has deterred direct conflict between the major powers since the end of World War II. The collapse of Communism in Eastern Europe has effectively ended the confrontation between East and West. The signature of the Charter of Paris in November 1990 formally ended the Cold War, but large nuclear stockpiles remain. However, fear of superpower imbalance has been replaced by fear of 'proliferation' – the spread of nuclear capability to powers outside the major blocs (see p. 40).

Until 1989–90 the greatest danger of conflict seemed to lie in Europe. Soviet forces withdrew from Hungary and the former Czechoslovakia in 1991, and being removed from Poland and the former East Germany. A number of US bases in western Europe have also closed. Local or regional conflicts in other parts of the world are now seen as a greater threat, for example the Iraqi invasion of Kuwait in August 1990 (see p. 39).

NATO

The North Atlantic Treaty Organization came into existence in April 1949 and into force in August 1949. NATO is a collective defence organization whose member countries agree to treat an armed attack on any one of them as an attack against all. The North Atlantic Council is the highest authority of the alliance. It comprises 16 permanent representatives – one from each member state – and is chaired by the Secretary General of NATO. The foreign ministers of the member states meet at least twice a year. The defence of the NATO area is the responsibility of the Defence Planning Committee. France is not a member of the DPC, which meets regularly at ambassadorial level and twice a year at ministerial level (see p. 40).

Headquarters: Brussels, Belgium. **Secretary General:** Manfred Wörner (*Germany*). **Members:** Belgium (founder member), Canada (founder member), Denmark (founder member), France (founder member), Germany (West Germany admitted on 5 May 1955; the former East Germany was included as part of reunified Germany on 3 Oct 1990), Greece (admitted 18 February 1952), Iceland (founder member), Italy (founder member), Luxembourg (founder member), Netherlands (founder member), Norway (founder member), Portugal (founder member), Spain (admitted on 30 May 1982), Turkey (admitted on 18 February 1952), United Kingdom (founder member), and USA (founder member).

OTHER DEFENCE ORGANIZATIONS

Several other organizations have a role to play in defence, particularly on a regional basis. ANZUS was set up in 1951 to form a collective defence policy for the preservation of peace in the Pacific. Its members are Australia, New Zealand and the USA. The Arab League (see p. 36) and the Cooperation Council for the Arab States of the Gulf (see p. 34) have a security role in the Middle East, and ECOWAS (see p. 36) has a defence policy for West Africa.

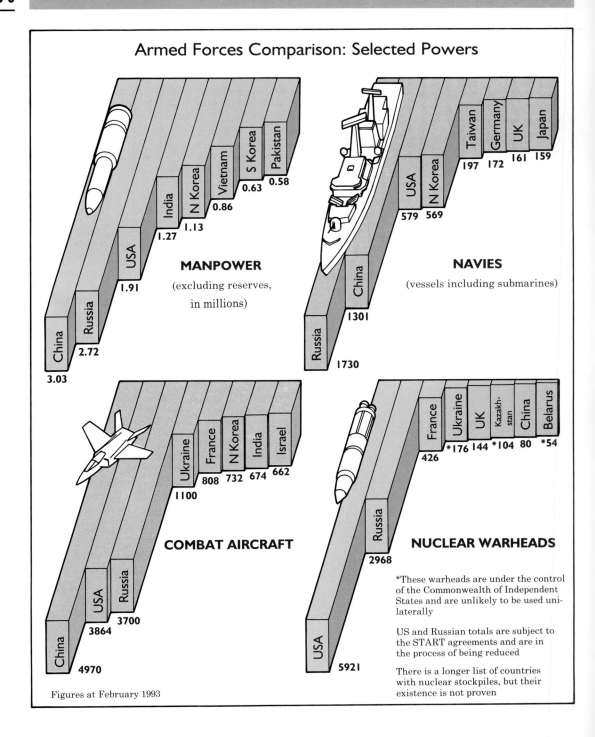

Armed Forces Comparison: Selected Powers

MANPOWER
(excluding reserves, in millions)

China 3.03
Russia 2.72
USA 1.91
India 1.27
N Korea 1.13
Vietnam 0.86
S Korea 0.63
Pakistan 0.58

NAVIES
(vessels including submarines)

Russia 1730
China 1301
USA 579
N Korea 569
Taiwan 197
Germany 172
UK 161
Japan 159

COMBAT AIRCRAFT

China 4970
USA 3864
Russia 3700
Ukraine 1100
France 808
N Korea 732
India 674
Israel 662

NUCLEAR WARHEADS

USA 5921
Russia 2968
France 426
Ukraine *176
UK 144
Kazakh-stan *104
China 80
Belarus *54

*These warheads are under the control of the Commonwealth of Independent States and are unlikely to be used unilaterally

US and Russian totals are subject to the START agreements and are in the process of being reduced

There is a longer list of countries with nuclear stockpiles, but their existence is not proven

Figures at February 1993

WARS IN THE 1990s

The conflicts listed below (chronologically) started or continued in the 1990s.

Ethiopia (1961–1991): Rebel forces in Eritrea and Tigre fought government forces for independence. Eritrea effectively seceded; spasmodic fighting continues, especially in Tigre.

Chad (1965–): Civil wars between the Muslim Arab North and the Christian and animist Black African South – Idriss Deby successfully led rebel forces against the government (1989). Unrest continues in the north.

Northern Ireland (1969–): Sectarian conflict between Protestant extremists intent on remaining part of the UK and Catholic extremists intent on reuniting Ireland. British troops – initially deployed in a peacekeeping role – are opposed by paramilitary groups such as the Ulster Defence Association (UDA) and the Provisional Irish Republican Army (IRA).

Lebanon (1975–): Civil war between Christian and Muslim forces reduced Lebanon to ungovernable chaos. Syria and Israel intervened and a Syrian-backed government imposed a semblance of order (1991), but spasmodic fighting in the South between Hizbollah fundamentalists and Israeli-backed forces continues.

Mozambique (1975–): Mozambique virtually disintegrated in civil war between the Front for Liberation of Mozambique (FRELIMO) government and the Mozambique National Resistance Organization (RENAMO). Peace moves have been made, but fighting continues.

Sri Lanka (1975–): Indian intervention (1987–90) led to a bitter counter-insurgency operation of the civil war between the ruling Sinhalese and the ethnic-Indian Tamils (particularly the Tamil Tigers), who are fighting for an independent Tamil state.

Angola (1976–): UNITA (National Union for the Total Independence of Angola) forces – initially aided by South Africa – fought the left-wing MPLA (People's Movement for the Liberation of Angola) government. The MPLA won the civil war of 1975–76, but continued to be opposed by UNITA rebels. A UN-supervised ceasefire (1991) was breached in 1992.

Afghanistan (1979–): Civil war was triggered by the Soviet invasion (1979). Mujahaddin guerrillas (Muslim fundamentalists) fought government forces even after the Soviet withdrawal (1989). In 1992 fundamentalists took Kabul and formed a provisional government, but factional – largely ethnic – fighting continues.

Cambodia (1979–1991): The 1991 ceasefire ended civil war between the Vietnamese-backed government and Pol Pot's Khmer Rouge. A UN Transitional Authority was established but spasmodic fighting continues.

El Salvador (1980–91): A UN-supervised peace agreement ended civil war between the government and left-wing Farabundo Marti National Liberation Front (FMLN) guerrillas.

Peru (1980–): Revolutionary activities of the Maoist Sendero Luminoso ('Shining Path') group triggered a counter-insurgency campaign by the government.

Sudan (1983–): Civil war continues between Islamic government forces and the Christian and pagan guerrillas of the Sudan People's Liberation Army (SPLA). The latter is subject to violent internal fighting. Western humanitarian aid has been disrupted.

Palestinian Intifada (1987–): The Palestinian uprising in the West Bank and Gaza Strip against Israeli occupying forces has been characterized by riots and shootings. Unrest continues despite on-going peace negotiations in the Middle East.

Myanmar (Burma; 1988–): Military despotic rule since 1988 has been opposed by a variety of political and nationalist groups. Non-Burman minorities have joined forces to fight against the military.

Somalia (1988–): An Ethiopian-backed uprising in N Somalia (1988) began armed opposition to President Barre, who fled (1991) after guerrillas attacked the capital, Mogadishu. The rebels have since fought among themselves and Somalia has descended into chaos. US Marines intervened (1992) to deliver humanitarian aid.

Liberia (1989–): ECOWAS deployed a peacekeeping force (1990) to end a civil war initially between the National Patriotic Front of Liberia (NLFL) and government forces, but fighting flared up between NLFL and rival rebel groups (1992) and is still continuing.

Kuwait (1990–91): Iraqi troops invaded Kuwait in 1990. A US-led multi-national force – under the auspices of the UN – used air attacks on Iraq and a 100-hour ground campaign to liberate Kuwait in 1991. Since then, the UN has monitored the border and the USA has initiated air strikes to deter Iraqi aggression.

Iraq (1991–): After the Gulf War (see Kuwait), Saddam Hussein faced uprisings by Shi'ite Muslims in the south and Kurds in the north. Allied 'no-fly zones' in these areas (and threats of intervention) have restrained Iraq, but small-scale attacks on the Shi'ites continue.

Georgia (1991–): Civil war between supporters and opponents of President Gamsakhurdia (1992), was followed by continuing secessionist wars as Muslims in Abkhazia and South Ossetia press for independence.

Croatia (1991–): War between Croats and ethnic Serbs in Krajina and parts of Slavonia following the break-up of Yugoslavia. A ceasefire was negotiated in early 1992 and a UN force deployed, but fighting resumed in 1993.

Bosnia-Herzegovina (1991–): Bosnian Serbs fought against Croats and Muslims (although the latter also fought each other) for control of what was central Yugoslavia. A UN force was deployed in 1992 to supervise the delivery of humanitarian aid. Peace negotiations are taking place, but fighting continues.

Armenia-Azerbaijan (1992–): Azeri and Armenian forces are fighting for control of Nagorno Karabakh, an enclave of Orthodox Christian Armenians surrounded by the Shi'ite Muslim Azeris.

Tajikistan (1992–): The ex-Communist rulers of this former Soviet republic have effectively defeated Islamic fundamentalists in the north.

NEW INTERNATIONAL DEFENCE COMMITMENTS

Since 1990 the map of Europe has changed dramatically. Germany has reunified, the Warsaw Pact has been disbanded and the USSR has disintegrated, producing a number of new independent states. Elsewhere, Yugoslavia has collapsed under the pressure of ethnic hatred and Czechoslovakia has been divided in two. The common denominator is the collapse of Communism, leaving the countries of the West relieved but without a tangible and predictable 'enemy'. This in turn has called into question the future of a number of international alliances and relationships that owed their creation to the identification of a common fear.

DEFENCE ORGANIZATIONS

The North Atlantic Treaty Organization (NATO; see p. 37), formed in April 1949 by Western states fearful of Soviet aggression, is the alliance most clearly affected. Recognition of the new reality was apparent as early as November 1991 when a North Atlantic Cooperation Council (NACC) was established to create a relationship between the existing NATO allies, former members of the Warsaw Pact (including the then USSR) and the Baltic republics of Estonia, Latvia and Lithuania. In June 1992 the NACC took the process further by offering the expertise and resources of NATO for crisis management and the settlement of disputes.

However, NATO, by the terms of its charter, cannot initiate involvement in international disputes; it has to respond to requests from other bodies. The most obvious of these is the United Nations (UN; see p. 25), which already has its own experienced crisis-management organization. Moreover, the UN, freed from the constraints of the superpower deadlock, is much more able to deal effectively with incidents on the world stage. Other organizations therefore tend to concentrate on regional crises, particularly if the response has to be one of peacemaking (intervening to ensure a settlement) rather than peacekeeping (deploying to keep rival factions apart in the aftermath of a ceasefire).

In Europe, the alternatives to the UN are the Western European Union (WEU; see p. 31), the European Community (EC; see p. 29) and the Conference on Security and Cooperation in Europe (CSCE; see p. 29). The WEU has been developed primarily as a European pillar of NATO and, since the Maastricht Treaty (1991), as an instrument of the European Union. As such, it has offered military units of its member states for humanitarian and rescue tasks, peacekeeping tasks, and tasks of combat forces in crisis management, including peacemaking. In July 1992 the WEU coordinated the deployment of a multinational naval force to the Adriatic to take part in monitoring sanctions imposed on Serbia and Montenegro. This leaves the CSCE – a body that represents all the states of Europe – as the institution most likely to take up the NATO offer of help in crisis management, although the CSCE may ask for such help only if requested to do so by a unanimous decision of all its member states, except the one against which measures are envisaged. NATO would then have to endorse such a request by its own unanimous vote.

NUCLEAR PROLIFERATION

Such a plethora of responses implies that any European crises will be dealt with. The degeneration of the former Yugoslavia into civil war shows the limits of effectiveness, raising the question of military intervention to enforce a settlement. However, conflicts and problems outside Europe are much more difficult. The proliferation of nuclear-weapon capability to states in unstable or potentially unstable regions in the world, is a cause for growing concern. This concern was epitomized by the policies of the UN towards Iraq in the aftermath of the Gulf War of 1991, where elements of Saddam Hussein's nuclear industry have been sought out and destroyed. In some cases, arrangements to control nuclear weapons have been effective. In late 1991 those former Soviet republics with nuclear weapons on their soil (Belarus, Kazakhstan and Ukraine) were quick to indicate that they would adhere to the Treaty on the Non-Proliferation of Nuclear Weapons (NPT) and become non-nuclear states as soon as possible. Both France and China have now also agreed to accede to NPT.

The real worries lie elsewhere. Although North Korea has signed the NPT, allowing inspectors from the International Atomic Energy Agency (IAEA) to visit nuclear sites, assurances that weapons are not being developed have not yet been accepted. In addition, a number of states are thought to be close to developing nuclear capability, including India, Pakistan, Argentina and Brazil, but until they sign the NPT, no-one can be sure. Local agreements, such as that between Argentina and Brazil (1991), may open the door to IAEA inspection, but are still restricted in scope. With ex-Soviet nuclear scientists looking for well-paid jobs elsewhere, the potential for the spread of nuclear capability is apparent.

The same is true of chemical and biological weapons – the 'poor man's nuclear capability' – with the added problem that factories producing them are almost impossible to distinguish from those engaged in more peaceful pursuits. Again, international and local agreements may be negotiated, but it is the verification of promises that is difficult to check. Such weapons in fact indicate a deeper problem – that of the spread of advanced technology, capable of inflicting precise and devastating damage on an enemy without the need for expensive mobilization of armies. Long range missiles such as the Soviet-designed Scud are a case in point, particularly as they can be used to deliver anything from a high-explosive warhead to chemical or even nuclear devices. Once a state in an unstable region gains access to such delivery means, its rivals will feel threatened and demand the same; something that has happened in the Middle East in recent years. The danger is that, should a conflict break out in such a region, no amount of crisis management will prevent escalation. The world is still a dangerous place.

TOWARDS A NEW WORLD ORDER

At a US Congress session in September 1990, shortly after America began orchestrating a collective response to Saddam Hussein's invasion of Kuwait, President Bush spoke of his hope for 'a new world order ... in which the nations of the world, East and West, North and South, can prosper and live in harmony ... a world where the rule of law supplants the rule of the jungle'. Similarly, in a speech made in April 1991, in the aftermath of the Gulf War, Bush expressed the hope that with the end of the Cold War a new world order, a new partnership of major powers working together for peace, had become a possibility.

Bush's references to a 'new world order' during and after the Gulf crisis of 1990–91 were dismissed by some observers as presidential rhetoric. He was accused of using idealism to mask self-interest in order to rally American opinion behind intervention in the Gulf. Yet Bush had done much to draw international attention to the possibilities that might flow from a profound change in the international political system. The adversarial relationship between the world's two most powerful states, the USA and the USSR, had at last ended. With the demise of the Soviet bloc and the Soviet Union itself, and with the Soviet Union's main successor state, Russia, apparently espousing Western ideology, East-West confrontation might now be replaced by cooperation. The Western powers and Russia, Bush suggested, could become partners on the management of the emerging new world order, one based on Western democratic notions such as the rule of law and pluralist democracy.

Bush's call for a new partnership of nations echoed those made by Western leaders after World Wars I and II. It differed from these earlier endeavours, however, in that it came not after a direct, all-out conflict but after a global proxy war. It also differed from earlier calls in that this time the leaders of the victorious alliance were not proposing to establish new international organizations to manage the affairs of the world – such as the League of Nations and the United Nations after World War I and World War II respectively – but to adopt and improve existing machinery, notably the UN, NATO and various European organizations.

THE CHANGING ROLE OF INTERNATIONAL AND REGIONAL ORGANIZATIONS

In the immediate aftermath of the demise of Marxist states in Eastern Europe, European bodies and institutions were at the forefront of efforts to manage the resultant dangers and opportunities. At the EC Maastricht meeting in December 1991 EC leaders seemed to recognize that without the Soviet threat European security problems might be manageable without the need to call on the USA for assistance. This was reflected in July 1992 in the Western European Union's (WEU; see p. 31) deployment of a multinational force to the Adriatic to take part in enforcing sanctions against Serbia (and Montenegro). European countries also responded to the changes in Eastern Europe through NATO (see p. 37) when, in November 1991, they helped set up the North Atlantic Cooperation Council (NACC). The NACC was established to create a relationship between the existing NATO allies, former members of the Warsaw Pact (including the then USSR) and the Baltic Republics.

If the collapse of the old order has given rise to an expanded role for organizations and bodies such as the EC (see p. 29), WEU and NATO, it has done much the same for the United Nations (see pp. 25–28). Founded in 1945 with a primary purpose of maintaining international peace and security, the UN's efforts to 'maintain the peace' were undermined from the very outset by deep political divisions, particularly those associated with the Cold War. With the Security Council hampered by a lack of unanimity among its great power members, the UN has been able only to exercise its enforcement powers, although it did manage to carry out several 'peace keeping' operations in which forces from member-states acted as buffers between states or factions at the request of the government(s) concerned. However, as Cold War tensions eased and then finally ceased, the UN was enabled (by its member-states) to play a more effective role in promoting international peace and security. This was demonstrated most readily by the Security Council's response to Saddam Hussein's invasion of Kuwait in 1990. It has also found expression in the UN's rapidly increasing number of 'peace keeping' operations; about a dozen by the end of 1992.

The Bush administration came to speak of the UN as fundamental to its hopes of creating a new world order, while Bush's successor, Bill Clinton, has spoken of the UN as a cornerstone of his world construct.

CHALLENGES FOR THE FUTURE

Whether the UN can live up to these high expectations remains to be seen. Bodies such as the UN can only be as effective as their member-states will allow them to be. The countries that have advocated a new world order might not be willing, or able, to bear the costs associated with collective actions against aggressors. In any event Western states, whether working multilaterally through international agencies or unilaterally, will face a plethora of problems in constructing a new world order. Although they no longer face the task of managing East-West hostility they are already encountering a series of challenges that have not been eased – and in some cases have even been exacerbated by – the collapse of the Eastern bloc. These challenges include the proliferation of weapons of mass destruction, resource depletion, environmental pollution and Third World poverty and associated mass migrations and, most notably, the resurgence of mutually antagonistic nationalisms. In the former Yugoslavia, for example, UN sanctions against Serbia have been flouted, UN resolutions ignored and even UN relief convoys have been attacked. The inability of the UN and other international bodies to halt the conflict in the former Yugoslavia is but one of numerous elements of actual and potential disorder to threaten the emerging new world order.

EASTERN EUROPE: TOWARDS A MARKET ECONOMY

The year of the Single Market for Western Europe was a sombre one for Eastern Europe. Real progress was made on privatization, on the rationalization of state industry, on the setting up of new intra-regional trading and payments arrangements, and on the development of economic relationships with the West. Yet the overall picture is still negative: output has fallen, by as much as 33% in Lithuania. High rates of inflation, associated with menacingly large budget deficits, has led to hyper-inflation (over 2000% in Russia and Ukraine). Unemployment has risen (13% in Slovakia), and the East – particularly the CIS countries (see p. 34) – has chronic trading deficits and payments difficulties with the West. The worldwide recession and continuing uncertainly about basic economic and political trends in Eastern Europe has limited the flow of Western aid and investment.

It is not difficult to find exceptions to all these negative trends. Industrial production in Poland is now trending upwards, while inflation fell from 70% in 1991 to 45% in 1992. The most encouraging aspect of the Polish record is that inflation has been brought under control even though the budget remains substantially in deficit. It seems, on the basis of Poland's experience, that if budgetary deficits can be reduced to not much more than 5% of GNP, inflation can be contained. Equally encouraging for other East European states is the indication that the IMF (see p. 28) will accept this proposition and release substantial new credits for Poland on that basis. In the former Czechoslovakia, the rate of inflation remained under 10% in 1992, and unemployment in the new Czech Republic was recorded at just over 4%. While industrial output in the Czech Republic and Slovakia fell in accordance with the general regional pattern, total retail sales grew substantially in both republics, with around half of that total being attributed to the private sector. The consolidated (combined central, regional and local) budget of the former Czechoslovakia is reported to have shown a small surplus. In Hungary, despite continued difficulties with the budget and signs of growing social discontent with unemployment, inflation and falling real wages, the flow of foreign private investment remains relatively buoyant. In conjunction with a privatization strategy that has been sustained rather than headlong, this marks out Hungary as the country with the best economic prospects.

NATIONALISM AND STATEHOOD

Nationalism and statehood are perhaps the most critical areas for the political and economic future of Eastern Europe. Poland and Hungary excepted, the entire region has been overtaken by an overwhelming tendency to ethnically-based fragmentation. In the case of the Czech Republic and Slovakia the transition has been peaceful enough so far, while in Yugoslavia it has produced full-scale civil war. Within the old Soviet Union, with its myriad nationalities, there are cases that might qualify for the soubriquet 'velvet divorce' and a few that have rather followed the Bosnian model, with the majority coming somewhere in between.

The reemergence of nationalism as a dominant political force in the region was no doubt inevitable once the ideology and repression of Communism had passed. The new nationalisms of Eastern Europe were, in the main, genuinely spontaneous mass movements. In the majority of cases, however, those mass movements have found their leaders among the cadres of the old Communist parties. The emergence of the ex-Communist capitalist was closely followed – particularly in 1992 – by the emergence of the ex-Communist nationalist. It is worth noting that countries as diverse as Croatia, Serbia, Slovenia, Romania, Slovakia and Ukraine are currently all ruled – in the name of nationalism – by men who were formerly members of the Communist Party. Perhaps the most significant political result of 1992 was the electoral defeat of anti-Communist nationalist Landsbergis by the former Communist nationalist Brazauskas in Lithuania. The severe economic decline in Lithuania may have been a factor.

Brazauskas's victory in the Lithuanian election genuinely represented the will of the people, as did the election of ex-communist nationalists President Milosevic in Serbia, President Kravchuk in Ukraine, and Prime Minister Meciar in Slovakia. They all won overwhelmingly in (more or less) fair elections in recent years. Virtually all the new leaders of Eastern Europe, nationalist or not, can lay claim to democratic credentials, at least at the level of electoral procedures. Under the ex-Communist nationalist regimes, however, traditionally Communist authoritarian patterns continue to prevail in everyday life. Similarly privatization programmes are often used as a smokescreen for effective nationalization, or simple transfer of property rights from the old Communist state to the new 'nationalist' elites. This represents a perfect marriage between ex-Communist nationalism and ex-Communist capitalism.

There are no grounds to suppose that ex-Communist nationalist regimes are bound to produce worse economic policies than more liberal-democratic regimes. It is nevertheless striking that Ukraine, under an ex-Communist nationalist regime, has been the slowest of all the ex-Soviet republics to deal with the basics of economic transformation. Within Russia it has been the regions under liberal-democratic local leaders that have made most progress with transformation policies and are having greatest success attracting foreign business. Slovakia is an example of the political and economic dangers of ex-Communist nationalism in power. Faced with rising unemployment and an uncontrollable budget deficit, Prime Minister Meciar has announced plans to increase the production and exports of arms, its traditional specialization under Communist rule. At the same time, the dispute between Slovakia and Hungary over the Gabcikovo dam on the river Danube, which separates the two countries, has become increasingly bitter. Budapest has accused Bratislava of reneging on an EC-sponsored agreement aimed at limiting the ecological damage caused by the project. This drama has unfolded against a background of growing tension between the two countries over the treatment of the 600 000-strong Hungarian minority in Slovakia.

PRIVATIZATION

There are two main models of privatization that have been implemented in the region. The 'top-down' holding company model, based on the German *Treuhandanstalt* system was widely employed in Poland and in the Yugoslav successor states. The 'bottom-up' voucher system was pioneered in the former Czechoslovakia and introduced in Russia in late 1992. Starting in May 1992, a substantial proportion of Czech and Slovak industry was privatized in the course of four rounds of selling-off. Every citizen received vouchers to a certain value, which could then be exchanged for shares in enterprises or in the investment funds. In the event, some 72% of the vouchers issued over the initial rounds of privatization were exchanged for shares in investment funds.

In Russia the pattern has been different in that the vouchers (privatization cheques) issued have been largely sold for cash (roubles) on the stock markets of the Federation. While there is great interest in the idea of investment funds in Russia, there is no proper legislation to cover their activities, and those operating do so at their own risk. As a result, Russian citizens are faced with the choice of investing their vouchers directly in enterprises or turning them into cash. In practice they have largely done the latter.

There can be no doubt that the Czecho-Slovak voucherization initiative has succeeded in creating a viable model of privatization capable of setting up a large number of independent industrial enterprises faster than alternative models. Substantial doubts remain as to the extent to which the voucher system is being used as a way of laundering former Communist and mafia money, and there are worries that such elements might start interfering in the management of enterprises. There is no evidence yet that this is going to be a major problem, but it is too early to make a definitive asessment.

The Russian voucherization experiment was not only a relative failure but caused fresh currency problems. The rouble actually strengthened against the dollar towards the end of 1992, as dealers bought roubles in order to buy up vouchers. But interest in vouchers then began to tail off, which in turn resulted in a drop in the demand for roubles. This, combined with underlying inflationary trends, precipitated a cumulative fall in the value of the rouble against the dollar on the Moscow exchange of around 40% through January 1993. The currency drop signalled a new dimension of crisis in the Russian economy.

INTRA-REGIONAL TRADE AND PAYMENTS

The early years of the post-Communist era saw a dangerous drop in the volume of intra-regional trade. This was caused partly by the breakdown of the Comecon system which, although clumsy and ineffi-

cient, did provide some kind of a basis for trade. It has also been caused by the inclination of ex-Communist nationalist governments for self-sufficieny and the discouragement of imports. Recent developments have offered some hope that the region may begin to move towards a functional system of economic cooperation. Most significant was the signature, in December 1992, of a Central European Free Trade Agreement (CEFTA), between Poland, the Czech Republic, Slovakia and Hungary (the so-called Visegard Group). The agreement sets out a path towards free trade between the four by the year 2001, though with all the reservations about 'sensitive' industrial sectors like textiles, steel and cars, and also agriculture, with which we are so familiar in the EC. In establishing CEFTA the member states have recognized that it is better to try to build free trade in their own backyard than to hang around hoping for admission to the EC. Perhaps most important of all, it is an alliance of the three front-runners – Poland, the Czech Republic and Hungary – which could, in time, build a new regional market of respectable proportions, to which neighbouring countries would then be drawn.

It is not so easy to be hopeful about the CIS agreement on the setting up of an Inter-State Bank (January 1993), which would provide the financial basis for multilateral clearing of trade balances between republics and create a framework for the coordination of monetary and budgetary policy. As long as the rouble remains so weak (as a result of the weakness of Russian economic policy), it will be impossible for an effective rouble zone to be created. At the same time, even weak roubles can be used to finance local budget deficits, so that the republics have an incentive to string along with the existing messy state of affairs, printing local 'coupons' and other forms of substitute money to supplement rather than supplant the rouble.

The brightest star on the East European horizon is the CEFTA. All the members of CEFTA have existing association agreements with the EC, and there is a real chance that markets can build on markets to create a genuine impetus for economic integration. With the exception of Slovenia, prospects throughout the former Yugoslavia are blighted by civil war, and in the Baltic region the problem of trading with Russia for oil will have to be sorted out before sustained progress can be made. In the CIS, the critical factor is Russian economic policy. The first year of an independent Russia was marked by a progressive loss of control of the macro-economy (national income, consumption and investment). The decline was paralleled by a progressive haemorrage of political power from liberal democrats to an alliance of conservative industrialists and ex-Communist nationalists. In January 1993 the Russian government announced an ambitious programme of macroeconomic stabilization that looks frankly unrealistic. But without a large measure of stabilization it will be difficult to move forward with the restructuring of the Russian economy, and impossible to create the new inter-republican financial mechanisms envisaged by the 1993 Minsk meeting of CIS states. East of Brest and south of Szeged the fate of the market still hangs in the balance.

DEVELOPMENT AND CONSERVATION

The Third World comprises the developing countries of Africa, Asia and Latin America. The term 'Third World' was coined in France to evoke a comparison with the three 'Estates' of French society before the revolution of 1789. The Third Estate had very few political rights, and was considerably impoverished. Similarly today, the Third World experiences great economic difficulties, and lacks political power in the world's financial and trading institutions. Its negotiating posture in the UN and elsewhere has always reflected this concern.

The conditions for development in the Third World have changed substantially as a result of the end of the Cold War and attempts to find global solutions to problems on the environment and international trade. The difficulties encountered in these areas were well demonstrated in 1992 by the Rio Conference on the Environment (UNCED) and the discussions within the Uruguay Round at the GATT. The Third World (or 'South') has become more than ever a victim of the debates within the First (or 'North').

The changes in Eastern Europe have created a new problem for developing countries because these newly democratic European states are drawing both money and resources, especially from international development agencies, that would otherwise have been concentrated in the South. This is not necessarily a disaster, partly because the Northern response to Eastern Europe has not been spectacularly successful, but also because developing countries now look more stable than the old Eastern Bloc. The most significant rise in direct inward investment in 1992 was to Latin America. Developing countries might also find new and lucrative markets in Eastern Europe. They might also benefit from the necessary reforms of the EC's Common Agricultural Policy, which will tend to increase the prices of agricultural products by reducing EC stocks. This, in turn, will reduce the dumping of such surpluses, often under the pseudonym of 'aid'. The creation of the Single Market in 1993 (see p. 29) might produce increased export possibilities for the developing countries, as promised by the 1988 Cecchini Report, but it might also increase the chances of the emergence of a European bloc that excludes developing countries.

The main short and medium-term concern must focus on the changes within Third World countries themselves. Internally driven demands for democracy and accountability (as in Eastern Europe, Latin America, much of Africa, as well as in China) have been taken up by international agencies (especially the World Bank) in the name of 'conditionality'. For the first time agencies are imposing political as well as economic conditions on loans and grants to finance structural adjustment and debt repayment. A debate has also emerged between some developing countries who are prepared to open radically their economies along the lines advocated by the World Bank and those who advocate the old policies of import substitution and government intervention.

Developing countries vary enormously in their present conditions and future prospects. The gap between the newly industrializing countries like Taiwan, South Korea and Brazil and the small, often island or landlocked, lesser developed countries like Chad, Zambia or Haiti, continues to grow. While capital stocks in Asian and Latin American developing countries have generally been growing since 1980, in Africa they have usually declined. The World Bank defines more than 50 Third World countries as falling within its lowest income groups (i.e. those with less than $610 GNP per capita). A further 90 states are defined as middle-income economies (i.e. having between $611–$2465 GNP per capita). To complicate matters, 26 of the low income states and 15 of the middle-income countries are also seen as 'severely indebted'.

INTERNATIONAL TRADE

Since the early 1980s accusations of 'unfair' trading practices have mainly been made by the great trading nations (or indeed 'blocs', like the EC) against each other. These countries dominate world trade, but when giants fall out and indulge in 'managed trade', 'regionalism' and 'unilateralism' the developing countries get hurt, as they have fewer possibilities for retaliation. This has not been helped by the inability of the North to agree on a final text for the Uruguay Round of GATT. International trade could receive a huge boost from a successful conclusion to the Uruguay Round, as it would reduce tariffs and other obstacles to international trade. The ability of developing countries to benefit from this will depend on their individual circumstances, such as their inherent ability to improve their terms of trade and their overall economic, political and social stability.

Developing countries have a much bigger stake in the current GATT Round than in any previous one, with over 80 of them participating. Many developing countries have embarked on reform programmes to fulfil their economic needs and the Rule of the GATT. These reforms have varied from putting more stress on export-led growth, or a reduction of import substitution policies, to a more general opening of markets. However, tariffs on goods from developing countries to the richer North remain high, and have actually increased recently. Since the 1986 GATT meeting developing countries have been particularly concerned about trade in agriculture and services, which are the main sticking points of the present Round. Developing countries have entered into novel alliances, such as with agricultural exporting developed countries like Australia and New Zealand in the Cairns Group. The GATT Round has not met with success yet, mainly because of disputes between the EC and the USA. Developing countries will also be paying particular attention to Northern promises to abolish the Multifibre Arrangement of the GATT which imposes quotas on their export of textiles.

The commitment of developing countries to the GATT process may prove a cruel deception if the Round fails, given the inevitable restructuring that many of the economies of the developing countries have endured to fulfil GATT requirements. Much will depend on the actual (as opposed to feared) emergence of trading blocs, within which some developing countries seem likely to be included (as with the US 'Enterprise for the Americas' scheme and NAFTA; see p. 36), and some excluded. Market access for developing countries will determine their trading futures.

ENVIRONMENTAL ISSUES

Environmental issues, as discussed at the 1992 Rio Conference, largely reflect the concerns of the developed world, especially the issues of deforestation, greenhouse gases and biodiversity. The environment is not a problem for developing countries in the same way as it is for the developed world. Poverty, the development of infrastructure and economic activity (as a way out of poverty) are their major concerns. There is a significant danger than politicians in the West will use the environmental card to impose restrictions on exports from developing countries as a form of Green protectionism. Since primary commodities – the most polluting – make up a significant proportion of the exports from developing countries this could severely limit their ability to repay debt and finance development. On the other hand environmental degradation, usually as a result of poverty, has led to some of the worst excesses of deforestation and desertification as population growth forces the use of marginal lands. This is not in the long-term interest of developing countries with growing populations.

The ideal answer would be a form of 'sustainable development', an idea first popularized by the Brundtland Commission. One way that has the support of the World Bank is to stress the economic efficiency that will derive from withdrawing subsidies to (often heavily polluting) state-controlled industries and investing funds instead in water purification and sanitation that will create jobs while helping the environment. At the same time there should be an improvement in governmental institutions to protect the environment, even if the market must generally guide development. It is a balancing act that might prove difficult. Recently Brazil's Environment Minister, with strong Green convictions, was dismissed for being over-zealous and threatening industrial interests.

Large developing countries, such as China and India, risk engendering social problems such as unemployment when trying to fulfil OECD demands for reductions, or stabilisation, of industry-related pollution, such as CFCs. Attempts to reduce greenhouse gases, especially carbon dioxide, are also problematic since the environmental costs of alternatives, such as hydro-electric dams and nuclear power stations, are well documented. A Global Environment Facility financed by donor countries has so far about $1.3 billion to distribute, mainly to biodiversity issues. Biodiversity is of more concern to the developed world than to the Third World. Drug companies in the North want to conserve species in the rain forest that may be a source of new compounds. Equally, there is little evidence that the preservation of wild animal species, another key Northern concern, is a great priority for developing countries, except in the maintenance of the tourist trade. The Rio Conference did not do much to provide new resources, without which it will be difficult to encourage developing countries to implement painful environmental policies.

It is difficult to see that the needs of conservation, in such areas as rain forest maintenance, carbon emissions or biodiversity, are obviously congruent with those of development. Most major international organizations are trying to make the case for this being true in the long term. However, developing countries may well take a short-term view of the problem – despite pressure from aid donors. This tendency may well be exacerbated by the new-born democratic forces in many of developing countries, who have more pressing priorities.

DEBT AND THE ENVIRONMENT

Although the debt crisis has long been with us, it has now developed an environmental dimension. The main solution that links the two concerns – 'debt-for-nature swaps' – has been espoused by non-governmental organizations (such as Greenpeace) as a way of exchanging the national debts of developing countries for a promise not to damage the environment of a given area. The idea, though neat, has made little headway against the huge totals of debt in existence which necessitate the production and export of as many (often environmentally sensitive) products as possible to service the debt.

The main initiatives suggested to reduce the debts of developing countries in the 1980s were the Brady Initiative of 1989, the OECD Paris Club, and bilateral deals. Although these initiatives have reduced debt totals, the price has often been high in terms of the 'conditionality' imposed by lenders such as the International Monetary Fund (IMF). Lending states and private lenders have not yet recovered from the shock of unilateral debt moratoria declared by some of the big developing countries in the early 1980s. In 1990 the level of capital flow to developing countries was still 40% below its 1981 level. Indeed it has been calculated that there are now net capital outflows to the North from the South. However, since most of this decline has been due to private flows it is now seen in some quarters as worrying that 'debt fatigue' is causing aid to be reduced, although there are those who think that aid is part of the problem, not the solution. The IMF and the World Bank have increasingly become the linchpin of the process of debt reduction and structural adjustment for developing countries.

The debt crisis also affects Eastern Europe, and the 'aid fatigue' that concerns developing countries is partly linked with the need to reduce debt and promote structural adjustment in Europe. There are limits to global resources faced with such gigantic tasks. The signs for Eastern Europe are not promising, with only a fraction of the $20 billion promised in Washington in February 1992 having been transferred. The first World Bank report on Russia in August 1992 identified a need for at least this amount per year for the next several years. If no new 'Marshall Plan' for Eastern Europe is to materialize, it is even less likely to materialize for the Third World. The best that developing countries can hope for is success in the Uruguay Round of the GATT talks and that debt restructuring continues, albeit at a snail's pace. These factors together are the best hope for a more integrated global economy although they appear merely as crumbs falling from the rich man's table.

THE DECLINE OF THE USA

The USA is undergoing a profound transition that is more than the beginning of a new administration under President Clinton. It is fundamentally a consequence of a period of massive upheaval in world affairs. Many commentators have seen the transition as one of decline, but it is likely that the outcome will prove more complex. The 1990s offer opportunities as well as challenges for America's role in the world.

ECONOMIC CRISIS

The disintegration of the USSR and discrediting of Communism has ended the Cold War. It seems paradoxical that the talk should be of American decline at a time when the USA – as the leading defender of the liberal democratic alternative – has triumphed over Communism. The explanation lies in the fact that much of America's power during the Cold War era stemmed from the existence of the USSR. Confronted with the perceived Soviet threat, America constructed a nuclear umbrella under which its allies sheltered and indeed prospered. With the removal of the external enemy the need for this protection has vanished and America's world role is reduced in consequence. The problem, however, is more acute. The Western alliance also acted as a discipline on America's allies, dependent as they were on its protection. That restraint has now disappeared and has left the USA open to economic competition from its erstwhile subordinates in the alliance. The USA does not appear to be well placed to meet this challenge, for there has been a gradual decline in American economic competitiveness that was masked by its political and military power in the Cold War.

To some extent decline was inevitable. American pre-eminence after World War II was the result of the ravages war imposed on other major economies; an unnatural state of affairs that could not last. Moreover, the revival of allied economies was the central purpose of US policy, both to create the prosperity that would act as a bulwark against the advance of Socialism, and to provide markets for American goods and capital. In this sense America created its own rivals and their current power is testament to the strength of the post-war western capitalist order the USA created. In a sense America has been a victim of its own success.

Whatever its past success, the pressing need for the USA now is to come to terms with the present and future threats to its competitiveness. One reason for the American economic crisis is the cost of political and military commitments associated with its superpower status. Maintaining these has diverted resources away from long-term investment in the civilian sector, and this has undermined productivity growth and export potential. The German and Japanese economies have been relieved of these imperial burdens and focussed their resources in more productive areas and increased their competitiveness (at America's expense), even while they benefited from its protection.

However, America's economic problems go beyond imperial overstretch. Its economy has developed a chronic imbalance between consumption and investment that has undermined the growth in the rate of productivity, which declined from 2.7% in 1947–68 to 1.4% in the 1980s. This was accentuated by the free market policies of the Reagan and Bush administrations which eschewed government involvement in a partnership with business and labour. The partnership – designed to promote the long-term planning of industrial development – has characterized the more successful economies. In its place there was a strategy of tax cuts to promote personal consumption and investment. It was intended that the benefits of this kind of growth would trickle down through society. However, in reality the policy has increased inequality and its attendant social problems, and encouraged a 'get rich quick' mentality that only reinforces the fundamental imbalances in the economy. The results were a massive federal budget deficit, which grew from 1% of GNP in the 1960s to 4.5% in the 1980s, and a balance of payments deficit which turned the USA from the world's largest creditor nation in 1980 to the largest debtor nation by the end of the decade. In addition a decline of national savings has led to a mountain of personal debt. These imbalances will have to be redressed in the 1990s, and will act as a constraint on economic growth.

THE CLINTON ADMINISTRATION

President Clinton was elected because awareness of these problems had become so pervasive and faith in the free market solution had weakened. His promise to focus on domestic problems is often seen as a move away from Bush's preoccupation with ensuring America's leading role in the New World Order. However, the shift is more apparent than real since Clinton is not advocating a new isolationism; rather he is suggesting that unless America rebuilds its domestic economic strength it will be unable to play a leading role in world affairs. Domestic strength and international leadership must be seen as complementary, with the former the essential precondition of the latter. The Clinton administration therefore remains committed to the spread of liberal democracy across the globe and to the free trade that has underpinned the post-war economic success. But the revitalization of the American economy will require substantial sacrifices. Pressures to resort to protectionism to cushion the process remain strong. There is a danger that free trade will be replaced by three trading blocs centred on the USA, the EC and Japan. The newly formed North American Free Trade Area (NAFTA; see p. 36) may be seen as an attempt by the USA to prepare for such a possibility.

There is widespread awareness that in the absence of the constraints imposed by the Cold War, the new era will require strong leadership if the threat of economic and political strife is to be avoided. The USA remains the country with the best combination of political, ideological, military and economic strengths to meet such a challenge. If Clinton can reinvigorate America's economy, he will have laid the groundwork for a role in world affairs in which the USA is less dominant than it once was, but where it remains first among equals.

THE RESURGENCE OF DEMOCRACY IN THE THIRD WORLD

The shift away from authoritarian military and single-party regimes began in Latin America in 1982, and later spread to Africa and other parts of the Third World. In both continents internal pressures for change were strengthened in varying degress by Western encouragement – sometimes including economic and military coercion – and by the ending of the Cold War. Although the changes were undoubtedly dramatic, by 1993, their permanence, especially in Africa, was far from assured. Elsewhere, major reverses included the suppression of the pro-democracy movement in China, following the brutal massacre in Tiananmen Square in 1989, and continuing military rule in Myanmar (Burma).

CHANGES IN LATIN AMERICA

In Latin America, democracy has vied with dictatorship since independence was achieved in the early 19th century, but by the 1970s the vast majority of the population lived under military or militarized regimes. Only three of the twenty Latin American countries could be regarded as democratic. The abuse of human rights was widespread, and was often tolerated by the West in the name of anti-Communism. By 1990, briefly and for the first time in its history, the whole of mainland America enjoyed constitutional rule. Elections in 1982 in Brazil, by far the largest and most populous Latin American country, helped to establish a trend. This was reinforced in the same year when Argentina's defeat by Britain over the Falkland Islands (Islas Malvinas) discredited its military rulers and paved the way for the return to civilian rule under President Raúl Alfonsín. In 1990, following similar changes in other South American countries, popular opposition to General Pinochet's rule in Chile succeeded in returning the country to its long democratic tradition. In Central America the active hostility of the USA to left-wing governments (as in Nicaragua) and left-wing popular movements (as in El Salvador), greatly complicated and delayed but did not halt the process for change. In its invasions of Grenada in 1983 and Panama in 1989, the USA could claim to be on the side of reform, although there was no such intervention to rescue the short-lived civilian regime of Father Aristide in Haiti.

Although immediate economic difficulties helped make the South American military rulers lose their nerve, it was economic growth over the longer term that underpinned the democracy movement. Economic growth decisively expanded 'civil society ' through the effects of urbanization, education, and the spread of networks of participatory voluntary organizations. A major contribution to the latter came from the development of 'liberation theology' within a part of the Roman Catholic Church. Liberation theology insists that Christianity involves a 'preferential option for the poor' and the active involvement of the oppressed in their own emancipation, including violence, if necessary. While this outlook directly encouraged many of the urban poor and discontented into political activism, it also encouraged middle-class support for democratic reform as a way of pre-empting the more radical social message of liberation theology. Meanwhile, as the power of Communism waned, the West increasingly voiced the cause of human rights, lending still greater legitimacy to the democratic movement.

CHANGES IN AFRICA

In contrast to Latin America, Africa's previous experience of democracy was limited to a very short period at independence (c. 1960 for the majority of African states). Colonial rule had itself been authoritarian, and independence was soon followed in most African countries by the personal rule of one-party presidents or by military despots who had seized power. The Black majority in South Africa have long been denied political rights, but by the mid-1980s its white regime was under severe internal and external pressure to end apartheid and introduce democracy.

Elsewhere, internal oppositions favouring a return to democracy were perceptible throughout the continent, but without appearing to have much chance of success. However, economic distress and national indebtedness forced many African governments to accept stringent 'structural adjustment programmes' formulated by the International Monetary Fund and the World Bank (see p. 28). The programmes prescribed what was called 'good governance', as well as the hardships of economic liberalization as a cure for African ills. As Soviet power diminished, Western governments made improved human rights and moves towards democracy a condition of further aid.

This, together with the demonstration effects of the destruction of the Berlin Wall and the fall of Communism in Eastern Europe, finally unleashed a wave of apparent democratization in 1990–92. The Mengistu dictatorship was overthrown in Ethiopia and there were peace accords in Angola and Mozambique. Throughout French-speaking Africa, national conferences refused to disband until political change was conceded: in English-speaking African countries multi-party systems were also grudgingly accepted. Some leaders were voted out (most notably in Zambia, Benin and Congo), others clung to office by holding elections before the opposition had time to organize (as in Côte d'Ivoire and Gabon) or by undue interference with the elections (Ghana and Kenya). In some countries, such as Ghana and Kenya, the democratic opposition contributed to their defeat through internal divisions. Some leaders were toppled by popular demonstrations or with the help of the army, while others just fled. Delaying tactics have been common, and many critical elections remain to be held, as in three of Africa's largest countries, Nigeria, Mozambique and Zaïre. In Angola, elections were held, but the losers, UNITA, refused to accept a democratic result and re-opened the civil war. The formidable economic and social problems facing the continent make the prospects for political stability and for genuine democracy uncertain at best.

ISLAM AND POLITICS

Islam as a political force burst onto the international stage in 1979 with the revolution in Iran. Encouraged, and sometimes financed, by Ayatollah Khomeini, political groups inspired by Islam mushroomed across the Muslim states of the Middle East, Africa and Asia. The 1980s were the decade of Islamic fundamentalism. The explosive mixture of radical politics and militant Islam threatened stability wherever it arose. Social and political upheaval accompanied the Iranian revolution. Iraq began its eight-year war with Iran to keep revolutionary Islam at bay. In Egypt Islamic militants assassinated President Sadat, and in Lebanon a generation of hostage-taking gangs claimed inspiration from fundamentalist Islam.

The aims of Islamic fundamentalism vary but a number of aims are common to most fundamentalist groups. These include the introduction of government based on Islamic *sharia* law; the banning of alcohol; the enforcement of strict dress codes for women; the separate education of boys and girls; and the strict observance of fasting during daylight hours in the Islamic holy month of Ramadan. On economics, there is much variation as some groups veer towards socialism, while others believe strongly in individual property rights. Many groups contain a powerful streak of religious intolerance; Baha'is, Jews and Christians have been persecuted in Islamic Iran.

THE REVIVAL OF ISLAMIC FUNDAMENTALISM

Islam has seen many religious revivals in its long history. The latest wave began in a small way in the mid-19th century with calls from Islamic scholars for the recreation of a pristine society that followed the 7th-century teachings of the Prophet Muhammad. These ideas were transformed into a more radical political creed in the present century by Muslim thinkers appalled by the domination of the Middle East by European powers. The latest generation of fundamentalists is more radical still. Many of them have called for a *jihad*, or holy war, to rescue the *umma*, the Islamic community of nations, from the corrupt standards of secular governments. What makes the latest movement more effective than earlier ones is its popularity.

The Islamic wave has its roots in the spiritual and cultural dislocation experienced by Muslims trying to reconcile traditional beliefs with the onslaught of Western culture. While many Muslims welcome the technological and material benefits of Western civilization they do not want the liberal social baggage that goes with it. The movement draws strength from the failure of secular ideologies of nationalism, socialism and free-market capitalism to ease this sense of cultural dislocation or raise the standard of living for the masses. It feeds on a nostalgic desire to restore the Islamic world to its former glory – to reverse centuries of decline that many Muslims blame on the degeneration of their faith and the malign influence of Western culture. Denunciation of Western culture is a feature of many fundamentalist groups. The Iranian revolution was in part a reaction of the educated and religious classes against what they perceived as Westernization and social degradation, and partly a result of the anger of the Iranian poor that they had not shared in the country's oil wealth.

THE SPREAD OF ISLAMIC FUNDAMENTALISM

The success of the Islamic fundamentalists has been limited. They rule only in Iran, Sudan and Afghanistan, and even in the two latter cases they are not in complete control. In Sudan the junta is dominated by the fundamentalist National Islamic Front. In Afghanistan the ruling regime has nationalist and Islamic strands inextricably mixed. In some countries, such as Syria, Iraq and Libya fundamentalist groups have been ruthlessly suppressed. In others, such as Egypt and Jordan, governments have attempted to separate extremists in the Islamic movement from moderates, crushing the former and drawing the latter into the political system. At the same time they have promoted state Islam and their own Islamic credentials.

The general failure of Islamic fundamentalists to take power by force persuaded Islamic groups in some countries to work within the existing political system, and seek power by democratic means. But in most Muslim countries that allow political parties, religiously-based parties are banned and fundamentalists are hunted down. The closest an Islamic party has come to winning power through the ballot box was in Algeria in 1991. However, when it looked as if the Algerian Islamic Salvation Front would win the general election in the final vote, the army stepped in to cancel the vote and outlaw the Front.

The future of Islamic fundamentalism is uncertain. Iran's influence as a source of radical Islam has waned since the death of Ayatollah Khomeini. Needing the West's help to rebuild an economy battered by revolution and war, Iran's leaders have been obliged to temper their efforts to export Islamic revolution. The clear failure of Islamic government in Iran to meet the material needs of the people, and the social dislocation caused by the revolution, means that the example of Iran no longer shines as brightly as it once did. Saudi Arabia, which has been run along fundamentalist lines since the 1920s, has cut the flow of funds it used to supply to Islamic groups when most of them backed Saddam Hussein in the Gulf War.

However, the Islamic wave has not yet broken. In Egypt the struggle between the government and Islamic extremists continues. A radical Palestinian Islamic movement, Hamas, has emerged as a major threat to both Israel and the PLO. Islamic activists have launched a guerrilla campaign against the government in Algeria. In the former Soviet Central Asian states, the Islamic Republican Party and other Islamic groups pose a potent challenge to secular governments. However, secular Muslim Turkey offers a different role model for the emerging Central Asian republics. In Malaysia and Indonesia political Islam has provided a home for those excluded from the political system. Islamic fundamentalism has triumphed, so far, in few places but it remains a potent political force.

THE ECONOMIC WORLD

POPULATION

Somewhere between 24 June and 11 July 1987, the human population of the planet Earth reached 5 billion. Yet, two hundred years before that, when the world's population was barely more than one billion, political economists such as Thomas Malthus and David Ricardo were already predicting that the human species would breed itself into starvation. Nevertheless, despite their predictions the human population keeps increasing – but so too does the food supply.

A direct relationship bewteen population and hunger was indicated 1800 years ago by Tertullian, an early Christian writer from North Africa, when he said 'We weigh upon the world; its resources hardly suffice to support us. As our needs grow larger, so do our protests that already nature does not sustain us.' Over thepast 200 years this concern has intensified. With more effective means of communication and more accurate record keeping, knowledge about living conditions of peoples all over the world has become more accessible. The Chinese famine of 1876–79 claimed approximately 13 000 000 lives, the 1943 Bengal famine 3 000 000 and the Ethiopian famine of 1984 up to 1 000 000.

Two contending views have emerged concerning the extent to which burgeoning populations affect food supply. The first is that population must be controlled if persistent malnutrition and starvation are not to become the inevitable lot for a substantial portion of the globe. The second is that, even with a projected global population of 10 billion by the year 2070 there is sufficient food to feed everyone.

POPULATION INCREASE
In 1990, every day the population of the world increased by an estimated 210 000 people – that is an additional 76 000 000 people in one year. The rate of increase varies from an average of 0.75% per annum in Europe to 3.05% in Africa. In the period between 1980 and 1985 the population of Kenya grew by 4.12% per annum at one extreme while the population of Suriname declined by an average of 0.42% per annum.

URBANIZATION
Urbanization – the increased migration of rural dwellers into cities – has been a particular feature of the second half of the 20th century. In 1950 under 30% of the population of the world lived in urban regions, but by 1990 almost 44% lived in cities, towns or their suburbs. The greatest proportion of urban dwellers is to be found in countries of the developed world. Almost 95% of the population of Belgium, for example, is urban.

On the map showing the world's largest cities (p. 51) the population figures given relate to the agglomeration or urban area; that is the city, its suburbs and surrounding built-up area rather than for local government districts.

POPULATION GROWTH

Period	World population
Neolithic period	5 000 000 – 10 000 000
4000 BC	c. 50 000 000
AD 500	c. 100 000 000
AD 800	c. 200 000 000
c. 1550	c. 500 000 000
1805	1 000 000 000
1926	2 000 000 000
1960	3 000 000 000
1974	4 000 000 000
1987	5 000 000 000
1998 (projected)	6 000 000 000
2010 (projected)	7 000 000 000
2023 (projected)	8 000 000 000
2040 (projected)	9 000 000 000
2070 (projected)	10 000 000 000

HIGHEST LIFE EXPECTANCY

Country	Life expectancy* average
Japan	79 years
Iceland	78 years
Sweden	78 years
Switzerland	78 years
Australia	77 years
Canada	77 years
France	77 years
Italy	77 years
Netherlands	77 years
Norway	77 years
San Marino	77 years

LOWEST LIFE EXPECTANCY

Country	Life expectancy* average
Guinea-Bissau	39 years
Afghanistan	42 years
Sierra Leone	42 years
Guinea	43 years
Gambia	44 years
Niger	45 years
Angola	46 years
Malawi	46 years
Burundi	47 years
Chad	47 years
Equatorial Guinea	47 years
Mauritania	47 years
Mozambique	47 years
Senegal	47 years
Uganda	47 years

* average life expectancy for 1990.

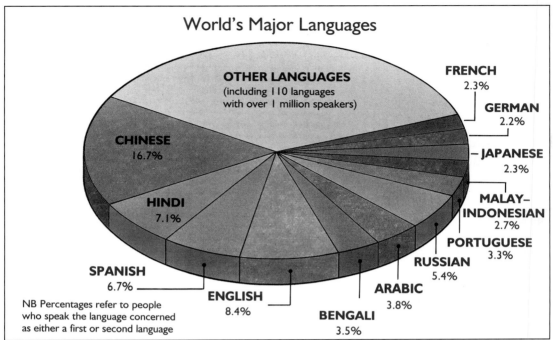

World's Major Languages

OTHER LANGUAGES
(including 110 languages
with over 1 million speakers)

FRENCH
2.3%

GERMAN
2.2%

JAPANESE
2.3%

CHINESE
16.7%

MALAY–
INDONESIAN
2.7%

PORTUGUESE
3.3%

HINDI
7.1%

RUSSIAN
5.4%

ARABIC
3.8%

SPANISH
6.7%

ENGLISH
8.4%

BENGALI
3.5%

NB Percentages refer to people
who speak the language concerned
as either a first or second language

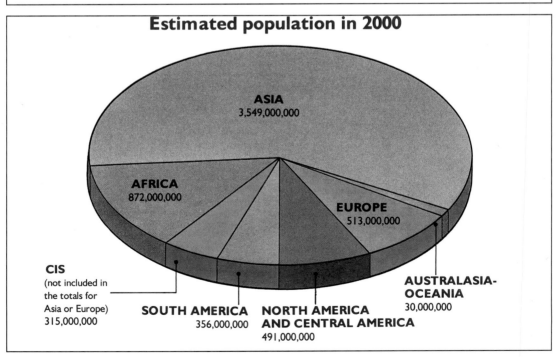

Estimated population in 2000

ASIA
3,549,000,000

AFRICA
872,000,000

EUROPE
513,000,000

CIS
(not included in
the totals for
Asia or Europe)
315,000,000

SOUTH AMERICA
356,000,000

NORTH AMERICA
AND CENTRAL AMERICA
491,000,000

AUSTRALASIA-
OCEANIA
30,000,000

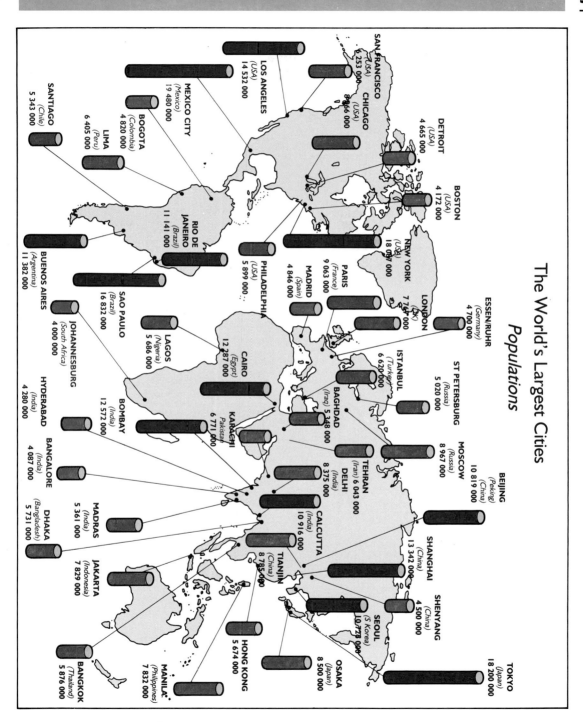

The World's Largest Cities
Populations

SAN FRANCISCO
(USA)
6 253 000

LOS ANGELES
(USA)
14 532 000

CHICAGO
(USA)
8 066 000

DETROIT
(USA)
4 665 000

BOSTON
(USA)
4 172 000

NEW YORK
(USA)
18 087 000

MEXICO CITY
(Mexico)
19 480 000

SANTIAGO
(Chile)
5 343 000

BOGOTA
(Colombia)
4 820 000

LIMA
(Peru)
6 405 000

RIO DE
JANEIRO
(Brazil)
11 141 000

BUENOS AIRES
(Argentina)
11 382 000

SAO PAULO
(Brazil)
16 832 000

PHILADELPHIA
(USA)
5 899 000

MADRID
(Spain)
4 846 000

PARIS
(France)
9 063 000

LONDON
(UK)
7 750 000

ESSEN/RUHR
(Germany)
4 700 000

JOHANNESBURG
(South Africa)
4 000 000

HYDERABAD
(India)
4 280 000

LAGOS
(Nigeria)
5 686 000

CAIRO
(Egypt)
12 287 000

KARACHI
(Pakistan)
6 771 000

BOMBAY
(India)
12 572 000

BANGALORE
(India)
4 087 000

DHAKA
(Bangladesh)
5 731 000

MADRAS
(India)
5 361 000

DELHI
(India)
8 375 000

TEHRAN
(Iran)
6 043 000

BAGHDAD
(Iraq)
5 348 000

ISTANBUL
(Turkey)
6 620 000

ST PETERSBURG
(Russia)
5 020 000

MOSCOW
(Russia)
8 967 000

CALCUTTA
(India)
10 916 000

JAKARTA
(Indonesia)
7 829 000

BANGKOK
(Thailand)
5 876 000

MANILA
(Philippines)
7 832 000

HONG KONG
5 674 000

TIANJIN
(China)
8 785 000

SHANGHAI
(China)
13 342 000

SHENYANG
(China)
4 500 000

SEOUL
(S Korea)
10 778 000

BEIJING
(Peking)
(China)
10 819 000

OSAKA
(Japan)
8 500 000

TOKYO
(Japan)
18 200 000

URBAN POPULATION

The definitions of 'urban' vary from country to country, often quite markedly, and these variations influence the positions of countries within the tables. Rapid urbanization is characteristic of the Third World. Conversely, in developed countries there is little scope for further growth in the level of urbanization. Indeed, in developed states the pattern of net population movement from country to town has been succeeded by a net movement from town to country ('counterurbanization').

Territories with the highest % of urban population

Country or territory*	Births per thousand
Gaza Strip	*100.0*
Macau	*100.0*
Monaco	100.0
Singapore	100.0
Vatican City	100.0
Belgium	97.0
Kuwait	96.0
Andorra	94.8
Hong Kong	*93.1*
Iceland	90.4
San Marino	90.4
Israel	89.9
UK	89.0
Uruguay	88.8
Netherlands	88.6

* non-sovereign territories are indicated in italics

Territories with the lowest % of urban population

Country or territory	Births per thousand
Bhutan	5.0
Burundi	5.0
Rwanda	8.0
Burkina Faso	9.0
Nepal	10.0
Ethiopia	12.1
Malawi	14.6
Bangladesh	16.0
Afghanistan	17.7
Vanuatu	18.4
Papua New Guinea	18.9
Lesotho	20.0
Niger	20.0

FERTILITY

In the following tables the crude birth rate measures the number of births per year per thousand. In the table listing territories with the highest crude birth rates, the figures given refer to the period 1985–90 (except for Mali and Malawi where earlier estimates are given).

Territories with the highest crude live birth rates

Country or territory	Births per thousand
Uganda	52.2
Rwanda	51.2
Zambia	51.1
Guinea	51.0
Tanzania	50.5
Somalia	50.1
Ivory Coast	49.9
Benin	49.2
Mali	48.7
Ethiopia	48.6
Botswana	48.5
Nigeria	48.5
Malawi	48.3
Sierra Leone	48.2

Territories with the lowest crude live birth rates

Country or territory*	Births per thousand
Falkland Islands	*7.5 (1988)*
Italy	9.7 (1989)
Japan	9.9 (1990)
Norfolk Island	*10.0 (1981)*
Greece	10.1 (1989)
San Marino	10.1 (1989)
Spain	10.7 (1988)
Austria	11.6 (1990)
Hungary	11.6 (1990)
Hong Kong	*11.7 (1990)*
Portugal	11.9 (1988)
Germany	11.4 (1989)
Belgium	12.0 (1988)
Isle of Man	*12.1 (1989)*
Andorra	12.2 (1990)

* non-sovereign territories are indicated in italics

POPULATION DENSITY

The least densely populated territories are to be found in high latitudes (e.g. Greenland and the Falkland Islands), in the major desert areas (e.g. Mongolia, Western Sahara, Mauritania and Namibia), or in parts of the world where tropical rain forests still remain the dominant vegetation type. The most densely-populated territories are mostly very small states or former colonial trading outposts with the character of city-states, or relatively small islands with diverse economies. Among the most populous states in the table is one low income country that is heavily dependent on the productivity of its rich soils (Bangladesh), one middle income country now rapidly industrializing (South Korea), and one major high-income country (The Netherlands).

Territories with the greatest density of population

Country or territory*	Population per km² (1990)
Macau	*29 962*
Monaco	28 500
Hong Kong	*5551*
Gibraltar	*5083*
Singapore	4859
Vatican City	1705
Gaza Strip	*1698*
Bermuda	*1144*
Malta	1120
Bangladesh	803
Guernsey	*760*
Bahrain	742
Maldives	722
Jersey	*714*
Barbados	594
Mauritius	531
Nauru	457
South Korea	432

Puerto Rico	*405*
San Marino	385
Tuvalu	373
The Netherlands	366

* non-sovereign territories are indicated in italics

Bulgaria	19
France	19
Hungary	19
Luxembourg	19

Territories with the least density of population

Country or territory*	Population per km² (1990)
Greenland	*0.03*
Falkland Islands	*0.16*
Guyane (French Guiana)	*1.10*
Mongolia	1.40
Western Sahara	*1.50*
Mauritania	1.97
Namibia	2.16
Australia	2.22
Botswana	2.22
Iceland	2.48
Libya	2.58
Suriname	2.58
Canada	2.66
Guyana	3.70
Gabon	4.38
Chad	4.42
Central African Republic	4.88

* non-sovereign territories are indicated in italics

POPULATION BY AGE

Third World countries with high birth rates tend to have young populations; developed countries with low birth rates tend to have more elderly populations.

Territories with the youngest population

Country	% of population under 25
Kenya	50
Uganda	50
Yemen	50
Botswana	49
Malawi	49
Rwanda	49
Tanzania	49
Zambia	49
Côte d'Ivoire	48
Niger	48
Nigeria	48
Comoros	47
Mali	47
Somalia	47
Swaziland	47
Zaïre	47

Territories with the oldest population

Country	% of population over 60
Sweden	23
Belgium	21
Norway	21
UK	21
Austria	20
Denmark	20
Greece	20
Italy	20
Switzerland	20

GNP PER HEAD

The growth in GNP of many Third World countries is not sustained at a level greater than their population growth, meaning that per capita GNP in such countries declines persistently.

Highest GNP per head (1990–92 est)

Country	GNP per head (US $)
Switzerland	35 500
Japan	32 018
Luxembourg	31 080
Sweden	29 600
Denmark	28 200
Norway	28 200
Finland	24 400
Belgium	22 600
Iceland	22 580
USA	22 520
Canada	21 710
Netherlands	21 400
Liechtenstein	21 020
Italy	20 200
United Arab Emirates	19 680
Singapore	18 143
Australia	17 320
UK	17 300

Lowest GNP per head (1989–92 est)

Country	GNP per head (US $)
Mozambique	80
Tajikistan	90
Uzbekistan	100
Turkmenistan	110
Ethiopia	120
Kyrgyzstan	120
Tanzania	120
Somalia	150
Kazakhstan	155
Nepal	170
Guinea-Bissau	180
Bhutan	190
Chad	190
Albania	200
Bangladesh	200
Laos	200
Malawi	200
Uganda	200
Ukraine	200

NATIONAL ECONOMIES

The gross national product (GNP) and the gross national product per head of the population is given for each sovereign state. Figures (in US $) are also given for total imports and total exports, along with the currency of each state.

Afghanistan *GNP ($ million):* 3100 (1988); *per head:* $220. *Imports ($ million):* 930 (1990). *Exports ($ million):* 235 (1990). 1 afghani = 100 pulis.

Albania *GNP ($ million):* 3800 (1988); *per head:* $200. *Imports ($ million):* 446.5 (1990). *Exports ($ million):* 267.4 (1990). 1 new lek = 100 quindarka (quintars).

Algeria *GNP ($ million):* 47 200 (1992); *per head:* $1696. *Imports ($ million):* 7396 (1988). *Exports ($ million):* 8164 (1988). 1 dinar = 100 centimes.

Andorra *GNP ($ million):* 892 (1992); *per head:* $16 600. *Imports ($ million):* 700.4 (1987). *Exports ($ million):* 24.6 (1987). Uses French and Spanish currency.

Angola *GNP ($ million):* 6010 (1989); *per head:* $620. *Imports ($ million):* 443 (1987). *Exports ($ million):* 2147 (1987). 1 new kwanza = 100 lwei.

Antigua and Barbuda *GNP ($ million):* 363 (1990); *per head:* $4600. *Imports ($ million):* 225 (1988). *Exports ($ million):* 22 (1988). 1 East Caribbean dollar = 100 cents.

Argentina *GNP ($ million):* 273 000 (1992); *per head:* $8142. *Imports ($ million):* 4076 (1990). *Exports ($ million):* 12 353 (1990). 1 peso = 100 centavos.

Armenia *GNP ($ million):* 2030 (1992); *per head:* $601. *Imports ($ million):* n/a. *Exports ($ million):* n/a. Uses Russian currency; to be replaced the dram.

Australia *GNP ($ million):* 308 700 (1992); *per head:* $17 320. *Imports ($ million):* 38 542 (1991). *Exports ($ million):* 41 793 (1991). 1 Australian dollar = 100 cents.

Austria *GNP ($ million):* 190 000 (1992); *per head:* $23 800. *Imports ($ million):* 50 740 (1991). *Exports ($ million):* 41 086 (1991). 1 Schilling = 100 Groschen.

Azerbaijan *GNP ($ million):* 3834 (1992); *per head:* $537. *Imports ($ million):* n/a. *Exports ($ million):* n/a. Uses Russian currency; to be replaced by the manat.

Bahamas *GNP ($ million):* 2913 (1990); *per head:* $11 510. *Imports ($ million):* 3001 (1989). *Exports ($ million):* 2786 (1989). 1 Bahamian dollar = 100 cents.

Bahrain *GNP ($ million):* 3120 (1989); *per head:* $6380. *Imports ($ million):* 3711 (1990). *Exports ($ million):* 3758 (1990). 1 Bahrain dinar = 1000 fils.

Bangladesh *GNP ($ million):* 22 579 (1990); *per head:* $200. *Imports ($ million):* 3405 (1990). *Exports ($ million):* 1690 (1991). 1 taka = 100 poisha.

Barbados *GNP ($ million):* 1680 (1990); *per head:* $6540. *Imports ($ million):* 695 (1991). *Exports ($ million):* 202 (1991). 1 Barbados dollar = 100 cents.

Belarus *GNP ($ million):* 9472 (1992); *per head:* $923. *Imports ($ million):* n/a. *Exports ($ million):* n/a. 1 Belarussian rouble = 100 kopeks; to be replaced by 1 taler = 100 grosches.

Belgium *GNP ($ million):* 225 000 (1992); *per head:* $22 600. *Imports ($ million):* 119 756 (1990). *Exports ($ million):* 117 989 (1990). 1 Belgian franc (frank) = 100 centimes (centiemen).

Belize *GNP ($ million):* 373 (1990); *per head:* $1970. *Imports ($ million):* 211 (1990). *Exports ($ million):* 129 (1990). 1 Belizean dollar = 100 cents.

Benin *GNP ($ million):* 1716 (1990); *per head:* $360. *Imports ($ million):* 288 (1984). *Exports ($ million):* 167 (1984). 1 CFA franc = 100 centimes.

Bhutan *GNP ($ million):* 273 (1990); *per head:* $190. *Imports ($ million):* 48 (1986). *Exports ($ million):* 22 (1986). 1 ngultrum = 100 chetrums.

Bolivia *GNP ($ million):* 4526 (1990); *per head:* $620. *Imports ($ million):* 942 (1991). *Exports ($ million):* 858 (1991). 1 boliviano = 100 centavos.

Bosnia-Herzegovina No figures available. 1 dinar = 100 para. (Croatian and Serbian/Yugoslav currency also in use.)

Botswana *GNP ($ million):* 2561 (1990); *per head:* $2040. *Imports ($ million):* 1780 (1990). *Exports ($ million):* 1779 (1990). 1 pula = 100 thebe.

Brazil *GNP ($ million):* 393 000 (1992); *per head:* $2466. *Imports ($ million):* 21 004 (1991). *Exports ($ million):* 31 622 (1991). 1 cruzeiro = 100 centavos.

Brunei *GNP ($ million):* 3302 (1989); *per head:* $13 290. *Imports ($ million):* 883 (1989). *Exports ($ million):* 1894 (1989). 1 Brunei dollar = 100 cents.

Bulgaria *GNP ($ million):* 8800 (1992); *per head:* $1021. *Imports ($ million):* 12 893 (1990). *Exports ($ million):* 13 347 (1990). 1 lev = 100 stotinki (stotinka).

Burkina Faso *GNP ($ million):* 2955 (1990); *per head:* $330. *Imports ($ million):* 322 (1989). *Exports ($ million):* 95 (1989). 1 CFA franc = 100 centimes.

Burundi *GNP ($ million):* 1151 (1990); *per head:* $210. *Imports ($ million):* 236 (1990). *Exports ($ million):* 75 (1990). 1 Burundi franc = 100 centimes.

Cambodia *GNP ($ million):* 4000 (1989 est); *per head:* $450. *Imports ($ million):* 118 (1985 est). *Exports ($ million):* 12 (1985 est). 1 new riel = 100 sen.

Cameroon *GNP ($ million):* 11 233 (1990); *per head:* $940. *Imports ($ million):* 1271 (1988). *Exports ($ million):* 924 (1988). 1 CFA dollar = 100 centimes.

Canada *GNP ($ million):* 588 000 (1992); *per head:* $21 710. *Imports ($ million):* 118 119 (1991). *Exports ($ million):* 126 883 (1991). 1 Canadian dollar = 100 cents.

Cape Verde *GNP ($ million):* 331 (1990); *per head:* $890. *Imports ($ million):* 112 (1991). *Exports ($ million):* 7 (1989). 1 Cape Verde escudo = 100 centavos.

Central African Republic *GNP ($ million):* 1194 (1990); *per head:* $390. *Imports ($ million):* 145 (1991). *Exports ($ million):* 74 (1991). 1 CFA franc = 100 centimes.

Chad *GNP ($ million):* 1074 (1990); *per head:* $190. *Imports ($ million):* 419 (1988). *Exports ($ million):* 141 (1988). 1 CFA franc = 100 centimes.

Chile *GNP ($ million):* 46 000 (1992); *per head:* $3074. *Imports ($ million):* 7424 (1990). *Exports ($ million):* 8924 (1991). 1 Chilean peso = 100 centavos.

China *GNP ($ million):* 475 900 (1992); *per head:* $399. *Imports ($ million):* 63 791 (1991). *Exports ($ million):* 71 910 (1991). 1 yuan (or renminbiao) = 10 jiao (chiao) = 100 fen.

China (Taiwan) *GNP ($ million):* 241 000 (1992); *per head:* $11 500. *Imports ($ million):* 54 716 (1990). *Exports ($ million):* 67 020 (1990). 1 new Taiwan dollar = 100 cents.

Colombia *GNP ($ million):* 40 805 (1988); *per head:* $1240. *Imports ($ million):* 5590 (1990). *Exports ($ million):* 6745 (1990). 1 Colombian peso = 100 centavos.

Comoros *GNP ($ million):* 227 (1990); *per head:* $480. *Imports ($ million):* 43 (1989). *Exports ($ million):* 18 (1989). 1 CFA franc = 100 centimes.

Congo *GNP ($ million):* 2296 (1990); *per head:* $1010. *Imports ($ million):* 600 (1990). *Exports ($ million):* 976 (1990). 1 CFA franc = 100 centimes.

Costa Rica *GNP ($ million):* 5342 (1990); *per head:* $1910. *Imports ($ million):* 1853 (1991). *Exports ($ million):* 1543 (1991). 1 Costa Rica colón = 100 céntimos.

Côte d'Ivoire (Ivory Coast) *GNP ($ million):* 8920 (1990); *per head:* $730. *Imports ($ million):* 2185 (1989). *Exports ($ million):* 2931 (1989). 1 CFA franc = 100 centimes.

Croatia *GNP ($ million):* 14 000 (1990); *per head:* $2941. *Imports ($ million):* 4430 (1990). *Exports ($ million):* 2910 (1990). 1 Croatian dinar = 100 para.

Cuba *GNP ($ million):* 20 900 (1989); *per head:* $2000. *Imports ($ million):* 7579 (1988). *Exports ($ million):* 5518 (1989). 1 Cuban peso = 100 centavos.

Cyprus *GNP ($ million):* 5633 (1990); *per head:* $8040. *Imports ($ million):* 2621 (1991). *Exports ($ million):* 960 (1991). 1 Cyprus pound = 100 cents. (Turkish currency is used in northern Cyprus.)

Czech Republic *GNP ($ million):* 26 600 (1992); *per head:* $2562. *Imports ($ million):* 6970 (1990 est). *Exports ($ million):* 7600 (1990 est). 1 Czech koruna = 100 haléru (haler).

Denmark *GNP ($ million):* 145 000 (1992); *per head:* $28 200. *Imports ($ million):* 32 257 (1991). *Exports ($ million):* 35 812 (1991). 1 Danish krone = 100 ore.

Djibouti *GNP ($ million):* 407 (1988); *per head:* $600. *Imports ($ million):* 215 (1990). *Exports ($ million):* 25 (1990). 1 Djibouti franc = 100 centimes.

Dominica *GNP ($ million):* 160 (1990); *per head:* $1940. *Imports ($ million):* 118 (1990). *Exports ($ million):* 55 (1990). 1 East Caribbean dollar = 100 cents.

Dominican Republic *GNP ($ million):* 5847 (1990); *per head:* $820. *Imports ($ million):* 1788 (1990). *Exports ($ million):* 734 (1990). 1 Dominican peso = 100 centavos.

Ecuador *GNP ($ million):* 10 112 (1990); *per head:* $960. *Imports ($ million):* 2399 (1991). *Exports ($ million):* 2851 (1991). 1 sucre = 100 centavos.

Egypt *GNP ($ million):* 42 700 (1992); *per head:* $751. *Imports ($ million):* 9202 (1990). *Exports ($ million):* 2582 (1990). 1 Egyptian pound = 100 piastres = 1000 millièmes.

El Salvador *GNP ($ million):* 5767 (1990); *per head:* $1100. *Imports ($ million):* 902 (1990). *Exports ($ million):* 412 (1990). 1 Salvadorian colón = 100 centavos.

Equatorial Guinea *GNP ($ million):* 136 (1990); *per head:* $330. *Imports ($ million):* 39 (1987). *Exports ($ million):* 41 (1989). 1 CFA franc = 100 centimes.

Estonia *GNP ($ million):* 968 (1992); *per head:* $613. *Imports ($ million):* n/a. *Exports ($ million):* n/a. 1 kroon = 100 cents.

Ethiopia *GNP ($ million):* 6041 (1990); *per head:* $120. *Imports ($ million):* 1076 (1990). *Exports ($ million):* 294 (1990). 1 birr = 100 cents.

Fiji *GNP ($ million):* 1326 (1990); *per head:* $1770. *Imports ($ million):* 652 (1991). *Exports ($ million):* 451 (1991). 1 Fiji dollar = 100 cents.

Finland *GNP ($ million):* 105 000 (1992); *per head:* $24 400. *Imports ($ million):* 21 711 (1991). *Exports ($ million):* 23 111 (1991). 1 markka (Finnmark) = 100 penniä (penni).

France *GNP ($ million):* 1 360 000 (1992); *per head:* $23 900. *Imports ($ million):* 230 786 (1991). *Exports ($ million):* 213 299 (1991). 1 French franc = 100 centimes.

Gabon *GNP ($ million):* 3654 (1990); *per head:* $3220. *Imports ($ million):* 767 (1989). *Exports ($ million):* 1288 (1987). 1 CFA franc = 100 centimes.

Gambia *GNP ($ million):* 229 (1990); *per head:* $260. *Imports ($ million):* 200 (1990). *Exports ($ million):* 41 (1990). 1 dalasi = 100 butut.

Georgia *GNP ($ million):* 3609 (1992); *per head:* $661. *Imports ($ million):* n/a. *Exports ($ million):* n/a. Uses Russian currency; to be replaced by the lary.

Germany *GNP ($ million):* 1 950 000 (1992); *per head:* $24 120. *Imports ($ million):* 382 050 (1991). *Exports ($ million):* 391 295 (1991). 1 Deutschmark = 100 Pfennige.

Ghana *GNP ($ million):* 5824 (1990); *per head:* $390. *Imports ($ million):* 1275 (1991). *Exports ($ million):* 1024 (1991). 1 new cedi = 100 pesewas.

Greece *GNP ($ million):* 80 000 (1992); *per head:* $7600. *Imports ($ million):* 21 582 (1991). *Exports ($ million):* 8653 (1991). 1 drachma = 100 leptae (lepta).

Grenada *GNP ($ million):* 199 (1990); *per head:* $2120. *Imports ($ million):* 92 (1988). *Exports ($ million):* 32 (1987). 1 East Caribbean dollar = 100 cents.

Guatemala *GNP ($ million):* 8309 (1990); *per head:* $900. *Imports ($ million):* 1674 (1991). *Exports ($ million):* 1033 (1991). 1 quetzal = 100 centavos.

Guinea *GNP ($ million):* 2756 (1990); *per head:* $480. *Imports ($ million):* 491 (1988). *Exports ($ million):* 548 (1988). 1 franc guineén = 100 centimes.

Guinea-Bissau *GNP ($ million):* 176 (1990); *per head:* $180. *Imports ($ million):* 39 (1984). *Exports ($ million):* 19 (1984). 1 Guinea peso = 100 centavos.

Guyana *GNP ($ million):* 293 (1990); *per head:* $370. *Imports ($ million):* 512 (1990). *Exports ($ million):* 255 (1990). 1 Guyanese dollar = 100 cents.

Haiti *GNP ($ million):* 2400 (1990); *per head:* $370. *Imports ($ million):* 374 (1991). *Exports ($ million):* 103 (1991). 1 gourde = 100 centimes.

Honduras *GNP ($ million):* 3023 (1990); *per head:* $590. *Imports ($ million):* 981 (1990). *Exports ($ million):* 912 (1990). 1 lempira = 100 centavos.

Hungary *GNP ($ million):* 40 200 (1992); *per head:* $3896. *Imports ($ million):* 11 532 (1991). *Exports ($ million):* 10 301 (1991). 1 forint = 100 fillér.

Iceland *GNP ($ million):* 5456 (1990); *per head:* $22 580. *Imports ($ million):* 1720 (1991). *Exports ($ million):* 1554 (1991). 1 new Icelandic krona = 100 aurar (eyrir).

India *GNP ($ million):* 236 000 (1992); *per head:* $269. *Imports ($ million):* 23 267 (1990). *Exports ($ million):* 17 663 (1990). 1 Indian rupee = 100 paisa (paise).

Indonesia *GNP ($ million):* 140 000 (1992); *per head:* $740. *Imports ($ million):* 21 931 (1990). *Exports ($ million):* 25 675 (1990). 1 rupiah = 100 sen.

Iran *GNP ($ million):* 60 300 (1992); *per head:* $957. *Imports ($ million):* 11 989 (1990). *Exports ($ million):* 13 200 (1986). 1 Iranian rial = 100 dinars.

Iraq *GNP ($ million):* 20 800 (1992); *per head:* $1000. *Imports ($ million):* 4834 (1990). *Exports ($ million):* 392 (1990). 1 Iraqi dinar = 20 dirhams = 1000 fils.

Ireland *GNP ($ million):* 50 000 (1992); *per head:* $14 700. *Imports ($ million):* 20 761 (1990). *Exports ($ million):* 24 232 (1990). 1 punt (Irish pound) = 100 pence (penny).

Israel *GNP ($ million):* 71 000 (1992); *per head:* $12 241. *Imports ($ million):* 16 906 (1990). *Exports ($ million):* 11 889 (1990). 1 new Israel shekel = 100 agorot (agora).

Italy *GNP ($ million):* 1 170 000 (1992); *per head:* $20 200. *Imports ($ million):* 182 554 (1991). *Exports ($ million):* 169 399 (1991). 1 Italian lira (lire) = 100 centisimi.

Jamaica *GNP ($ million):* 3606 (1990); *per head:* $1510. *Imports ($ million):* 1864 (1990). *Exports ($ million):* 1116 (1990). 1 Jamaican dollar = 100 cents.

Japan *GNP ($ million):* 4 000 000 (1992); *per head:* $32 018. *Imports ($ million):* 236 744 (1991). *Exports ($ million):* 314 525 (1991). 1 yen = 100 sen.

Jordan *GNP ($ million):* 3408 (1990); *per head:* $1076. *Imports ($ million):* 2512 (1991). *Exports ($ million):* 902 (1991). 1 Jordanian dinar = 1000 fils.

Kazakhstan *GNP ($ million):* 2600 (1992); *per head:* $155. *Imports ($ million):* n/a. *Exports ($ million):* n/a. Uses Russian currency; to be replaced by the tan'ga.

Kenya *GNP ($ million):* 8100 (1992); *per head:* $320. *Imports ($ million):* 2226 (1990). *Exports ($ million):* 1052 (1990). 1 Kenya shilling = 100 cents.

Kiribati *GNP ($ million):* 54 (1990); *per head:* $760. *Imports ($ million):* 27 (1990). *Exports ($ million):* 3 (1990). Uses Australian currency.

Korea (North) *GNP ($ million):* 28 000 (1990); *per head:* $1240. *Imports ($ million):* 2900 (1989). *Exports ($ million):* 1800 (1989). 1 won = 100 chon (jun).

Korea (South) *GNP ($ million):* 354 000 (1992); *per head:* $8040. *Imports ($ million):* 81 557 (1991). *Exports ($ million):* 71 898 (1991). 1 won = 10 hwan = 100 chun (jeon).

Kuwait *GNP ($ million):* 33 089 (1989); *per head:* $16 160. *Imports ($ million):* 6303 (1989). *Exports ($ million):* 11 476 (1989). 1 Kuwaiti dinar = 1000 fils.

Kyrgyzstan *GNP ($ million):* 520 (1992); *per head:* $118. *Imports ($ million):* n/a. *Exports ($ million):* n/a. Uses Russian currency.

Laos *GNP ($ million):* 848 (1990); *per head:* $200. *Imports ($ million):* 162 (1988). *Exports ($ million):* 81 (1988). 1 new kip = 100 at.

Latvia *GNP ($ million):* 744 (1992); *per head:* $279. *Imports ($ million):* n/a. *Exports ($ million):* n/a. 1 Latvian rouble = 100 cents; to be replaced by the lat.

Lebanon *GNP ($ million):* 1800 (1990); *per head:* $690. *Imports ($ million):* 2580 (1989). *Exports ($ million):* 570 (1989). 1 Lebanese pound = 100 piastres.

Lesotho *GNP ($ million):* 832 (1990); *per head:* $470. *Imports ($ million):* 587 (1988). *Exports ($ million):* 64 (1988). 1 loti (maloti) = 100 lisente.

Liberia *GNP ($ million):* 1030 (1987); *per head:* $440. *Imports ($ million):* 272 (1988). *Exports ($ million):* 382 (1987). 1 Liberian dollar = 100 cents; the US dollar is also legal tender.

Libya *GNP ($ million):* 23 333 (1989); *per head:* $5310. *Imports ($ million):* 4723 (1987). *Exports ($ million):* 8766 (1987). 1 Libyan dinar = 100 dirhams.

Liechtenstein *GNP ($ million):* 610 (1992); *per head:* $21 020. *Imports ($ million):* 535 (1989). *Exports ($ million):* 989 (1989). Uses Swiss currency.

Lithuania *GNP ($ million):* 996 (1992); *per head:* $265. *Imports ($ million):* n/a. *Exports ($ million):* n/a. 1 Lithuanian 'rouble coupon' = 100 kopeks; to be replaced by the litas.

Luxembourg *GNP ($ million):* 11 225 (1992); *per head:* $31 080. *Imports ($ million):* 6193 (1990). *Exports ($ million):* 5402 (1989). 1 Luxembourg franc = 100 centimes.

Madagascar *GNP ($ million):* 2710 (1990); *per head:* $230. *Imports ($ million):* 426 (1991). *Exports ($ million):* 306 (1991). 1 Malagasy franc = 100 centimes.

Malawi *GNP ($ million):* 1662 (1990); *per head:* $200. *Imports ($ million):* 705 (1991). *Exports ($ million):* 473 (1991). 1 Malawi kwacha = 100 tambala.

Malaysia *GNP ($ million):* 66 000 (1990); *per head:* $3468. *Imports ($ million):* 36 699 (1991). *Exports ($ million):* 34 375 (1991). 1 ringgit (Malaysian dollar) = 100 sen.

Maldives *GNP ($ million):* 96 (1990); *per head:* $440. *Imports ($ million):* 129 (1990). *Exports ($ million):* 52 (1990). 1 rufiyaa (Maldivian rupee) = 100 laari (larees).

Mali *GNP ($ million):* 2292 (1990); *per head:* $270. *Imports ($ million):* 500 (1990). *Exports ($ million):* 271 (1989). 1 CFA franc = 100 centimes.

Malta *GNP ($ million):* 2342 (1990); *per head:* $6630. *Imports ($ million):* 1953 (1990). *Exports ($ million):* 1126 (1990). 1 Maltese lira (Maltese pound) = 100 cents = 1000 mils.

Marshall Islands *GNP ($ million):* 63 (1989); *per head:* $1500. *Imports ($ million):* 34 (1988). *Exports ($ million):* 2 (1988). Uses US currency.

Mauritania *GNP ($ million):* 987 (1990); *per head:* $500. *Imports ($ million):* 351 (1989). *Exports ($ million):* 451 (1989). 1 ouiguiya = 5 khoums.

Mauritius *GNP ($ million):* 2422 (1990); *per head:* $2250. *Imports ($ million):* 1619 (1990). *Exports ($ million):* 1193 (1990). 1 Mauritian rupee = 100 cents.

Mexico *GNP ($ million):* 382 000 (1992); *per head:* $4186. *Imports ($ million):* 29 993 (1990). *Exports ($ million):* 26 524 (1990). 1 Mexican peso = 100 centavos.

Micronesia *GNP ($ million):* 99 (1989); *per head:* $980. *Imports ($ million):* 68 (1988). *Exports ($ million):* 2 (1988). Uses US currency.

Moldova *GNP ($ million):* 2706 (1992); *per head:* $620. *Imports ($ million):* n/a. *Exports ($ million):* n/a. Uses Russian currency.

Monaco *GNP ($ million):* 375 (1992 est); *per head:* $12 609. *Imports ($ million):* n/a. *Exports ($ million):* n/a. Uses French currency.

Mongolia *GNP ($ million):* 1161 (1988); *per head:* $473. *Imports ($ million):* 2030 (1988). *Exports ($ million):* 812 (1988). 1 tugrik = 100 möngös.

Morocco *GNP ($ million):* 23 788 (1990); *per head:* $950. *Imports ($ million):* 6919 (1990). *Exports ($ million):* 4229 (1990). 1 dirham = 100 francs (centimes).

Mozambique *GNP ($ million):* 1208 (1990); *per head:* $80. *Imports ($ million):* 715 (1989). *Exports ($ million):* 101 (1989). 1 metical = 100 centavos.

Myanmar *GNP ($ million):* 16 330 (1989–90); *per head:* $400. *Imports ($ million):* 616 (1991). *Exports ($ million):* 412 (1991). 1 kyat = 100 pyas.

Namibia *GNP ($ million):* 1600 (1988); *per head:* $1300. *Imports ($ million):* 861 (1988). *Exports ($ million):* 940 (1988). Uses South African currency.

Nauru *GNP ($ million):* 90 (1989); *per head:* $10 000. *Imports ($ million):* 14 (1988). *Exports ($ million):* 74 (1988). Uses Australian currency.

Nepal *GNP ($ million):* 3289 (1990); *per head:* $170. *Imports ($ million):* 790 (1991). *Exports ($ million):* 273 (1991). 1 Nepalese rupee = 100 paisa.

Netherlands *GNP ($ million):* 330 000 (1992); *per head:* $21 400. *Imports ($ million):* 125 906 (1990). *Exports ($ million):* 133 554 (1991). 1 Netherlands gulden (guilder) or florin = 100 cents.

New Zealand *GNP ($ million):* 43 185 (1990); *per head:* $12 680. *Imports ($ million):* 8522 (1991). *Exports ($ million):* 9720 (1991). 1 New Zealand dollar = 100 cents.

Nicaragua *GNP ($ million):* 2911 (1987); *per head:* $830. *Imports ($ million):* 923 (1987). *Exports ($ million):* 300 (1987). 1 córdoba oro = 100 centavos.

Niger *GNP ($ million):* 2365 (1990); *per head:* $310. *Imports ($ million):* 345 (1985). *Exports ($ million):* 209 (1985). 1 CFA franc = 100 centimes.

Nigeria *GNP ($ million):* 27 800 (1992); *per head:* $301. *Imports ($ million):* 3419 (1989). *Exports ($ million):* 13 649 (1990). 1 naira = 100 kobo.

Norway *GNP ($ million):* 120 000 (1992); *per head:* $28 200. *Imports ($ million):* 25 244 (1991). *Exports ($ million):* 34 034 (1990). 1 Norwegian krone (kroner) = 100 ore.

Oman *GNP ($ million):* 7756 (1989); *per head:* $4770. *Imports ($ million):* 2681 (1990). *Exports ($ million):* 5215 (1990). 1 rial Omani = 100 baiza.

Pakistan *GNP ($ million):* 53 000 (1992); *per head:* $430. *Imports ($ million):* 8427 (1991). *Exports ($ million):* 6471 (1991). 1 Pakistani rupee = 100 paisa.

Panama *GNP ($ million):* 4414 (1990); *per head:* $1830. *Imports ($ million):* 1695 (1991). *Exports ($ million):* 342 (1991). 1 balboa = 100 centésimos; US currency is also legal tender.

Papua New Guinea *GNP ($ million):* 3372 (1990); *per head:* $860. *Imports ($ million):* 1403 (1991). *Exports ($ million):* 1283 (1991). 1 Kina = 100 toea.

Paraguay *GNP ($ million):* 4796 (1990); *per head:* $1110. *Imports ($ million):* 695 (1989). *Exports ($ million):* 1163 (1989). 1 guaraní = 100 céntimos.

Peru *GNP ($ million):* 25 149 (1990); *per head:* $1160. *Imports ($ million):* 2885 (1990). *Exports ($ million):* 3276 (1990). 1 new sol = 100 céntimos.

Philippines *GNP ($ million):* 54 000 (1992); *per head:* $823. *Imports ($ million):* 13 042 (1990). *Exports ($ million):* 8186 (1990). 1 Philippine peso = 100 centavos.

Poland *GNP ($ million):* 63 700 (1992); *per head:* $1660. *Imports ($ million):* 14 261 (1991). *Exports ($ million):* 14 460 (1991). 1 zloty = 100 groszy.

Portugal *GNP ($ million):* 80 000 (1992); *per head:* $7600. *Imports ($ million):* 26 113 (1991). *Exports ($ million):* 16 281 (1991). 1 escudo = 100 centavos.

Qatar *GNP ($ million):* 6962 (1990); *per head:* $15 860. *Imports ($ million):* 1326 (1989). *Exports ($ million):* 2687 (1989). 1 Qatar riyal = 100 dirhams.

Romania *GNP ($ million):* 15 800 (1992); *per head:* $680. *Imports ($ million):* 5600 (1991). *Exports ($ million):* 4124 (1991). 1 leu (lei) = 100 bani.

Russia *GNP ($ million):* 137 800 (1992); *per head:* $929. *Imports ($ million):* n/a. *Exports ($ million):* n/a. 1 rouble = 100 kopeks.

Rwanda *GNP ($ million):* 2214 (1990); *per head:* $310.

Imports ($ million): 369 (1988). *Exports ($ million):* 101 (1988). 1 Rwanda franc (Franc rwandais) = 100 centimes.

St Christopher and Nevis *GNP ($ million):* 133 (1990); *per head:* $3330. *Imports ($ million):* 79 (1987). *Exports ($ million):* 28 (1987). 1 East Caribbean dollar = 100 cents.

St Lucia *GNP ($ million):* 286 (1990); *per head:* $1900. *Imports ($ million):* 221 (1988). *Exports ($ million):* 119 (1988). 1 East Caribbean dollar = 100 cents.

St Vincent and the Grenadines *GNP ($ million):* 184 (1990); *per head:* $1610. *Imports ($ million):* 98 (1987). *Exports ($ million):* 52 (1987). 1 East Caribbean dollar = 100 cents.

San Marino *GNP ($ million):* 205 (1992); *per head:* $8590. *Imports ($ million):* n/a. *Exports ($ million):* n/a. Uses Italian currency.

São Tomé e Principé *GNP ($ million):* 47 (1990); *per head:* $380. *Imports ($ million):* 13 (1987). *Exports ($ million):* 7 (1987). 1 dobra = 100 cêntimos.

Saudi Arabia *GNP ($ million):* 122 000 (1992); *per head:* $7463. *Imports ($ million):* 24 069 (1990). *Exports ($ million):* 44 417 (1990). 1 Saudi riyal = 100 halalah.

Senegal *GNP ($ million):* 5260 (1990); *per head:* $710. *Imports ($ million):* 1023 (1987). *Exports ($ million):* 606 (1987). 1 CFA franc = 100 centimes.

Seychelles *GNP ($ million):* 318 (1990); *per head:* $4670. *Imports ($ million):* 173 (1991). *Exports ($ million):* 48 (1991). 1 Seychelles rupee = 100 cents.

Sierra Leone *GNP ($ million):* 981 (1990); *per head:* $240. *Imports ($ million):* 164 (1990). *Exports ($ million):* 143 (1990). 1 leone = 100 cents.

Singapore *GNP ($ million):* 52 000 (1992); *per head:* $18 143. *Imports ($ million):* 66 108 (1991). *Exports ($ million):* 59 046 (1991). 1 Singapore dollar = 100 cents.

Slovakia *GNP ($ million):* 10 000 (1992); *per head:* $1898. *Imports ($ million):* 2990 (1990). *Exports ($ million):* 3260 (1990). 1 Slovak koruna = 100 haléru.

Slovenia *GNP ($ million):* 14 000 (1990 est); *per head:* $7132. *Imports ($ million):* n/a. *Exports ($ million):* n/a. 1 tolar = 100 cents.

Solomon Islands *GNP ($ million):* 187 (1990); *per head:* $580. *Imports ($ million):* 92 (1990). *Exports ($ million):* 70 (1990). 1 Solomon Islands dollar = 100 cents.

Somalia *GNP ($ million):* 946 (1990); *per head:* $150. *Imports ($ million):* 132 (1987). *Exports ($ million):* 104 (1987). 1 Somali shilling = 100 cents.

South Africa *GNP ($ million):* 123 000 (1992); *per head:* $3312. *Imports ($ million):* 17 506 (1991). *Exports ($ million):* 17 052 (1990). 1 rand = 100 cents.

Spain *GNP ($ million):* 540 000 (1992); *per head:* $13 600. *Imports ($ million):* 93 314 (1991). *Exports ($ million):* 60 182 (1991). 1 Spanish peseta = 100 céntimos.

Sri Lanka *GNP ($ million):* 7971 (1990); *per head:* $470. *Imports ($ million):* 3083 (1991). *Exports ($ million):* 1965 (1990). 1 Sri Lanka rupee = 100 cents.

Sudan *GNP ($ million):* 28 906 (1990); *per head:* $390.

Imports ($ million): 1060 (1988). *Exports ($ million):* 672 (1989). 1 dinar = 100 piastres.

Suriname *GNP ($ million):* 1365 (1990); *per head:* $3050. *Imports ($ million):* 294 (1987). *Exports ($ million):* 306 (1987). 1 Surinam gulden (guilder) or florin = 100 cents.

Swaziland *GNP ($ million):* 645 (1990); *per head:* $820. *Imports ($ million):* 590 (1989). *Exports ($ million):* 468 (1989). 1 lilangeni (emalangeni) = 100 cents.

Sweden *GNP ($ million):* 260 000 (1992); *per head:* $29 600. *Imports ($ million):* 49 751 (1991). *Exports ($ million):* 55 129 (1990). 1 Swedish krona (kroner) = 100 öre.

Switzerland *GNP ($ million):* 240 000 (1992); *per head:* $35 500. *Imports ($ million):* 66 517 (1991). *Exports ($ million):* 61 537 (1991). 1 Swiss franc (Schweizer Franken) = 100 Rappen (centimes).

Syria *GNP ($ million):* 12 404 (1990); *per head:* $990. *Imports ($ million):* 3151 (1991). *Exports ($ million):* 3143 (1991). 1 Syrian pound = 100 piastres.

Tajikistan *GNP ($ million):* 483 (1992); *per head:* $90. *Imports ($ million):* n/a. *Exports ($ million):* n/a. Uses Russian currency.

Tanzania *GNP ($ million):* 2779 (1990); *per head:* $120. *Imports ($ million):* 1495 (1988). *Exports ($ million):* 337 (1988). 1 Tanzanian shilling = 100 cents.

Thailand *GNP ($ million):* 117 000 (1992); *per head:* $1605. *Imports ($ million):* 33 379 (1990). *Exports ($ million):* 23 068 (1990). 1 baht = 100 satangs.

Togo *GNP ($ million):* 1474 (1990); *per head:* $410. *Imports ($ million):* 487 (1988). *Exports ($ million):* 242 (1988). 1 CFA franc = 100 centimes.

Tonga *GNP ($ million):* 100 (1990); *per head:* $1010. *Imports ($ million):* 65 (1990). *Exports ($ million):* 13 (1990). 1 pa'anga = 100 seniti.

Trinidad and Tobago *GNP ($ million):* 4458 (1990); *per head:* $3470. *Imports ($ million):* 1222 (1990). *Exports ($ million):* 2049 (1990). 1 Trinidad and Tobago dollar = 100 cents.

Tunisia *GNP ($ million):* 11 592 (1990); *per head:* $1420. *Imports ($ million):* 5189 (1991). *Exports ($ million):* 3713 (1991). 1 Tunisian dinar = 1000 millimes.

Turkey *GNP ($ million):* 130 000 (1992); *per head:* $2170. *Imports ($ million):* 20 019 (1991). *Exports ($ million):* 13 603 (1990). 1 Turkish lira = 100 kurus.

Turkmenistan *GNP ($ million):* 400 (1992); *per head:* $110. *Imports ($ million):* n/a. *Exports ($ million):* n/a. Uses Russian currency; to be replaced by the manat.

Tuvalu *GNP ($ million):* 4.6 (1990); *per head:* $530. *Imports ($ million):* 4 (1989). *Exports ($ million):* 0.06 (1989). Uses Australian currency.

Uganda *GNP ($ million):* 3814 (1990); *per head:* $220. *Imports ($ million):* 544 (1988). *Exports ($ million):* 152 (1990). 1 new Uganda shilling = 100 cents.

Ukraine *GNP ($ million):* 10 000 (1992); *per head:* $200.

Imports ($ million): n/a. *Exports ($ million):* n/a. Karbovanets (karbovantsi) – no subdivisions; to be replaced by 1 hryvnia = 100 kopeks.

United Arab Emirates *GNP ($ million):* 31 613 (1990); *per head:* $19 680. *Imports ($ million):* 11 199 (1990). *Exports ($ million):* 15 837 (1990). 1 UAE dirham = 100 fils.

UK *GNP ($ million):* 1 000 000 (1992); *per head:* $17 300. *Imports ($ million):* 210 019 (1991). *Exports ($ million):* 185 212 (1991). 1 pound sterling = 100 new pence.

USA *GNP ($ million):* 5 670 000 (1992); *per head:* $22 520. *Imports ($ million):* 509 320 (1991). *Exports ($ million):* 421 850 (1991). 1 US dollar = 100 cents.

Uruguay *GNP ($ million):* 7929 (1990); *per head:* $2560. *Imports ($ million):* 1619 (1991). *Exports ($ million):* 1590 (1991). 1 Uruguayan new peso = 100 centésimos.

Uzbekistan *GNP ($ million):* 2000 (1992); *per head:* $100. *Imports ($ million):* n/a. *Exports ($ million):* n/a. Uses Russian currency; to be replaced by the soum.

Vanuatu *GNP ($ million):* 167 (1990); *per head:* $1060. *Imports ($ million):* 97 (1990). *Exports ($ million):* 19 (1990). Vatu (no subdivisions).

Vatican City Uses Italian currency.

Venezuela *GNP ($ million):* 66 000 (1992); *per head:* $3110. *Imports ($ million):* 9963 (1991). *Exports ($ million):* 17 586 (1991). 1 bolivar = 100 céntimos.

Vietnam *GNP ($ million):* 14 200 (1989); *per head:* $210. *Imports ($ million):* 3050 (1989). *Exports ($ million):* 1502 (1989). 1 đong = 10 hào = 100 xu.

Western Samoa *GNP ($ million):* 121 (1990); *per head:* $730. *Imports ($ million):* 76 (1988). *Exports ($ million):* 15 (1988). 1 tala = 100 sene.

Yemen *GNP ($ million):* 7203 (1989); *per head:* $640. *Imports ($ million):* 1378 (1987). *Exports ($ million):* 101 (1987. 1 Yemen rial = 100 fils.

Yugoslavia *GNP ($ million):* 28 400 (1990); *per head:* $2729. *Imports ($ million):* n/a. *Exports ($ million):* n/a. 1 new dinar = 100 para.

Zaïre *GNP ($ million):* 8117 (1990); *per head:* $230. *Imports ($ million):* 886 (1990). *Exports ($ million):* 999 (1990). 1 Zaïre = 100 makuta (likuta) = 10 000 sengi.

Zambia *GNP ($ million):* 3391 (1990); *per head:* $420. *Imports ($ million):* 1243 (1990). *Exports ($ million):* 899 (1990). 1 Zambian kwacha = 100 ngwee.

Zimbabwe *GNP ($ million):* 4100 (1992); *per head:* $412. *Imports ($ million):* 1850 (1990). *Exports ($ million):* 1723 (1990). 1 Zimbabwe dollar = 100 cents.

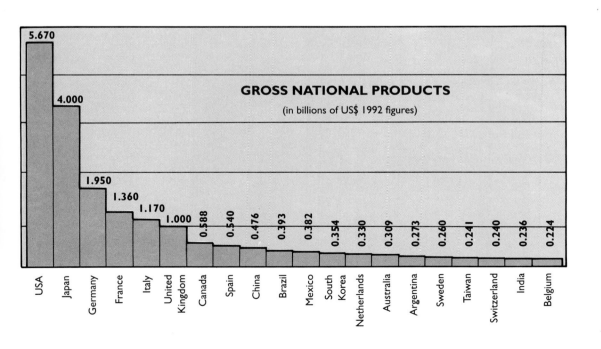

GROSS NATIONAL PRODUCTS
(in billions of US$ 1992 figures)

USA	5.670
Japan	4.000
Germany	1.950
France	1.360
Italy	1.170
United Kingdom	1.000
Canada	0.588
Spain	0.540
China	0.476
Brazil	0.393
Mexico	0.382
South Korea	0.354
Netherlands	0.330
Australia	0.309
Argentina	0.273
Sweden	0.260
Taiwan	0.241
Switzerland	0.240
India	0.236
Belgium	0.224

PRODUCTION FIGURES

Most of the annual production figures given below are for 1990. In some cases the latest comparable figures were for 1989, which are indicated with an *.

MAJOR MINERAL ORES

Bauxite*
Country	Production (in tonnes)
Australia	38 600 000 p.a
Guinea	17 500 000 p.a
Jamaica	9 400 000 p.a
Brazil	7 900 000 p.a
Russia	5 800 000 p.a
India	4 300 000 p.a

Coal (bituminous)
Country	Production (in tonnes)
China	1 000 000 000 p.a
USA	860 000 000 p.a
Russia	415 000 000 p.a
India	198 000 000 p.a
South Africa	180 000 000 p.a
Australia	162 000 000 p.a

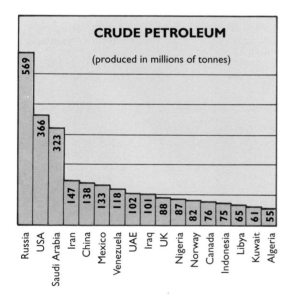

CRUDE PETROLEUM

(produced in millions of tonnes)

Russia 569, USA 366, Saudi Arabia 323, Iran 147, China 138, Mexico 133, Venezuela 118, UAE 102, Iraq 101, UK 88, Nigeria 87, Norway 82, Canada 76, Indonesia 75, Libya 65, Kuwait 61, Algeria 55

Copper*
Country	Production (in tonnes)
USA	2 900 000 p.a
Japan	1 600 000 p.a
Chile	1 100 000 p.a
Germany	750 000 p.a
Russia	550 000 p.a
Canada	550 000 p.a

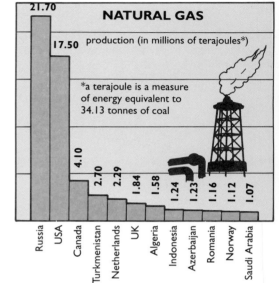

NATURAL GAS

production (in millions of terajoules*)

*a terajoule is a measure of energy equivalent to 34.13 tonnes of coal

Russia 21.70, USA 17.50, Canada 4.10, Turkmenistan 2.70, Netherlands 2.29, UK 1.84, Algeria 1.58, Indonesia 1.24, Azerbaijan 1.23, Romania 1.16, Norway 1.12, Saudi Arabia 1.07

Diamonds
Country	Production (in carats)
Australia	36 000 000 p.a
Zaïre	24 000 000 p.a
Botswana	17 300 000 p.a
Russia	15 000 000 p.a
South Africa	8 500 000 p.a
Angola	1 300 000 p.a

Gold
Country	Production (in tonnes)
South Africa	610 p.a
USA	295 p.a
Russia	280 p.a
Australia	241 p.a
Canada	165 p.a
China	80 p.a

Iron Ore
Country	Production (in tonnes)
Brazil	104 500 000 p.a
China	84 700 000 p.a
Australia	70 400 000 p.a
Ukraine	66 300 000 p.a
Russia	60 500 000 p.a
USA	34 900 000 p.a

Uranium

Country	Production (in tonnes)
Russia	31 200 p.a
Canada	8 700 p.a
Australia	3 500 p.a
USA	3 500 p.a
Namibia	3 200 p.a
Germany	3 000 p.a

Zinc*

Country	Production (in tonnes)
Russia	940 000 p.a
Japan	840 000 p.a
Canada	670 000 p.a
USA	600 000 p.a
Germany	480 000 p.a
China	450 000 p.a

MAJOR CROPS

Barley

Country	Production (in tonnes)
Russia	28 000 000 p.a
Ukraine	14 000 000 p.a
Germany	13 300 000 p.a
Canada	13 200 000 p.a
France	10 000 000 p.a
Spain	9 300 000 p.a

Maize

Country	Production (in tonnes)
USA	201 500 000 p.a
China	82 300 000 p.a
Brazil	21 400 000 p.a
Mexico	12 000 000 p.a
South Africa	9 200 000 p.a
Romania	9 200 000 p.a

Rice

Country	Production (in tonnes)
China	188 400 000 p.a
India	112 500 000 p.a
Indonesia	44 500 000 p.a
Bangladesh	29 400 000 p.a
Vietnam	19 200 000 p.a
Thailand	18 500 000 p.a

Cocoa beans

Country	Production (in tonnes)
Ivory Coast	740 000 p.a
Brazil	372 000 p.a
Ghana	299 000 p.a
Malaysia	250 000 p.a
Nigeria	170 000 p.a
Cameroon	109 000 p.a

Coffee

Country	Production (in tonnes)
Brazil	1 440 000 p.a
Colombia	780 000 p.a
Indonesia	390 000 p.a
Mexico	309 000 p.a
Guatemala	240 000 p.a
Côte d'Ivoire	220 000 p.a

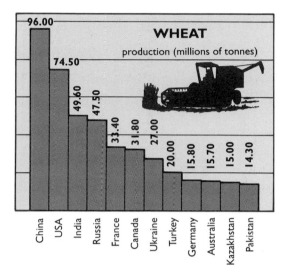

WHEAT
production (millions of tonnes)

China	USA	India	Russia	France	Canada	Ukraine	Turkey	Germany	Australia	Kazakhstan	Pakistan
96.00	74.50	49.60	47.50	33.40	31.80	27.00	20.00	15.80	15.70	15.00	14.30

Cotton Lint

Country	Production (in tonnes)
China	4 400 000 p.a
USA	3 200 000 p.a
Uzbekistan	2 600 000 p.a
Pakistan	1 500 000 p.a
India	1 500 000 p.a
Brazil	660 000 p.a

Potatoes

Country	Production (in tonnes)
Russia	38 000 000 p.a
Poland	36 300 000 p.a
China	28 000 000 p.a
USA	17 800 000 p.a
Germany	17 500 000 p.a
Ukraine	16 700 000 p.a

Rubber

Country	Production (in tonnes)
Malaysia	1 420 000 p.a
Indonesia	1 300 000 p.a
Thailand	930 000 p.a
India	290 000 p.a
China	250 000 p.a
Philippines	180 000 p.a

Sugar Beet

Country	Production (in tonnes)
Ukraine	44 000 000 p.a

Country	Production
Russia	33 900 000 p.a
France	29 900 000 p.a
Germany	28 900 000 p.a
USA	25 000 000 p.a
Poland	15 200 000 p.a

Sugar Cane

Country	Production (in tonnes)
Brazil	272 500 000 p.a
India	210 000 000 p.a
Cuba	85 900 000 p.a
China	61 800 000 p.a
Pakistan	38 000 000 p.a
Mexico	34 900 000 p.a

Tea*

Country	Production (in tonnes)
India	735 000 p.a
China	521 000 p.a
Sri Lanka	225 000 p.a
Kenya	193 000 p.a
Indonesia	165 000 p.a
Turkey	140 000 p.a

LIVESTOCK

Cattle

Country	Number
India	197 300 000
Brazil	140 000 000
USA	99 300 000
China	77 000 000
Russia	60 000 000
Argentina	50 600 000

Sheep

Country	Number
Australia	167 800 000
China	113 500 000
Russia	62 000 000
New Zealand	58 300 000
India	54 800 000
Iran	34 000 000

Pigs

Country	Number
China	360 600 000
USA	53 900 000
Russia	39 200 000
Germany	34 200 000
Brazil	33 200 000
Poland	19 800 000

AGRICULTURAL FORESTRY AND FISHING PRODUCTS

Beef and Veal*

Country	Production (in tonnes)
USA	10 700 000 p.a
Russia	5 000 000 p.a
Argentina	2 600 000 p.a
Brazil	2 500 000 p.a
Germany	2 000 000 p.a
Mexico	1 800 000 p.a

Butter (and Ghee)*

Country	Production (in tonnes)
Russia	900 000 p.a
India	840 000 p.a
Germany	690 000 p.a
USA	570 000 p.a
France	540 000 p.a
Pakistan	330 000 p.a

Cow's Milk*

Country	Production (in tonnes)
USA	65 400 000 p.a
Russia	52 800 000 p.a
Germany	33 500 000 p.a
France	27 300 000 p.a
Ukraine	24 500 000 p.a
India	23 000 000 p.a

Fishing Catch (Maritime and Freshwater)

Country	Catch (in tonnes; 1988)
Japan	11 900 000 p.a
China	10 400 000 p.a
Russia	10 000 000 p.a
Peru	6 600 000 p.a
USA	6 000 000 p.a
Chile	5 200 000 p.a

Paper

Country	Production (in tonnes; 1988)
USA	69 500 000 p.a
Japan	24 600 000 p.a
Canada	16 600 000 p.a
China	14 100 000 p.a
Germany	11 900 000 p.a
Finland	8 700 000 p.a

Roundwood – Coniferous

Country	Production (in cubic metres; 1988)
USA	345 000 000 p.a
Russia	300 000 000 p.a
Canada	164 000 000 p.a
China	134 000 000 p.a
Sweden	44 200 000 p.a
Brazil	41 800 000 p.a

Roundwood – non-Coniferous

Country	Production (in cubic metres; 1988)
India	243 000 000 p.a
USA	185 000 000 p.a
Indonesia	172 000 000 p.a
Brazil	170 000 000 p.a

China   142 000 000 p.a
Nigeria   96 200 000 p.a

Sheep Meat*
Country	Production (in tonnes)
New Zealand	570 000 p.a
Australia	540 000 p.a
China	420 000 p.a
Russia	420 000 p.a
UK	350 000 p.a
Turkey	300 000 p.a

Sugar*
Country	Production (in tonnes)
India	10 200 000 p.a
Cuba	8 200 000 p.a
Brazil	7 400 000 p.a
USA	6 500 000 p.a
China	5 600 000 p.a
Ukraine	4 700 000 p.a

Wine*
Country	Production (in tonnes)
Italy	6 000 000 p.a
France	5 900 000 p.a
Spain	3 000 000 p.a
Argentina	2 000 000 p.a
USA	1 800 000 p.a
Germany	1 200 000 p.a

Wool
Country	Production (in tonnes)
Australia	1 100 000 p.a
New Zealand	320 000 p.a
China	240 000 p.a
Russia	210 000 p.a
Argentina	160 000 p.a
Kazakhstan	110 000 p.a

Aluminium*
Country	Production (in tonnes)
USA	6 100 000 p.a
Russia	2 400 000 p.a
Canada	1 700 000 p.a
Germany	1 300 000 p.a
Australia	1 300 000 p.a
Japan	1 100 000 p.a

Cement
Country	Production (in tonnes)
China	204 000 000 p.a
Russia	84 500 000 p.a
Japan	84 400 000 p.a
USA	70 900 000 p.a
India	43 200 000 p.a
Germany	40 000 000 p.a

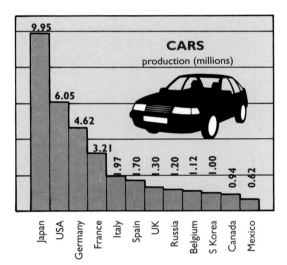

CARS
production (millions)

Japan 9.95; USA 6.05; Germany 4.62; France 3.21; Italy .97; Spain 1.70; UK 1.30; Russia 1.20; Belgium 1.12; S Korea 1.00; Canada 0.94; Mexico 0.62

MANUFACTURED GOODS

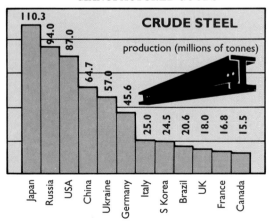

CRUDE STEEL
production (millions of tonnes)

Japan 110.3; Russia 94.0; USA 87.0; China 64.7; Ukraine 57.0; Germany 45.6; Italy 25.0; S Korea 24.5; Brazil 20.6; UK 18.0; France 16.8; Canada 15.5

Shipping (Merchant)
Country	Launched (tonnes)
Japan	6 500 000 p.a
South Korea	3 300 000 p.a
Germany	860 000 p.a
China	450 000 p.a
Denmark	400 000 p.a
Spain	380 000 p.a

Television Sets
Country	Production (1988)
Japan	17 700 000 p.a
China	16 700 000 p.a
USA	13 700 000 p.a
South Korea	7 800 000 p.a
Russia	6 000 000 p.a
Germany	4 400 000 p.a

WORLD RAILWAYS

Figures are given for the total route length (in km and miles) of the principal railway systems of the world. 'Metros' are both above and below ground.

USA 261 124 km (162 254 mi). There are 'metros' in New York (373 km/232 mi), Chicago (156 km/97 mi), Washington DC (118 km/73 mi), San Francisco (115 km/71 mi), Boston (70 km/43 mi), Philadelphia (39 km/24 mi), Atlanta, Baltimore, Buffalo, Cleveland, Detroit, Los Angeles and Miami.

Russia 86 300 km (53 624 mi). There are 'metros' in Moscow (242 km/151 mi), St Petersburg 83 km (52 mi), Nizhny Novgorod (formerly Gorky), Novosibirsk, Samara (formerly Kubyshev) and Yekaterinburg (formerly Sverdlovsk).

Canada 63 549 km (39 487 mi). There are 'metros' in Montreal 64 km (40 mi), Toronto 64 km (40 mi) and Vancouver.

India 61 976 km (38 510 mi). There is a 'metro' in Calcutta.

China c. 54 000 km (c. 33 500 mi). There are 'metros' in Beijing (Peking) and Tianjin (Tientsin).

Germany 41 039 km (25 500 mi). There are 'metros' in Berlin (168 km/104 mi), Hamburg (90 km/56 mi), Frankfurt, Munich, Nürnberg and Wuppertal.

Australia 38 803 km (24 111 mi). No 'metros'.

France 34 680 km (21 549 mi). There are 'metros' in Paris (307 km/191 mi), Lille, Lyon, Marseille and Toulouse.

Argentina c. 34 500 km (c. 21 400 mi). There is a 'metro' in Buenos Aires.

Poland 27 137 km (16 862 mi). No 'metros'.

South Africa 23 619 km (14 676 mi). No 'metros'.

Ukraine 22 760 km (14 142 mi). There are 'metros' in Dneipropetrovsk, Kharkov and Kiev.

Brazil 22 417 km (13 929 mi). There are 'metros' in Rio de Janeiro and São Paulo.

Japan 20 984 km (13 038 mi). There are 'metros' in Tokyo (151 km/94 mi), Osaka (91 km/57 mi), Nagoya (69 km/43 mi), Fukuoka, Kobe, Kyoto, Sapporo, Sendai and Yokohama.

Mexico 20 306 km (12 618 mi). There is a 'metro' in Mexico City (141 km/88 mi).

United Kingdom 16 915 km (10 510 mi). There are 'metros' in London (408 km/254 mi), Glasgow, Manchester and Newcastle.

Italy 15 982 km (9931 mi). There are 'metros' in Milan (66 km/41 mi), Naples and Rome.

Kazakhstan 14 550 km (9041 mi). No 'metros'.

Spain 12 691 km (7886 mi). There are 'metros' in Madrid (112 km/70 mi) and Barcelona (71 km/44 mi).

Romania 11 127 km (6914 mi). There is a 'metro' in Bucharest.

Sweden 11 119 km (6909 mi). There is a 'metro' in Stockholm.

MAJOR PORTS

The figures in the list of the world's largest ports are in millions of tonnes (tons) of goods handled in 1990.

Rotterdam (Netherlands)	287.7
Singapore (Singapore)	187.8
Kobe (Japan)	171.5
Shanghai (China)	133.0
Nagoya (Japan)	128.9
Yokohama (Japan)	123.9
Antwerp (Belgium)	102.0
Osaka (Japan)	97.4
Kitakyushu (Japan)	95.2
Marseille (France)	90.3
Hong Kong (Hong Kong)	89.0
Tokyo (Japan)	79.3
Kaohsiung (Taiwan)	78.0
Long Beach (USA)	74.8
Philadelphia (USA)	68.6
Los Angeles (USA)	67.9

MAJOR SHIP CANALS

Major ship canals used by ocean-going shipping include:

St Lawrence Seaway (from Montreal to Lake Ontario, Canada-USA); opened 1959; 304 km (189 mi) – canalized section of the St Lawrence Seaway that enables shipping to sail 3769 km (2342 mi) inland.

Main-Danube Canal (from Bamberg on the Main to Kelheim on the Danube, Germany); opened 1992; 171 km (106 mi).

Suez Canal (from the Mediterranean to the Red Sea, Egypt); opened 1869; 162 km (101 mi).

Albert Canal (from the Maas to the Scheldt, Belgium); opened 1939; 129 km (80 mi).

Kiel Canal (from the North Sea to the Baltic, Germany); opened 1895; 99 km (62 mi).

Alfonso XIII Canal (from Seville to the Gulf of Cadiz, Spain); opened 1926; 85 km (53 mi).

Panama Canal (from the Pacific to the Caribbean, Panama); opened 1914; 81 km (50 mi).

CAR OWNERSHIP

	Persons per car	Total no. of cars
USA	1.8	148 081 443
Japan	3.4	36 621 085
Germany	2.3	34 051 299
Italy	2.4	24 307 000
France	2.5	23 010 000
United Kingdom	3.0	19 266 000
Brazil	10.2	14 995 837
Canada	2.1	12 811 318
Spain	3.7	10 787 500

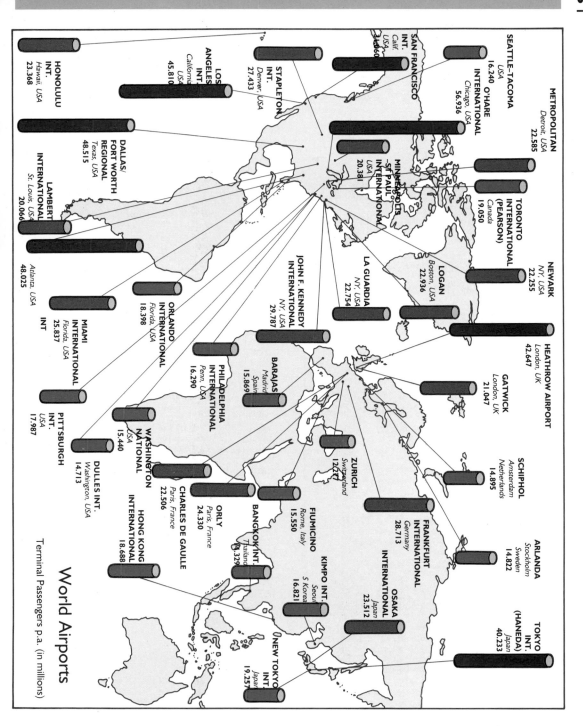

World Airports

Terminal Passengers p.a. (in millions)

SEATTLE-TACOMA
INT.
USA
16,240

SAN FRANCISCO
INT.
Calif.
USA
31,060

O'HARE
INTERNATIONAL
Chicago, USA
56,936

METROPOLITAN
Detroit, USA
22,585

LOS
ANGELES
INT.
California,
USA
45,810

STAPLETON
INT.
Denver, USA
27,433

HONOLULU
INT.
Hawaii, USA
23,368

MINNEAPOLIS
-ST PAUL
INTERNATIONAL
USA
20,381

TORONTO
INTERNATIONAL
(PEARSON)
Canada
19,050

NEWARK
NY, USA
22,255

DALLAS/
FORT WORTH
REGIONAL
Texas, USA
48,515

LAMBERT
INTERNATIONAL
St. Louis, USA
20,066

Atlanta, USA
48,025

LOGAN
Boston, USA
22,936

LA GUARDIA
NY, USA
22,754

JOHN F. KENNEDY
INTERNATIONAL
NY, USA
29,787

HEATHROW AIRPORT
London, UK
42,647

MIAMI
INTERNATIONAL
Florida, USA
25,837

ORLANDO
INTERNATIONAL
Florida, USA
18,398

INT
30

PITTSBURGH
INT.
USA
17,987

WASHINGTON
NATIONAL
USA
15,440

PHILADELPHIA
INTERNATIONAL
Penn, USA
16,290

BARAJAS
Madrid,
Spain
15,869

GATWICK
London, UK
21,047

SCHIPHOL
Amsterdam
Netherlands
14,895

DULLES INT.
Washington, USA
14,713

CHARLES DE GAULLE
Paris, France
22,506

ORLY
Paris, France
24,330

ZURICH
Switzerland
12,277

FIUMICINO
Rome, Italy
15,550

FRANKFURT
INTERNATIONAL
Germany
28,713

ARLANDA
Stockholm
Sweden
14,822

HONG KONG
INTERNATIONAL
18,688

BANGKOK INT.
Thailand
13,329

KIMPO INT.
Seoul
S Korea
16,821

OSAKA
INTERNATIONAL
Japan
23,512

TOKYO
INT.
(HANEDA)
Japan
40,233

NEW TOKYO
INT.
Japan
19,257

COUNTRIES OF THE WORLD

AFGHANISTAN

Official name: Jamhuria Afghanistan (Republic of Afghanistan).

Member of: UN.

Area: 652 225 km² (251 773 sq mi).

Population: 16 121 000 (1990 est). There are almost 3 500 000 (1990 est) Afghan refugees in Pakistan and Iran.

Capital and major cities: Kabul 1 425 000 (including suburbs), Kandahar (Qandahar) 226 000, Herat 177 000, Mazar-i-Sharif 131 000, Qonduz 108 000, Charikar 100 000 (1988 est).

Languages: Pushto (52%), Dari (Persian; 30%) - both official.

Religions: Sunni Islam (74%), Shia Islam (25%).

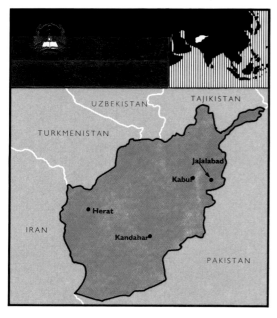

GOVERNMENT The constitution provides for a two-chamber National Assembly, elected by universal adult suffrage. The Loya Jirgha (the supreme state body) consists of the National Assembly and the Cabinet, and provincial, legal and tribal representatives. The Loya Jirgha elects the President, who appoints a Prime Minster, who, in turn, appoints the Council of Ministers. A provisional government was formed in 1992. Various political groupings are active, but political parties do not currently operate within a recognizable constitutional framework.

President: Burhanuddin Rabbani.

Prime Minister: Abdul Sabur Farid.

GEOGRAPHY The central highlands, dominated by the Hindu Kush, cover over three quarters of the country and contain several peaks over 6400 m (21 000 ft). North of the highlands are plains, an important agricultural region, while the southwest of the country is desert and semidesert. *Principal rivers:* Helmand, Amu Darya (Oxus). *Highest point:* Noshaq 7499 m (24 581 ft).

ECONOMY Over 60% of the labour force is employed in agriculture. Most of the usable land is pasture, mainly for sheep, but cereal crops, particularly wheat and maize, are also important. Principal exports include fresh and dried fruit, wool and cotton. Natural gas, found in the northern plains, is also exported, but rich deposits of coal and iron ore are comparatively underdeveloped. Economic development has been held back by civil war, and much of the basic infrastructure of the country has been damaged.

RECENT HISTORY Afghanistan secured its independence in 1921 after three wars with the British. A period of unrest followed until a more stable monarchy was established in 1933. A coup in 1973 overthrew the monarchy. A close relationship with the USSR resulted from the 1978 Saur Revolution, but the Soviet invasion (1979) led to civil war. In 1989 the Soviets withdrew, leaving the cities in the hands of the government and Muslim fundamentalist guerrillas controlling the countryside. In 1992 fundamentalists took Kabul and formed a provisional government, but factional – largely ethnic – fighting continues.

ALBANIA

Official name: Republika e Shqipërisë (Republic of Albania).

Member of: UN, CSCE.

Area: 28 748 km² (11 100 sq mi).

Population: 3 303 000 (1991 est).

Capital and major cities: Tirana (Tiranë) 238 000, Durrës 83 000, Elbasan 81 000, Shkodër 80 000, Vlorë 72 000 (1989 est).

Languages: Albanian (Gheg and Tosk dialects). Tosk is the official language.

Religions: Sunni Islam (20%), small Greek Orthodox and Roman Catholic minorities. The practice of religion was banned from 1967 to 1990.

GOVERNMENT A President and the 140-member Assembly are elected under a system of proportional representation by universal adult suffrage for four years. The Assembly elects a Prime Minister and a Council of Ministers. The principal political parties are the (centre) Democratic Party and the (former Communist) Socialist Party.
President: Sali Berisha.
Prime Minister: Aleksandr Meksi.

GEOGRAPHY Coastal lowlands support most of the country's agriculture. Mountain ranges cover the greater part of Albania. *Principal rivers:* Semani, Drini, Vjosa. *Highest point:* Mount Korab 2751 m (9025 ft).

ECONOMY Albania is poor by European standards. The state-owned economy is mainly based on agriculture and the export of chromium. In 1990 Albania ended self-imposed economic isolation and sought financial, technical and humanitarian assistance. Nevertheless, the country has experienced famine, emigration and the collapse of much of its industrial infrastructure.

RECENT HISTORY Independence from the Ottoman (Turkish) Empire was declared in 1912. The country was occupied in both the Balkan Wars and World War I, and the formation of a stable government within recognized frontiers did not occur until the 1920s. Interwar Albania

was dominated by Ahmed Zogu (1895–1961), who made himself king (as Zog I) in 1928 and used Italian loans to develop his impoverished country. He fled when Mussolini invaded in 1939. Communist-led partisans took power when the Germans withdrew (1944). Under Enver Hoxha (1908–85), the regime pursued rapid modernization on Stalinist lines, allied, in turn, to Yugoslavia, the USSR and China, before opting (in 1978) for self-sufficiency and isolation. In 1990, a power struggle within the ruling Communist Party was won by the more liberal wing led by President Alia, who instituted a programme of economic, political and social reforms. The Communist Party retained a majority in multi-party elections held in April 1991, but – as the Socialist Party – was defeated in 1992. The new centrist government faces severe economic problems.

ALGERIA

Official name: El Djemhouria El Djazaïria Demokratia Echaabia (the Democratic and Popular Republic of Algeria).
Member of: UN, OAU, Arab League, OPEC.
Area: 2 381 741 km² (919 595 sq mi).
Population: 25 888 000 (1991 est).
Capital and major cities: Algiers (El Djazaïr or Alger) 1 722 000, Oran (Ouahran) 664 000, Constantine (Qacentina) 449 000 Annaba 348 000, Blida (el-Boulaïda) 191 000, Sétif (Stif) 187 000 (all including suburbs; 1989 est).
Languages: Arabic (official), French, Berber.
Religion: Sunni Islam (official).

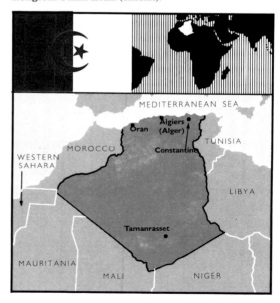

GOVERNMENT The constitution provides for the election of a President, who is executive head of state, and a 296-member National People's Assembly by universal adult suffrage every five years. In 1992 the constitution was suspended and a military council – whose chairman is President – was appointed. The principal political parties are the (banned fundamentalist) Islamic Salvation Front (FIS), the (socialist) National Liberation Front (FLN) and the (largely Berber) Socialist Forces Front (FFS).

President: Ali Kafi.
Prime Minister: Belaid Abdelsalam.

GEOGRAPHY Over 85% of Algeria is covered by the Sahara Desert. To the north lie the Atlas Mountains which enclose a dry plateau. In the southeast are the Hoggar mountains. Along the Mediterranean coast are plains and lower mountain ranges. *Principal river:* Chéliff. *Highest point:* Mont Tahat 2918 m (9573 ft).

ECONOMY Petroleum and natural gas are the main exports and the basis of important industries. The country faces severe economic problems including high unemployment. Nearly one quarter of the adult population is involved in agriculture, but lack of rain and suitable land mean that Algeria has to import two thirds of its food. The small amount of arable land mainly produces wheat, barley, fruit and vegetables, while arid pasturelands support sheep, goats and cattle.

RECENT HISTORY Nationalist riots against French colonial rule were ruthlessly suppressed in 1945, and in 1954 the FLN initiated a revolt that became a bitter war. A rising by French settlers, in favour of the integration of Algeria with France, led to the crisis that returned de Gaulle to power in France (1958). Despite two further risings by the settlers, and the activities of the colonists' terrorist organization, the OAS, Algeria gained independence in 1962. The first president, Ahmed Ben Bella (1916–   ), was overthrown in 1965 by Colonel Houari Boumédienne (1932–78), who aimed to re-establish the principles of the 1963 socialist constitution. His successor, Colonel Benjedid Chadli (1929–) began to steer Algeria towards democracy in the late 1980s. Multi-party local elections in 1990 were won by the newly-formed fundamentalist FIS (Islamic Salvation Front). In 1992 the second round of national multi-party elections was cancelled when the FIS gained a large lead in the first round. The military took power and suspended political activity. Tension increased when the new military-appointed president was assassinated.

ANDORRA

Official name: Les Valls d'Andorrà (The Valleys of Andorra).
Member of: Andorra is not a member of any major international organizations.
Area: 467 km² (180 sq mi).

Population: 55 400 (1991 est).
Capital: Andorra la Vella 33 400 (town 20 400; Les Escaldes 13 000; 1990 est).
Languages: Catalan (30%; official), Spanish (59%), French (6%).
Religion: Roman Catholic.

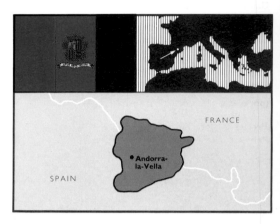

GOVERNMENT Andorra has joint heads of state (co-princes) – the president of France and the Spanish bishop of Urgel – who delegate their powers to permanent representatives who retain certain rights of veto. The 28-member General Council – four councillors from each parish – is elected for four years by universal adult suffrage, and (since 1981) chooses an Executive Council (government). There are no political parties.

Head of government (President of the Executive Council): Oscar Ribas Reig.

GEOGRAPHY Situated in the eastern Pyrenees, Andorra is surrounded by mountains. *Principal river*: Valira. *Highest point*: Pla del'Estany 3011 m (9678 ft).

ECONOMY The economy used to be based mainly on sheep and timber. Tourism has been encouraged by the development of ski resorts and by the duty-free status of consumer goods.

RECENT HISTORY The country's joint allegiance to French and Spanish co-princes has made difficulties for Andorra in obtaining international recognition. However, reforms in 1993 included a proposed new constitution and independent diplomatic representation.

ANGOLA

Official name: A República de Angola (The Republic of Angola).
Member of: UN, OAU, SADCC.

Area: 1 246 700 km² (481 354 sq mi).

Population: 10 284 000 (1991 est).

Capital and major cities: Luanda 1 200 000 (1988; including suburbs), Huambo 203 000, Benguela 155 000, Lobito 150 000, Lubango 105 000 (1982–3 est).

Languages: Portuguese (official), Kimbundu (27%), Umbundu (38%), Lunda (13%), Kikongo (11%).

Religions: Roman Catholic (over 60%), animist (20%).

GOVERNMENT A 318-member Assembly is elected by universal adult suffrage for three years. The President – who is directly-elected for five years – appoints a Prime Minister and a Council of Minsters. The principal political movements are the (former Marxist-Leninist) People's Liberation Movement of Angola (MPLA) and (pro-Western) National Union for the Total Independence of Angola (UNITA).

President: José Eduardo dos Santos.

Prime Minster: Fernando Van Dunem.

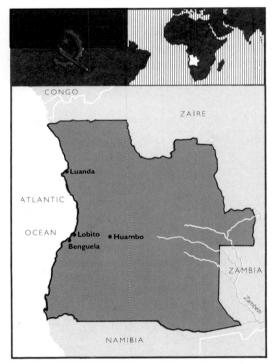

GEOGRAPHY Plateaux, over 1000 m (3300 ft), cover 90% of Angola. In the west is a narrow coastal plain and in the southwest is desert. *Principal rivers*: Cunene (Kunene), Cuanza (Kwanza), Congo (Zaïre), Cuando (Kwando), Zambezi. *Highest point*: Serra Mòco 2610 m (8563 ft).

ECONOMY The development of Angola has been hampered by war. The country is, however, rich in minerals, particularly diamonds, iron ore and petroleum. Although less than 5% of the land is arable, over half the adult population is engaged in agriculture, mainly producing food crops. The main export crop is coffee.

RECENT HISTORY In the 20th century, forced labour, heavy taxation and discrimination from Portuguese colonial settlers helped to stimulate nationalism. Portugal's repression of all political protest led to the outbreak of guerrilla wars in 1961. When independence was finally conceded (1975), three rival guerrilla movements fought for control of the country. With Soviet and Cuban support, the MPLA, under Dr Agostinho Neto (1922–79), gained the upper hand and also managed to repulse an invasion from South Africa. In the 1980s, Cuban troops continued to support the MPLA government against Jonas Savimbi's South African-aided UNITA movement in the South. Foreign involvement in the civil war ended in 1990. A ceasefire ended the civil war in 1991, but fighting between MPLA and UNITA forces resumed after the latter refused to accept the results of multi-party elections in 1992.

ANTIGUA AND BARBUDA

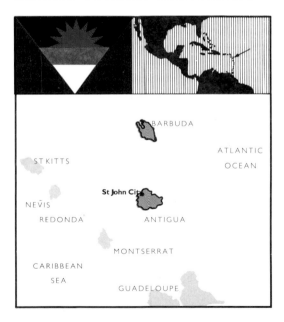

Member of: UN, Commonwealth, OAS, CARICOM.

Area: 442 km² (170.5 sq mi).

Population: 81 600 (1991 est).

Capital: St John's 36 000 (1986 est.).
Language: English.
Religion: Anglican (44%), Moravian.

GOVERNMENT The 17-member House of Representatives is elected by universal adult suffrage for five
years. The Senate, which also has 17 members, is
appointed. Government is by a Cabinet of Ministers. A
Prime Minister, commanding a majority in the lower
house, is appointed by the Governor General, the
representative of the British Queen as sovereign of
Antigua. The main political party is the Antigua Labour
Party.
Prime Minister: Vere C. Bird.

GEOGRAPHY Antigua is a low limestone island,
rising in the west. Barbuda – 45 km / 25 mi to the north –
is a flat wooded coral island. Redonda is a rocky outcrop.
There are no significant rivers. *Highest point*: Boggy
Peak 402 m (1319 ft).

ECONOMY Tourism is the mainstay of the country. In
an attempt to diversify the economy, the government has
encouraged agriculture, but the lack of water on Antigua island is a problem.

RECENT HISTORY The British colonies of Antigua
and Barbuda were united in 1860. Britain granted
Antigua complete internal self-government in 1967 and
independence in 1981.

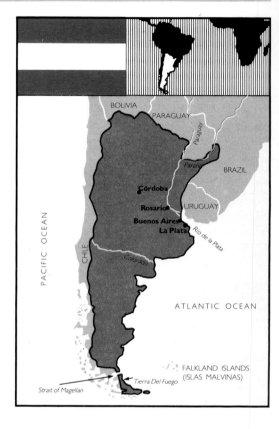

ARGENTINA

Official name: República Argentina (the Argentine
Republic).
Member of: UN, OAS, ALADI, Mercosur.
Area: 2 766 889 km² (1 068 302 sq mi), excluding terri-
tories claimed by Argentina: the Falkland Islands (Islas
Malvinas), South Georgia, South Sandwich Islands, and
parts of the Antarctic.
Population: 32 880 000 (1990 est).
Capital and major cities: Buenos Aires 11 382 000,
Córdoba 1 167 000, Rosario 1 096 000, Mendoza 729 000,
La Plata 644 000, San Miguel de Tucumán 626 000, Mar
del Plata 523 000, San Juan 358 000 (all including sub-
urbs; 1990 est).
Languages: Spanish (95%; official), Guarani (3%).
Religion: Roman Catholic (nearly 93%).

GOVERNMENT The President and Vice-President
are elected for a six-year term of office by an electoral
college of 600 members who are chosen by universal
adult suffrage. The lower house of Congress (the Chamber of Deputies) has 254 members elected by universal
suffrage for four years, with one half of its members
retiring every two years. The 46 members of the upper
house (the Senate) are chosen by provincial legislatures
to serve for nine years, with 18 members retiring every

three years. The main political parties are the Radical
Civil Union (UCR), the Partido Justicialista (Peronist),
and the Union of the Democratic Centre.
President: Carlos Saul Menem.

GEOGRAPHY The Andes extend as a rugged barrier
along the border with Chile. South of the Colorado River
is Patagonia, an important pastureland – although
much of it is semidesert. Nearly 80% of the population
lives in the pampas, whose prairies form one of the
world's most productive agricultural regions. The subtropical plains of northeast Argentina contain part of
the Gran Chaco prairie and rain forests. *Principal
rivers*: Paraná, Colorado, Negro, Salado, Chubut. *Highest point*: Cerro Aconcagua 6960 m (22 834 ft).

ECONOMY Argentina is one of the world's leading
producers of beef, wool, mutton, wheat and wine. The
pampas produce cereals, while fruit and vines are
important in the northest. Pasturelands cover over 50%
of Argentina – for beef cattle in the pampas and for sheep
in Patagonia. However, manufacturing (including
chemicals, steel, cement, paper, pulp and textiles) now
makes the greatest contribution to the economy. The
country is rich in natural resources, including petrol-

eum, natural gas, iron ore and precious metals, and has great potential for hydroelectric power. Argentina is remarkably self-sufficient, although its status as an economic power has declined owing to political instability and massive inflation. Financial reforms in the 1990s improved the prospects of the economy.

RECENT HISTORY Argentinian economic prosperity was ended by the Depression, and, in 1930, the long period of constitutional rule was interrupted by a military coup. In 1946, a populist leader, Juan Perón (1895–1974), came to power with the support of the unions. His wife Eva was a powerful and popular figure, and after her death (1952), Perón was deposed (1955) because of his unsuccessful economic policies, and his anticlericalism. Succeeding civilian governments were unable to conquer rampant inflation, and the military took power again (1966–73). An unstable period of civilian rule (1973–76) included Perón's brief second presidency. In the early 1970s, urban terrorism grew and the economic crisis deepened, prompting another coup. The military junta that seized control in 1976 received international condemnation when thousands of opponents of the regime were arrested or disappeared. In April 1982, President Galtieri ordered the invasion of the Falkland Islands and its dependencies, which had long been claimed by Argentina. A British task force recaptured the islands in June 1982, and Galtieri resigned. Constitutional rule was restored in 1983 under President Raul Alfonsin.

ARGENTINIAN EXTERNAL TERRITORY
Argentine Antarctic Territory see Other Territories, following this chapter.

ARMENIA

Official name: Haikakan (Armenia).
Member of: UN, CIS, CSCE.
Area: 29 800 km² (11 500 sq mi).
Population: 3 376 000 (1989 census).
Capital and major cities: Yerevan 1 215 000, Kumayri (formerly Leninakan) 228 000, Karaklis 169 000 (1989 census).
Languages: Armenian (official; 93%), Azeri (3%), Kurdish (2%).
Religions: Armenian Orthodox majority.
GOVERNMENT A 259-member Assembly and an executive President are elected by universal adult suffrage for four years. A new constitution is to be drafted. The principal political party is the Armenian National Movement.
President: Levon Ter-Petrosyan.
Prime Minister: Grant Bagratyan.
GEOGRAPHY All of Armenia is mountainous – only 10% of the country is under 1000 m (3300 ft). *Principal*

rivers: Araks, Zanga. *Highest point:* Mt Aragats at 4090 m (13 418 ft).

ECONOMY The diverse industrial sector includes chemicals, metallurgy, textiles, precision goods and food processing. Major projects have provided hydroelectric power as well as irrigation water for agriculture. Steps have been taken to introduce a market economy, but an effective blockade by Azerbaijan has devastated the economy.

RECENT HISTORY Russia took E Armenia between 1813 and 1828. The W Armenians (under Ottoman rule) suffered persecution and, in 1896 and again in 1915, large-scale massacres. During World War I Turkey deported nearly 2 000 000 Armenians (suspected of pro-Russian sympathies) to Syria and Mesopotamia. The survivors contributed to an Armenian diaspora in Europe and the USA. Following the collapse of Tsarist Russia, an independent Armenian state emerged briefly (1918–22), but faced territorial wars with all its neighbours. Armenia became part of the Transcaucasian Soviet Republic in 1922 and a separate Union Republic within the USSR in 1936. After the abortive coup by Communist hardliners in Moscow (September 1991), Armenia declared independence and received international recognition when the USSR was dissolved (December 1991). Since 1990 Azeri and Armenian irregular forces have been involved in a violent dispute concerning the status of Nagorno Karabakh, an enclave of Orthodox Christian Armenians surrounded by the Shiite Muslim Azeris.

AUSTRALIA

Official name: The Commonwealth of Australia.
Member of: UN, Commonwealth, ANZUS, OECD, South Pacific Forum.
Area: 7 682 300 km² (2 966 150 sq mi).

Population: 17 211 000 (1991 est).

Capital and major cities: Canberra 310 000, Sydney 3 657 000, Melbourne 3 081 000, Brisbane 1 302 000, Perth 1 193 000, Adelaide 1 050 000, Newcastle 429 000, Gold Coast 266 000, Wollongong 238 000, Hobart 184 000, Geelong 151 000, Townsville 114 000, Launceston 89 000, Toowoomba 80 000, Cairns 76 000, Ballarat 75 000, Darwin 73 000, Bendigo 62 000, Rockhampton 61 000 (all including suburbs; 1990 est).

Language: English.

Religions: Anglican (26%), Roman Catholic (26%), Uniting Church in Australia (8%), Orthodox.

GOVERNMENT The Federal Parliament consists of two chambers elected by compulsory universal adult suffrage. The Senate has 76 members elected by proportional representation – 12 senators elected from each state for six years, 2 from both territories elected for three years. The House of Representatives has 148 members elected for three years. A Prime Minister, who commands a majority in the House of Representatives, is appointed by the Governor General, who is the representative of the British Queen as sovereign of Australia. The Prime Minister chairs the Federal Executive Council (or Cabinet), which is responsible to Parliament. Each state has its own government. The main political parties are the Australian Labor Party, the Australian Democrats (liberal), the Liberal Party of Australia (conservative), and the National Party of Australia (conservative).

Prime Minister: Paul Keating.

STATES AND TERRITORIES New South Wales
Area: 801 600 km² (309 500 sq mi). *Population*: 5 862 000 (1991 est). *Capital*: Sydney.

Queensland *Area*: 1 727 200 km² (666 875 sq mi). *Population*: 2 939 000 (1991 est). *Capital*: Brisbane.

South Australia *Area*: 984 000 km² (379 925 sq mi). *Population*: 1 448 000 (1991 est). *Capital*: Adelaide.

Tasmania *Area*: 67 800 km² (26 175 sq mi). *Population*: 459 000 (1991 est). *Capital*: Hobart.

Victoria *Area*: 227 600 km² (87 875 sq mi). *Population*: 4 407 000 (1991 est). *Capital*: Melbourne.

Western Australia *Area*: 2 525 500 km² (975 100 sq mi). *Population*: 1 650 000 (1991 est). *Capital*: Perth.

Australian Capital Territory *Area*: 2400 km² (925 sq mi). *Population*: 289 000 (1991 est). *Capital*: Canberra –

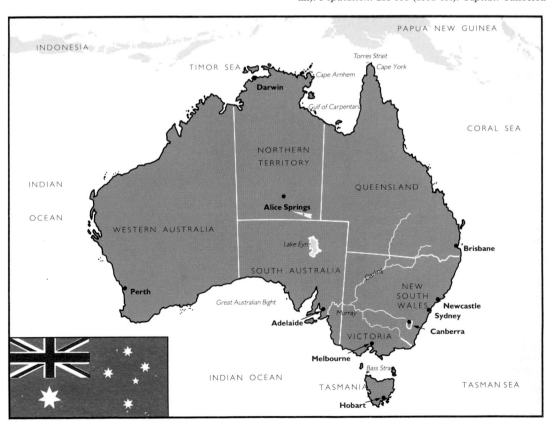

the population given above for Canberra includes suburbs in New South Wales.

Northern Territory *Area*: 1 346 200 km² (519 750 sq mi). *Population*: 158 000 (1991 est). *Capital*: Darwin.

GEOGRAPHY Vast areas of desert cover most of the land in central and western Australia, a region of plateaux between 400 and 600 m (1300–2000 ft) with occasional higher regions, such as the Kimberley Plateau. In contrast to this arid, scarcely populated area – which covers more than 50% of the country – are the narrow coastal plains of the fertile, well-watered east coast where the majority of Australians live. Behind the plains – which range from temperate forest in the south, through subtropical woodland to tropical rain forest in Queensland – rise the Eastern Uplands, or Great Dividing Range. This is a line of ridges and plateaux, interrupted by basins, stretching from Cape York Peninsula in the north to the island of Tasmania. West of the uplands is the Great Artesian Basin extending from the Gulf of Carpentaria to the Murray River and Eyre Basins. Landforms in the basin include rolling plains, plateaux, salt lakes and river valleys, while the natural vegetation ranges from savannah and mixed forest to arid steppe and desert. Between the Murray River and Eyre Basins are the Flinders and Mount Lofty Ranges. Many of Australia's rivers flow intermittently. *Principal rivers*: Murray, Darling, Lachlan, Flinders, Diamentina, Ashburton, Fitzroy. *Highest point*: Mount Kosciusko 2230 m (7316 ft).

ECONOMY Since World War II, Australia's economy has been dominated by mining, and minerals now account for over 30% of the country's exports. Australia has major reserves of coal, petroleum and natural gas, uranium, iron ore, copper, nickel, bauxite, gold and diamonds. Manufacturing and processing are largely based upon these resources: iron and steel, construction, oil refining and petrochemicals, vehicle manufacturing and engineering are all prominent. The food-processing and textile industries are based upon agriculture. Australia's reliance on the agricultural sector has fallen considerably and in the 1990s there has been a planned reduction of the sheep population. However, the country is still the world's leading producer of wool. Major interests include sheep, cattle, cereals (in particular wheat), sugar (in Queensland) and fruit. A strong commercial sector, with banks and finance houses, adds to the diversity of the economy.

RECENT HISTORY In 1901, the Commonwealth of Australia was founded when the six British colonies of New South Wales, Queensland, South Australia, Tasmania, Victoria, and Western Australia came together in a federation. Australia made an important contribution in World War I – one fifth of its servicemen were killed in action. The heroic landing at Gallipoli in the Dardenelles is marked by a national day of remembrance in Australia. The Depression hit the country badly, but the interwar years did see international recognition of Australia's independence. World War II, during which the north was threatened by Japan, strengthened links with America. Australian troops fought in Vietnam and

important trading partnerships have been formed with Asian countries. Since 1945, migrants from all over Europe have gained assisted passage to Australia, further diluting the British connection. Australia now has a close relationship with the USA and is a regional power in the South Pacific region.

AUSTRALIAN EXTERNAL TERRITORIES
Ashmore and Cartier Islands *Area*: 5 km² (2 sq mi). *Population*: uninhabited.

Australian Antarctic Territory see Other Territories, following this chapter.

Christmas Island *Area*: 135 km² (52 sq mi). *Population*: 1770 (1991 est). *Capital*: Flying Fish Cove.

Cocos (Keeling) Islands *Area*: 14 km² (5.5 sq mi). *Population*: 600 (1990 census). *Capital*: Bantam Village (on Home Island).

Coral Sea Islands Territory *Area*: 8 km² (5 sq mi) of land in a sea area of 780 000 km² (300 000 sq mi). *Population*: no permanent inhabitants. A meteorological station is staffed by 3 officers.

Heard and MacDonald Islands *Area*: 292 km² (113 sq mi). *Population*: no permanent inhabitants.

Norfolk Island *Area*: 34.5 km² (13.3 sq mi). *Population*: 1980 (1986 census). *Capital*: Kingston.

AUSTRIA

Official name: Republik Österreich (Republic of Austria)

Member of: UN, EFTA, OECD, CSCE, Council of Europe.

Area: 83 855 km² (32 367 sq mi).

Population: 7 812 000 (1991 census).

Capital and major cities: Vienna (Wien) 2 045 000 (city 1 533 000), Linz 434 000 (city 203 000), Graz 395 000 (city 232 000), Salzburg 267 000 (city 144 000), Innsbruck 235 000 (city 115 000), Klagenfurt 135 000 (city 90 000), Villach 55 000, Wels 53 000, Sankt Pölten 50 000, Dornbirn 41 000 (1991 census).

Language: German (official; 96%).

Religion: Roman Catholic (84%); various Protestant Churches (6%).

GOVERNMENT Executive power is shared by the Federal President – who is elected by universal adult suffrage for a six-year term – and the Council of Ministers (Cabinet), led by the Federal Chancellor. The President appoints a Chancellor who commands a majority in the Federal Assembly's lower chamber, the Nationalrat, whose 183 members are elected by universal adult suffrage according to proportional representation for a term of four years. The 63 members of the upper chamber – the Bundesrat – are elected by the assemblies of the nine provinces of the Federal Republic. The main political parties are the (socialist) Social Democratic Party (SPO), (conservative) People's Party

(OVP), (right-wing) Freedom Party (FPO) and the Greens (VGO).

Federal President: Thomas Klestil.

Federal Chancellor: Franz Vranitzky.

PROVINCES (Länder) Burgenland *Area*: 3966 km² (1531 sq mi). *Population*: 274 000 (1991 census). *Capital*: Eisenstadt.

Carinthia (Kärnten) *Area*: 9533 km² (3681 sq mi). *Population*: 552 000 (1991 census). *Capital*: Klagenfurt.

Lower Austria (Niederösterreich) *Area*: 19 171 km² (7402 sq mi). *Population*: 1 481 000 (1991 census). *Capital*: Sankt Pölten.

Salzburg *Area*: 7154 km² (2762 sq mi). *Population*: 484 000 (1991 census). *Capital*: Salzburg.

Styria (Steiermark) *Area*: 16 387 km² (6327 sq mi). *Population*: 1 185 000 (1991 census). *Capital*: Graz.

Tirol *Area*: 12 647 km² (4883 sq mi). *Population*: 630 000 (1991 census). *Capital*: Innsbruck.

Upper Austria (Oberösterreich) *Area*: 11 979 km² (4625 sq mi). *Population*: 1 340 000 (1991 census). *Capital*: Linz.

Vienna (Wien) *Area*: 415 km² (160 sq mi). *Population*: 1 533 000 (1991 census). *Capital*: Vienna.

Vorarlberg *Area*: 2601 km² (1004 sq mi). *Population*: 333 000 (1991 census). *Capital*: Dornbirn.

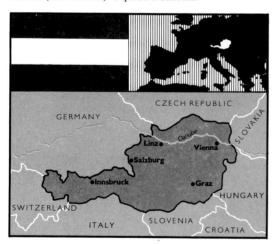

GEOGRAPHY The Alps – much of which are covered by pastures and forests – occupy nearly two thirds of Austria. Lowland Austria – in the east – consists of low hills, the Vienna Basin and a flat marshy area beside the Neusiedler See on the Hungarian border. Along the Czech border is a forested massif rising to 1200 m (4000 ft). *Principal rivers*: Danube (Donau), Inn, Mur. *Highest point*: Grossglockner 3798 m (12 462 ft).

ECONOMY Although Austria produces about 90% of its own food requirements, agriculture employs only 8% of the labour force. The arable land in the east has fertile soils producing good yields of cereals, as well as grapes for wine. Dairy produce is an important export from the pasturelands in the east and in the Alps. The mainstay of the economy is manufacturing industry, including machinery and transport equipment, iron and steel products, refined petroleum products, cement and paper. Natural resources include magnesite and iron ore, as well as hydroelectric power potential and the most considerable forests in central Europe. The Alps attract both winter and summer visitors, making tourism a major earner of foreign currency. Austria retains economic links with countries in Central Europe that were once part of the Habsburg empire.

RECENT HISTORY In 1918–19, the Austro-Hungarian Habsburg empire was dismembered. An Austrian republic was established as a separate state, despite considerable support for union with Germany. Unstable throughout the 1920s and 1930s, Austria was annexed by Germany in 1938 (the Anschluss). Austria was liberated in 1945, but Allied occupation forces remained until 1955 when the independence of a neutral republican Austria was recognized. The upheavals in Central Europe in 1989–90 encouraged Austria to renew traditional links with Hungary, the Czech Republic, Slovenia, Croatia and Slovakia – all once part of the Habsburg Empire. Austria is a candidate for membership of the EC.

AZERBAIJAN

Official name: Azarbaijchan (Azerbaijan).

Member of: UN, CSCE.

Area: 86 600 km² (33 400 sq mi).

Population: 7 137 000 (1989 census).

Capital and major cities: Baku 1 757 000, Gyanzha (formerly Kirovabad) 270 000, Sumgait 234 000 (1989 census).

Languages: Azeri (83%), Russian (6%), Armenian (2%).

Religions: Shia Islam majority.

GOVERNMENT An executive President and a 350-member Assembly are elected by universal adult suffrage for four years. A new constitution is to be drafted. Party politics are at an early stage and there are many small Azeri parties and political groupings. The main parties are the Popular Front of Azerbaijan and the Social Democratic Group.

President: Albulfaz Elchibey.

Prime Minister: Rakhim Guseynov.

GEOGRAPHY Azerbaijan comprises lowlands beside the Caspian Sea, part of the Caucasus Mountains in the N and the Little Caucasus in the SW. The republic includes the Nakhichevan enclave to the W of Armenia. *Principal rivers*: Kura, Araks. *Highest point*: Bazar-Dyuzi 4480 m (14 694 ft).

ECONOMY Important reserves of oil and natural gas are the mainstay of the economy and the basis of heavy industries. Although industry dominates the economy, agriculture contributes a variety of exports including cotton and tobacco. Sturgeon are caught in the Caspian Sea for the important caviar industry. Initial steps have been taken to introduce a market economy, and trade agreements have been concluded with Turkey.

RECENT HISTORY Russia took northern Azerbaijan in 1813, and Nakhichevan and the rest of the present state in 1828. However, the greater part of the land of the Azeris remained under Persian rule. During World War I, a nationalist Azeri movement became allied with the Turks. An independent Azeri state was founded with Turkish assistance (1918), but was invaded by the Soviet Red Army in 1920. Azerbaijan was part of the Transcaucasian Soviet Republic from 1922 until 1936 when it became a separate Union Republic within the USSR. Independence was declared following the abortive coup in Moscow by Communist hardliners (September 1991) and was internationally recognized when the USSR was dissolved (December 1991). Since 1990 Azeri and Armenian irregular forces have been involved in a violent dispute concerning the status of Nagorno Karabakh, an enclave of Orthodox Christian Armenians surrounded by the Shiite Muslim Azeris. Azerbaijan withdrew from the CIS in 1992 and established close links with Turkey.

BAHAMAS

Official name: The Commonwealth of the Bahamas.

Member of: UN, Commonwealth, OAS, CARICOM (Community only).

Area: 13 939 km² (5382 sq mi).

Population: 255 000 (1990 census).

Capital: Nassau 169 000, Freeport 25 000 (1990 census).

Language: English.

Religions: Baptist (29%), Anglican (21%), Roman Catholic (26%).

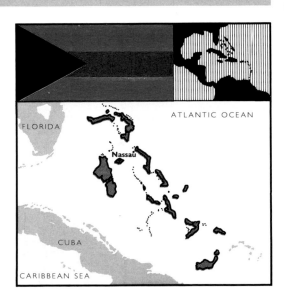

GOVERNMENT The Senate (the upper house of Parliament) has 16 appointed members. The House of Assembly (the lower house) has 49 members elected by universal adult suffrage for five years. A Prime Minister, who commands a majority in the House, is appointed by the Governor General, who is the representative of the British Queen as sovereign of the Bahamas. The Prime Minister chairs the Cabinet, which is responsible to the House. The main political parties are the Progressive Liberal Party and the Free National Movement.

Prime Minister: Hubert A. Ingraham.

GEOGRAPHY The Bahamas comprises some 700 long, flat, narrow islands, and over 2000 barren rocky islets. There are no significant rivers. *Highest point*: Mount Alvernia, Cat Island 63 m (206 ft).

ECONOMY Tourism – mainly from the USA – is the major source of income, and, with related industries, it employs the majority of the labour force. The islands have become a tax haven and financial centre.

RECENT HISTORY Britain granted internal self-government to the Bahamas in 1964. Since independence in 1973, the Bahamas have developed close ties with the USA, although the relationship has been strained at times owing to an illegal drug trade through the islands.

BAHRAIN

Official name: Daulat al-Bahrain (The State of Bahrain).

Member of: UN, Arab League, OPEC, GCC.

Area: 691 km^2 (267 sq mi).
Population: 516 000 (1991 est).
Capital: Manama 152 000, al-Muharraq 78 000 (1988 est).
Language: Arabic.
Religions: Sunni Islam (33%), Shia Islam (60%).

GOVERNMENT Bahrain is ruled directly by an Amir (a hereditary monarch), who appoints a Prime Minister and a Cabinet of Ministers. The 1973 Constitution provides for a National Assembly consisting of Cabinet plus 30 other members elected by popular vote. However, the Assembly was dissolved in 1975 and has not been reconvened. The Amir appoints an advisory Council.
Amir: HH Shaikh Isa II bin Sulman Al-Khalifa (succeeded upon the death of his father, 2 November 1961).
Prime Minister:HH Shaikh Khalifa bin Sulman Al-Khalifa.

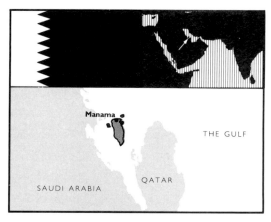

GEOGRAPHY Bahrain Island is the largest of six principal and 29 very small islands that comprise the Bahrain archipelago. It consists mainly of sandy plains and salt marshes, and is linked to Saudi Arabia by causeway. There are no rivers. *Highest point:* Jabal al-Dukhan 134 m (440 ft).

ECONOMY The wealth of Bahrain is due to its petroleum and natural gas resources, and the oil-refining industry. As reserves began to wane in the 1970s, the government encouraged diversification. As a result, Bahrain is now one of the Gulf's major banking and communication centres.

RECENT HISTORY Bahrain was a British protected state until 1971, when complete independence was obtained. Since then there has been tension between the Sunni and Shiite communities. Responding to threats from revolutionary Shiite Iran, Bahrain entered defence agreements with Saudi Arabia and other Gulf states, and joined the coalition forces against Iraq after the invasion of Kuwait (August 1990). Since 1986 Bahrain has been in dispute with Qatar over several small (but potentially petroleum-rich) islands.

BANGLADESH

Official name: Gana Praja Tantri Bangla Desh (People's Republic of Bangladesh).
Member of: UN, Commonwealth, SAARC.
Area: 143 998 km^2 (55 598 sq mi).
Population: 107 992 000 (1991 census).
Capital and major cities: Dhaka 5 731 000, Chittagong 2 133 000, Khulna 1 029 000, Rajshahi 427 000, Mymensingh 191 000, Comilla 185 000, Sylhet 169 000, Barisal 159 000 (1991 census).
Languages: Bengali (official; 97%), tribal dialects.
Religion: Sunni Islam (over 85%), Hindu (12%).

GOVERNMENT The Parliament (Jatiya Sangsad) comprises 300 members elected for five years by universal suffrage and 30 women chosen by the elected members. Parliament elects a President – who serves for five years – and a Prime Minister who appoints a Council of Ministers. The main political parties include the Jatiya Party, the Awami League, Jamit-i-Islami and the BNP (Bangladesh Nationalist Party).
President: Abdur Rahman Biswas.
Prime Minister: Begum Khaleda Zia-ur-Rahman.

GEOGRAPHY Most of Bangladesh comprises alluvial plains in the deltas of the rivers Ganges and Brahmaputra, which combine as the Padma. The swampy plains – generally less than 9 m (30 ft) above sea level – are dissected by rivers dividing into numerous distributaries with raised banks. The south and southeast coastal regions contain mangrove forests (the Sundarbans). The only uplands are the Sylhet Hills in the northeast and the Chittagong hill country in the east. *Principal rivers:* Ganges, Brahmaputra. *Highest point:* Keokradong 1230 m (4034 ft).

ECONOMY With a rapidly increasing population, Bangladesh is among the world's poorest countries and is heavily dependent on foreign aid. Over 70% of the population is involved in agriculture. Rice is produced on over three quarters of the cultivated land, but although the land is fertile, crops are often destroyed by floods and cyclones. A major Flood Action Plan, started in 1992, will alter the course of rivers and raise embankments. The main cash crops are jute – Bangladesh yields 90% of the world's production – and tea. Industries include those processing agricultural products – jute, cotton and sugar. Mineral resources are few, but there are reserves of natural gas.

RECENT HISTORY On the partition of British India in 1947, as the majority of its inhabitants were Muslim, the area became the eastern province of an independent Pakistan. Separated by 1600 km (1000 mi) from the Urdu-speaking, politically dominant western province, East Pakistan saw itself as a victim of economic and ethnic injustice. Resentment led to civil war in 1971 when Indian aid to Bengali irregulars gave birth to an

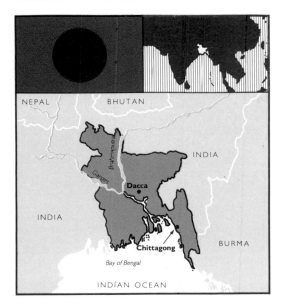

PM appoints a Cabinet responsible to the House. The main political parties are the Democratic Labour Party and the Barbados Labour Party.
Prime Minister: L. Erskine Sandiford.

GEOGRAPHY Barbados is generally flat and low, except in the north. There are no significant rivers. *Highest point:* Mount Hillaby (340 m/1115 ft).

ECONOMY Tourism – which employs about one third of the labour force – is the main source of income. The government has encouraged diversification, and there has been a growth in banking and insurance. Sugar – once the mainstay of Barbados – remains the main crop.

independent People's Republic of Bangladesh ('Free Bengal') under Sheik Mujib-ur-Rahman. The Sheik's assassination in 1975 led eventually to a takeover by General Zia-ur-Rahman, who amended the constitution to create an 'Islamic state'. The General in turn was assassinated in 1981, and General Ershad took power in 1982. Martial law was lifted in 1986 when the constitution was amended and a civilian government took office. Following a period of unrest, President Ershad was deposed in 1990 and charged with corruption. In March 1991 multi-party elections were won by the BNP led by the widow of General Zia. Bangladesh has since switched from a presidential to a parliamentary system of government.

RECENT HISTORY In the British colony of Barbados in the 1930s, economic and social conditions for black Barbadians were miserable. Riots in 1937 led to reforms and also greatly increased black political consciousness. As a result, Barbadians, such as Grantley Adams and Errol Barrow, became prominent in Caribbean politics. Barbados gained independence in 1966 and has become an important influence among the smaller islands of the Lesser Antilles.

BARBADOS

Member of: UN, Commonwealth, OAS, CARICOM.
Area: 430 km² (166 sq mi).
Population: 257 000 (1990 census).
Capital: Bridgetown 102 000 (city 7500; 1990 census).
Language: English.
Religions: Anglican (40%), Pentacostalist (8%), Methodist (7%).

GOVERNMENT The 21 members of the Senate are appointed; the 27 members of the House of Assembly are elected by universal adult suffrage for five years. The Governor General, the representative of the British Queen as sovereign of Barbados, appoints a Prime Minister who commands a majority in the House. The

BELARUS (BYELORUSSIA)

Official name: Respublika Belarus. Formerly known as Byelorussia.
Member of: UN, CIS, CSCE.
Area: 207 600 km² (80 200 sq mi).
Population: 10 260 000 (1989 census).
Capital and major cities: Minsk (Mensk) 1 589 000, Gomel (Homel) 500 000, Mogilev (Mahilyou) 359 000, Vitebsk 347 000, Grodno 263 000, Brest 238 000 (1989 census).
Languages: Belarussian (also known as Belorussian) (79%), Russian (13%), Polish (4%).

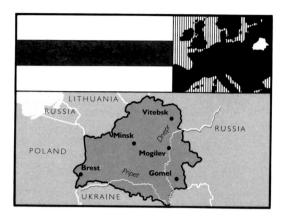

republic. A perceived lack of Soviet concern for the republic at the time of the accident at the Chernobyl nuclear power station (just over the Ukrainian border) strengthened a reawakening Belarussian national identity. Contamination from Chernobyl affected about 20% of the republic, causing some areas to be sealed off and necessitating the eventual resettlement of up to 2 000 000 people. Byelorussia declared independence following the abortive coup by Communist hardliners in Moscow (September 1991) and – as Belarus (pronounced 'By-ella-roose') – received international recognition when the USSR was dissolved (December 1991).

Religions: Russian Orthodox majority, Roman Catholic (5%).

GOVERNMENT A 360-member legislature and a President – who appoints a Council of Ministers – are elected by universal adult suffrage for four years. A new constitution is to be drafted. Many small political parties and groups are active. The largest is the Belarussian Popular Front (BNF).

President: Stanislav Shushkevich.
Prime Minister: Vyacheslav Kebich.

GEOGRAPHY Belarus comprises lowlands covered with glacial debris in the N, fertile well-drained tablelands and ridges in the centre, and the low-lying Pripet Marshes in the S and E. Much of the country is flat. *Principal rivers:* Dnepr, Pripyat, Dvina, Neman. *Highest point:* Dzyarzhynskaya Mountain 346 m (1135 ft).

ECONOMY Although Belarus has few natural resources, its economy is overwhelmingly industrial. Major heavy engineering, chemical, fertilizer, oil refining and synthetic fibre industries were established as part of the centrally-planned Soviet economy. Belarus is dependent upon trade with other former Soviet republics from which it imports the raw materials for its industries and upon which it relies as a market for its industrial goods. Little progress towards establishing a market economy has been made and the country faces severe economic problems. Agriculture is dominated by raising fodder crops for beef cattle, pigs and poultry. Flax is grown for export and the local linen industry. Extensive forests supply important woodworking and paper industries.

RECENT HISTORY The Belarussians came under Russian rule as a result of the three partitions of Poland (1772, 1793 and 1795). The region suffered some of the fiercest fighting between Russia and Germany during World War I. Following the Russian Revolution, a Byelorussian Soviet republic was proclaimed (1919). The republic was invaded by the Poles in the same year and divided between Poland and the Soviet Union in 1921. Byelorussia was devastated during World War II. In 1945 the Belarussians were reunited in a single Soviet

BELGIUM

Official name: Royaume de Belgique or Koninkrijk België (Kingdom of Belgium).
Member of: UN, NATO, EC, CSCE, WEU, Council of Europe, OECD.
Area: 30 519 km² (11 783 sq mi).
Population: 9 849 000 (1991 census).
Capital and major cities: Brussels (Bruxelles or Brussel) 960 000, Antwerp (Antwerpen or Anvers) 920 000 (city 468 000), Liège (Luik) 590 000 (city 185 000), Ghent (Gent or Gand) 485 000 (city 230 000), Charleroi 429 000 (city 207 000), Malines (Mechelen) 293 000 (city 75 000), Courtrai (Kortrijk) 275 000 (city 76 000), Namur (Namen) 264 000 (city 104 000), Bruges (Brugge) 260 000 (city 117 000), Mons (Bergen) 92 000, Ostend (Oostende or Ostende) 69 000 (1990 est).
Languages: Flemish (a dialect of Dutch; 58%), French (42%). (10% of the population is officially bilingual.)
Religion: Roman Catholic (86%).

GOVERNMENT Belgium is a constitutional monarchy. The Chamber of Deputies (the lower house of Parliament) comprises 212 members elected by universal adult suffrage for four years under a system of proportional representation. The Senate (the upper house) has 182 members: 106 directly elected, 50 chosen by provincial councils, 25 co-opted, plus the heir to the throne. The King appoints a Prime Minister, who commands a majority in the Chamber, and, upon the PM's advice, other members of the Cabinet. The main political parties are two Christian Social Parties – the (Flemish) CVP (Christelijke Volkspartei) and its French-speaking equivalent the Parti social chrétien (PSC), the two Socialist parties – Socialistische Partei (SP) and the Parti socialiste belge (FS), two liberal parties – the (Flemish) Liberal Freedom and Progress Party (PVV) and the (French-speaking) Liberal Reform Party (PRL), and Flemish and Walloon regional parties such as the (Flemish) Vlaams Blok and Volksunie. The directly elected regional councils of Flanders, Wallonia and Brussels have very considerable powers.

King: HM Baudouin I, King of the Belgians (succeeded upon the abdication of his father, 15 July 1951).
Prime Minister: Jean-Luc Dehaene.

REGIONS   Brussels (Bruxelles/Brussel) *Area*: 162 km² (63 sq mi). *Population*: 960 000 (1991 census). *Administrative centre*: Brussels.
Flanders (Vlaanderen) *Area*: 13 512 km² (5217 sq mi). *Population*: 5 725 000 (1991 census). *Administrative centre*: Ghent.
Wallonia (Wallonie) *Area*: 16 844 km² (6503 sq mi). *Population*: 3 165 000 (1991 census). *Administrative centre*: Namur.

GEOGRAPHY The forested Ardennes plateau occupies the southeast of the country. The plains of central Belgium, an important agricultural region, are covered in fertile loess. The north, which is flat and low-lying, contains the sandy Kempenland plateau in the east and the plain of Flanders in the west. Enclosed by dykes behind coastal sand dunes are polders – former marshes and lagoons reclaimed from the sea. *Principal rivers*: Scheldt (Schelde or Escaut), Meuse (Maes), Sambre. *Highest point*: Botrange 694 m (2272 ft).

ECONOMY Belgium is a small, densely populated industrial country with few natural resources. In the centre and the north, soils are generally fertile and the climate encourages high yields of wheat, sugar beet, grass and fodder crops. Metalworking – originally based on small mineral deposits in the Ardennes – is the most important industry. Textiles, chemicals, ceramics, glass and rubber are also important, but, apart from coal, almost all the raw materials required by industry now have to be imported. Economic problems in the 1970s and 1980s have mirrored Belgium's linguistic divide, with high unemployment largely confined to the French-speaking (Walloon) south, while the industries of the Flemish north have prospered. Banking, commerce and,

in particular, administration employ increasing numbers, and Brussels has benefited from its role as the unofficial 'capital' of the EC.

RECENT   HISTORY Belgium's neutrality was broken by the German invasion in 1914 (which led to Britain's declaration of war against Germany). The brave resistance of King Albert in 1914–18 earned international admiration; the capitulation of Leopold III when Belgium was again occupied by Germany (1940–45) was severely criticized. The Belgian Congo (Zaïre), acquired as a personal possession by Leopold II (1879), was relinquished amidst scenes of chaos in 1960. Belgium is now the main centre of administration of the EC and of NATO, but the country is troubled by the acute rivalry between its Flemish and French speakers and a federal system based on linguistic regions has gradually evolved.

BELIZE

Member of: UN, Commonwealth, CARICOM, OAS.
Area: 22 965 km² (8867 sq mi).
Population: 191 000 (1991 est).
Capital and major cities: Belmopan 4000, Belize City 50 000, Orange Walk 10 500, Corozal 8500, Dangriga 8000 (1989 est).
Languages: English (majority; official), Creole (33%), Spanish (32%), Garifuna (7%).
Religion: Roman Catholic (62%), various Protestant Churches (28% – mainly Anglican and Methodist).

GOVERNMENT The eight members of the Senate

(the upper house of the National Assembly) are appointed by the Governor General, the representative of the British Queen as sovereign of Belize. The 28 members of the House of Representatives (the lower house) are elected by universal adult suffrage for five years. The Governor General appoints a Prime Minister, who commands a majority in the House, and – on the PM's advice – a Cabinet, which is responsible to the House. The main political parties are the People's United Party and the United Democratic Party.

Prime Minister: George Price.

GEOGRAPHY   Tropical jungle covers much of Belize. The south contains the Maya Mountains. The north is mainly swampy lowlands. *Principal rivers*: Hondo, Belize. *Highest point*: Victoria Peak 1122 m (3681 ft).

ECONOMY   The production of sugar, bananas and citrus fruit for export dominates the economy.

RECENT HISTORY   The colony of British Honduras was renamed Belize in 1973 and gained independence in 1981. Following a severe hurricane in 1961, the capital was moved inland from Belize City to a purpose-built new town, Belmopan. Guatemala continued to claim Belize as part of her territory until 1991.

BENIN

Official name: La République du Bénin (the Republic of Benin).

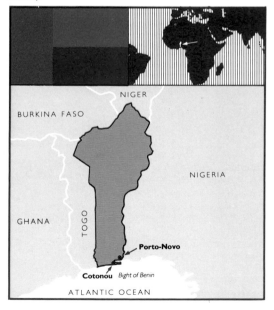

Member of: UN, OAU, ECOWAS.

Area: 112 622 km² (43 484 sq mi).

Population: 4 776 000 (1991 est).

Capital and major cities: Porto-Novo 208 000, Cotonou 487 000, Parakou 66 000 (1983 est).

Languages: French (official), Fon (47%), Adja (12%).

Religions: Animist (61%), Sunni Islam (16%), various Christian Churches (22% – mainly Roman Catholic).

GOVERNMENT   An executive President and an 80-member National Assembly are elected by universal adult suffrage for four years. Multi-party elections in 1991 were contested by 34 political parties.

President: Nicephore Soglo.

GEOGRAPHY   In the northwest lies the Atacora Massif; in the northeast, plains slope down to the Niger Valley. The plateaux of central Benin fall in the south to a low fertile region. A narrow coastal plain is backed by lagoons. *Principal rivers*: Ouémé, Niger. *Highest point*: Atacora Massif 635 m (2083 ft).

ECONOMY   The economy is based on agriculture, which occupies the majority of the labour force. The main food crops are cassava (manioc), yams and maize; the principal cash crop is palm oil. In the late 1980s, central planning was abandoned in favour of a market economy.

RECENT HISTORY   Benin was known as Dahomey until 1975. Political turmoil followed independence from France in 1960, and five army coups took place between 1963 and 1972. The regime established by Colonel Kerekou in 1972 brought some stability, and after 1987, experiments with state socialism were moderated. In 1989 President Kerekou disavowed Marxist-Leninism, and appointed a civilian administration to guide Benin towards becoming a market economy. Kerekou was defeated in multi-party presidential elections in 1991. Benin has since sought Western assisance.

BHUTAN

Official name: Druk-yul (Realm of the Dragon).

Member of: UN, SAARC.

Area: 46 500 km² (17 954 sq mi).

Population: 1 442 000 (1990 UN est; 1992 Bhutanese government estimates give a population of over 700 000).

Capital: Thimphu 60 000 (1987 est).

Language: Dzongkha (Tibetan; official 70%), Nepali (30%).

Religion: Buddhist (70%), Hindu (30%).

GOVERNMENT   Bhutan is a hereditary monarchy without a written constitution. The King shares power with a Council of Ministers, the National Assembly and the head of Bhutan's 5000 Buddhist monks. Of the 150

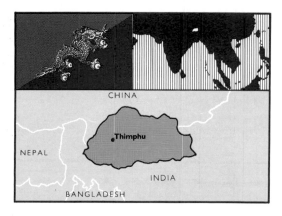

CHINA

NEPAL

Thimphu

INDIA

BANGLADESH

members of the National Assembly, 100 are directly elected by universal adult suffrage for a three-year term; the remainder include the Royal Advisory Council, the Ministers and 10 religious representatives. There are no political parties.

King: HM the *Druk Gyalpo* Jigme Singhye Wangchuk, King of Bhutan (succeeded on the death of his father, 24 July 1972).

GEOGRAPHY The Himalaya make up most of the country. The valleys of central Bhutan are wide and fertile. The narrow Duars Plain – a subtropical jungle – lies along the Indian border. *Principal rivers*: Amo-chu, Wang-chu, Machu. *Highest point*: Khula Kangri 7554 m (24 784 ft).

ECONOMY Bhutan is one of the poorest and least developed countries in the world. About 90% of the labour force is involved in producing food crops.

RECENT HISTORY In 1907 the governor of Tongsa became the first king of Bhutan. In 1949 India returned territory to Bhutan (partially annexed by British India in 1865) but assumed influence over its external affairs. Bhutan remains largely closed to outside influences and measures taken in the 1990s discriminate against the Nepali population in favour of the Bhutanese.

BOLIVIA

Official name: República de Bolivia (Republic of Bolivia).

Member of: UN, OAS, ALADI, Andean Pact.

Area: 1 098 581 km² (424 164 sq mi).

Population: 7 530 000 (1991 est).

Capital and major cities: La Paz (administrative capital) 1 050 000, Sucre (legal capital) 96 000, Santa Cruz 615 000, Cochabamba 377 000, Oruro 195 000, Potosí 114 000, Tarija 68 500 (1988 est).

Languages: Spanish (official; 55%), Quéchua (5%), Aymara (22%).

Religion: Roman Catholic (official; 95%).

GOVERNMENT The President (who appoints a Cabinet), the 27-member Senate and the 130-member Chamber of Deputies are elected for four-year terms by universal adult suffrage. The main political parties are the Movimiento Nacionalista Revolucionario and Acción Democrática Nacionalista.

President: Jaime Paz Zamora.

GEOGRAPHY The Andes divide into two parallel chains between which is an extensive undulating depression (the Altiplano), containing Lake Titicaca, the highest navigable lake in the world. In the east and northeast, a vast lowland includes tropical rain forests (the Llanos), subtropical plains and semiarid grasslands (the Chaco). *Principal rivers*: Beni, Mamoré, Pilcomayo, Paraguay. *Highest point*: Sajama 6542 m (21 463 ft).

ECONOMY Bolivia is a relatively poor country, despite being rich in natural resources such as petroleum and tin. Lack of investment, political instability and the high cost of extraction have retarded development. Agriculture, which is labour intensive, produces domestic foodstuffs (potatoes and maize), as well as export crops (sugar cane and cotton). The illegal cultivation of coca (the source of cocaine) is causing concern.

BRAZIL

PERU

Lake Titicaca

La Paz

Santa Cruz

PACIFIC OCEAN

Sucre

CHILE   ARGENTINA

PARAGUAY

RECENT HISTORY In three devastating wars – the War of the Pacific (1879–83), and the Chaco Wars (1928–30 and 1933–35) – Bolivia sustained great human and territorial losses. After 1935, the political instability of the 19th century continued with a succession of military and civilian governments. Since 1982, however, Bolivia has had democratically elected governments.

BOSNIA-HERZEGOVINA

Official name: Bosna i Hercegovina (Bosnia-Herzegovina).

Member of: UN, CSCE.

Area: 51 129 km² (19 741 sq mi).

Population: 4 365 000 (1991 census); 2 000 000 (late 1992 est; some 2 000 000 refugees left Bosnia in 1992 and over 200 000 people were killed in the war.)

Capital and major cities: Sarajevo 526 000 (city 416 000; by late 1992 the population of Sarajevo was c. 200 000), Banja Luka 143 000, Tuzla 122 000, Mostar 110 000 (1991 census).

Languages: Serbo-Croat – a single language with two written forms.

Religions: Sunni Islam (44%), Serbian Orthodox (33%), Roman Catholic (17%).

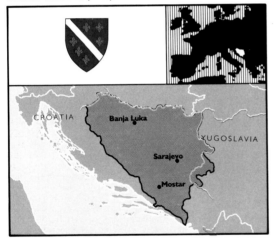

GOVERNMENT: There is constitutional provision for an Assembly and a President – who appoints a Prime Minister and a Cabinet – to be directly elected by universal adult suffrage for four years. In early 1993 government authority was restricted to about 10% of central Bosnia.

GEOGRAPHY Ridges of the Dinaric Mountains, rising to over 1800 m (6000 ft), occupy the greater part of the country and in places form arid karst limestone plateaux. The N comprises restricted lowlands in the valley of the River Sava. The combined length of two tiny coastlines on the Adriatic is less than 20 km (13 mi). *Principal rivers*: Sava, Bosna, Drina. *Highest point*: Maglic 2387 m (9118 ft).

ECONOMY The economy was devastated by war in 1992. Central and E Bosnia is forested. Agriculture is a major employer and sheep, maize, olives, grapes and citrus fruit were important. Bosnia has little industry

but possesses natural resources including coal, lignite, copper and asphalt.

HISTORY A major Bosnian revolt (1875–6) against Turkish rule attracted international concern, but the great powers overrode Bosnia's pan-Slavic aspirations at the Congress of Berlin (1877–8; see p. 429) and assigned Bosnia-Herzegovina to Habsburg Austro-Hungarian rule. In Sarajevo in 1914, Gavrilo Princip, a Bosnian student (ethnically a Serb), assassinated Archduke Franz Ferdinand, the heir to the Austro-Hungarian Empire – an event that helped precipitate World War I (see p. 436). In 1918, Bosnia became part of the new Kingdom of Serbs, Croats and Slovenes, which was renamed Yugoslavia in 1929. Following the German invasion (1941), Bosnia was included in the Axis-controlled puppet state of Croatia. In 1945, when Yugoslavia was reorganized by Marshal Tito on Soviet lines, Bosnia-Herzegovina became a republic within the Communist federation. After the secession of Slovenia and Croatia and the beginning of the Yugoslav civil war (1991), tension grew between Serbs and Croats in Bosnia. The Muslim Bosnians reasserted their separate identity. In 1992, a referendum – which was boycotted by the Serbs – gave a majority in favour of Bosnian independence. International recognition of Bosnia-Herzegovina was gained in April 1992 but Bosnian Serbs, encouraged by Serbia, seized 70% of the country, killing or expelling Muslims and Croats in a campaign of 'ethnic cleansing'. International peace and humanitarian efforts were attempted.

BOTSWANA

Official name: The Republic of Botswana.

Member of: UN, OAU, Commonwealth, SADCC.

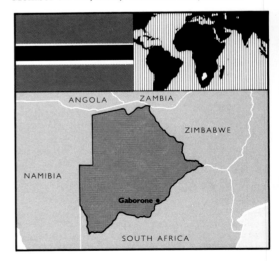

Area: 582 000 km² (224 711 sq mi).

Population: 1 320 000 (1991 est).

Capital and major cities: Gaborone 130 000 (1991 est), Francistown 56 000, Selibi-Pikwe 53 000 (1990 est).

Languages: English (official), Setswana (national).

Religions: Animist (over 50%), various Protestant Churches (50%) – mainly Congregational, Anglican and Roman Catholic.

GOVERNMENT Thirty-four of the 40 members of the National Assembly are elected by universal adult suffrage for five years. Of the remainder, four are nominated by the President and specially elected; the Speaker and Attorney General are non-voting members. The President, who chairs and appoints a Cabinet, is elected for five years by the Assembly. (There is also a 15-member House of Chiefs whose sole brief is to deal with tribal, constitutional and chieftancy matters.) The main political parties are the Botswana Democratic Party and the Botswana National Front.

President: Dr Quett Masire.

GEOGRAPHY A central plateau divides a flat near-desert in the east of Botswana from the Kalahari Desert and Okavango Swamps in the west. *Principal rivers*: Chobe, Shashi. *Highest point*: Tsodilo Hill 1375 m (4511 ft).

ECONOMY Nomadic cattle herding and the cultivation of subsistence crops occupies the majority of the labour force. The mainstay of the economy is mining for diamonds, copper-nickel and coal.

HISTORY Nationalism in the British protectorate of Bechuanaland was late to develop, and independence – as Botswana – was granted without a struggle in 1966. Under the first president, Sir Seretse Khama, and his successor, Botswana has succeeded in remaining a democracy.

BRAZIL

Official name: A República Federativa do Brasil (the Federative Republic of Brazil).

Member of: UN, OAS, ALADI, Mercosur.

Area: 8 511 965 km² (3 286 488 sq mi).

Population: 153 322 000 (1991 est).

Capital and major cities: Brasília 1 864 000 (city 1 841 000), São Paulo 16 832 000 (city 9 700 000), Rio de Janeiro 11 141 000 (city 5 480 000), Belo Horizonte 3 446 000 (city 2 103 000), Recife 2 924 000 (city 1 336 000), Pôrto Alegre 2 924 000 (city 1 255 000), Salvador 2 362 000 (city 2 075 000), Fortaleza 2 169 000 (city 1 709 000), Curitiba 1 926 000 (city 1 248 000), Nova Iguaçu (part of the Rio de Janeiro agglomeration) 1 325 000, Belém 1 296 000 (city 1 236 000), Goiânia 998 000 (1991 est).

Language: Portuguese (official).

Religion: Roman Catholic (89%), various Protestant Churches (7%), Candomble.

GOVERNMENT The President – who appoints and chairs a Cabinet – is elected for a five-year term by universal adult suffrage. The lower house of the National Congress (the Chamber of Deputies) has 503 members elected for four years by compulsory universal adult suffrage. The 91 members of the upper house (the Federal Senate) are elected directly for an eight-year term – one third and two thirds of the senators retiring alternately every four years. Each of the 26 states and the Federal District of Brasília has its own legislature. The principal political parties are the (moderate) PMDB (Brazilian Democratic Movement), the (moderate) PFL (Liberal Front), the (conservative) National Reconstruction Party, the (socialist) PT (Worker's Party) and the Democratic Labour Party. A referendum in 1993 will decide whether Brazil will retain its present presidential system, adopt a parliamentary system or restore the monarchy.

President: Itamar Franco.

STATES AND TERRITORIES **Acre** *Area*: 152 589 km² (58 915 sq mi). *Population*: 428 000 (1991 est). *Capital*: Rio Branco.

Alagoas *Area*: 27 731 km² (10 707 sq mi). *Population*: 2 459 000 (1991 est). *Capital*: Maceió.

Amazonas *Area*: 1 564 445 km² (604 032 sq mi). *Population*: 2 055 000 (1991 est). *Capital*: Manaus.

Bahia *Area*: 561 026 km² (216 612 sq mi). *Population*: 11 953 000 (1991 est). *Capital*: Salvador.

Ceará *Area*: 150 630 km² (58 158 sq mi). *Population*: 6 587 000 (1991 est). *Capital*: Fortaleza.

Espírito Santo *Area*: 45 597 km² (17 605 sq mi). *Population*: 2 571 000 (1991 est). *Capital*: Vitória.

Goiás *Area*: 364 770 km² (140 838 sq mi). *Population*: 4 036 000 (1991 est). *Capital*: Goiânia.

Maranhão *Area*: 328 663 km² (126 897 sq mi). *Population*: 5 287 000 (1991 est). *Capital*: São Luis.

Mato Grosso *Area*: 881 001 km² (340 154 sq mi). *Population*: 1 776 000 (1991 est). *Capital*: Cuiaba.

Mato Grosso do Sul *Area*: 350 548 km² (135 347 sq mi). *Population*: 1 838 000 (1991 est). *Capital*: Campo Grande.

Minas Gerais *Area*: 587 172 km² (226 707 sq mi). *Population*: 16 071 000 (1991 est). *Capital*: Belo Horizonte.

Pará *Area*: 1 250 722 km² (482 904 sq mi). *Population*: 5 142 000 (1991 est). *Capital*: Belém.

Paraíba *Area*: 56 372 km² (21 765 sq mi). *Population*: 3 294 000 (1991 est). *Capital*: João Pessoa.

Paraná *Area*: 199 554 km² (77 048 sq mi). *Population*: 9 340 000 (1991 est). *Capital*: Curitiba.

Pernambuco *Area*: 98 281 km² (37 946 sq mi). *Population*: 7 482 000 (1991 est). *Capital*: Recife.

Piauí *Area*: 250 934 km² (96 886 sq mi). *Population*: 2 715 000 (1991 est). *Capital*: Teresina.

Rio de Janeiro *Area*: 44 268 km² (17 092 sq mi). *Population*: 13 351 000 (1991 est). *Capital*: Rio de Janeiro.

Rio Grande do Norte *Area*: 53 015 km² (20 469 sq mi). *Population*: 2 360 000 (1991 est). *Capital*: Natal.

Rio Grande do Sul *Area*: 282 184 km² (108 951 sq mi). *Population*: 9 298 000 (1991 est). *Capital*: Pôrto Alegre.

Rondônia *Area*: 243 044 km² (93 839 sq mi). *Population*: 1 135 000 (1991 est). *Capital*: Pôrto Velho.

Santa Catarina *Area*: 95 985 km² (37 060 sq mi). *Population*: 4 536 000 (1991 est). *Capital*: Florianópolis.

São Paulo *Area*: 247 898 km² (95 714 sq mi). *Population*: 33 777 000 (1991 est). *Capital*: São Paulo.

Sergipe *Area*: 21 994 km² (8492 sq mi). *Population*: 1 440 000 (1991 est). *Capital*: Aracaju.

Tocantins *Area*: 277 322 km² (107 075 sq mi). *Population*: 1 009 000 (1991 est). *Capital*: Palmas.

Amapá (territory) *Area*: 140 276 km² (54 161 sq mi). *Population*: 264 000 (1991 est). *Capital*: Macapá.

Federal District (Distrito Federal) *Area*: 5814 km² (2245 sq mi). *Population*: 1 925 000 (1991 est). *Capital*: Brasília.

Fernando de Noronha (territory) *Area*: 26 km² (10 sq mi). *Population*: 1300 (1991 est). *Capital*: the island territory is administered from the mainland.

Roraima (territory) *Area*: 230 104 km² (88 843 sq mi). *Population*: 124 000 (1991 est). *Capital*: Boa Vista.

GEOGRAPHY Nearly one half of Brazil is drained by the world's largest river system, the Amazon, whose wide, low-lying basin is still largely covered by tropical rain forest, although pressure on land has led to extensive deforestation. North of the Amazon Basin, the Guiana Highlands contain Brazil's highest peak. A central plateau of savannah grasslands lies south of the Basin. The east and south of the country contain the Brazilian Highlands – a vast plateau divided by fertile valleys and mountain ranges. A densely populated narrow coastal plain lies at the foot of the Highlands. *Principal rivers*: Amazon, Paraná, São Francisco, Madeira, Juruá, Purus. *Highest point*: Pico da Neblina 3014 m (9888 ft).

ECONOMY Agriculture employs about one quarter of the labour force. The principal agricultural exports include coffee, sugar cane, soyabeans, oranges, beef cattle and cocoa. Timber was important, but environmental concern is restricting its trade. Rapid industrialization since 1945 has made Brazil a major manufacturing country. While textiles, clothing and food processing are still the biggest industries, the iron and steel, chemical, petroleum-refining, cement, electrical, motor-vehicle and fertilizer industries have all attained international stature. Brazil has enormous – and, in part, unexploited – natural resources, including iron ore, phosphates, uranium, copper, manganese, bauxite, coal and vast hydroelectric-power potential. In the last two decades, rampant inflation has hindered development.

RECENT HISTORY In 1889 a coup ended the long reign of the liberal Emperor Pedro II, and established a federal republic. The republic was initially stable, but social unrest mounted and, in 1930, Getúlio Vargas seized power. Vargas attempted to model Brazil on Mussolini's Italy, but was overthrown by the military in 1945. In 1950, Vargas was elected president again, but he committed suicide rather than face impeachment (1954). Short-lived civilian governments preceded a further period of military rule (1964–85), during which the economy expanded rapidly, but political and social rights were restricted. Brazil returned to civilian rule in 1985 and in 1990 Brazilians were able to vote for a president for the first time in 29 years. The country faces problems concerning the development of the Amazon Basin and in balancing the needs of developers and landless peasants on the one hand and the advice of conservationists and the interests of tribal peoples on the other.

BRUNEI

Official name: Negara Brunei Darussalam (Sultanate of Brunei).

Member of: UN, Commonwealth, ASEAN.

Area: 5765 km² (2226 sq mi).

Population: 264 000 (1991 est).

Capital: Bandar Seri Begawan 52 000 (1988 est).

Languages: Malay (official; over 50%), Chinese (26%), English.

Religion: Sunni Islam (official; 66%), Buddhist (12%), various Christian Churches (9%).

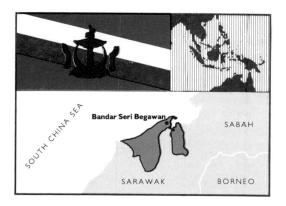

GOVERNMENT The Sultan, a hereditary monarch, rules by decree, assisted by a Council of Ministers whom he appoints. There are no political parties.
Sultan: HM Haji Hassanal Bolkiah, Sultan of Brunei (succeeded upon the abdication of his father, 5 October 1967).

GEOGRAPHY Brunei consists of two coastal enclaves. The (larger) western part is hilly; the eastern enclave is more mountainous and forested. *Principal river*: Brunei River. *Highest point*: Bukit Pagon (on the border with Malaysia) 1850 m (6070 ft).

ECONOMY Exploitation of substantial deposits of petroleum and natural gas has given Brunei one of the world's highest per capita incomes. Most of the country's food has to be imported.

RECENT HISTORY Formerly a pirates' paradise, Britain established a protectorate in the region from 1888 to 1971. Oil was discovered in 1929. Full independence was restored in 1984 under the absolute rule of Sultan Hassanal Bolkiah, allegedly the richest man in the world.

BULGARIA

Official name: Republika Bulgariya (Republic of Bulgaria).
Member of: UN, CSCE, Council of Europe.
Area: 110 912 km² (42 823 sq mi).
Population: 9 005 000 (1991 est).
Capital and major cities: Sofia (Sofiya) 1 221 000, Plovdiv 379 000, Varna 315 000, Burgas 205 000, Ruse 192 000, Stara Zagora 165 000, Pleven 138 000, Dobrich (formerly Tolbukhin) 116 000, Sliven 112 000, Shumen 111 000 (1990 est).
Languages: Bulgarian (official; 89%), Turkish (11%).
Religions: Orthodox (80%), Sunni Islam (8%).

GOVERNMENT The 240-member National Assembly is elected every five years by universal adult suffrage using a system of proportional representation. The President – who is directly elected for five years – appoints a Prime Minister and a Council of Ministers that enjoy a majority in the Assembly. The main political parties are the (centre) Union of Democratic Forces, the (former Communist) Socialist Party and the (Turkish) Movement for Rights and Freedom.
President: Zhelo Zhelev.
Prime Minister: Lyuben Berov.

GEOGRAPHY The Balkan Mountains run from east to west across central Bulgaria. To the north, low-lying hills slope down to the River Danube. To the south, a belt of lowland separates the Balkan Mountains from a high, rugged massif, which includes Bulgaria's highest peak. *Principal rivers*: Danube, Iskur, Maritsa. *Highest point*: Musala 2925 m (9596 ft).

ECONOMY With fertile soils, and few other natural resources, Bulgaria's has a strong agricultural base. Production is centred on large-scale, mechanized cooperatives. The principal crops include: cereals (wheat, maize, barley), fruit (grapes) and, increasingly, tobacco. Agricultural products are the basis of the food-processing, wine and tobacco industries. Eastern bloc grants helped develop industry including engineering, fertilizers and chemicals. Trade patterns were disrupted in Eastern Europe in 1990 and 1991 following the social, economic and political upheavals that had swept the region. Bulgaria – whose trade links with the USSR had been particularly close – suffered more than most East European countries, with severe shortages of many commodities including oil. Industrial production declined but progress has been made towards the privatization of industry and agriculture.

RECENT HISTORY Bulgaria was on the losing side in the final Balkan War (1913) and in World Wars I and II

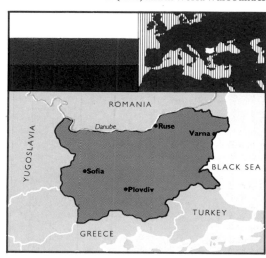

(1915–1918 and 1941–1944), and forfeited territory. After the Red Army invaded (1944), a Communist regime, tied closely to the USSR, was established and the king was exiled (1946). Following popular demonstrations in 1989, the hardline leader Todor Zhivkov (1911–) was replaced by reformers who promised free elections and renounced the leading role of the Communist Party. Free elections were held in June 1990, when the Bulgarian Socialist Party (BSP) – formerly the Bulgarian Communist Party – was returned to power. Faced by severe economic problems, the BSP was unable to govern alone and a coalition government with a non-party premier took office in 1991. Short-lived coalitions involving various combinations of the three main parties have followed.

BURKINA FASO

Official name: Burkina Faso or République de Burkina (previously Upper Volta).

Member of: UN, OAS, ECOWAS.

Area: 274 200 km² (105 869 sq mi).

Population: 9 261 000 (1991 est).

Capital and major cities: Ouagadougou 442 000, Bobo-Dioulasso 229 000, Koudougou 52 000, Ouahigouya 39 000, Banfora 35 500 (1985 est).

Languages: French (official), Mossi (48%), Fulani (10%).

Religions: Animist (49%), Sunni Islam (40%), various Christian Churches (11% – mainly Roman Catholic).

GOVERNMENT The constitution provides for the election by universal adult suffrage of a 77-member Assembly for four years and a President for seven years. The Chamber of Representatives (the upper house) is

indirectly elected. The main political party is the (coalition) Popular Front (FP).

Head of state: Capt. Blaise Campoare.

Prime Minister: Youssouf Ouedraogo.

GEOGRAPHY The country consists of plateaux about 500 m (1640 ft) high. *Principal rivers*: Mouhoun (Black Volta), Nakambe (White Volta), Nazinon (Red Volta). *Highest point*: Mt Tema 749 m (2457 ft).

ECONOMY Burkina Faso, one of the world's poorest states, has been severely stricken by drought in the last two decades. Nomadic herdsmen and subsistence farmers – producing mainly sorghum, sugar cane and millet – form the bulk of the population. Cotton, manganese and zinc are exported.

RECENT HISTORY Burkina Faso was the French colony of Upper Volta. Since independence in 1960, the country – which changed its name to Burkina Faso in 1984 – has had a turbulent political history, with a succession of military coups. In 1990 and 1991, pressure for liberalization and civilian rule came from local students and from foreign-aid donors, upon whom the country is heavily dependent. A new constitution was introduced in 1991 and a multi-party system restored in 1992.

BURMA (see MYANMAR)

BURUNDI

Official name: La République du Burundi or Republika y'Uburundi (The Republic of Burundi).

Member of: UN, OAU.

Area: 27 834 km² (10 747 sq mi).

Population: 5 611 000 (1991 est).

Capital and major city: Bujumbura 227 000, Gitega 95 000 (1990 est).

Languages: Kirundi (majority) and French – both official, Kiswahili.

Religion: Roman Catholic (65%).

GOVERNMENT Power is held by a 31-member military committee, whose Chairman is President. The Committee has appointed a civilian Council of Ministers. In 1992 it was announced that a multi-party system would be reintroduced.

President: Maj. Pierre Buyoya.

Prime Minister: Adrien Sibomana.

GEOGRAPHY Burundi is a high plateau, rising from Lake Tanganyika in the west. *Principal rivers*: Kagera, Ruzizi. *Highest point*: Mt Hela 2685 m (8809 ft).

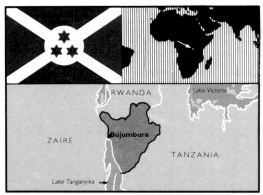

ECONOMY   Over 92% of the labour force is involved in agriculture, producing both subsistence crops and crops for export, such as coffee.

RECENT HISTORY   Colonized by Germany in 1890, Burundi was taken over by Belgium after World War I under a League of Nations mandate. Independence came in 1962, after much conflict throughout the country. Following a military coup in 1966, a republic was established. The killing of the deposed king in 1972 led to a massacre of the Hutu people. There have since been further coups. Serious ethnic unrest in 1988 led to an exodus of Hutu refugees to Rwanda.

CAMBODIA

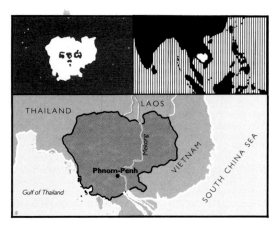

Official name: Roat Kampuchea (The State of Cambodia) – previously known as the Khmer Republic and Kampuchea.

Member of: UN.

Area: 181 035 km² (69 898 sq mi).

Population: 8 780 000 (1991 est).

Capital and major cities: Phnom-Penh 900 000 (1991 est), Battambang 45 000, Kampong Cham 32 000 (1987 est).

Languages: Khmer (official), French.

Religion: Buddhist (official; majority).

GOVERNMENT Internationally supervised multi-party elections will be held in 1993 for a 123-member National Assembly, which will draft a new constitution. Government remains in the hands of the existing administration, assisted by the UN, although sovereignty is temporarily vested in the hands of a 12-member Supreme National Council. The principal political parties are the (monarchist) FUNCINPEC, the (left-wing) Khmer People's National Liberation Front (KPNLF), the (former Communist) Cambodian People's Party and the (Khmer Rouge) Party of Democratic Kampuchea.

Head of state: Heng Samrin.

Prime Minister: Hun Sen.

GEOGRAPHY Central Cambodia consists of fertile plains in the Mekong River valley and surrounding the Tonle Sap (Great Lake). To the north and east are plateaux covered by forests and savannah. The southern Phnom Kravanh mountains run parallel to the coast. *Principal river*: Mekong. *Highest point*: Phnum Aoral 1813 m (5947 ft).

ECONOMY Invasion, civil wars, massacres of the civilian population (1976–79) and the (temporary) abolition of currency (in 1978) all but destroyed the economy. Aided by the Vietnamese since 1979, agriculture and – to a lesser extent – industry have been slowly rebuilt, but Cambodia remains one of the world's poorest nations. Rice yields – formerly exported – still fall short of Cambodia's own basic needs.

RECENT HISTORY A French protectorate was established in 1863 and continued, apart from Japanese occupation during World War II, until independence was regained in 1953. Throughout the colonial period, Cambodia's monarchy remained in nominal control. In 1955, King (now Prince) Norodom Sihanouk abdicated to lead a broad coalition government, but he could not prevent Cambodia's involvement in the Vietnam War or allay US fears of his sympathies for the Communists. In 1970 he was overthrown in a pro-US military coup. The military regime was attacked by Communist Khmer Rouge guerrillas, who sought to create a self-sufficient workers' utopia. The Khmer Rouge were finally victorious in 1975. Under Pol Pot, they forcibly evacuated the towns and massacred up to 2 000 000 of their compatriots. In 1978 Vietnam – Cambodia's traditional foe – invaded, overthrowing the Khmer Rouge. The hostility between the two countries had been sharpened by the Sino-Soviet split in which they took different sides. After Vietnamese troops withdrew in 1989, resistance forces of the exiled tripartite coalition government – led by Prince Sihanouk and including the Khmer Rouge – became active in much of western and southern Cambodia. In 1991 the country's warring factions agreed a peace plan that included free elections and UN supervision, and reduction of all Cambodian forces. A large UN peace keeping force was deployed (1992) and UN participation in the administration of Cambodia was agreed. However, violence resumed when the Khmer Rouge effectively withdrew from the peace plan.

CAMEROON

Official name: La République unie du Cameroun (The United Republic of Cameroun).
Member of: UN, OAU.
Area: 475 442 km² (183 569 sq mi).
Population: 12 239 000 (1991 est).
Capital and major cities: Yaoundé 712 000, Douala 1 117 000, Nkongsamba 112 000, Maroua 106 000, Bafoussam 99 000 (1987 est).
Languages: French, English (both official), Fulani, Sao, Bamileke.
Religions: Animist (40%), Sunni Islam (20%), Roman Catholic (20%).

GOVERNMENT The 180 members of the National Assembly are elected for a five-year term by universal adult suffrage. The President – who is also directly elected for a five-year term – appoints a Council of Ministers and a Prime Minister. The main political parties are the (former monopoly) Cameroon People's Democratic Movement (RDPC), the Cameroon People's Union (UPC) and the Democratic Movement for the Defence of the Republic (RDDR).
President: Paul Biya.
Prime Minister: Simon Achidi Achu.

GEOGRAPHY In the west, a chain of highlands rises to the volcanic Mont Cameroun. In the north, savannah plains dip towards Lake Chad. The coastal plains and plateaux in the south and the centre are covered with tropical forest. *Principal rivers*: Sanaga, Nyong. *Highest point*: Mont Cameroun 4069 m (13 353 ft).

ECONOMY Cameroon is a major producer of cocoa, and other export crops include bananas, coffee, cotton, rubber and palm oil. The diversity of Cameroon's agriculture, and the rapid development of the petroleum industry, have given the country one of the highest standards of living in tropical Africa.

RECENT HISTORY After World War I, the former German colony Kamerun was divided between the UK and France. The French Cameroons became independent in 1960. Following a plebiscite (1961), the north of the British Cameroons merged with Nigeria; the south federated with the former French territory. A unitary state replaced the federation in 1972. A number of arrests followed attempts to establish an opposition political party in 1990. Political pluralism returned in 1992, when multi-party elections were held.

CANADA

Member of: UN, Commonwealth, OAS, NATO, CSCE, G7, NAFTA.
Area: 9 970 610 km² (3 849 674 sq mi).
Population: 26 991 000 (1991 est).
Capital and major cities: Ottawa 864 000 (city 301 000), Toronto 3 752 000 (city 612 000), Montréal 3 068 000 (city 1 015 000), Vancouver 1 547 000 (city 431 000), Edmonton 824 000 (city 574 000), Calgary 723 000 (city 636 000), Winnipeg 647 000 (city 595 000), Québec 622 000 (city 165 000), Hamilton 595 000 (city 307 000), London 368 000 (city 269 000), St Catharine's–Niagara (St Catharine's city 123 000), Kitchener 346 000 (city 151 000), Halifax 312 000 (city 114 000), Victoria 279 000 (city 66 000), Windsor 261 000 (city 193 000), Oshawa 245 000 (city 124 000), Saskatoon 201 000 (city 178 000), Regina 187 000 (city 175 000), St John's 162 000 (city 69 000). (1990 est; city populations 1986 census.)
Languages: English (62% as a first language; official), French (25% as a first language; official), bilingual English–French (16%).
Religions: Roman Catholic (45%), United Church of Canada (15%), Anglican (10%).

GOVERNMENT The Canadian Federal Parliament has two houses – a Senate of 118 members appointed by

NIGER

Lake Chad

CHAD

NIGERIA

CENTRAL AFRICAN REPUBLIC

Douala

Yaoundé

Gulf of Guinea

ZAIRE

EQUATORIAL GUINEA

GABON

CONGO

the Governor General to represent the provinces, and the House of Commons, whose 295 members are elected for five years by universal adult suffrage. A Prime Minister, commanding a majority in the House of Commons, is appointed by the Governor General, who is the representative of the British Queen as sovereign of Canada. The PM, in turn, appoints a Cabinet of Ministers which is responsible to the House. Each province has its own government and legislature. The main political parties are the Liberal Party, the Progressive Conservative Party, the (socialist) New Democratic Party, the (radical) Reform Party and the (nationalist) Parti Québecois.

Prime Minister: Brian Mulroney.

Nova Scotia *Area*: 55 490 km² (21 425 sq mi). *Population*: 892 000. *Capital*: Halifax.

Ontario *Area*: 1 068 582 km² (412 582 sq mi). *Population*: 9 748 000. *Capital*: Toronto.

Prince Edward Island *Area*: 5657 km² (2184 sq mi). *Population*: 130 000. *Capital*: Charlottetown.

Québec *Area*: 1 540 680 km² (594 860 sq mi). *Population*: 6 771 000. *Capital*: Québec.

Saskatchewan *Area*: 651 900 km² (251 700 sq mi). *Population*: 1 000 000. *Capital*: Regina.

Northwest Territories *Area*: 3 379 285 km² (1 304 903 sq mi). *Population*: 54 000. *Capital*: Yellowknife. In 1990

CANADIAN PROVINCES AND TERRITORIES
Population figures are for 1990.

Alberta *Area*: 661 199 km² (255 285 sq mi). *Population*: 2 473 000. *Capital*: Edmonton.

British Columbia *Area*: 948 596 km² (366 255 sq mi). *Population*: 3 139 000. *Capital*: Victoria.

Manitoba *Area*: 650 087 km² (251 000 sq mi). *Population*: 1 091 000. *Capital*: Winnipeg.

New Brunswick *Area*: 73 437 km² (28 354 sq mi). *Population*: 724 000. *Capital*: Fredericton.

Newfoundland and Labrador *Area*: 404 517 km² (156 185 sq mi). *Population*: 573 000. *Capital*: St John's.

agreement was reached to divide the Northwest Territories into two separate territories – Nunavut Territory with an Inuit (Eskimo) majority in the east and Nenedeh Territory with a native Canadian (Indian) majority in the west.

Yukon Territory *Area*: 482 515 km² (186 299 sq mi). *Population*: 26 000. *Capital*: Whitehorse.

GEOGRAPHY Nearly one half of Canada is covered by the Laurentian (or Canadian) Shield, a relatively flat region of hard rocks stretching round Hudson's Bay and penetrating deep into the interior. Inland, the Shield ends in a scarp that is pronounced in the east, beside the lowlands around the St Lawrence River and the Great Lakes. To the west, a line of major lakes (including Lake Winnipeg) marks the boundary with the interior plains, the Prairies. A broad belt of mountains – over 800 km (500 mi) wide – lies west of the plains. This western cordillera comprises the Rocky, Mackenzie, Coast and St Elias Mountains – which include Canada's highest point. A lower, more discontinuous, chain of highlands borders the east of Canada, running from Baffin Island, through Labrador and into New Brunswick and Nova Scotia. *Principal rivers*: Mackenzie, Slave, Peace, St Lawrence, Yukon, Nisutlin, Nelson, Saskatchewan.

Highest point: Mount Logan 5951 m (19 524 ft).

ECONOMY Canada enjoys one of the highest standards of living in the world, due, in part, to great mineral resources. There are substantial deposits of zinc, nickel, gold, silver, iron ore, uranium, copper, and lead, as well as major reserves of petroleum and natural gas, and enormous hydroelectric-power potential. These resources are the basis of such industries as petroleum refining, motor vehicles, metal refining, chemicals, and iron and steel. Canada is one of the world's leading exporters of cereals – in particular, wheat from the Prairie provinces. Other agricultural interests include fruit (mainly apples), beef cattle and potatoes. Vast coniferous forests have given rise to large lumber, wood-pulp and paper industries. Rich Atlantic and Pacific fishing grounds have made Canada the world's leading exporter of fish and seafood. The country has an important banking and insurance sector, and the economy is closely linked with that of the USA – within NAFTA.

RECENT HISTORY The Dominion of Canada was formed in 1867 with the confederation of four provinces. All the remaining provinces joined between 1870 and 1905 except Newfoundland which only became part of Canada in 1949. The late 19th century saw important mineral finds, and the western provinces developed rapidly. In World War I, Canadian forces distinguished themselves at Vimy Ridge, and Canada won itself a place as a separate nation at the peace conferences after the war. The Statute of Westminster (1931) recognized Canadian independence. The Depression of the 1930s had a severe impact on Canada – Newfoundland, for example, went bankrupt. Canada played an important role in World War II and the Korean War, and was a founder member of NATO. Throughout the 1970s and 1980s, there was friction over the use and status of the French language, and separatism became an issue in Québec. The Canadian constitution was redefined in 1982, but Québec refused to ratify it. A series of constitutional amendments – the Meech Lake accord – was formulated to persuade Québec to adhere to the constitution, but a number of English-speaking provinces would not agree to Québec being declared 'a distinct society' with additional powers. The failure of the Meech Lake accord (1990) encouraged the nationalist party in Québec (the Parti Québecois) to call for 'sovereignty association' (a politically independent Québec in economic association with Canada).

CAPE VERDE

Official name: A República de Cabo Verde (The Republic of Cape Verde).
Member of: UN, OAU, ECOWAS.
Area: 4033 km² (1557 sq mi).
Population: 341 000 (1991 est).
Capital: Praia 62 000, Mindelo 47 000 (1990 est).
Languages: Portuguese (official), Crioulu (majority).
Religion: Roman Catholic (over 92%).

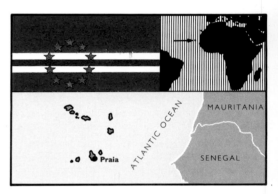

GOVERNMENT The 83-member National Assembly is elected for five years by universal adult suffrage. The Assembly elects a President – also for five years – who appoints a Council of Ministers. The main political parties are the (centre) Movement for Democracy (MPD) and the (socialist) PAICV party.
President: Antonio Mascarenhas.
Prime Minister: Carlos Veiga.

GEOGRAPHY Cape Verde consists of ten volcanic, semi-arid islands. There are no significant rivers. *Highest point*: Monte Fogo 2829 m (9281 ft).

ECONOMY Lack of surface water hinders agriculture, and over 90% of Cape Verde's food has to be imported. Money sent back by over 600 000 Cape Verdeans living abroad is vital to the economy.

RECENT HISTORY Cape Verde – a former Portuguese colony – was linked with Guinea-Bissau in the struggle against colonial rule, but gained independence separately in 1975. The PAICV party offended Catholics by decriminalizing abortion and unrest grew in 1987–88. Social and political reforms were agreed in 1990, and in 1991 the PAICV was overwhelmingly defeated in elections by a newly legalized opposition group – the Movement for Democracy. A free market economy has since been introduced.

CENTRAL AFRICAN REPUBLIC

Official name: La République Centrafricaine (The Central African Republic).

Member of: UN, OAU.

Area: 622 984 km² (240 535 sq mi).

Population: 2 937 000 (1991 est).

Capital and major cities: Bangui 598 000 (1988 est), Bambari 52 000, Bouar 49 000 (1987 est).

Languages: French (official), Sangho (national).

Religions: Various Protestant Churches (48%), Roman Catholic (32%), animist (20%).

GOVERNMENT The President – who appoints a Council of Ministers and a Prime Minister – is elected for a six-year term by universal adult suffrage. The Congress consists of a 52-member National Assembly (elected directly for a five-year term) and an Economic and Regional Council (half of whose members are elected by the Assembly; the remainder are appointed by the President). The main political parties are the (former monopoly) Rassemblement démocratique centrafricain (RDC) and the Mouvement pour la libération du peuple centrafricain (MLPC).

President: Gen. André-Dieudonné Kolingba.

Prime Minister: Edouard Franck.

GEOGRAPHY The country is a low plateau, rising along the border with Sudan to the Bongos Mountains and in the west to the Monts Karre. *Principal rivers:* Oubangui, Zaïre, Chari. *Highest point:* Mt Gaou 1420 m (4659 ft).

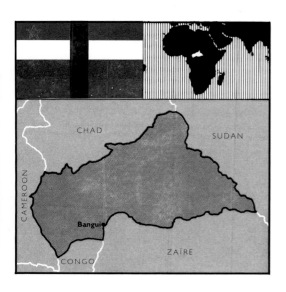

ECONOMY Subsistence farming dominates, although cotton and coffee are produced for export. Diamonds contribute over 25% of the country's foreign earnings. The country is one of the poorest in the world, and – largely owing to mismanagement during Bokassa's rule – its economy has declined since independence.

RECENT HISTORY The region became the French colony of Oubangi-Chari in 1903. It suffered greatly from the activities of companies that were granted exclusive rights to large areas of the colony. Independence – as the Central African Republic – was gained in 1960. Jean-Bédel Bokassa took power in a coup in 1965. In 1976 he declared himself emperor and was crowned in an extravagantly expensive ceremony. Revolts by students and schoolchildren helped to end his murderous regime in 1979. A multi-party system has been permitted since 1991.

CHAD

Official name: La République du Tchad (The Republic of Chad).

Member of: UN, OAU.

Area: 1 284 000 (495 750 sq mi).

Population: 5 823 000 (1991 est).

Capital and major cities: N'Djamena 594 000, Sarh 113 000, Moundou 102 000 (1988 est).

Languages: French and Arabic (both official), plus over 100 local languages.

Religions: Sunni Islam (50%), animist (25%).

GOVERNMENT The constitution provides for a 123-member National Assembly and a President to be elected by universal adult suffrage for five years. Following a military coup in 1991, these provisions have been suspended but multi-party elections have been agreed in principle. Legislative power is currently exercised by a 31-member Consultative Provisional Republican Council.

President: Idriss Deby.

Prime Minister: Joseph Yodoyman.

GEOGRAPHY Deserts in the north include the Tibesti Mountains, the highest part of the country. Savannah and semidesert in the centre slope down to Lake Chad. The Oubangui Plateau in the south is covered by tropical rain forest. *Principal river:* Chari. *Highest point:* Emi Koussi 3415 m (11 204 ft).

ECONOMY Chad – one of the poorest countries in the world – has been wracked by civil war and drought. With few natural resources, it relies on subsistence farming. exports of cotton and on foreign aid.

RECENT HISTORY The area around Lake Chad became French in the late 19th century. The French conquest of the north was not completed until 1916.

Since independence in 1960, Chad has been torn apart by a bitter civil war between the Muslim Arab north and the Christian and animist Black African south. Libya and France intervened forcefully on several occasions, but neither was able to achieve its aims. In October 1988, the civil war was formally ended. However, from March 1989 the former Chadian army chief, Idriss Deby, led a rebel force from bases in Sudan against the government in N'Djamena and took control of the whole country late in 1990. Recurrent unrest continues in the north.

CHILE

Official name: República de Chile (The Republic of Chile).

Member of: UN, OAS, ALADI.

Area: 756 945 km² (292 258 sq mi).

Population: 13 385 000 (1991 est).

Capital and major cities: Santiago (capital) 5 343 000, Valparaiso (legislative capital) 277 000, Concepción 307 000, Viña del Mar 281 000, Talcahuano 247 000, Antofagasta 219 000, Temuco 212 000 (1991 est).

Language: Spanish, Araucanian (5%).

Religion: Roman Catholic (79%), various Protestant Churches.

GOVERNMENT Executive power is held by the President, who appoints a Cabinet of Ministers. Under the constitution introduced in 1990, the President is elected by universal adult suffrage for a single eight-year term. The National Congress has an upper chamber – of 38 senators directly elected for eight years and 10 senators appointed by the President – and a lower chamber of 120 deputies elected for a four-year term by universal adult suffrage. Since 1990, the National Con-

gress has met in Valparaiso. The principal political parties include the (conservative) Christian Democrat Party, the (centrist) National Renovation Party, the Socialist Party, and the (right-wing) Independent Democratic Union.

President: Patricio Aylwin.

GEOGRAPHY For almost 4000 km (2500 mi), the Andes form the eastern boundary of Chile. Parallel to the Andes is a depression, in which lies the Atacama Desert in the north and fertile plains in the centre. A mountain chain runs between the depression and the coast, and, in the south, forms a string of islands. *Principal rivers*: Loa, Maule, Bio-Bio. *Highest point*: Ojos del Salado 6895 m (22 588 ft).

ECONOMY The main agricultural region is the central plains, where cereals (mainly wheat and maize) and fruit (in particular grapes) are important. Excellent fishing grounds yield one of the world's largest catches of fish. There are considerable mineral resources and great hydroelectric-power potential. Chile is the world's largest exporter of copper, and has major reserves of iron ore, coal, petroleum, and natural gas.

RECENT HISTORY During the century following independence (1821) conservative landowners held power. Between the late 1920s and the 1940s, Chile was governed by liberal and radical regimes, but social and economic change was slow. The election of the Christian Democrats (1964) brought some reforms, but not until Salvador Allende's Marxist government was elected in 1970 were major changes – including land reform – realized. Chile was polarized between right and left, and political chaos resulted in an American-backed military

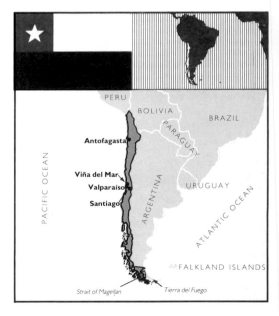

coup led by General Augusto Pinochet in 1973. Tens of thousands of leftists were killed, imprisoned or exiled by the junta. Pinochet reversed Allende's reforms, restructuring the economy in favour of landowners and exporters. Pressure on the dictatorship from within Chile and abroad encouraged the junta to return the country to democratic rule in 1990.

CHILEAN EXTERNAL TERRITORY
Chilean Antarctic Territory see Other Territories, following this chapter.

CHINA

Official name: Zhonghua Renmin Gongheguo (The People's Republic of China).
Member of: UN.
Area: 9 571 300 km² (3 695 500 sq mi).
Population: 1 150 000 000 (1991 est), Han (Chinese; 92%), with Mongol, Tibetan, Uighur, Manchu and other minorities.
Capital and major cities: Beijing (Peking) 10 819 000, Shanghai 13 342 000, Tianjin (Tientsin) 8 785 000, Shenyang 4 500 000, Wuhan 3 710 000, Guangzhou (Canton) 3 540 000, Chongquin 2 960 000, Harbin 2 800 000, Chengdu 2 780 000, Xian 2 710 000, Nanjing (Nanking) 2 471 000, Zibo 2 430 000, Dalian (Darien) 2 370 000, Jinan 2 290 000, Changchun 2 070 000, Qingdao (Tsingtao) 2 040 000, Taiyuan 1 900 000, Zhengzhou 1 660 000, Kunming 1 500 000, Guiyang (Kweiyang), 1 490 000, Tangshan 1 490 000, Lanzhou (Lanchow) 1 480 000, Anshan 1 370 000, Qiqihar (Tsitsihar) 1 370 000, Fushun 1 330 000, Hangzhou 1 330 000, Nanchang 1 330 000, Changsha 1 300 000, Shijiazhuang (Shihkiachwang) 1 300 000, Fuzhou (Foochow) 1 270 000, Jilin (Kirin) 1 250 000, Baotou (Paotow) 1 180 000, Huainan 1 170 000, Luoyang 1 160 000, Urümqi 1 110 000, Datong 1 090 000, Handan 1 090 000, Ningbo 1 070 000, Nanning 1 050 000, (1990 census). Twenty other municipalities – with overwhelmingly rural populations – have over 1 000 000 inhabitants.
Languages: Chinese (Guoyo or 'Mandarin' dialect in the majority, with local dialects in south and southeast, e.g. Cantonese), with small Mongol, Tibetan and other minorities.
Religions: Officially atheist but those religions and philosophies practised include Confucianism and Daoism, (over 20% together), Buddhism (c. 15%).

PROVINCES **Anhui** *Area:* 139 900 km² (54 020 sq mi). *Population:* 56 180 000 (1990 census). *Capital:* Hefei.
Beijing (Peking; municipal province) *Area:* 17 800 km² (6870 sq mi). *Population:* 10 819 000 (1990 census). *Capital:* Beijing (Peking).
Fujian *Area:123 100 km² (47 530 sq mi). Population:* 30 048 000 (1990 census). *Capital:* Fushu.

Gansu *Area:*530 000 km² (204 600 sq mi). *Population:* 22 371 000 (1990 census). *Capital:* Lanzhou.
Guangdong *Area:* 197 900 km² (76 400 sq mi). *Population:* 62 829 000 (1990 census). *Capital:* Guangzhou (Canton).
Guangxi Zhuang (autonomous province) *Area:* 220 400 km² (85 100 sq mi). *Population:* 42 246 000 (1990 census). *Capital:* Nanning.
Guizhou *Area:* 174 000 km² (67 200 sq mi). *Population:* 32 391 000 (1990 census). *Capital:* Guiyang.
Hainan *Area:* 33 570 km² (12 960 sq mi). Population: *6 557 000 (1990 census). Capital:* Haikou.
Hebei *Area:* 202 700 km² (78 260 sq mi). *Population:* 61 082 000 (1990 census). *Capital:* Shijiazhuang (Shihkiachwang).
Heilongjiang *Area:* 463 600 km² (179 000 sq mi). *Population:* 35 215 000 (1990 census). *Capital:* Harbin.
Henan *Area:* 167 000 km² (64 480 sq mi). *Population:* 85 510 000 (1990 census). *Capital:* Zhengzhou.
Hubei *Area* 187 500 km² (72 400 sq mi). *Population:* 53 969 000 (1990 census). *Capital:* Wuhan.
Hunan *Area:* 210 500 km² (81 270 sq mi). *Population:* 60 660 000 (1990 census). *Capital:* Changsha.
Jiangsu *Area:* 102 200 km² (39 460 sq mi). *Population:* 67 057 000 (1990 census). *Capital:* Nanjing (Nanking).
Jiangxi *Area:* 164 800 km² (63 630 sq mi). *Population:* 37 710 000 (1990 census). *Capital:* Nanchang.
Jilin *Area:* 187 000 km² (72 200 sq mi). *Population:* 24 659 000 (1990). *Capital:* Changchun.
Liaoning *Area:* 151 000 km² (58 300 sq mi). *Population:* 39 460 000 (1990 census). *Capital:* Shenyang.
Nei Monggol (Inner Mongolia) (autonomous province) *Area:* 450 000 km² (173 700 sq mi). *Population:* 21 457 000 (1990 census). *Capital:* Hohhot (Huhehot).
Ningxia Hui (autonomous province) *Area:* 170 000 km² (65 600 sq mi). *Populatiooon:* 4 655 000 (1990 census). *Capital:* Yinchuan.
Qinghai *Area:* 721 000 km² (278 400 sq mi). *Population:* 4 457 000 (1990 census). *Capital:* Xining.
Shaanxi *Area:* 195 800 km² (75 600 sq mi). *Population:* 32 882 000 (1990 census). *Capital:* Xian.
Shandong *Area:* 153 300 km² (59 190 sq mi). *Population:* 84 393 000 (1990 census). *Capital:* Jinan.
Shanghai (municipal province) *Area:* 5800 km² (2240 sq mi). *Population:* 13 342 000 (1990 census). *Capital:* Shanghai.
Shanxi *Area:* 157 100 km² (60 660 sq mi). *Population:* 28 759 000 (1990 census). *Capital:* Taiyuan.
Sichuan *Area:* 569 000 km² (219 700 sq mi). *Population:* 107 218 000 (1990 census). *Capital:* Chengdu.
Tianjin (municipal province) *Area:* 4000 km² (1540 sq mi). *Population:* 8 785 000 (1990 census). *Capital:* Tianjin.
Xinjiang Uygur (Sinkiang) (autonomous province) *Area:* 1 646 900 km² (635 870 sq mi). *Population:* 15 156 000 (1990 census). *Capital:* Urumqi.
Xizang (Tibet) (autonomous province) *Area:* 1 221 600 km² (471 660 sq mi). *Population:* 2 196 000 (1990 census). *Capital:* Lhasa.

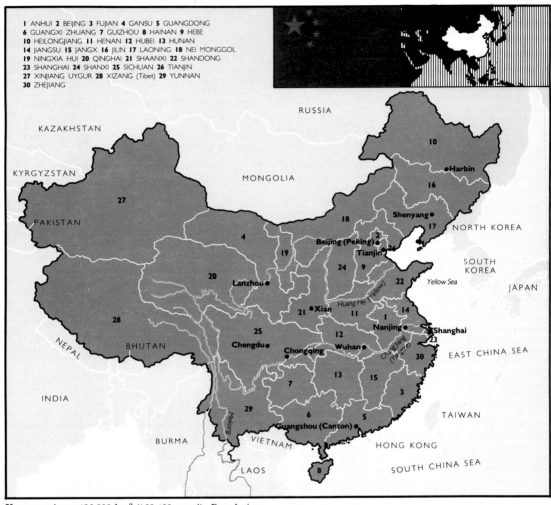

1 ANHUI 2 BEIJING 3 FUJIAN 4 GANSU 5 GUANGDONG
6 GUANGXI ZHUANG 7 GUIZHOU 8 HAINAN 9 HEBE
10 HEILONGJIANG 11 HENAN 12 HUBEI 13 HUNAN
14 JIANGSU 15 JANGX 16 JILIN 17 LAONING 18 NEI MONGGOL
19 NINGXIA HUI 20 QINGHAI 21 SHAANXI 22 SHANDONG
23 SHANGHAI 24 SHANXI 25 SICHUAN 26 TIANJIN
27 XINJIANG UYGUR 28 XIZANG (Tibet) 29 YUNNAN
30 ZHEJIANG

Yunnan *Area:* 436 200 km² (168 420 sq mi). *Population:* 36 973 000 (1990 census). *Capital:* Kunming.

Zheijiang *Area:* 101 800 km² (39 300 sq mi). *Population:* 41 446 000 (1990 census). *Capital:* Hangzhou.

President: Jiang Zemin.
Prime Minister: Li Peng.
General Secretary of the Communist Party: Jiang Zemin.

GOVERNMENT The 2978 deputies of the National People's Congress are elected for a five-year term by the People's Congresses of the 22 provinces, five autonomous provinces and three municipal provinces, and by the People's Liberation Army. The Congress elects a Standing Committee, a President (for a five-year term), a Prime Minister and a State Council (or Cabinet) – all of whom are responsible to the Congress. The only legal party is the Chinese Communist Party, which holds a Congress every five years. The Party Congress elects a Central Committee, which in turn elects a Politburo, and it is these two bodies that hold effective power.

GEOGRAPHY China is the third largest country in the world in area and the largest in population. Almost half of China comprises mountain chains, mainly in the west, including the Altaï and Tien Shan Mountains in Xinjiang Uygur, and the Kun Lun Mountains to the north of Tibet. The Tibetan Plateau – at an altitude of 3000 m (10 000 ft) – is arid. In the south of Tibet is the Himalaya, containing 40 peaks over 7000 m (23 000 ft). In the far south, the Yunnan Plateau rises to nearly 3700 m (12 000 ft), while in the far northeast, ranges of hills and mountains almost enclose the Northeast Plain, more usually known as Manchuria. Crossing central China – and separating the basins of the Yellow (Huang He) and Yangtze (Chang Jiang) rivers – is the Nan Ling Range of hills and mountains. In east and central China, three great lowlands support intensive agriculture and dense populations – the plains of central China, the Sichuan Basin and the flat North China Plain. A vast loess plateau, deeply dissected by ravines, lies between the Mongolian Plateau – which contains the Gobi Desert – and the deserts of the Tarim and Dzungarian Basins in the northwest. *Principal rivers*: Yangtze (Chang Jiang), Huang He (Yellow River), Xijiang (Sikiang or Pearl River), Heilongjiang (Amur). *Highest point*: Mount Everest 8863 m (29 078 ft).

ECONOMY Agriculture occupies over 60% of the labour force. All large-scale production is on collective farms, but traditional and inefficient practices remain. Nearly two thirds of the arable land is irrigated, and China is the world's largest producer of rice. Other major crops include wheat, maize, sweet potatoes, sugar cane and soyabeans. Livestock, fruit, vegetables and fishing are also important, but China is still unable to supply all its own food. The country's mineral and fuel resources are considerable and, for the most part, underdeveloped. They include coal, petroleum, natural gas, iron ore, bauxite, tin, antimony and manganese in major reserves, as well as huge hydroelectric power potential. The economy is centrally planned, with all industrial plant owned by the state. Petrochemical products account for nearly one quarter of China's exports. Other major industries include iron and steel, cement, vehicles, fertilizers, food processing, clothing and textiles. The most recent five-year plans have promoted modernization and reform, including an 'open-door' policy under which joint ventures with other countries and foreign loans have been encouraged, together with a degree of small-scale private enterprise. Most of this investment went into light industry and textiles. Special Economic Zones and 'open cities' were designated in the south and central coastal areas to encourage industrial links with the west. Although foreign investment temporarily diminished after the 1989 pro-democracy movement was suppressed, sustained economic growth has been achieved in southern China, in particular Guangdong where the new city of Shenzhen (near Hong Kong) is the centre of major industrial development.

RECENT HISTORY At the beginning of the 20th century China was in turmoil. The authority of the emperor had been weakened in the 19th century by outside powers greedy for trade and by huge rebellions which had left large areas of the country beyond the control of the central government. In 1911 a revolution, led by the Guomintang (Kuomintang or Nationalists) under Sun Zhong Shan (Sun Yat-sen; 1866–1925), overthrew the last of the Manchu emperors. Strong in the south (where Sun had established a republic in 1916), the Nationalists faced problems in the north, which was ruled by independent warlords. Sun's successor, Jiang Jie Shi (Chiang Kai-shek; 1887–1975), made some inroads in the north, only to be undermined by the emergent Communist Party.

After a series of disastrous urban risings, the Communist Mao Zedong (Mao Tse-tung; 1893–1976) concentrated on rural areas. After being forced to retreat from Jiangxi in 1934, Mao led his followers for 12 months on a 9000 km (5600 mi) trek, the 'Long March', to the remote province of Shaanxi. In 1931 the Japanese seized Manchuria and established a puppet regime. After the Japanese occupied Beijing (Peking) and most of coastal China in 1937, Jiang and Mao combined against the invaders but were able to achieve little against superior forces. After World War II, the Soviets tried to ensure that Mao's Communists took over China. In 1946 Mao marched into Manchuria, beginning a civil war that lasted until 1949 when Mao declared a People's Republic in Beijing and Jiang fled to the offshore island of Taiwan, where a Nationalist government was set up (see below).

In 1950 Chinese forces invaded Tibet – an independent state since 1916. Repressive Communist rule alienated the Tibetans, who, loyal to their religious leader the Dalai Lama, unsuccessfully rose in revolt in 1959. Chinese 'volunteers' were active in the Korean War on behalf of the Communist North Koreans (1950–53). China has been involved in a number of border disputes and conflicts, including clashes with the USSR in the late 1950s, with India in 1962 and with Vietnam in 1979. Relations with the USSR deteriorated in the 1950s, triggered by ideological clashes over the true nature of Communism. The Sino-Soviet rift led to the acceleration of Chinese research into atomic weapons – the first Chinese bomb was tested in 1964 – and a rapprochement with the USA in the early 1970s.

The 'Great Leap Forward', an ambitious programme of radicalization in the 1950s, largely failed. In the 1960s Mao tried again to spread more radical revolutionary ideas in the so-called Cultural Revolution. Militant students formed groups of 'Red Guards' to attack the existing hierarchy. Thousands died as the students went out of control, and the army had to restore order. Since Mao's death (1976), China has effectively been under the leadership of Deng Xiaoping (1904–), although he holds none of the major state or party offices. A more careful path has been followed both at home and abroad; a rapprochement with the USSR was achieved in 1989, and agreement has been reached with the UK for the return of Hong Kong to Chinese rule in 1997. China was opened to foreign technology and investment, together with a degree of free enterprise, but this led to internal pressures for political change, culminating in massive pro-democracy demonstrations by students and workers early in 1989. These were brutally suppressed in the massacre of students in Tiananmen Square (June 1989) and hardline leaders such as President Yang Shangkun have gained in influence.

Economic progress has been a priority in the 1990s. Living standards have improved drastically, and the southern provinces and Shanghai have experienced very high economic growth rates. However, an ageing political leadership continued to deny many basic human rights. Relations with the UK became strained when Britain proposed to widen the suffrage in the British colony of Hong Kong, which is due to revert to China in 1997.

CHINA, REPUBLIC OF (TAIWAN)

Official name: Chung-hua Min Kuo (The Republic of China).

Member of: Taiwan is not a member of any major international organization.

Area: 35 981 km² (13 893 sq mi).

Population: 20 489 000 (1991 est).

Capital and major cities: Taipei 2 720 000, Kaohsiung 1 393 000, Taichung 762 000, Tainan 683 000, Panchiao 539 000 (1990 est).

Language: Chinese (northern or Amoy dialect).

Religions: Buddhist (24%), Daoist (14%), Roman Catholic (14%).

GOVERNMENT Under the terms of a new constitution (1991), the National Assembly comprises 325 members elected by universal adult suffrage for six years. The Assembly elects a President for a six-year term. The President appoints a Prime Minister and a Council of Ministers. The principal political parties are the (Nationalist) Guomintang (Kuomintang) and the (Taiwanese) National Democratic Progressive Party.

President: Lee Teng-hui.

Prime Minister: Lien Chan.

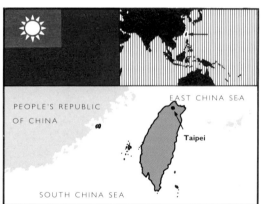

GEOGRAPHY Taiwan is an island 160 km (100 mi) off the southeast coast of mainland China with a mountainous interior. Most of the inhabitants live on the coastal plain in the west. The Republic of China also includes the small islands of Quemoy and Matsu close to the Chinese mainland. *Principal rivers*: Hsia-tan-shui Chi, Chosui Chi. *Highest point*: Yu Shan 3997 m (13 113 ft).

ECONOMY Despite Taiwan's diplomatic isolation, the island is a major international trading nation, exporting machinery, electronics, and textiles. Taiwan has achieved high economic growth rates over the past four decades. Mineral resources include coal, marble, gold, petroleum and natural gas. Despite the fertility of the soil, agriculture has declined in relative importance.

RECENT HISTORY In 1895 Japan annexed the Chinese province of Taiwan – formerly Formosa – and modernized its agriculture, transport and education. In 1949, the Nationalist forces of Jiang Jie Shi (Chiang Kai-shek) were driven onto Taiwan by the Communist victory on the mainland (see China above). Under US protection, the resulting authoritarian regime on Taiwan declared itself the Republic of China, and claimed to be the legitimate government of all China. America's rapprochement with the mainland People's Republic of China lost Taiwan its UN seat in 1971 and US recognition in 1978. By the late 1980s Taiwan was moving cautiously towards democracy, although its international status remained problematic. In 1988 a native Taiwanese became president and in 1990 an agreement was reached to speed up the retirement of Guomintang 'life members' from Taiwan's political bodies. A new constitution in 1991 marked the transition to a more Taiwanese, less Chinese, identity.

COLOMBIA

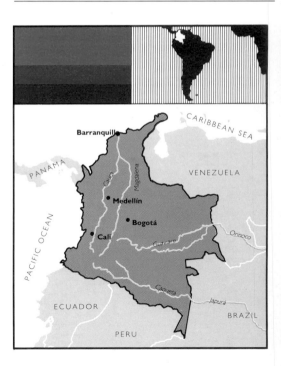

Official name: La República de Colombia (The Republic of Colombia).

Member of: UN, OAS, ALADI, Andean Pact.

Area: 1 141 748 km² (440 831 sq mi).

Population: 33 613 000 (1991 est).

Capital and major cities: Bogotá (officially known as Santa Fé de Bogotá, DE – DE stands for Distrito Especial – Special District) 4 820 000, Medellín 2 121 000, Cali 1 637 000, Barranquilla 1 029 000, Cartagena 564 000, Cúcuta 407 000, Bucaramanga 364 000, Manizales 310 000, Ibagué 306 000, Pereira 302 000 (all including suburbs; 1990 est).

Languages: Spanish, over 150 Indian languages.

Religions: Roman Catholic (official; over 95%).

GOVERNMENT A President (who appoints a Cabinet of 13 members), a Senate of 102 members and a House of Representatives of 161 members are elected for a four-year term by universal adult suffrage. The main political parties are the Liberal Party, the Social Conservative Party, the (leftist) M-19 (April 19th Movement), and the (leftist) UP (Patriotic Union).

President: Cesar Gaviria.

GEOGRAPHY The Andes run north to south through Colombia with the greater part of the country lying to the east of the mountains in the mainly treeless grassland plains of the Llanos and the tropical Amazonian rain forest. A coastal plain lies to the west of the Andes. *Principal rivers*: Magdalena, Cauca, Amazon (Amazonas). *Highest point*: Pico Cristóbal Colón 5775 m (18 947 ft).

ECONOMY Colombian coffee is the backbone of the country's exports; other cash crops include bananas, sugar cane, flowers and tobacco. However, profits from the illegal cultivation and export of marijuana and cocaine probably produce the greatest revenue. Mineral resources include iron ore, silver and platinum as well as coal, petroleum and natural gas. The main industries are food processing, petroleum refining, fertilizers, cement, textiles and clothing, and iron and steel.

RECENT HISTORY Since Colombia's independence in 1819 the centralizing pro-clerical Conservatives and the federalizing anti-clerical Liberals have struggled for control, leading to civil wars (1899–1902 and 1948–1957) in which 400 000 people died. From 1957 to 1974 there were agreements between the Liberals and Conservatives to protect a fragile democracy. In the 1980s, Colombia was threatened by left-wing guerrillas, right-wing death squads and powerful drug-trafficking cartels. The 1990 presidential and legislative elections were disrupted by the assassination of several candidates, but the uncomprising stand taken against the drug cartels by President Virgilio Barco and his successor Cesar Gaviria paid dividends. Violence decreased and a number of leading drug-traffickers were arrested. In a separate development, left-wing former guerrillas – such as M-19 – had abandoned their armed struggle in favour of legitimate political activity.

COMOROS

Official name: La République fédérale islamique des Comores (The Federal Islamic Republic of the Comoros).

Member of: UN, OAU.

Area: 1862 km² (719 sq mi; excluding Mayotte which is administered by France).

Population: 479 000 (1991 est; excluding Mayotte).

Capital: Moroni 60 000 (city 22 000), Mutsamudu 14 000 (1987 est).

Languages: French and Arabic (official languages), Comoran (a blend of Swahili and Arabic).

Religion: Sunni Islam (official; 99 %).

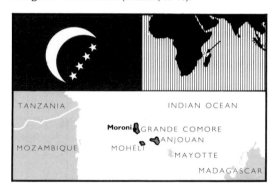

GOVERNMENT The President – who is elected for a six-year term by universal adult suffrage – appoints a Council of Ministers. The 42 members of the Federal Assembly are directly elected for five years. The main political parties are the (former monopoly) Udzima party and Rachade (a breakaway movement).

President: Siad Mohamed Djohar.

Prime Minister: to be appointed.

GEOGRAPHY Ngazidja (Grande Comore) – the largest island – is dry and rocky, rising to an active volcano. Ndzouani (Anjouan) is a heavily eroded volcanic massif. Moili (Mohéli) is a forested plateau with fertile valleys. There are no significant rivers. *Highest point*: Mont Kartala (an active volcano) 2361 m (7746 ft).

ECONOMY Poor and eroded soils, overpopulation and few resources combine to make these underdeveloped islands one of the world's poorest countries. Subsistence farming occupies the majority of the population, although vanilla, cloves and ylang-ylang are produced for export.

RECENT HISTORY The four Comoran islands became a French colony in 1912. In a referendum in 1974, three islands voted to become independent, which they declared themselves without French agreement. The fourth island, Mayotte, voted against independence, and remains under French rule. Following a coup in 1978, an Islamic republic was proclaimed, and a single-party state established. In 1989, the third attempted coup in a decade resulted in the assassination of the president and a brief period of rule by European mercenaries. Civilian rule was restored in December 1989. A multi-party system was restored in 1990, although Udzima retains all the seats in the Assembly.

CONGO

Official name: La République populaire du Congo (The People's Republic of the Congo).

Member of: UN, OAU.

Area: 342 000 km² (132 047 sq mi).

Population: 2 411 000 (1991 est).

Capital and major cities: Brazzaville 760 000, Pointe-Noire 388 000, Loubomo 62 000 (1990 est).

Languages: French (official), Lingala patois (50%), Monokutuba patois (over 40%), Kongo (45%), Teke (20%).

Religion: Roman Catholic (53%), various Protestant Churches (22%), animist (25%).

GOVERNMENT The 153-member Assembly and the President are elected for a five-year term by universal adult suffrage. The President appoints a Prime Minister and a Council of Ministers. The main political parties are the (former Communist) Congolese Party of Labour (PCT), the Movement for Democracy and for Development (MDD), the (liberal) Union for Congolese Democracy (UDC), the Union for Development and Social Progress (UDPS), and the Union for the Progress of the Congolese People (UPPC).

President: Pascal Lissouba.

Prime Minister: André Milongo.

GEOGRAPHY Behind a narrow coastal plain, the plateaux of the interior are covered by tropical rain forests and rise to over 700 m (2300 ft). *Principal rivers*: Zaïre (Congo), Oubangui. *Highest point*: Mont de la Lékéti 1040 m (3412 ft).

ECONOMY Until 1991, Congo had a centrally-planned economy. Privatization has begun but the country is crippled by the highest per capita external debt in Africa. Petroleum and timber are the main exports. Subsistence agriculture – chiefly for cassava – occupies over a third of the labour force.

RECENT HISTORY In 1905 the region became the French colony of Moyen-Congo. Independence was gained in 1960. In 1963, following industrial unrest, a Marxist-Leninist state was established. Since then, ethnic tensions have led to political unrest and military coups. A multi-party system was restored in 1991.

COSTA RICA

Official name: República de Costa Rica (The Republic of Costa Rica).

Member of: UN, OAS, CACM.

Area: 51 100 km² (19 730 sq mi).

Population: 3 088 000 (1991 est).

Capital and major cities: San José 1 040 000 (city 294 000), Alajuela 158 000, Cartago 109 000, Puntarenas 92 000, Limón 68 000 (1990 est).

Language: Spanish (official).

Religions: Roman Catholic (official).

GOVERNMENT Executive power is vested in the President, who is assisted by two Vice-Presidents and by a Cabinet of Ministers that he appoints. The President, Vice-Presidents and the 57-member Legislative Assembly are elected for four-year terms by compulsory universal adult suffrage. The principal political parties are the PUSC (Social Christian Unity Party) and the PLN (National Liberation Party).

President: Rafael Angel Calderón Fournier.

GEOGRAPHY Between a narrow plain on the Pacific coast and a wider plain along the Caribbean coast rise a central plateau and mountain ranges. *Principal river*: Rio Grande. *Highest point*: Chirripó Grande 3820 m (12 533 ft).

ECONOMY Coffee is Costa Rica's major export. Bananas, sugar cane, beef cattle, cocoa and timber are also important.

RECENT HISTORY In the 19th century, Costa Rica developed largely in isolation from its neighbours.

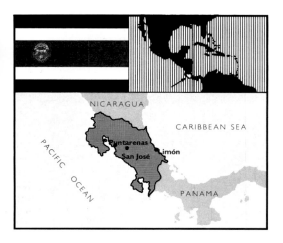

Dominated by small farms, Costa Rica prospered, attracted European immigrants, and developed a stable democracy. Following a brief civil war in 1948, the army was disbanded. Costa Rica has since adopted the role of peacemaker in Central America.

COTE D'IVOIRE

Official name: La République de la Côte d'Ivoire (The Republic of the Ivory Coast). Since 1986 Côte d'Ivoire has been the only official name.

Member of: UN, OAU, ECOWAS.

Area: 322 462 km² (124 503 sq mi).

Population: 12 464 000 (1991 est.).

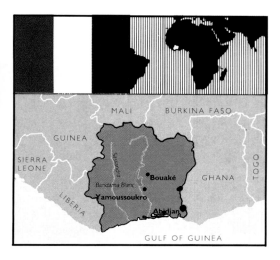

Capital and major cities: Yamoussoukro (de jure and administrative capital) 120 000, Abidjan (de facto and legislative capital) 1 850 000, Bouaké 220 000 (1987 est.).

Languages: French (official), Bete (20%), Senufo (14%), Baoulé (12%).

Religions: Animist (60%), Christian, mainly Roman Catholic (20%), Sunni Islam (20%).

GOVERNMENT The President – who is elected for a five-year term by universal adult suffrage – appoints a Council of Ministers who are responsible to him. The 175-member National Assembly is also directly elected for five years. The main political parties are the Democratic Party, the Ivorian Popular Front, the Workers' Party, the Socialist Party and the Social Democratic Party.

President: Felix Houphouët-Boigny.

Prime Minister: Alassane Ouattara.

GEOGRAPHY The north is a savannah-covered plateau. In the south, tropical rain forest – increasingly cleared for plantations – ends at the narrow coastal plain. *Principal rivers:* Sassandra, Bandama, Komoé. *Highest point:* Mont Nimba 1752 m (5748 ft).

ECONOMY The country depends on exports of cocoa, coffee and timber, and suffered in the 1980s when prices for these commodities fell. Natural resources include petroleum, natural gas and iron ore. Political stability has helped economic growth.

RECENT HISTORY Colonized by France in the 19th century, the Ivory Coast became a relatively prosperous part of French West Africa. Independence was gained in 1960 under the presidency of Félix Houphouët-Boigny (1905–), who has kept close links with France in return for aid and military assistance, and is Africa's longest-serving president. Multi-party elections were held in 1990, but opposition parties claimed electoral fraud.

CROATIA

Official name: Republika Hrvatska (The Republic of Croatia).

Area: 56 538 km² (21 829 sq mi), including the area (about one third) that is controlled by Serb forces.

Population: 4 760 000 (1991 census). Since early 1992 Croatia has received over 400 000 refugees from Bosnia.

Capital and major cities: Zagreb 1 175 000 (city 704 000), Split 236 000 (city 189 000), Rijeka 193 000 (city 168 000), Osijek 159 000 (city 105 000). (1991 census).

Languages: Serbo-Croat – a single language with two written forms, Croat (75%), Serbian (24%).

Religions: Roman Catholic majority, Orthodox minority.

GOVERNMENT The 356-member Parliament and an executive President are directly elected. A Prime

Minister and Cabinet are appointed by the President. The main political parties are the (nationalist) Croatian Democratic Union, the (former Communist) Social Democratic Party-Party of Democratic Reform, the Croatian Democratic Party and the Croatian Peasants Party.

President: Franjo Tudjman.

Prime Minister: Franjo Greguric.

GEOGRAPHY Croatia comprises plains in the E (Slavonia), hills around Zagreb, and barren limestone ranges running parallel to the Dalmatian coast. Dubrovnik is detached from the rest of Croatia. *Principal rivers:* Sava, Danube, Drava. *Highest point:* Troglav 1913 m (6275 ft).

ECONOMY Manufacturing (aluminium, textiles and chemicals), mining (bauxite) and oil dominate the economy. Slavonia grows cereals, potatoes and sugar beet. In 1991–2 the economy was damaged by the Yugoslav civil war, and the lucrative Dalmatian tourist industry collapsed.

HISTORY At the start of the 20th century Croatia was part of Hungary within the Habsburg Empire. A Croat national revival looked increasingly to independent Serbia to create a South ('Yugo') Slav state. After World War I when the Habsburg Empire was dissolved (1918), the Croats joined the Serbs, Slovenes and Montenegrins in the state that was to become Yugoslavia in 1929. However, the Croats soon resented the highly centralized Serb-dominated kingdom. Following the German invasion (1941), the occupying Axis powers set up an 'independent' Croat puppet state that adopted anti-Serb

policies. In 1945 Croatia was reintegrated into a federal Communist Yugoslav state by Marshal Tito, but after Tito's death (1980), the Yugoslav experiment faltered in economic and nationalist crises. Separatists came to power in Croatia in free elections (1990) and declared independence (June 1991). Serb insurgents, backed by the Yugoslav federal army, occupied one third of Croatia including those areas with an ethnic Serb majority – Krajina and parts of Slavonia. The fierce Serbo-Croat war came to an uneasy halt in 1992 after Croatian independence had gained widespread diplomatic recognition and a UN peace-keeping force was agreed. Fighting in Krajina recommenced in 1993.

CUBA

Official name: La República de Cuba (The Republic of Cuba).

Member of: UN, OAS (suspended).

Area: 110 860 km² (42 803 sq mi).

Population: 10 700 000 (1991 est.).

Capital and major cities: Havana (La Habana) 2 096 000, Santiago de Cuba 405 000, Camagüey 283 000, Holguín 228 000, Guantánamo 200 000, Santa Clara 194 000 (1990 est.).

Language: Spanish.

Religion: Roman Catholic (39%).

GOVERNMENT The Communist Party is the only legal political party. A constitutional amendment in 1993 replaced the indirectly-elected parliamentary system with a directly-elected 499-member National Assembly. The Assembly elects 31 of its members to form the Council of State, whose President – as head of state and government – appoints a Council of Ministers.

President: Fidel Castro Ruz.

GEOGRAPHY Three ranges of hills and mountains run east to west across Cuba. *Principal river*: Cauto. *Highest point*: Pico Turquino 1971 m (6467 ft).

ECONOMY Sugar (the leading export), tobacco and coffee are the main crops. State-controlled farms occupy most of the land but are unable to meet Cuba's food needs. Rationing is in force. Production of nickel – Cuba's second most important export – is increasing. The disruption of trading patterns that has followed the adoption of market economies in Eastern Europe and the end of Soviet subsidies have severely damaged the Cuban economy which is on the verge of collapse.

RECENT HISTORY Spain relinquished the colony of Cuba in 1898, but independence was not confirmed until after two periods of American administration (1899–1901 and 1906–09). Under a succession of corrupt governments, the majority of Cubans suffered abject poverty. In 1959, the dictatorship of Fulgencio Batista was overthrown by the guerrilla leader Fidel Castro

AUSTRIA
HUNGARY
ITALY
SLOVENIA
Zagreb
Drava
Danube
Osijek
Rijeka
Sava
BOSNIA-
HERZEGOVINA
ADRIATIC
SEA
Split
Dubrovnik

(1926–), whose revolutionary movement merged with the Communist Party to remodel Cuba on Soviet lines. In 1961, US-backed Cuban exiles attempted to invade at the Bay of Pigs, and relations with America deteriorated further in 1962 when the installation of Soviet missiles on Cuba almost led to world war. Castro has encouraged revolutionary movements throughout Latin America, and his troops have bolstered Marxist governments in Ethiopia and Angola. Despite being a close ally of the USSR, Cuba became a leading Third World power, but the upheavals in the USSR and Eastern Europe in 1989–90 left the Cuban government increasingly isolated as a hardline Marxist state.

CYPRUS

Official name: Kypriaki Dimokratia (in Greek) or Kibris Cumhuriyeti (in Turkish) (The Republic of Cyprus).

Member of: UN, Commonwealth, CSCE, Council of Europe.

Area: 9251 km² (3572 sq mi).

Population: 748 000 (1991 est).

Capital and major cities: Nicosia 338 000 (including the Turkish Cypriot zone Lefkosa), Limassol 135 000, Larnaca 63 000 (1990 est).

Languages: Greek (80%), Turkish (19%).

Religions: Orthodox (80%), Sunni Islam (19%).

GOVERNMENT   A 56-member House of Representatives is elected by universal adult suffrage in the Greek Cypriot community for five years – an additional 24 seats for the Turkish Cypriot community remain unfilled. The President – who appoints a Council of Ministers – is elected from the Greek Cypriot community by universal adult suffrage for a five-year term. There is provision in the constitution for a Vice President to be similarly elected from the Turkish Cypriot community. In 1975, the administration of the Turkish Cypriot community unilaterally established the 'Turkish Republic of Northern Cyprus', which is unrecognized internationally except by Turkey. The main political parties are the Democratic Rally (DISY), the Liberal Party, the (Communist) AKEL party and the Democratic Party. In the Turkish zone, the main political parties are the National Union Party, the New Dawn Party and the Free Democratic Party.

President: Glafcos Clerides.

GEOGRAPHY   The south of the island is covered by the Troodos Mountains. Running east to west across the centre of Cyprus is a fertile plain, north of which are the Kyrenian Mountains and the Karpas Peninsula. *Principal rivers*: Seranhis, Pedieas. *Highest point*: Mount Olympus 1951 m (6399 ft).

ECONOMY   Potatoes, fruit, wine, clothing and textiles are exported from the Greek Cypriot area, in which ports, resorts and an international airport have been constructed to replace facilities lost since partition. The Turkish Cypriot area – which exports fruit, potatoes and tobacco – relies heavily on aid from Turkey. Tourism is important in both zones.

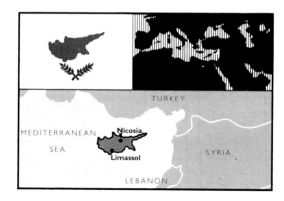

RECENT   HISTORY   British   administration   in Cyprus was established in 1878. During the 1950s, Greek Cypriots – led by Archbishop (later President) Makarios III (1913–77) – campaigned for Enosis (union with Greece). The Turkish Cypriots advocated partition, but following a terrorist campaign by the Greek Cypriot EOKA movement, a compromise was agreed. In 1960 Cyprus became an independent republic. Power was shared by the two communities, but the agreement broke down in 1963, and UN forces intervened to stop intercommunal fighting. The Turkish Cypriots set up their own administration. When pro-Enosis officers staged a coup in 1974, Turkey invaded the north. Cyprus was effectively partitioned. Over 200 000 Greek Cypriots were displaced from the north, into which settlers arrived from Turkey. Since then, UN forces have manned the 'Attila Line' between the Greek south and

Turkish north, but attempts to reunite Cyprus as a federal state have been unsuccessful.

CZECH REPUBLIC

Official name: Ceská Republika (Czech Republic).
Member of: UN, CSCE, Council of Europe.
Area: 78 880 km² (30 456 sq mi).
Population: 10 299 000 (1991 census).
Capital and major cities: Prague (Praha) 1 212 000, Brno 388 000, Ostrava 328 000, Olomouc 224 000, Zlin 197 000, Plzen 174 000, Ceské Budejovice 173 000, Hradec Kralové 163 000, Pardubice 162 000, Liberec 160 000 (1991 census).
Languages: Czech.
Religions: Roman Catholic (39%), Hussite (8%).

GOVERNMENT   The 200-member Assembly is elected by universal adult suffrage for five years. The Assembly elects a President who appoints a Prime Minister and a Council of Ministers, responsible to the Assembly. The main political parties are the (conservative) Civic Democratic Party, the (conservative) Civic Democratic Alliance, the Social Democratic Party, the (Moravian and Silesian nationalist) MAD – SMS, the Christian Democratic Party and the Communist Party.
President: Václav Havel.
Prime Minister: Václav Klaus.

GEOGRAPHY   In the west (Bohemia), the Elbe basin

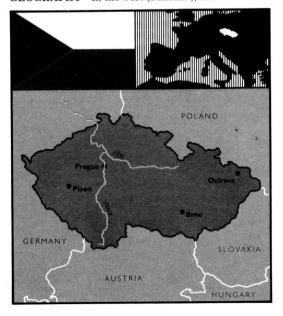

is ringed on three sides by uplands. The Moravian plain lies to the east of Bohemia. *Principal rivers*: Elbe (Labe), Vltava. *Highest point*: Snezka 1603 m (5259 ft).

ECONOMY   Apart from coal, there are few mineral resources, but the country is heavily industrialized. Some areas have suffered heavy pollution. Manufactures include industrial machinery, motor vehicles and consumer goods. The country is switching from a centrally planned to a free-market economy. The majority of businesses have been privatized. The Czech Republic has attracted considerable foreign investment (80% German) and its economy is increasingly linked to that of Germany. The timber industry is important. The main crops include wheat, maize, potatoes, barley and sugar beet.

RECENT HISTORY   On the collapse of the Habsburg Empire, the Czechs and Slovaks united in an independent state (1918) – largely due to the efforts of Thomas Masaryk, who became Czechoslovakia's first president. In 1938, Hitler demanded that Germany be granted the Sudetenland, where Germans predominated. Lacking allies, Czechoslovakia was dismembered – Bohemia and Moravia became German 'protectorates'. The Nazi occupation included the massacre of the inhabitants of Lidice (1942). Following liberation (1945), a coalition government was formed, but the Communists staged a takeover in 1948. In 1968, moves by Party Secretary Alexander Dubček to introduce political reforms met with Soviet disapproval, and invasion by Czechoslovakia's Warsaw Pact allies. The conservative wing of the Communist party regained control until 1989, when student demonstrations developed into a peaceful revolution led by the Civic Forum movement. Faced by overwhelming public opposition, the Communist Party renounced its leading role and hardline leaders were replaced by reformers. A new government, in which Communists were in a minority, was appointed and Civic Forum's leader – the playwright Václav Havel – was elected president. In 1990 free multi-party elections were held, Soviet troops were withdrawn and the foundations of a market economy were laid. Increased Slovak separatism led to the division of the country in 1993, when the secession of poorer, more rural Slovakia left the more developed Czech Republic as a likely future EC member.

DENMARK

Official name: Kongeriget Danmark (Kingdom of Denmark).
Member of: UN, EC, NATO, Council of Europe, CSCE, OECD, WEU (associate).
Area: 43 092 km² (16 638 sq mi) – metropolitan Denmark, excluding dependencies.
Population: 5 194 000 (including the Faeroe Islands; 1991 census).
Capital and major cities: Copenhagen (København) 1 337 000 (city 465 000), Aarhus (Århus) 264 000, Odense

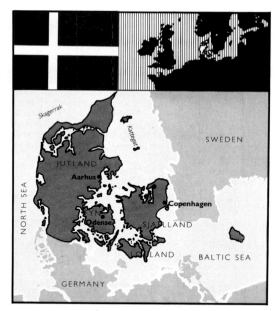

manufacturing, with iron- and metal-working, food processing and brewing, engineering and chemicals as the most important industries. The high cost of imported fuel has been a problem for the economy, but this has been partly alleviated by petroleum and natural gas from the North Sea.

RECENT HISTORY In the 20th century, Denmark's last colonial possessions were either sold (Virgin Islands) or given independence (Iceland) or autonomy (Greenland and the Faeroe Islands). In 1920 northern Schleswig – surrendered to Germany in 1864 – was returned to Denmark. The country was occupied by Nazi Germany (1940–45), and has since been a member of the Western Alliance. From the 1960s, Denmark's economic and political ties have increasingly been with Germany, the UK and the Netherlands, rather than the traditional links with the Nordic countries (Norway and Sweden). Thus, in 1973 Denmark joined the EC, but the political consequence of joining the Common Market has been a further fragmentation of the country's political parties, which has made the formation of coalition and minority governments a protracted and difficult process. The failure of the Danish electorate to approve the EC Maastricht Treaty (1992) halted moves towards European integration.

DANISH AUTONOMOUS DEPENDENCIES
Faeroe Islands (Faeroerne) *Area*: 1399 km² (540 sq mi). *Population*: 48 400 (1990 est). *Capital*: Tórshavn 16 200 (1990 est).
Greenland (Gronland or **Kalaallit)** *Area*: 2 175 600 km² (840 000 sq mi). *Population*: 55 500 (1991 est). *Capital*: Nuuk (formerly Godthab) 12 200 (1991 est).

178 000, Aalborg (Ålborg) 156 000, Esbjerg 82 000, Randers 61 000, Kolding 58 000, Helsingor 57 000, Horsens 55 000 (all including suburbs; 1991 census).
Language: Danish.
Religion: Lutheran (91%).

GOVERNMENT Denmark is a constitutional monarchy. The 179 members of Parliament (the Folketing) are elected by universal adult suffrage under a system of proportional representation for a four-year term. Two members are elected from both of the autonomous dependencies. The Monarch appoints a Prime Minister, who commands a majority in the Folketing. The PM, in turn, appoints a State Council (Cabinet), which is responsible to the Folketing. The main political parties are the Liberal Party, the Conservative People's Party, the Social Democratic Party, the Socialist People's Party, the Progress Party, the Centre Democrats, the Christian People's Party, and the Radical Liberals.
Queen: HM Queen Margrethe II (succeeded upon the death of her father, 14 January 1972).
Prime Minister: Poul Nyrup Rasmussen.

GEOGRAPHY Denmark is a lowland of glacial moraine – only Bornholm, in the Baltic, has ancient hard surface rocks. The islands to the east of Jutland make up nearly one third of the country. *Principal river:* Gudená. *Highest point:* Yding Skovhøj 173 m (568 ft).

ECONOMY Denmark has a high standard of living, but few natural resources. Danish agriculture is organized on a cooperative basis, and produces cheese and other dairy products, bacon and beef – all mainly for export. About one fifth of the labour force is involved in

DJIBOUTI

Official name: Jumhuriya Jibuti (The Republic of Djibouti).
Member of: UN, OAU, Arab League.
Area: 23 200 km² (8950 sq mi).
Population: 541 000 (1991 est).

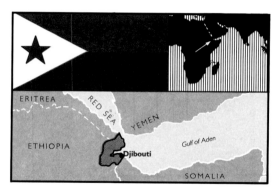

Capital: 290 000 (1988 est).
Languages: Arabic and French (both official), Somali (Issa; 37%).
Religion: Sunni Islam.

GOVERNMENT Every five years the 65-member Chamber of Deputies is elected by universal adult suffrage. The President – who is directly elected every six years – appoints a Prime Minister and Council of Ministers who are responsible to him. The main political party is the (former monopoly) Rassemblement populaire pour le progrès.
President: Hassan Gouled Aptidon.
Prime Minister: Barkat Gourad Hamadou.

GEOGRAPHY Djibouti is a low-lying desert – below sea level in two basins, but rising to mountains in the north. There are no significant rivers. *Highest point:* Musa Ali Terara 2062 m (6768 ft).

ECONOMY Lack of water largely restricts agriculture to grazing sheep and goats. The economy depends on the expanding seaport and railway, which both serve Ethiopia.

RECENT HISTORY France established the colony of French Somaliland in 1888. In the 1950s and 1970s, the Afar tribe and Europeans voted to remain French, while the Issas (Somalis) opted for independence. In 1977, the territory became the Republic of Djibouti, but the new state has suffered ethnic unrest and drought. From 1981 to 1992 Djibouti was a single-party state.

DOMINICA

Official name: Commonwealth of Dominica.
Member of: UN, Commonwealth, CARICOM, OAS.
Area: 751 km² (290 sq mi).

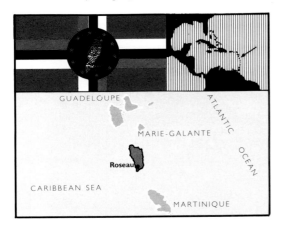

Population: 83 400 (1991 est).
Capital: Roseau 22 000 (city 8300); Portsmouth 5000 (town 2200) (1991 est).
Languages: English (official), French patois.
Religion: Roman Catholic (80%).

GOVERNMENT Every five years, 21 members of the House of Assembly are elected by universal adult suffrage and nine are appointed by the President, who is elected for a five-year term by the House. The President appoints a Prime Minister and Cabinet. The main political parties are the (conservative) Dominica Freedom Party, the United Dominica Labour Party, and the Dominica Labour Party.
President: Clarence Seignoret.
Prime Minister: Eugenia Charles.

GEOGRAPHY Dominica is surrounded by steep cliffs with a forested mountainous interior. *Principal river*: Layou. *Highest point*: Morne Diablotin 1447 m (4747 ft).

ECONOMY Dominica is a poor island. It produces bananas, timber and coconuts, and exports water to drier neighbours. Tourism is increasing in importance.

RECENT HISTORY A former British colony, Dominica was a member of the West Indies Federation (1958–62), gained autonomy in 1967 and independence in 1978.

DOMINICAN REPUBLIC

Official name: República Dominicana (The Dominican Republic).
Member of: UN, OAS, CARICOM.
Area: 48 422 km² (18 696 sq mi).
Population: 7 320 000 (1991 est).
Capital and major cities: Santo Domingo 1 600 000, Santiago 308 000, La Romana 101 000, San Pedro 87 000 (all including suburbs; 1986).
Language: Spanish.
Religions: Roman Catholic (official; over 90%).

GOVERNMENT The President and the National Congress – a 30-member Senate and a 120-member Chamber of Deputies – are elected for four years by universal adult suffrage. The President appoints a Cabinet. The main political parties are the (conservative) PR (Partido Reformista), the (left-wing) PRD (Partido Revolucionario Dominicano) and the (left-wing) PLD (Partido de la Liberación Dominicana).
President: Joaquin Balaguer.

GEOGRAPHY The republic consists of the eastern two thirds of the island of Hispaniola. The fertile Cibao

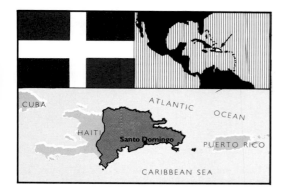

Valley in the north is an important agricultural region. Most of the rest of the country is mountainous. *Principal river:* Yaque del Norte. *Highest point:* Pico Duarte 3175 m (10 417 ft).

ECONOMY Sugar is the traditional mainstay of the economy, but nickel and iron ore have become the principal exports. Tourism is now the greatest foreign-currency earner.

RECENT HISTORY The 19th century witnessed a succession of tyrants, and by 1900 the republic was bankrupt and in chaos. The USA intervened (1916–24). Rafael Trujillo (1891–1961) became president in 1930 and ruthlessly suppressed opposition. He was assassinated in 1961. Civil war in 1965 ended after intervention by US and Latin American troops. Since then, an infant democracy has survived violent elections. The country faces grave economic problems.

ECUADOR

Official name: República del Ecuador (The Republic of Ecuador).
Member of: UN, OAS, ALADI, Andean Pact.
Area: 270 670 km² (104 506 sq mi).
Population: 10 782 000 (1990 census).
Capital and major cities: Quito 1 388 000 (city 1 101 000), Guayaquil 1 764 000 (city 1 531 000), Cuenca 272 000 (city 195 000), Ambato 229 000 (city 124 000), Portoviejo 201 000 (city 133 000), Esmeraldas 173 000, Riobamba 160 000 (1990 census).
Language: Spanish (official; 93%), Quéchua.
Religion: Roman Catholic (92%).

GOVERNMENT The President is elected by compulsory universal adult suffrage for a single term of 4 years. The 72-member Chamber of Representatives is also directly elected; 12 members are elected for four years on a national basis and 60 members for a single term of two years on a provincial basis. The President appoints a

Cabinet of Ministers. The principal political parties include the (conservative coalition) FRN (National Reconstruction Front), the (left-wing coalition) Front of Democratic Progress, and the Christian Democrat coalition.
President: Sixto Duran Ballen.

GEOGRAPHY The Andes divide the Pacific coastal plain in the west from the Amazonian tropical rain forest in the east. *Principal rivers:* Napo, Pastaza, Curaray, Daule. *Highest point:* Chimborazo 6267 m (20 561 ft).

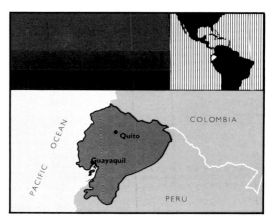

ECONOMY Agriculture is the largest single employer, and major export crops include cocoa, coffee and, in particular, bananas. Petroleum is the major foreign-currency earner. High inflation and foreign debt are severe problems.

RECENT HISTORY Since 1895 there have been long periods of military rule, but democratically elected governments have been in power since 1978. Relations with neighbouring Peru have long been tense – war broke out in 1941, when Ecuador lost most of its Amazonian territory, and there were border skirmishes in 1981. Emergency economic measures in 1988 led to a wave of strikes and unrest.

EGYPT

Official name: Jumhuriyat Misr al-'Arabiya (Arab Republic of Egypt).
Member of: UN, OAU, Arab League.
Area: 997 739 km² (385 229 sq mi).
Population: 54 609 000 (1991 est).
Capital and major cities: Cairo (El-Qahira) 12 287 000 (including suburbs), Alexandria (El-Iskandariyah) 3 170 000, El-Giza 2 156 000 and Shubrâ El-Kheima 811 000 are both part of the Cairo agglomeration, Port Said (Bur Sa'id) 461 000, Suez 392 000 (1990 est).

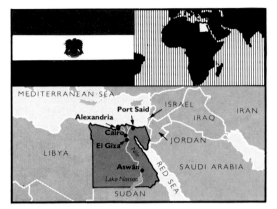

Language: Arabic (official).

Religion: Sunni Islam (90%), Coptic Christian (7%).

GOVERNMENT Every five years, 454 members are elected by universal adult suffrage to the Majlis ash-Sha'ab (People's Assembly); 10 additional members are appointed by the President, who is nominated by the Assembly and confirmed by referendum for a six-year term. The President appoints a Prime Minister, Ministers and Vice-President(s). The principal political parties include the (socialist) National Democratic Party, the (traditional) New Wafd Party, the Socialist Labour Party, and the Progressive Unionist Rally.

President: Mohammed Hosni Mubarak.

Prime Minister: Atef Sedki.

GEOGRAPHY Desert covers more than 90% of Egypt. The Western Desert – which stretches into Libya and Sudan – is low-lying. The Eastern Desert is divided by wadis and ends in the southeast in mountains beside the Red Sea. The vast majority of the population lives in the Nile River valley and delta, intensively cultivated lands that rely on irrigation by the annual flood of the Nile. East of the Suez Canal is the Sinai Peninsula. *Principal river:* Nile. *Highest point:* Mount Catherine (Jabal Katrina) 2642 m (8668 ft).

ECONOMY Over 40% of the labour force is involved in agriculture, producing maize, wheat, rice and vegetables for the domestic market, and cotton and dates mainly for export. Petroleum reserves (small by Middle Eastern standards), canal tolls and tourism are major foreign-currency earners. The economy is held back by rapid population growth and by the demands of a large public sector and food subsidies.

RECENT HISTORY The UK occupied Egypt (1882) and established a protectorate (1914–22). The corrupt regime of King Farouk was toppled in a military coup (1952) and a republic was established (1953). The radical Gamal Abdel Nasser (1918–70) became president in 1954. He nationalized the Suez Canal and made Egypt the leader of Arab nationalism. Nasser was twice defeated by Israel in Middle East wars (1967 and 1973), but his

successor, President Anwar Sadat, made peace with Israel (1979) and was ostracized by the Arab world. Since Sadat's assassination (1981), Egypt has regained its place in the Arab fold, and the prominent role played by Egypt in the coalition against Saddam Hussein's Iraq (1991) confirmed Egypt as one of the leaders of the Arab world. The country is faced by severe economic problems, and there is a growth in Islamic fundamentalism.

EL SALVADOR

Official name: La República de El Salvador (The Republic of El Salvador).

Member of: UN, OAS, CACM.

Area: 21 393 km^2 (8260 sq mi).

Population: 5 392 000 (1991 est).

Capital and major cities: San Salvador 1 151 000 (city 477 000), Santa Ana 224 000 (city 145 000), San Miguel 176 000 (city 93 000), Mejicanos 107 000 (city 96 000) (1987 est).

Language: Spanish (official).

Religion: Roman Catholic (over 90%).

GOVERNMENT The President – who appoints a Cabinet of Ministers – is elected by universal adult suffrage for a single five-year term. Every three years, direct elections are also held for the 60-member National Assembly. The main political parties are (right-wing) ARENA (the Nationalist Republican Alliance), the PCN (National Reconstruction Party), the (left-wing) Democratic Convergence, and the PDC (Christian Democratic Party).

President: Alfredo Cristiani.

GEOGRAPHY The country is mountainous, with ranges along the border with Honduras and a higher volcanic chain in the south. *Principal rivers:* Lempa, San Miguel. *Highest point:* Volcán de Santa Ana 2381 m (7812 ft).

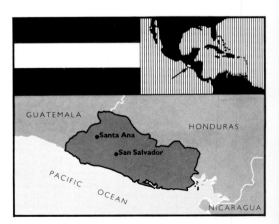

ECONOMY Agricultural products – in particular coffee and sugar cane – account for nearly two thirds of the country's exports. The economy has declined since the 1970s owing to the state of near civil war.

RECENT HISTORY Since independence in 1821, El Salvador has suffered frequent coups and political violence. In 1932 a peasant uprising – led by Agustín Farabundo Martí – was harshly suppressed. El Salvador's overpopulation has been partially relieved by migration to neighbouring countries. Following a football match between El Salvador and Honduras in 1969, war broke out because of illegal immigration by Salvadoreans into Honduras. Political and economic power is concentrated in the hands of a few families, and this has led to social tension. The country was in a state of virtual civil war from the late 1970s to 1992 with the US-backed military, assisted by extreme right-wing death squads, combating left-wing guerrillas – the FMLN-FDR (Farabundo Martí National Liberation Movement and Democratic Revolutionary Front). A peace agreement between these forces was reached in 1992 and constitutional multi-party rule was restored.

EQUATORIAL GUINEA

Official name: La República de Guinea Ecuatorial (The Republic of Equatorial Guinea).
Member of: UN, OAU.
Area: 28 051 km² (10 831 sq mi).
Population: 358 000 (1991 est).
Capital and major cities: Malabo 37 000, Bata 24 000 (1988 est).
Languages: Spanish (official), Fang, Bubi, Portuguese patois on Pagalu.
Religions: Roman Catholic majority.

GOVERNMENT The constitution provides for the election of a President for a seven-year term. However, effective power is in the hands of the Supreme Military Council, whose President is head of state and of government. A 41-member House of Representatives is directly elected for a five-year term. All candidates for election are nominated by the President and since 1987 all are members of the single party of government, the PDGE (Partido Democratico de Guinea Ecuatorial). In 1992, the restoration of a multi-party system was approved.
President: Brig. Gen. Teodoro Obiang.

GEOGRAPHY The republic consists of the fertile island of Bioko (formerly Fernando Póo), the much smaller islands of Pagalu (formerly Annobón) and the Corisco Group, and the district of Mbini (formerly Río Muni) on the African mainland. *Principal rivers:* Campo, Benito, Muni. *Highest point:* Pico de Moca (Moka) 2850 m (9350 ft).

ECONOMY Mbini exports coffee and timber, but cocoa production on Bioko slumped after the departure of Nigerian workers (1976). The economy relies heavily upon foreign aid.

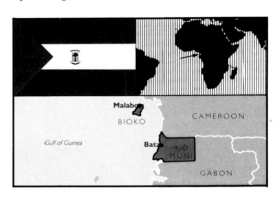

RECENT HISTORY Independence from Spain in 1968 began under the dictatorship of Francisco Nguema, who was overthrown by his nephew Teodoro Obiang in a military coup in 1979. Severe economic decline was experienced in the 1970s. Coups were attempted in 1981, 1983, 1986 and 1988. One-party rule was introduced in 1987 but the return of political pluralism is expected.

ESTONIA

Official name: Eesti Vabariik (Republic of Estonia).
Member of: UN, CSCE.
Area: 45 100 km² (17 413 sq mi).
Population: 1 589 000 (1991 est).
Capital and major cities: Tallinn 505 000, Tartu 115 000, Narva 82 000, Kohtla-Järve 77 000, Parnu 54 000 (1991 est).
Languages: Estonian (over 62%), Russian (30%).
Religions: Lutheran (30%), Orthodox (10%).

GOVERNMENT A 105-member Assembly and a President are elected by universal adult suffrage for four years. The President appoints a Prime Minister and a Council of Ministers who are responsible to the Assembly. The main political parties are the (nationalist) Popular Front of Estonia, the Christian Democratic Party, the Christian Democratic Union, the Social Democratic Party, the Liberal Democratic Party and the Communist Party.

President: Lennart Meri.
Prime Minister: Mart Laar.

GEOGRAPHY Estonia comprises a low-lying mainland and two main islands. *Principal river:* Narva. *Highest point:* Munamägi 318 m (1042 ft).

ECONOMY Major industries include engineering and food processing. Gas for heating and industry is extracted from bituminous shale. The important agricultural sector is dominated by dairying. Since 1991 severe economic difficulties have resulted from Estonia's heavy dependency upon trade with Russia. The economy is still largely state-run, but some progress towards privatization has been made.

RECENT HISTORY When the Communists took power in Russia (1917), Estonia seceded, but a German occupation and two Russian invasions delayed independence until 1919. Estonia's fragile democracy was replaced by a dictatorship in 1934. The Non-Aggression Pact (1939) between Hitler and Stalin assigned Estonia to the USSR, which invaded and annexed the republic

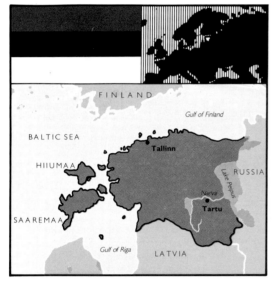

(1940). Estonia was occupied by Nazi Germany (1941–44). When Soviet rule was reimposed (1945), large-scale Russian settlement replaced over 120 000 Estonians who had been killed or deported to Siberia. In 1988, reforms in the USSR allowed Estonian nationalists to operate openly. Nationalists won a majority in the republic's parliament, gradually assumed greater autonomy and seceded following the failed coup by Communist hardliners in Moscow (August 1991). The USSR recognized Estonia's independence in September 1991. In 1992 the introduction of strict Estonian citizenship laws that denied full rights to most Russian-speakers increased tension with Russia, which halted the withdrawal of troops from Estonia.

ETHIOPIA

Official name: Ityopia (Ethiopia). Previously known as Abyssinia.

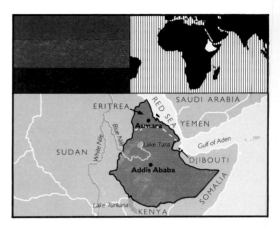

Member of: UN, OAU.

Area: 1 223 600 km² (472 435 sq mi).

Population: 51 617 000 (1991 est – including Eritrea).

Capital and major cities: Addis Ababa 1 739 000, Asmara (Asmera) 344 000, Dire Dawa 122 000, Gondar 88 000, Dese 78 000 (1991 est).

Languages: Amharic (official), Arabic, Oromo (40%).

Religions: Sunni Islam (45%), Ethiopian Orthodox (40%).

GOVERNMENT The constitution provides for elections every five years by universal adult suffrage for the 835-member National Assembly (Shengo), which elects the President and appoints the Cabinet. The main political parties are the Tigrayan People's Liberation Front, the Ethiopian People's Democratic Movement, the Oromo People's Democratic Organization and the Eritrean People's Liberation Front. In 1992 a plan for a federal system, including 14 autonomous regions, was announced. The region of Eritrea has *de facto* been an independent state since 1991.

President: Meles Zenawi.

Prime Minister: Tamirat Layne.

GEOGRAPHY The Western Highlands – including Eritrea, the Tigré Plateau and the Semien Mountains – are separated from the lower Eastern Highlands by a wide rift valley. *Principal rivers:* Blue Nile (Abay Wenz), Tekeze, Awash, Omo, Sagan. *Highest point:* Ras Dashen 4620 m (15 158 ft).

ECONOMY Secessionist wars have damaged an impoverished, underdeveloped economy. The majority of the population is involved in subsistence farming, but drought and overgrazing have led to desertification. Coffee is the main foreign-currency earner. The economy is in serious difficulties owing to the end of aid from the Eastern bloc.

RECENT HISTORY Ethiopia survived the European scramble for empire although the Italians occupied Ethiopia from 1936 to 1941. Emperor Haile Selassie

(1892–1975) played a prominent part in African affairs, but – failing to modernize Ethiopia or overcome its extreme poverty – he was overthrown in 1974. Allied to the USSR, a left-wing military regime instituted revolutionary change, but, even with Cuban help, it was unable to overcome secessionist guerrilla movements in Eritrea and Tigray. Drought, soil erosion and civil war brought severe famine in the 1980s. President Mengistu – who ruled a one-party Marxist state from 1979 to 1991 – was toppled by an alliance of Tigrayan, Oromo and other forces in 1991. Multi-party rule was restored and new constitutional arrangements to accommodate various regional secessionist movements are to be implemented. However, Eritrea has already effectively seceded and a referendum on the province's future status is scheduled for 1993.

ERITREA *Area:* 117 400 km² (45 300 sq mi). *Population:* 3 323 000 (1991 est). *Capital:* Asmara (Asmera) 344 000 (1991 est).

FIJI

Official name: Matanitu Ko Viti (Republic of Fiji).
Member of: UN, South Pacific Forum.
Area: 18 376 km² (7095 sq mi).
Population: 738 000 (1991 est).
Capital: Suva 141 000 (city 70 000), Lautoka 29 000 (1986 census).
Languages: English, Fijian (48%), Hindi (46%).
Religions: Methodist (45%), Hindu (over 40%).

GOVERNMENT The 70-seat House of Representatives is elected by universal adult suffrage for five years – 37 members by Fijians, 27 by Indians, 1 by Rotumans, 5 by others. The 34-member Senate comprises 24 members chosen by the traditional Council of Chiefs, 1 to represent Rotuma, 9 appointed by the President. The Council of Chiefs appoints the President for a five-year term. The President, in turn, appoints a PM who commands a majority in the House. The main political parties include

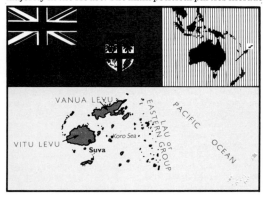

the Fijian Nationalist Party, the Fijian Political Party, the National Federation Party, the (right-wing) Taukei Solidarity Movement, the Fiji Labour Party and the (liberal) Western United Front.
President: Penaia Ganilau.
Prime Minister: Sitiveni Rabuka.

GEOGRAPHY The mountainous larger islands are volcanic in origin. The smaller islands are mainly coral reefs. *Principal rivers:* Rewa, Sigatoka. *Highest point:* Tomaniivi (Mount Victoria) 1323 m (4341 ft).

ECONOMY Fiji's economy depends on agriculture, with sugar cane as the main cash crop. Copra, ginger, fish and timber are also exported.

RECENT HISTORY Chief Cakobau ceded Fiji to Britain in 1874. Indian labourers arrived to work on sugar plantations, reducing the Fijians, who retained ownership of most of the land, to a minority. Since independence (1970), racial tension and land disputes have brought instability. A military takeover in 1987 overthrew an Indian-led government and established a Fijian-dominated republic outside the Commonwealth. Fiji returned to civilian rule in January 1990, with the resignation of the military officers from the cabinet. A new constitution guarantees political power for the native Melanese (Fijian) population.

FINLAND

Official name: Suomen Tasavalta (Republic of Finland).
Member of: UN, EFTA, CSCE, Council of Europe, OECD.
Area: 338 145 km² (130 557 sq mi).
Population: 4 999 000 (1990 census).
Capital and major cities: Helsinki (Helsingfors) 994 000 (city 492 000), Turku (Åbo) 265 000 (city 159 000), Tampere (Tammerfors) 261 000 (city 173 000), Espoo 173 000 and Vantaa 155 000 are part of the Helsinki agglomeration; Oulu (Uleaborg) 101 000, Lahti 93 000, Kuopio 81 000, Pori (Björneborg) 76 000 (1990 census).
Languages: Finnish (94%), Swedish (6%).
Religion: Lutheran (88%).

GOVERNMENT The 200-member Eduskunta (Parliament) is elected for four years under a system of proportional representation by universal adult suffrage. Executive power is vested in a President elected for six years by direct popular vote. The President appoints a Council of State (Cabinet) – headed by a Prime Minister – responsible to the Parliament. The main political parties include the Centre Party, the (conservative) National Coalition Party, the Social Democratic Party, the Left-Wing Alliance, the Green Union, the Swedish People's Party, the Liberal People's Party, the Rural Party, and the Communist Party. The Aland Islands have a considerable degree of self-government.

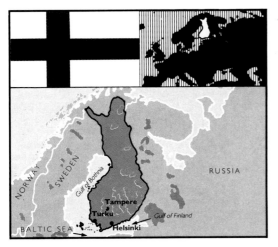

President: Mauno Koivisto.
Prime Minister: Esko Aho.

AUTONOMOUS COUNTY Aland Islands (Ahvenanmaa) *Area*: 1527 km² (590 sq mi). *Population*: 24 600 (1990 census). *Capital*: Mariehamn.

GEOGRAPHY Nearly one third of Finland lies north of the Arctic Circle and one tenth of the country is covered by lakes, some 50 000 in all. Saimaa – the largest lake – has an area of over 4400 km² (1700 sq mi). During the winter months the Gulfs of Bothnia (to the west) and of Finland (to the south) freeze, and ports have to be kept open by icebreakers. The land has been heavily glaciated, and except for mountains in the northwest most of the country is lowland. *Principal rivers:* Paatsjoki, Torniojoki, Kemijoki, Kokemäenjoki. *Highest point:* Haltiatunturi 1342 m (4344 ft).

ECONOMY Forests cover about two thirds of the country and wood products provide over one third of Finland's foreign earnings. Metalworking and engineering – in particular shipbuilding – are among the most important of Finland's industries, which have a reputation for quality and good design. Finland enjoys a high standard of living, although – apart from forests, copper and rivers suitable for hydroelectric power – the country has few natural resources. There is a large fishing industry, and the agricultural sector produces enough cereals and dairy products for export. The collapse of trade with Russia – traditionally a major trading partner – brought severe economic difficulties to Finland in 1991–92.

RECENT HISTORY After the Russian Revolution of 1917, civil war broke out in Russian-ruled Finland. The pro-Russian party was defeated and an independent republican constitution (still in force today) was established (1919). Finland's territorial integrity lasted until the Soviet invasion in 1939, after which land was ceded to the USSR. The failure of a brief alliance with Germany led to further cession of territory to the Soviet Union in 1944. Finland has, since 1945, retained its neutrality and independence. Finland has achieved some influence through the careful exercise of its neutrality, for example, hosting the initial sessions of CSCE (the 'Helsinki accords'). Government in Finland is characterized by multi-party coalitions, and since 1987 parties of the left have lost favour. Economically, Finland is integrated into Western Europe through membership of EFTA and OECD, and is a candidate for EC membership.

FRANCE

Official name: La République Française (The French Republic).
Member of: UN, EC, NATO, WEU, G7, OECD, CSCE, Council of Europe.
Area: 543 965 km² (210 026 sq mi) – 'metropolitan' France, excluding overseas départements and collectivités territoriales.
Population: 56 614 000 (1990 census) – 'metropolitan' France.
Capital and major cities: Paris 9 063 000 (city 2 175 000), Lyon 1 262 000 (city 422 000), Marseille 1 087 000 (city 808 000), Lille 950 000 (city 178 000), Bordeaux 686 000 (city 213 000), Toulouse 608 000 (city 366 000), Nantes 492 000 (city 252 000), Nice 476 000 (city 346 000), Toulon 438 000 (city 170 000), Grenoble 400 000 (city 154 000), Strasbourg 388 000 (city 256 000), Rouen 380 000 (city 105 000), Valenciennes 336 000 (town 39 000), Cannes 336 000 (city 69 000), Lens 323 000 (town 35 000), Saint-Etienne 313 000 (city 202 000), Nancy 311 000 (city 102 000), Tours 272 000 (city 133 000), Béthune 260 000 (town 26 000), Clermont-Ferrand 254 000 (city 140 000), Le Havre 254 000 (city 197 000), Rennes 245 000 (city 204 000), Orléans 243 000 (city 108 000), Dijon 226 000 (city 152 000), Mulhouse 224 000 (city 110 000), Reims 206 000 (city 185 000), Angers 206 000 (city 146 000), Brest 201 000 (city 153 000), Douai 200 000 (city 44 000), Dunkerque 193 000 (town 71 000), Metz 193 000 (city 124 000), Le Mans 189 000 (city 148 000), Caen 189 000 (city 116 000), Mantes-la-Jolie 189 000 (town 45 000), Avignon 181 000 (city 89 000), Limoges 170 000 (city 136 000) (1990 census).
Languages: French, with Breton and Basque minorities.
Religions: Roman Catholic (74%), Sunni Islam (4%).

GOVERNMENT Executive power is vested in the President, who is elected for a 7-year term by universal adult suffrage. The President appoints a Prime Minister and a Council of Ministers – both responsible to Parliament – but it is the President, rather than the PM, who presides over the Council of Ministers. Parliament has two chambers. The Senate (the upper house) comprises 321 members – 296 of whom represent individual départements and 13 of whom represent overseas départements and territories – elected by members of municipal, local and regional councils. The remaining

12 senators are elected by French citizens resident abroad. Senators serve for nine years, with one third of the Senate retiring every three years. The National Assembly (the lower house) comprises 577 deputies – including 22 for overseas départements and territories – elected for a five-year term by universal adult suffrage from single-member constituencies, with a second ballot for the leading candidates if no candidate obtains an absolute majority in the first round. The main political parties include the PS (Socialist Party), the (conservative Gaullist) RPR (Rally for the Republic), the (centrist) UDF (Union for French Democracy), the PC (Communist Party), the Centre Union, and the (right-wing) FN (National Front). Since 1982, the 96 metropolitan French départements have been grouped into 22 regions which have increased powers of local government.

President: François Mitterrand.
Prime Minister: Edouard Balladur.

REGIONS Alsace *Area*: 8280 km² (3197 sq mi). *Population*: 1 624 000 (1990 census). *Administrative centre*: Strasbourg.

Aquitaine *Area*: 41 308 km² (15 949 sq mi). *Population*: 2 796 000 (1990 census). *Administrative centre*: Bordeaux.

Auvergne *Area*: 26 013 km² (10 044 sq mi). *Population*: 1 321 000 (1990 census). *Administrative centre*: Clermont-Ferrand.

Brittany (Bretagne) *Area*: 27 208 km² (10 505 sq mi). *Population*: 2 796 000 (1990 census). *Administrative centre*: Rennes.

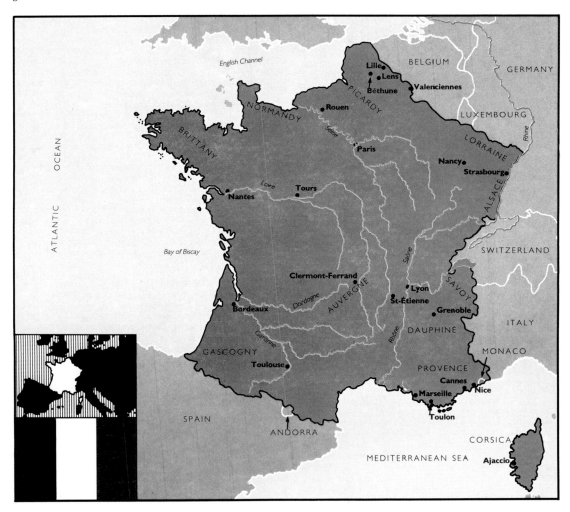

Burgundy (Bourgogne) *Area*: 31 582 km^2 (12 194 sq mi). *Population*: 1 609 000 (1990 census). *Administrative centre*: Dijon.

Centre *Area*: 39 151 km^2 (15 116 sq mi). *Population*: 2 371 000 (1990 census). *Administrative centre*: Orléans.

Champagne-Ardenne *Area*: 25 606 km^2 (9886 sq mi). *Population*: 1 348 000 (1990 census). *Administrative centre*: Reims.

Corsica (Corse) *Area*: 8680 km^2 (3351 sq mi). *Population*: 250 000 (1990 census). *Administrative centre*: Ajaccio.

Franche-Comté *Area*: 16 202 km^2 (6256 sq mi). *Population*: 1 097 000 (1990 census). *Administrative centre*: Besançon.

Ile-de-France *Area*: 12 012 km^2 (4638 sq mi). *Population*: 10 660 000 (1990 census). *Administrative centre*: Paris.

Languedoc-Roussillon *Area*: 27 376 km^2 (10 570 sq mi). *Population*: 2 115 000 (1990 census). *Administrative centre*: Montpellier.

Limousin *Area*: 16 942 km^2 (6541 sq mi). *Population*: 723 000 (1990 census). *Administrative centre*: Limoges.

Lorraine *Area*: 23 547 km^2 (9091 sq mi). *Population*: 2 306 000 (1990 census). *Administrative centre*: Nancy.

Lower Normandy (Basse Normandie) *Area*: 17 589 km^2 (6791 sq mi). *Population*: 1 391 000 (1990 census). *Administrative centre*: Caen.

Midi-Pyrénées *Area*: 45 348 km^2 (17 509 sq mi). *Population*: 2 431 000 (1990 census). *Administrative centre*: Toulouse.

Nord-Pas-de-Calais *Area*: 12 414 km^2 (4793 sq mi). *Population*: 3 965 000 (1990 census). *Administrative centre*: Lille.

Pays de la Loire *Area*: 32 082 km^2 (12 387 sq mi). *Population*: 3 059 000 (1990 census). *Administrative centre*: Nantes.

Picardy (Picardie) *Area*: 19 399 km^2 (7490 sq mi). *Population*: 1 811 000 (1990 census). *Administrative centre*: Amiens.

Poitou-Charentes *Area*: 25 810 km^2 (9965 sq mi). *Population*: 1 595 000 (1990 census). *Administrative centre*: Poitiers.

Provence-Côte d'Azur *Area*: 31 400 km^2 (12 124 sq mi). *Population*: 4 258 000 (1990 census). *Administrative centre*: Marseille.

Rhône-Alpes *Area*: 43 698 km^2 (16 872 sq mi). *Population*: 5 351 000 (1990 census). *Administrative centre*: Lyon.

Upper Normandy (Haute-Normandie) *Area*: 12 317 km^2 (4756 sq mi). *Population*: 1 737 000 (1990 census). *Administrative centre*: Rouen.

GEOGRAPHY The Massif Central – a plateau of old hard rocks, rising to almost 2000 m (6500 ft) – occupies the middle of France. The Massif is surrounded by four major lowlands, which together make up almost two thirds of the total area of the country. The Paris Basin – the largest of these lowlands – is divided by low ridges and fertile plains and plateaux, but is united by the river system of the Seine and its tributaries. To the east of the Massif Central is the long narrow Rhône-Saône Valley,

while to the west the Loire Valley stretches to the Atlantic. Southwest of the Massif Central lies the Aquitaine Basin, a large fertile region drained by the River Garonne and its tributaries. A discontinuous ring of highlands surrounds France. In the northwest the Armorican Massif (Brittany) rises to 411 m (1350 ft). In the southwest the Pyrenees form a high natural boundary with Spain. The Alps in the southeast divide France from Italy and contain the highest peak in Europe (outside the Caucasus). The lower Jura – in the east – form a barrier between France and Switzerland, while the Vosges Mountains separate the Paris Basin from the Rhine Valley. In the northeast, the Ardennes extend into France from Belgium. The Mediterranean island of Corsica is an ancient massif rising to 2710 m (8891 ft). *Principal rivers:* Rhine (Rhin), Loire, Rhône, Seine, Garonne, Saône. *Highest point:* Mont Blanc 4807 m (15 771 ft).

ECONOMY Nearly two thirds of France is farmed. The principal products include cereals (wheat, maize, barley and even rice), meat and dairy products, sugar beet, and grapes for wine. France is remarkably self-sufficient in agriculture, with tropical fruit and animal feeds being the only major imports. However, the small size of land holdings remains a problem, despite consolidation and the efforts of cooperatives. Reafforestation is helping to safeguard the future of the important timber industry. Natural resources include coal, iron ore, copper, bauxite and tungsten, as well as petroleum and natural gas, and plentiful sites for hydroelectric power plants. The major French industries include: textiles, chemicals, steel, food processing, motor vehicles, aircraft, and mechanical and electrical engineering. Traditionally French firms have been small, but mergers have resulted in larger corporations able to compete internationally. France is now the world's fourth industrial power after the USA, Japan and Germany. During the later 1980s many of the state-owned corporations were privatized. Over one half of the labour force is involved in service industries, in particular administration, banking, finance, and tourism.

RECENT HISTORY Georges Clemenceau (1841–1929) – who had led France as prime minister during the World War I – lost power in 1919 when the French electorate perceived the harsh peace terms as being too lenient to Germany. Between 1919 and 1939 French government was characterized by instability and frequent changes of administration. In 1936 Léon Blum (1872–1950) led a Popular Front (Socialist-Communist-Radical) coalition to power and instituted many important social reforms. In World War II (1939–45), Germany rapidly defeated the French in 1940 and completely occupied the country in 1942. Marshal Philippe Pétain (1856–1951) led a collaborationist regime in the city of Vichy, while General Charles de Gaulle (1890–1970) headed the Free French in exile in London from 1940. France was liberated following the Allied landings in Normandy in 1944. After the war, the Fourth Republic (1946–58) was marked by instability and the Suez Crisis of 1956 – when France and the UK sought to prevent Egypt's nationalization of the canal. The end of the colonial era was marked by nationalist revolts in some of the colonies, notably Vietnam – where the Communists defeated French colonial forces at Dien Bien Phu in 1954 – and Algeria. The troubles in Algeria – including the revolt of the French colonists and the campaign of their terrorist organization, the OAS – led to the end of the Fourth Republic and to the accession to power of General de Gaulle in 1959.

As first president of the Fifth Republic, de Gaulle granted Algerian independence in 1962. While the French colonial empire – with a few minor exceptions – was being disbanded, France's position within Western Europe was being strengthened, especially by vigorous participation in the European Community. At the same time, de Gaulle sought to pursue a foreign policy independent of the USA, building up France's nuclear capability and withdrawing French forces from NATO's integrated command structure. Although restoring political and economic stability to France, domestic dissatisfaction – including the student revolt of May 1968 – led de Gaulle to resign in 1969. De Gaulle's policies were broadly pursued by his successors as president, Georges Pompidou (in office 1969–74) and Valéry Giscard d'Estaing (1974–81). The modernization of France continued apace under the country's first Socialist president, François Mitterrand (1916–), who was elected in 1981.

FRENCH OVERSEAS DEPARTEMENTS The overseas départements are integral parts of the French Republic.
Guadeloupe *Area*: 1780 km² (687 sq mi). *Population*: 387 000 (1990 census). *Capital*: Basse-Terre 38 000 (town 14 000). *Largest town*: Pointe-à-Pitre 122 000 (town 26 000) (1990 census).
Guyane (French Guiana) *Area*: 90 000 km² (34 750 sq mi). *Population*: 115 000 (1990 census). *Capital*: Cayenne 42 000 (1990 census).
Martinique *Area*: 1100 km² (425 sq mi). *Population*: 360 000 (1990 census). *Capital*: Fort-de-France 102 000 (1990 census).
Réunion *Area*: 2512 km² (970 sq mi). *Population*: 597 000 (1990 census). *Capital*: Saint-Denis 122 000 (1990 census).

FRENCH COLLECTIVITES TERRITORIALES
The collectivités territoriales – a status between that of an overseas département and an overseas territory – are integral parts of the French Republic.
Mayotte *Area*: 376 km² (145 sq mi). *Population*: 94 400 (1990 census). *Capital*: Dzaoudzi 5900. *Largest town*: Mamoudzou 12 000 (1990 census).
Saint-Pierre-et-Miquelon *Area*: 242 km² (93 sq mi). *Population*: 6400 (1990 census). *Capital*: Saint-Pierre 5700 (1990 census).

FRENCH OVERSEAS TERRITORIES
French Polynesia *Area*: 4200 km² (1622 sq mi). *Population*: 199 000 (1991 est). *Capital*: Papeete (on Tahiti) 23 500 (1991 est).
New Caledonia *Area*: 19 103 km² (7376 sq mi). *Population*: 168 000 (1990 est). *Capital*: Nouméa 65 000 (1989 est).

Southern and Antarctic Territories *Area*: Kerguelen Archipelago 18 130 km² (7000 sq mi); Crozet Archipelago 1295 km² (500 sq mi), Amsterdam Island 155 km² (60 sq mi), St Paul Island 18 km² (7 sq mi). *Population*: there is a fluctuating population of scientific missions of c. 140. *Principal settlement*: Port-aux-Français (on Kerguelen) 100. (For information regarding the Antarctic Territories see Other Territories, following this chapter.)
Wallis and Futuna Islands *Area*: 274 km² (106 sq mi). *Population*: 13 700 (1990 est). *Capital*: Mata-Utu 810 (1990 est).

GABON

Official name: La République Gabonaise (The Gabonese Republic).
Member of: UN, OAU, OPEC.
Area: 267 667 km² (103 347 sq mi).
Population: 1 133 000 (1990 est).
Capital and major cities: Libreville 352 000, Port-Gentil 164 000, Masuku (formerly Franceville) 75 000 (1987 est).
Languages: French (official), 40 local languages including Fang (30%).
Religions: Roman Catholic (71%), animist (28%).

GOVERNMENT The President – who is elected by compulsory universal adult suffrage for a seven-year term – appoints a Council of Ministers (over which he presides) and a Prime Minister. The National Assembly has 120 members directly elected for five years. The main political parties are the (former monopoly) Gabonese Democratic Party (PDG), the Gabonese Progress Party (PGP), the African Forum for Reconstruction (FAR) and the Woodcutters' Union (RB).

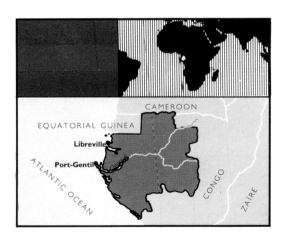

President: Omar Bongo.
Prime Minister: Casimir Oye Mba.

GEOGRAPHY Apart from the narrow coastal plain, low plateaux make up most of the country. *Principal river:* Ogooué. *Highest point:* Mont Iboundji 1580 m (5185 ft).

ECONOMY Petroleum, natural gas, manganese, uranium and iron ore – and a relatively small population – make Gabon the richest Black African country, although most Gabonese are subsistence farmers.

RECENT HISTORY Pro-French Léon M'Ba (1902–67) led the country to independence from France in 1960. Deposed in a coup (1964), he was restored to power by French troops. Under his successor, Omar Bongo, Gabon has continued its pro-Western policies. Pro-democracy demonstrations and strikes, followed by anti-government riots in 1990, prompted France to dispatch troops to Gabon to restore order. President Bongo appointed a transitional government and permitted the establishment of a multi-party system.

GAMBIA

Official name: The Republic of the Gambia.
Member of: UN, OAU, ECOWAS, Commonwealth.
Area: 11 295 km² (4361 sq mi).
Population: 883 000 (1991 est).
Capital and major cities: Banjul 147 000 (city 44 000), Brikama 24 000 (1986 est).
Language: English (official), local languages.
Religions: Sunni Islam (90%), various Protestant Churches (9%) – mainly Anglican.

GOVERNMENT The President and 36 of the 50 members of the House of Representatives are elected by universal adult suffrage every five years. The remaining members of the House are appointed. The President appoints a Vice-President – to lead the government in the House – and a Cabinet of Ministers. The main

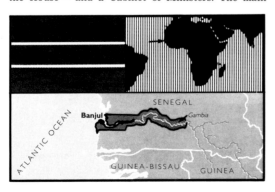

political parties are the People's Progressive Party and the National Convention Party.
President: Sir Dawda Kairaba Jawara.

GEOGRAPHY The Gambia is a narrow low-lying country on either bank of the River Gambia. *Principal river:* Gambia. *Highest point:* an unnamed point on the Senegalese border 43 m (141 ft).

ECONOMY The economy is largely based on the cultivation of groundnuts. Tourism is the major foreign-currency earner.

RECENT HISTORY The Gambia achieved independence from Britain in 1965 under Sir Dawda K. Jawara. In 1981 an attempted coup against his rule encouraged efforts to merge with the neighbouring French-speaking country of Senegal, but the confederation was dissolved in 1989. The Gambia remains a democracy.

GEORGIA

Official name: Sakartvelo (Georgia) or Sakartvelos Respublica (The Republic of Georgia).
Member of: UN, CSCE.
Area: 69 700 km² (26 900 sq mi).
Population: 5 464 000 (1991 census).
Capital and major cities: Tbilisi 1 264 000, Kutaisi 235 000, Rustavi 159 000, Batumi 136 000, Sukhumi 121 000 (1991 census).
Languages: Georgian (70%), Armenian (8%), Russian (6%), Azeri (3%), Ossetian (2%), Greek (2%), Abkhazian (2%).
Religions: Georgian Orthodox majority.

GOVERNMENT The constitution provides for the election by universal adult suffrage of a 250-member Assembly and a President – who appoints a Council of Ministers – for four years. A new constitution is to be drafted. The main political parties are the (coalition nationalist) Round-Table – Free Georgia, the National Democratic Party, the Social Democratic Party and the Georgian Monarchists' Party.
President: Eduard Shevardnadze.
Prime Minister: Tengiz Sigua.

GEOGRAPHY The spine of the Caucasus Mountains forms the N border of Georgia. A lower range, the Little Caucasus, occupies S Georgia. Central Georgia comprises the Kolkhida lowlands. *Principal rivers:* Kura, Rioni. *Highest point:* Elbrus 5642 m (18 510 ft).

ECONOMY Despite a shortage of cultivable land, Georgia has a diversified agricultural sector including tea, citrus fruit, tobacco, cereals, vines, livestock and vegetables. Natural resources include coal, manganese and plentiful hydroelectric power. Machine building, food processing and chemicals are major industries. The private sector is probably more highly developed than in

RUSSIA

BLACK SEA

Kutaisi

Tbilisi

Batumi

Rustavi

TURKEY

ARMENIA

any other former Soviet republic, but the economy was damaged by civil war (1991–92).

RECENT HISTORY Russia annexed Georgia by degrees (1801–78). Following the Russian Revolution (1918), a Georgian republic, allied to Germany, was proclaimed. A British occupation (1918–20) in favour of the Tsarist White Russians failed to win local support, and Georgia was invaded by the Soviet Red Army (1921). Georgia became part of the Transcaucasian Soviet Republic in 1921 and a separate Union Republic within the USSR in 1936. Following the abortive coup by Communist hardliners in Moscow (1991), Georgia declared independence. Locked into a fierce civil war, Georgia remained outside the Commonwealth of Independent States (the defence and economic community founded when the USSR was dissolved in 1991). A temporary state council – led by Eduard Shevardnadze, the former Soviet Foreign Minister – replaced a military council in 1992. The Abkhazian Muslims attempted secession in 1992.

GERMANY

Official name: Bundesrepublik Deutschland (The Federal Republic of Germany).

Member of: UN, EC, NATO, CSCE, WEU, G7, OECD, Council of Europe.

Area: 357 050 km² (137 857 sq mi).

Population: 79 096 000 (1991 est).

Capital and major cities: Berlin (capital in name only; the lower house of parliament is scheduled to move to Berlin in 1995) 3 410 000, Bonn (capital *de facto*) 284 000, Essen 4 700 000 (Essen/Ruhr; city 621 000), Hamburg 1 626 000, Munich (München) 1 218 000, Cologne (Köln) 940 000, Frankfurt 629 000, Dortmund (part of the Essen/ Ruhr agglomeration) 589 000, Düsseldorf 570 000, Stuttgart 566 000, Bremen 546 000, Leipzig 539 000, Duisburg (part of the Essen/Ruhr agglomeration) 530 000,

Dresden 516 000, Hannover 502 000, Nuremberg (Nürnberg) 482 000, Bochum (part of the Essen/Ruhr agglomeration) 390 000, Wuppertal 372 000, Bielefeld 313 000, Chemnitz 310 000, Mannheim 303 000, Magdeburg 290 000, Gelsenkirchen (part of the Essen/Ruhr agglomeration) 288 000, Karlsruhe 267 000, Wiesbaden 255 000, Rostock 255 000, Brunswick (Braunschweig) 254 000, Mönchengladbach 254 000, Münster 250 000, Augsburg 248 000, Kiel 241 000, Krefeld 237 000, Halle 235 000, Aachen 234 000, Oberhausen (part of the Essen/ Ruhr agglomeration) 221 000, Erfurt 220 000, Lübeck 211 000, Hagen 210 000, Kassel 190 000, Saarbrücken 189 000, Freiburg 185 000, Mülheim 176 000, Hamm 175 000, Herne (part of the Essen/Ruhr agglomeration) 175 000, Mainz 175 000, Solingen 162 000, Ludwigshafen 159 000, Leverkusen 158 000, Osnabrück 157 000 (1990 est).

Language: German.

Religions: various Protestant Churches (mainly Lutheran; 34%), Roman Catholic (35%).

GOVERNMENT Each of the 16 states (Länder; singular Länd) is represented in the 79-member upper house of Parliament – the Federal Council (Bundesrat) – by three, four or six members of the state government (depending on population). These members are appointed for a limited period. The lower house – the Federal Assembly (Bundestag) – has 662 members elected for four years by universal adult suffrage under a mixed system of single-member constituencies and proportional representation. Executive power rests with the Federal Government, led by the Federal Chancellor – who is elected by the Bundestag. The Federal President is elected for a five-year term by a combined sitting of the Bundesrat and an equal number of representatives of the states. The Parliament, Government, ministries and the Federal Chancellor and President are based in Bonn, although Berlin was named as capital in August 1990. The main political parties include the (socialist) SPD (Social Democratic Party), the (conservative) CDU (Christian Democratic Union) and CSU (Christian Social Union, its Bavarian equivalent), the (liberal) FDP (Free Democratic Party), Die Grünen (the Green Party), and the PDS (Party of Democratic Socialism; the former East German Communist Party). Each state has its own Parliament and Government.

Federal President: Dr Richard von Weizsäcker.
Federal Chancellor: Dr Helmut Kohl.

LANDER Baden-Württemberg *Area:* 35 752 km² (13 803 sq mi). *Population:* 9 619 000 (1990 est). *Capital:* Stuttgart.

Bavaria (Bayern) *Area:* 70 546 km² (27 238 sq mi). *Population:* 11 221 000 (1990 est). *Capital:* Munich (München).

Berlin *Area:* 883 km² (341 sq mi). *Population:* 3 410 000 (1990 est). *Capital:* Berlin.

Brandenburg *Area:* 28 016 km² (10 817 sq mi). *Population:* 2 641 000 (1990 est). *Capital:* Potsdam.

Bremen *Area:* 404 km² (156 sq mi). *Population:* 674 000 (1990 est). *Capital:* Bremen.

Hamburg *Area*: 755 km² (292 sq mi). *Population*: 1 626 000 (1990 est). *Capital*: Hamburg.

Hesse (Hessen) *Area*: 21 114 km² (8152 sq mi). *Population*: 5 661 000 (1990 est). *Capital*: Wiesbaden.

Lower Saxony (Niedersachsen) *Area*: 47 431 km² (18 313 sq mi). *Population*: 7 284 000 (1990 est). *Capital*: Hannover.

Mecklenburg-West Pomerania (Mecklenburg-Vorpommern) *Area*: 26 694 km² (10 307 sq mi). *Population*: 1 964 000 (1990 est). *Capital*: Schwerin.

North Rhine-Westphalia (Nordrhein-Westfalen) *Area*: 34 066 km² (13 153 sq mi). *Population*: 17 104 000 (1990 est). *Capital*: Düsseldorf.

Rhineland-Palatinate (Rheinland-Pfalz) *Area*: 19 848 km² (7663 sq mi). *Population*: 3 702 000 (1990 est). *Capital*: Mainz.

Saarland *Area*: 2571 km² (993 sq mi). *Population*: 1 065 000 (1990 est). *Capital*: Saarbrücken.

Saxony (Sachsen) *Area*: 17 713 km² (6839 sq mi). *Population*: 4 901 000 (1990 est). *Capital*: Dresden.

Saxony-Anhalt (Sachsen-Anhalt) *Area*: 20 297 km² (7837 sq mi). *Population*: 2 965 000 (1990 est). *Capital*: Magdeburg.

Schleswig-Holstein *Area*: 15 720 km² (6069 sq mi). *Population*: 2 595 000 (1990 est). *Capital*: Kiel.

Thuringia (Thüringen) *Area*: 15 209 km² (5872 sq mi). *Population*: 2 684 000 (1990 est). *Capital*: Erfurt.

GEOGRAPHY The North German Plain – a region of fertile farmlands and sandy heaths – is drained by the Rivers Elbe and Weser and their tributaries. In the west, the plain merges with the North Rhine lowlands which contain the Ruhr coalfield and over fifth of the country's population. A belt of plateaux, formed of old hard rocks, crosses the country from east to west and includes the Hunsrück and Eifel highlands in the Rhineland, the Taunus and Westerwald uplands in Hesse, and extends into the Harz and Erz Mountains in Thuringia. The Rhine cuts through these central plateaux in a deep gorge. In southern Germany, the Black Forest (Schwarzwald) separates the Rhine valley from the fertile valleys and scarplands of Swabia. The forested edge of the Bohemian uplands marks the Czech border, while the Bavarian Alps form the frontier with Austria. *Principal rivers*: Rhine (Rhein), Elbe, Danube (Donau), Oder, Moselle (Mosel), Neckar, Havel, Leine, Weser. *Highest point*: Zugspitze 2963 m (9721 ft).

ECONOMY Germany is the world's third industrial power after the USA and Japan. The country's recovery after World War II has been called the 'German economic miracle'. The principal industries include mechanical and electrical engineering, chemicals, textiles, food processing and vehicles, with heavy industry and engineering concentrated in the Ruhr, chemicals in cities on the Rhine, and motor vehicles in large provincial centres such as Stuttgart. From the 1980s, there has been a spectacular growth in high-technology industries. Apart from coal and brown coal, and relatively small deposits of iron ore, bauxite, copper ore, nickel, tin, silver, potash and salt, Germany has relatively few natural resources, and the country relies heavily upon imports. Labour has also been in short supply, and large numbers of 'guest workers' (Gastarbeiter) – particularly from Turkey and the former Yugoslavia – have been recruited. Since 1990 the labour shortage in the western part of the country has been met by migration from the east, the former German Democratic Republic. Service industries employ almost twice as many people as manufacturing industry. Banking and finance are major foreign-currency earners, and Frankfurt is one of the world's leading financial and business centres.

The unification of Germany in October 1990 presented a major problem for the German economy. The GDR's economy had previously been the most successful in CMEA (Comecon), but, compared with West Germany, it lagged in terms of production, quality, design, profitability and standards of living. A trust – the Treuhandanstalt – was established to oversee the privatization of the 8000 state-run firms in eastern Germany. The main industries of the former GDR include machinery and transportation equipment, steel, cement, chemicals, fertilizers and plastics, but many of these have been unable to compete with their western counterparts. The Trabant and Wartburg car firms, for example, ceased production in 1991, and, bought by West

German firms, began production of western models. However, many other East German firms have gone bankrupt, and by late 1992 unemployment in the former GDR stood at nearly 20%.

The main German agricultural products include hops (for beer), grapes (for wine), sugar beet, wheat, barley, and dairy products. The collectivized farms of the former GDR – which provided that country's basic food needs – were privatized in 1990–91. Forests cover almost one third of the country and support a flourishing timber industry.

RECENT HISTORY Defeat in World War I led to the loss of much territory in Europe and the colonies overseas, the end of the German monarchies, the imposition of a substantial sum for reparations, and the occupation of the Rhineland by Allied forces until 1930. The liberal Weimar republic (1919–33) could not bring economic or political stability. In the early 1930s the National Socialist German Workers', or Nazi, Party increased in popularity, urging the establishment of a strong centralized government, an aggressive foreign policy, 'Germanic character' and the overturn of the postwar settlement. In 1933, the Nazi leader Adolf Hitler (1889–1945) became Chancellor and in 1934 President.

His Third Reich (empire) annexed Austria (1938), dismembered Czechoslovakia (1939), and embarked on the extermination of the Jews and others that the Nazis regarded as 'inferior'. In furtherance of territorial claims in Poland, Hitler concluded the Nazi-Soviet Non-Aggression Pact (24 August), which allowed the USSR to annex the Baltic republics (Estonia, Latvia and Lithuania) and agreed to divide Poland between the Soviets and the Nazis. Invading Poland on 1 September1939, Hitler launched Germany into war.

Britain and France declared war on Germany two days later but could do nothing to help the Poles. After a pause known as the 'Phoney War', Hitler turned towards the west (1940) and invaded Denmark, Norway, Belgium, the Netherlands, Luxembourg and France. After Italy entered the war against the UK and France (1941), the Balkan Front opened up, when Italy invaded Albania and Greece. The German invasion of the USSR (1941) opened the Eastern Front. Also in 1941 Japan joined the Axis powers (Germany and Italy) by attacking the US naval base at Pearl Harbor, Hawaii. At the height of Axis power in 1942, Germany controlled – directly or through allies – virtually the whole of Europe except the British Isles, and neutral Switzerland, Sweden, Spain and Portugal. The tide against the Axis countries turned in North Africa late in 1942. In 1943, Italy surrendered, and Soviet forces started to push back the Germans. In 1944 the Allied landings in Normandy began the liberation of Western Europe, and advances into the Balkans cleared the Germans from Soviet territory. After massive Allied bombing attacks, the end came swiftly for Germany. Hitler committed suicide in April 1945 and Berlin fell to the Soviets early in May.

In 1945, Germany lost substantial territories to Poland, and was divided – as was its capital, Berlin – into four zones of occupation by the Allies (Britain, France, the USA and the USSR). Their intention was a united,

disarmed Germany, but cooperation between the Allies rapidly broke down, and in 1948–49 the USSR blockaded West Berlin. The western zones of Germany were merged economically in 1948. After the merger of the western zones to form the Federal Republic of Germany, the German Democratic Republic was proclaimed in the Soviet zone (October 1949). The GDR's economic progress suffered by comparison with that of the Federal Republic. Food shortages and repressive Communist rule led to an uprising in 1953. West Germany gained sovereignty – as a member of the Western alliance – in 1955.

The division of Germany was only grudgingly accepted in West Germany. Chancellor Konrad Adenauer (1876–1967) refused to recognize East Germany as a separate state and relations with the Soviet Union remained uncertain. Major problems with the Eastern bloc included the undefined status of the areas taken over by Poland in 1945 and the difficult position of West Berlin – a part of the Federal Republic isolated within Communist East Germany. Relations between the two Germanys were soured as large numbers of East Germans fled to the West, and this outflow was stemmed only when Walter Ulbricht (East German Communist Party leader 1950–71) ordered the building of the Berlin Wall (1961).

Adenauer strove to gain the acceptance of West Germany back into Western Europe through reconciliation with France and participation in the European Community. The economic revival of Germany begun by Adenauer continued under his Christian Democrat (conservative) successors as Chancellor – Ludwig Erhard (1963–66) and Georg Kiesinger (1966–69). Under the Social Democrat Chancellors – Willy Brandt (1969–74) and Helmut Schmidt (1974–82) – treaties were signed with the Soviet Union (1970) and Poland (recognizing the Oder-Neisse line as Poland's western frontier), and relations with the GDR were normalized (1972). Under Helmut Kohl – Christian Democrat Chancellor from 1982 – West Germany has continued its impressive economic development and enthusiastic membership of the EC.

In the late 1980s, West Germany acted as an economic and cultural magnet for much of Eastern Europe. The root causes of the GDR's problems remained, however, and resurfaced in the late 1980s. The ageing Communist leadership led by Erich Honecker proved unresponsive to the mood of greater freedom emanating from Gorbachov's USSR. In 1989 fresh floods of East Germans left the GDR for the West by way of Poland, Czechoslovakia and Hungary. Massive public demonstrations in favour of reform – led to the appointment of a new leader, Egon Krenz. The Berlin Wall was reopened (November 1989) allowing free movement between the two Germanys, but demonstrations in favour of more radical change continued. A government including members of opposition groups was appointed. Free elections were held in East Germany in March 1990 when the Communist Party was reduced to a minority. When the East German economy collapsed, the call for German reunification became unstoppable. Despite the initial opposition of the USSR, the reunification of Germany as a full EC and NATO member was agreed. German reunification took place on 3 October 1990 and all-German elections took place in December 1990. Soviet troops are scheduled to withdraw from the former GDR by 1994. Reunited Germany is the greatest economic power in Europe, and, after Russia, the most populous state. However, reunification has proved costly to the German economy.

GHANA

Official name: The Republic of Ghana.

Member of: UN, OAU, ECOWAS, Commonwealth.

Area: 238 537 km² (92 099 sq mi).

Population: 15 509 000 (1991 est).

Capital and major cities: Accra 1 580 000, Kumasi 490 000, Tema (part of the Accra agglomeration) 190 000, Sekondi-Takoradi 175 000, Tamale 170 000 (1988 est).

Languages: English (official), Asante, Ewe, Ga.

Religions: Various Protestant Churches (30%), Sunni Islam (20%), Roman Catholic (over 25%), animist (17%).

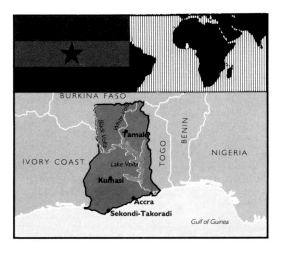

GOVERNMENT Under a new constitution (1992), a 140-member Assembly and a President are elected for four years by universal adult suffrage. The main political parties include the National Democratic Convention (NDC), the (Nkrumahist left-wing) People's National Convention Party and the New Patriotic Party.

President: Flight. Lt. Jerry Rawlings.

GEOGRAPHY Most of the country comprises low-lying plains and plateaux. In the centre, the Volta Basin – which ends in steep escarpments – contains the large Lake Volta reservoir. *Principal river:* Volta. *Highest point:* Afadjato 872 m (2860 ft).

ECONOMY Political instability and mismanagement have damaged the economy of Ghana. Nearly 50% of the labour force is involved in agriculture, with cocoa being the main cash crop. Forestry and mining for bauxite, gold and manganese are also important activities.

RECENT HISTORY After World War II, the prosperity of the cocoa industry, increasing literacy and the dynamism of Dr Kwame Nkrumah (1909–72) helped the Gold Coast set the pace for decolonization in Black Africa. After independence from Britain in 1957 – as Ghana – Nkrumah's grandiose policies and increasingly dictatorial rule led to his overthrow in a military coup in 1966. Ghana has since struggled to overcome its economic and political problems. There were six coups in 20 years, including two by Flight Lieutenant Jerry Rawlings (1979 and 1982). A multi-party system was restored in 1992.

GREECE

Official name: Ellenikí Dimokrátia (Hellenic Republic) or Ellás (Greece).

Member of: UN, EC, NATO, Council of Europe, CSCE, OECD, WEU (associate).

Area: 131 957 km² (50 949 sq mi).

Population: 10 269 000 (1991 census).

Capital and major cities: Athens (Athínai) 3 097 000, Thessaloníki (formerly known as Salonika) 706 000, Piraeus (Piraiévs; part of the Athens agglomeration) 196 000, Patras (Pátrai) 155 000, Volos 107 000, Lárisa 102 000, Heraklion (Iráklion, formerly known as Candia) 102 000, Kavalla 57 000, Canea (Khania) 48 000 (all including suburbs; 1991 census).

Language: Greek (official).

Religion: Orthodox (98%; official).

GOVERNMENT The 300-member Parliament is elected for four years by universal adult suffrage under a system of proportional representation. The President – who is elected for a five-year term by Parliament – appoints a Prime Minister (who commands a majority in Parliament) and other Ministers. The main political parties include the (conservative) NDP (New Democracy Party), PASOK (the Pan-Hellenic Socialist Party), the (centre) Democratic Renewal Party, and the (Communist-led) Left Alliance.

President: Konstantinos Karamanlis.

Prime Minister: Konstantinos Mitsotakis.

SELF-GOVERNING COMMUNITY Mount Athos (Ayion Oros) (an autonomous monks' republic) *Area:* 336 km² (130 sq mi). *Population:* 1400 (1990 est). *Capital:* Karyai.

GEOGRAPHY Over 80% of Greece is mountainous. The mainland is dominated by the Pindus Mountains, which extend from Albania south into the Peloponnese

when, with British and US aid, the monarchists emerged victorious. Continued instability in the 1960s led to a military coup in 1967. King Constantine II, who had not initially opposed the coup, unsuccessfully appealed for the overthrow of the junta and went into exile. The dictatorship of the colonels ended in 1974 when their encouragement of a Greek Cypriot coup brought Greece to the verge of war with Turkey. Civilian government was restored, and a new republican constitution was adopted in 1975. Greece has since forged closer links with Western Europe, in particular through membership of the EC (1981). Greek opposition prevented international recognition of the former Yugoslav republic of Macedonia in 1992.

Peninsula. The Rhodope Mountains lie along the Bulgarian border. Greece has some 2000 islands, of which only 154 are inhabited. *Principal rivers:* Aliákmon, Piniós, Akhelóös. *Highest point:* Mount Olympus 2911 m (9550 ft).

ECONOMY Agriculture involves over one quarter of the labour force. Much of the land is marginal – in particular the extensive sheep pastures. Greece is largely self-sufficient in wheat, barley, maize, sugar beet, fruit, vegetables and cheese, and produces enough wine, olives (and olive oil) and tobacco for export. The industrial sector is expanding rapidly and includes the processing of natural resources such as petroleum and natural gas, lignite, uranium and bauxite. Tourism, the large merchant fleet, and money sent back by Greeks working abroad are all important foreign-currency earners. Greece is burdened by a large state sector and receives special economic assistance from the EC.

RECENT HISTORY Greece in the 20th century has been marked by great instability. Eleuthérios Venizélos (1864–1936) dominated Greek politics from 1910 to 1935. A period of rivalry between republicans and royalists. An attempt by his rival King Constantine I to seize Anatolia from Turkey (1921–22) ended in military defeat and the establishment of a republic in 1924. The monarchy was restored in 1935, but it depended upon a military leader, General Ioannis Metaxas (1871–1941), who, claiming the threat from Communism as justification, ruled as virtual dictator. The nation was deeply divided. The German invasion of 1941 was met by rival resistance groups of Communists and monarchists, and the subsequent civil war between these factions lasted from 1945 to 1949,

GRENADA

Official name: The State of Grenada.
Member of: UN, OAS, Commonwealth, CARICOM.
Area: 344 km² (133 sq mi).
Population: 96 000 (1991 est).
Capital: St George's 36 000 (city 7500) (1989 est).
Language: English (official); French-African patios.
Religions: Roman Catholic (over 60%), Anglican.

GOVERNMENT The Governor General – the representative of the British Queen as sovereign of Grenada – appoints a Prime Minister (who commands a majority in the House of Representatives), other members of the Cabinet and the 13-member Senate (the upper house of Parliament). The 15-member House of Representatives is elected for five years by universal adult suffrage. The main political parties include the National Democratic Congress, the National Party, the United Labour Party, and the New National Party.
Prime Minister: Nicholas Braithwaite.

GEOGRAPHY A forested mountain ridge covers much of this well-watered island. The island of Carria-

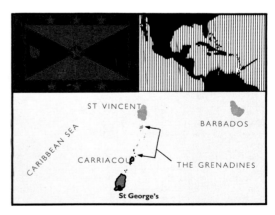

cou forms part of Grenada. *Principal rivers:* there are no significant rivers. *Highest point:* Mount St Catherine 840 m (2706 ft).

ECONOMY   The production of spices, in particular nutmeg, is the mainstay of a largely agricultural economy. Tourism is increasing in importance.

RECENT HISTORY   Independence from Britain was gained in 1974. The left-wing New Jewel Movement seized power in a coup in 1979. In 1983 the PM Maurice Bishop was killed in a further coup in which more extreme members of the government seized power. Acting upon a request from East Caribbean islands to intervene, US and Caribbean forces landed in Grenada. After several days' fighting, the coup leaders were detained. Constitutional rule was restored in 1984.

GUATEMALA

Official name: República de Guatemala (Republic of Guatemala).
Member of: UN, OAS, CACM.
Area: 108 889 km² (42 042 sq mi).
Population: 9 454 000 (1991 est).
Capital and major cities: Guatemala City 2 000 000, Puerto Barrios 338 000, Quezaltenango 246 000, Escuintla 61 000 (all including suburbs; 1989 est).
Language: Spanish (official); Mayan languages (45%).
Religions: Roman Catholic (official; 70%), various Protestant evangelical Churches (30%).

GOVERNMENT   A President – who appoints a Cabinet – and a Vice President are elected for a five-year term by universal adult suffrage. The 100-member National Congress is also directly elected for five years – 75 members are directly elected; the remaining 25 members are returned under a system of proportional represen-

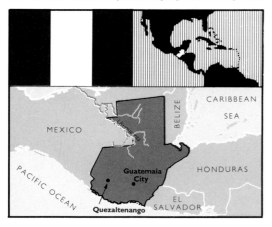

tation. The main political parties include the (right-wing) Christian Democratic Party (PDGC), the (centre) Union of National Centre (UCN), the (centre-right) Movement for Action and Solidarity (MAS), and the (coalition left-wing) Platforma NO-Venta.
President: Jorge Antonio Serrano.

GEOGRAPHY   Pacific and Atlantic coastal lowlands are separated by a mountain chain containing over 30 volcanoes. *Principal river:* Usumacinta, Montagua. *Highest point:* Tajumulco 4220 m (13 881 ft)

ECONOMY   More than one half of the labour force is involved in agriculture. Coffee is the major export, while the other main crops include sugar cane and bananas.

RECENT HISTORY   For the first half of the 20th century Guatemala was ruled by dictators allied to landowners. However, in the 1950s President Jacobo Arbenz expropriated large estates, dividing them among the peasantry. Accused of being a Communist, he was deposed by the army with US military aid (1954). For over 30 years, the left was suppressed, leading to the emergence of guerrilla armies. Thousands of dissidents were killed or disappeared. Civilian government was restored in 1986, but unrest continues and there have been serious abuses of human rights by the military.

GUINEA

Official name: La République de Guinée (The Republic of Guinea).
Member of: UN, OAU, ECOWAS.
Area: 245 857 (94 926 sq mi).
Population: 7 052 000 (1991 est).
Capital and major cities: Conakry 705 000, Kankan 89 000, Kindia 56 000 (1983 est).
Languages: French (official), Soussou (11%), Fulani (40%).
Religion: Sunni Islam (85%), Roman Catholic and animist minorities.

GOVERNMENT   Power is exercised by the Military Committee for National Recovery, whose President is head of state and of government. There are no political parties.
President: Gen. Lansana Conte.

GEOGRAPHY   Tropical rain forests cover the coastal plain. The interior highlands and plains are covered by grass and scrubland. There are mountains in the southwest. *Principal river:* Niger, Bafing, Konkouré, Kogon. *Highest point:* Mont Nimba 1752 m (5748 ft).

ECONOMY   Bauxite accounts for 80% of Guinea's exports. However, over 75% of the labour force is involved in agriculture, producing bananas, oil palm and citrus fruits for export, and maize, rice and cassava

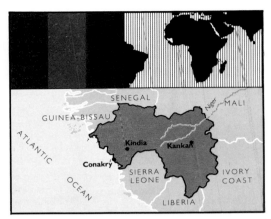

as subsistence crops. Despite mineral wealth, Guinea is one of the world's poorest countries and relies heavily on aid.

RECENT HISTORY Unlike the rest of French Africa, Guinea voted for a complete separation from France in 1958, suffering severe French reprisals as a result. The authoritarian radical leader Sékou Touré (1922–84) isolated Guinea, but he became reconciled with France in 1978. The leaders of a military coup (1984) have achieved some economic reforms.

GUINEA-BISSAU

Official name: Republica da Guiné-Bissau (Republic of Guinea-Bissau).

Member of: UN, OAU, ECOWAS.

Area: 36 125 km² (13 948 sq mi).

Population: 994 000 (1991 est).

Capital and major towns: Bissau 125 000 (1988 est), Bafatá 13 500 (1980 est).

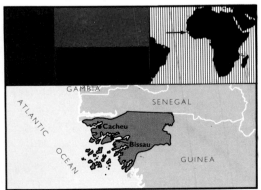

Languages: Portuguese (official), Crioulo.

Religions: Animist (55%), Sunni Islam (40%), Roman Catholic (5%).

GOVERNMENT The 150-member Assembly is elected for five years by universal adult suffrage. The Assembly elects a President, who appoints Ministers. The main political parties include the (former monopoly) PAIGC, the Guinea-Bissau Resistance-Bafata Movement (RGB-MB), the Democratic Front (FD) and the Social Democratic Front (FDS).

President: Brig. Gen. João Bernardo Vieira.

Prime Minister: Carlos Correia.

GEOGRAPHY Most of the country is low-lying, with swampy coastal lowlands and a flat forested interior plain. The northeast is mountainous. *Principal rivers:* Cacheu, Mansôa, Géba, Corubel. *Highest point:* an unnamed point in the Fouta Djallon plateau 180 m (591 ft).

ECONOMY The country has one of the lowest standards of living in the world. Its subsistence economy is based mainly on rice. Palm kernels and timber are exported.

RECENT HISTORY The colony of Portuguese Guinea was created in 1879. Failing to secure reform by peaceful means, the PAIGC movement mounted a liberation war (1961–1974). Independence was proclaimed in 1973 and recognized by Portugal in 1974. Following a military coup in 1980, the aim of union with Cape Verde was dropped. Multi-party politics were introduced in 1991.

GUYANA

Official name: The Cooperative Republic of Guyana.

Member of: UN, Commonwealth, OAS, CARICOM.

Area: 214 969 km² (83 000 sq mi).

Population: 760 000 (1991 est).

Capital and major cities: Georgetown 187 000, Linden 35 000 (including suburbs; 1986 est).

Languages: English (official), Hindu, Urdu.

Religions: Hinduism (34%), various Protestant Churches (34%) – mainly Anglican; Roman Catholic (18%), Sunni Islam (9%).

GOVERNMENT The 65-member National Assembly is elected for five years under a system of proportional representation by universal adult suffrage. The President – the leader of the majority in the Assembly – appoints a Cabinet led by the First Vice-President. The main political parties are the (left-wing) People's National Congress, the (left-wing) People's Progressive Party, the (conservative) United Force, and the (left-wing) Working People's Alliance.

President: Cheddi Jagan.

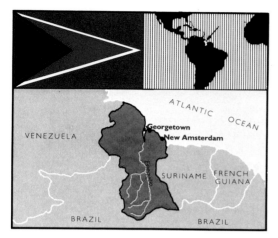

First Vice-President and Prime Minister: Samuel Hinds.

GEOGRAPHY A coastal plain is protected from the sea by dykes. Tropical rain forest covers much of the interior. *Principal rivers:* Essequibo, Courantyne, Mazaruni, Demarara. *Highest point:* Mt Roraima 2772 m (9094 ft).

ECONOMY Guyana depends on mining bauxite and growing sugar cane and rice. Nationalization and emigration have caused economic problems.

RECENT HISTORY Guyana is the former colony of British Guiana. From the 1840s large numbers of Indian and Chinese labourers were imported from Asia to work on sugar plantations. Racial tension between their descendants – now the majority – and the black community (descended from imported African slaves) led to violence in 1964 and 1978. Guyana has been independent since 1966. After 1987 President Hoyte introduced liberal economic reforms, but austerity measures have been in force since 1988.

HAITI

Official name: La République d'Haïti (Republic of Haiti).

Member of: UN, OAS, CARICOM.

Area: 27 750 km² (10 714 sq mi).

Population: 6 486 000 (1990 est).

Capital and major cities: Port-au-Prince 1 144 000, Jacmel 217 000, Les Cayes 215 000, Jérémie 152 000 (all including suburbs; 1988 est).

Languages: Creole (90%) and French (both official).

Religions: Voodoo (majority), Roman Catholic (official).

GOVERNMENT The constitution provides for elections by universal adult suffrage for a 27-member Senate, a 77-member Chamber of Deputies and a President, all to serve a five-year term. A large number of political parties were formed between 1987 and 1990, but constitutional rule was overturned by a military coup in 1991.

Acting President and Prime Minister: Marc Bazin.

GEOGRAPHY Haiti is the western part of the island of Hispaniola. Mountain ranges run from east to west, alternating with densely populated valleys and plains. *Principal river:* Artibonite. *Highest point:* Pic La Selle 2680 m (8793 ft).

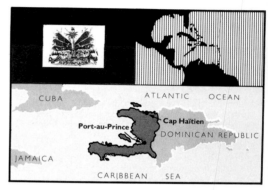

ECONOMY Two thirds of the labour force is involved in agriculture, mainly growing crops for domestic consumption. Coffee is the principal cash crop. With few resources, overpopulated Haiti is the poorest country in the western hemisphere.

RECENT HISTORY Coups, instability and tension between blacks and mulattos wracked modern Haiti until the US intervened (1915–35). President François Duvalier ('Papa Doc'; in office 1956–71) and his son Jean-Claude ('Baby Doc'; 1971–86) cowed the country into submission by means of their infamous private militia, the Tontons Macoutes. The military took control after the younger Duvalier fled during a period of violent popular unrest. A period of unrest preceded Haiti's only democratic multi-party elections in 1991. However, the victor – a radical priest, Fr. Aristide – was toppled by the military within seven months. Violence and intimidation by the Tontons Macoutes remains endemic. Many thousands of Haitians attempt to enter the USA illegally every year.

HONDURAS

Official name: La República de Honduras (Republic of Honduras).

Member of: UN, OAS, CACM.

Area: 112 088 km² (43 277 sq mi).

Population: 4 708 000 (1991 est).

Capital and major cities: Tegucigalpa 648 000, San Pedro Sula 301 000, La Ceiba 72 000 (all including suburbs; 1988 census).

Language: Spanish (official).

Religion: Roman Catholic (85%), various Protestant evangelical Churches (15%).

GOVERNMENT The President and the 134-member National Assembly are elected by universal adult suffrage for four years. The main political parties are the PLH (Liberal Party of Honduras), the (right-wing) PN (National Party), and PINU-SD (Party of Innovation and Unity).

President: Rafael Callejas.

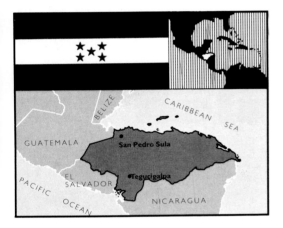

GEOGRAPHY Over three quarters of Honduras is mountainous, and there are small coastal plains. *Principal rivers:* Patuca, Ulúa. *Highest point:* Cerio las Minas 2849 m (9347 ft).

ECONOMY The majority of Hondurans work in agriculture, but despite agrarian reform, living standards remain low. Bananas and coffee are the leading exports. Fluctuations in the price of these commodities on the world market have caused economic problems since the 1980s. There are few natural resources.

RECENT HISTORY Between independence (1821) and the early 20th century, Honduras experienced constant political upheaval and wars with neighbouring countries. US influence was immense, largely owing to the substantial investments of the powerful United Fruit Company in banana production. After a short civil war in 1925, a succession of military dictators governed Honduras until 1980. Since then the country has had democratically elected pro-US centre-right civilian governments.

HUNGARY

Official name: Magyarország (Hungary) or Magyar Köztársásag (The Hungarian Republic)

Member of: UN, CSCE, Council of Europe.

Area: 93 036 km² (35 921 sq mi).

Population: 10 375 000 (1990 census).

Capital and major cities: Budapest 2 018 000, Debrecen 214 000, Miskolc 194 000, Szeged 176 000, Pécs 170 000, Györ 130 000, Nyíregyháza 115 000, Székésfehérvár 109 000, Kecskemét 104 000 (1990 census).

Language: Magyar (Hungarian) (97%), German (2%), Slovak (1%).

Religions: Roman Catholic (56%), Calvinist and Lutheran (22%).

GOVERNMENT The 386-member National Assembly is elected for five years by universal adult suffrage. It comprises 58 members elected from a national list under a system of proportional representation, 152 members elected on a county basis and 176 elected from single-member constituencies. An executive President – who is elected by the Assembly – appoints a Cabinet and a Prime Minister from the majority in the Assembly. The main political parties include the (centre right) Democratic Forum (MDF), the (liberal) Alliance of Free Democrats, the Socialist Party (formerly the Communist Party), the Smallholders' Party (ISP), the Federation of Young Democrats, and the Christian Democratic People's Party (KDNP).

President: Arpad Goncz.

Prime Minister: Jozsef Antall.

GEOGRAPHY Hungary west of the River Danube is an undulating lowland. There are thickly wooded highlands in the northeast. The southeast is a great expanse of flat plain. *Principal rivers:* Danube (Duna), Tisza, Drava. *Highest point:* Kékes 1015 m (3330 ft).

ECONOMY Nearly one fifth of the labour force is involved in agriculture. Major crops include cereals (maize, wheat and barley), sugar beet, fruit, and grapes for wine. Despite considerable reserves of coal, Hungary imports more than half of its energy needs. The steel, chemical fertilizer, pharmaceutical, machinery and vehicle industries are important. Since the early 1980s, private enterprise and foreign investment have been encouraged, and between 1989 and 1991 most of the large state enterprises were privatized.

RECENT HISTORY In the settlement after World War I, Hungary lost two thirds of its territory. The Regent, Admiral Miklás Horthy (1868–1957), cooperated with Hitler during World War II in an attempt to regain territory, but defeat in 1945 resulted in occupation by the Red Army, and a Communist People's Republic was established in 1949. The Hungarian Uprising in 1956 was a heroic attempt to overthrow Communist rule, but was quickly suppressed by Soviet forces, and its leader, Imre

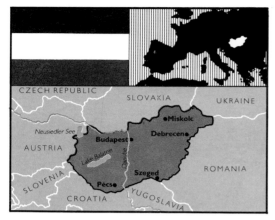

Nagy, was executed. János Kadar – Party Secretary 1956–88 – tried to win support with economic progress. However, in the late 1980s reformers in the Communist Party gained the upper hand, and talks with opposition groups led to agreement on a transition to a fully democratic, multi-party state. The (Communist) Hungarian Socialist Workers' Party transformed itself into the Socialist Party but was heavily defeated in the first free elections in May 1990 when conservative and liberal parties won most seats. Soviet troops left Hungary in 1990, and the country has joined Western European organizations and established a free-market economy. The status of over 3 000 000 Hungarians who are citizens of Slovakia, Romania and the former Yugoslavia has become an issue.

ICELAND

Official name: Lýdveldid Island (The Republic of Iceland).

Member of: UN, NATO, EFTA, Council of Europe, CSCE, OECD.

Area: 103 001 km² (39 769 sq mi).

Population: 258 000 (1991 est).

Capital and major cities: Reykjavik 146 000 (city 98 000), Kópavogur 16 000 and Hafnarfjördhur 15 000 are part of the Reykjavik agglomeration, Akureyri 14 000, Keflavik 7500 (1990 est).

Language: Icelandic (official).

Religion: Evangelical Lutheran (93%).

GOVERNMENT The 63-member Althing (Parliament) is elected under a system of proportional representation by universal adult suffrage for a four-year term. The Althing elects 20 of its members to sit as the Upper House and the remaining 43 members to sit as the Lower House. The President – who is also directly elected for four years – appoints a Prime Minister and a Cabinet

who are responsible to the Althing. The main political parties include the (conservative) Independence Party, the Progressive Party, the (socialist) People's Alliance, the Social Democratic Party, and the Women's Alliance.

President: Vigdis Finnbogadottir.
Prime Minister: David Oddsson.

GEOGRAPHY The greater part of Iceland has a volcanic landscape with hot springs, geysers and some 200 volcanoes – some of them active. Much of the country is tundra. The south and centre are covered by glacial icefields. *Principal rivers:* Thjórsá, Skjalfanda Fljót. *Highest point:* Hvannadalshnúkur 2119 m (6952 ft).

ECONOMY The fishing industry provides the majority of Iceland's exports. Hydroelectric power is used in the aluminium-smelting industry, while geothermal power warms extensive greenhouses. Ample grazing land makes the country self-sufficient in meat and dairy products. Economic problems include high inflation and over dependence upon a single export.

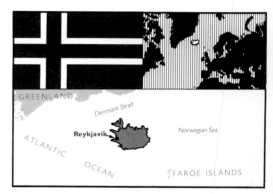

RECENT HISTORY Icelandic nationalism grew in the 19th century, and in 1918 Iceland gained independence from Denmark. However, the two countries remained linked by their shared monarchy. In World War II the Danish link was severed and a republic was declared (1944). Disputes over fishing rights in Icelandic territorial waters led to clashes with British naval vessels in the 1950s and 1970s.

INDIA

Official name: Bharat (Republic of India).

Member of: UN, Commonwealth, SAARC.

Area: 3 287 263 km² (1 269 212 sq mi) – including the Indian-held part of Jammu and Kashmir.

Population: 844 324 000 (1991 census) – including the Indian-held part of Jammu and Kashmir.

Capital and major cities: Delhi 8 375 000 (city 7 175 000), Bombay 12 572 000 (city 9 910 000), Calcutta

10 916 000 (city 4 388 00), Madras 5 361 000 (city 3 795 000), Hyderabad 4 280 000 (city 3 005 000), Bangalore 4 087 000 (city 2 651 000), Ahmedabad 3 298 000 (city 2 873 000), Pune (formerly Poona) 2 485 000 (city 1 560 000), Kanpur 2 111 000 (city 1 958 000), Nagpur 1 661 000 (city 1 622 000), Lucknow 1 642 000 (city 1 592 000), Surat 1 517 000 (city 1 497 000), Jaipur 1 514 000 (city 1 455 000), Kochi (formerly Cochin) 1 140 000 (city 564 000), Coimbatore 1 136 000 (city 853 000), Vadodara (formerly Baroda) 1 115 000 (city 1 021 000), Indore 1 104 000 (city 1 087 000), Patna 1 099 000 (city 917 000), Madurai 1 094 000 (city 952 000), Bhopal 1 064 000, Visakhapatnam 1 052 000 (city 750 000), Varanasi (formerly Banaras) 1 026 000, Kalyan (part of the Bombay agglomeration) 1 014 000, Ludhiana 1 012 000, Agra 956 000 (city 899 000), Hoara (part of the Calcutta agglomeration) 946 000, Jabalpur 887 000 (city 740 000), Allahabad 858 000 (city 806 000), Meerut 847 000 (city 752 000), Vijaywada 845 000 (city 701 000), Jamshedpur 835 000 (city 461 000) (1991 census).

Languages: Hindi (30%; official), English (official), Bengali (8%), Telugu (8%), Marathi (8%), Tamil (7%), Urdu (5%), Gujarati (5%), with over 1600 other languages.

Religions: Hindu (83%), Sunni Islam (11%), Christian (mainly Roman Catholic) (nearly 3%).

GOVERNMENT India is a federal republic in which each of the 25 states has its own legislature. The upper house of the federal parliament – the 250-member Council of States (Rajya Sabha) – consists of 12 members nominated by the President and 238 members elected by the assemblies of individual states. One third of the Council retires every two years. The lower house – the House of the People (Lok Sabha) – consists of 542 members elected for a five-year term by universal adult suffrage, plus two nominated members. The President – who serves for five years – is chosen by an electoral college consisting of the federal parliament and the state assemblies. The President appoints a Prime Minister – who commands a majority in the House – and a Council of Ministers, who are responsible to the House. The main political parties include the Congress (I) Party, the Janata Dal (People's Party), the (right-wing Hindu) Bharatiya Janata Party (Indian People's Party), the Communist Party of India – Marxist, the Communist Party of India, and a number of regional groupings.

President: Ramaswamy Venkataraman.
Prime Minister: P.V. Narasimha Rao.

STATES AND TERRITORIES Andhra Pradesh *Area*: 276 814 km² (106 878 sq mi). *Population*: 66 355 000 (1991 census). *Capital*: Hyderabad.

Arunachal Pradesh *Area*: 83 587 km² (32 269 sq mi). *Population*: 858 000 (1991 census). *Capital*: Itanagar.

Assam *Area*: 78 523 km² (30 310 sq mi). *Population*: 22 295 000 (1991 census). *Capital*: Gauhati.

Bihar *Area*: 173 876 km² (67 134 sq mi). *Population*: 86 339 000 (1991 census). *Capital*: Patna.

Goa *Area*: 3701 km² (1429 sq mi). *Population*: 1 169 000 (1991 census). *Capital*: Panaji.

Gujarat *Area*: 195 984 km² (75 669 sq mi). *Population*: 41 174 000 (1991 census). *Capital*: Gandhinagar.

Haryana *Area*: 44 222 km² (17 074 sq mi). *Population*: 16 318 000 (1991 census). *Capital*: Chandigarh (a separate Union Territory, see below).

Himachal Pradesh *Area*: 55 673 km² (21 495 sq mi). *Population*: 5 111 000 (1991 census). *Capital*: Simla.

Jammu and Kashmir *Area*: 101 283 km² (39 105 sq mi) – the Indian-held part of the state only. *Population*: 7 719 000 (1991 census) – the Indian-held part of the state only. *Capitals*: Srinagar (summer capital); Jammu (winter capital).

Karnataka *Area*: 191 773 km² (74 044 sq mi). *Population*: 44 806 000 (1991 census). *Capital*: Bangalore.

Kerala *Area*: 38 864 km² (15 005 sq mi). *Population*: 25 403 000 (1991 census). *Capital*: Thiruvananthapuram (formerly Trivandrum).

Madhya Pradesh *Area*: 442 841 km² (170 981 sq mi). *Population*: 66 136 000 (1991 census). *Capital*: Bhopal.

Maharashtra *Area*: 307 762 km² (118 827 sq mi). *Population*: 78 748 000 (1991 census). *Capital*: Bombay.

Manipur *Area*: 22 356 km² (8632 sq mi). *Population*: 1 827 000 (1991 census). *Capital*: Imphal.

Meghalaya *Area*: 22 429 km² (8660 sq mi). *Population*: 1 761 000 (1991 census). *Capital*: Shillong.

Mizoram *Area*: 21 090 km² (8143 sq mi). *Population*: 686 000 (1991 census). *Capital*: Aizawl.

Nagaland *Area*: 16 527 km² (6381 sq mi). *Population*: 1 216 000 (1991 census). *Capital*: Kohima.

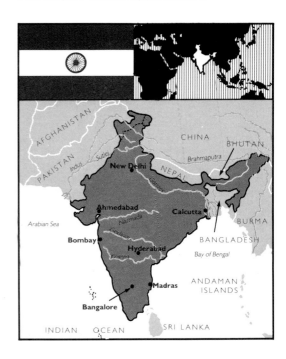

Orissa *Area*: 155 707 km² (60 118 sq mi). *Population*: 31 512 000 (1991 census). *Capital*: Bhubaneshwar.

Punjab *Area*: 50 376 km² (19 450 sq mi). *Population*: 20 191 000 (1991 census). *Capital*: Chandigarh (a separate Union Territory, see below).

Rajasthan *Area*: 342 239 km² (132 138 sq mi). *Population*: 43 881 000 (1991 census). *Capital*: Jaipur.

Sikkim *Area*: 7298 km² (2818 sq mi). *Population*: 406 000 (1991 census). *Capital*: Gangtok.

Tamil Nadu *Area*: 130 357 km² (50 331 sq mi). *Population*: 55 638 000 (1991 census). *Capital*: Madras.

Tripura *Area*: 10 477 km² (4045 sq mi). *Population*: 2 745 000 (1991 census). *Capital*: Agartala.

Uttar Pradesh *Area*: 294 413 km² (113 673 sq mi). *Population*: 139 031 000 (1991 census). *Capital*: Lucknow.

West Bengal *Area*: 87 853 km² (33 920 sq mi). *Population*: 67 983 000 (1991 census). *Capital*: Calcutta.

Andaman and Nicobar Islands (territory) *Area*: 8293 km² (3202 sq mi). *Population*: 279 000 (1991 census). *Capital*: Port Blair.

Chandigarh *Area*: 114 km² (44 sq mi). *Population*: 641 000 (1991 census). *Capital*: Chandigarh (which is also the capital of Haryana and Punjab).

Dadra and Nagar Haveli (territory) *Area*: 491 km² (190 sq mi). *Population*: 138 000 (1991 census). *Capital*: Silvassa.

Daman and Diu *Area*: 112 km² (43 sq mi). *Population*: 101 000 (1991 census). *Capital*: Daman.

Delhi (territory) *Area*: 1485 km² (573 sq mi). *Population*: 9 370 000 (1991 census). *Capital*: Delhi.

Lakshadweep (territory) *Area*: 32 km² (12 sq mi). *Population*: 52 000 (1991 census). *Capital*: Kavaratti.

Pondicherry (territory) *Area*: 492 km² (190 sq mi). *Population*: 807 000 (1991 census). *Capital*: Pondicherry.

GEOGRAPHY The Himalaya cut the Indian subcontinent off from the rest of Asia. Several Himalayan peaks in India rise to over 7000 m (23 000 ft). South of the Himalaya, the basins of the Rivers Ganges and Brahmaputra and their tributaries are intensively farmed and densely populated. The Thar Desert stretches along the border with Pakistan. In south India, the Deccan – a large plateau of hard rocks – is bordered in the east and west by the Ghats, discontinuous ranges of hills descending in steps to coastal plains. Natural vegetation ranges from tropical rain forest on the west coast and monsoon forest in the northeast and far south, through dry tropical scrub and thorn forest in much of the Deccan to Alpine and temperate vegetation in the Himalaya. *Principal rivers:* Ganges (Ganga), Brahmaputra, Sutlej, Yamuna, Tapti, Godavari, Krishna. *Highest point:* Kangchenjunga 8598 m (28 208 ft).

ECONOMY Two thirds of the labour force are involved in subsistence farming, with rice and wheat as the principal crops. Cash crops tend to come from large plantations and include tea, cotton, jute and sugar cane – all grown for export. The monsoon rains and irrigation make cultivation possible in many areas, but drought and floods are common. India is one of the ten largest industrial powers in the world. Major coal reserves provide the power base for industry. Other mineral deposits include diamonds, bauxite, and titanium, copper and iron ore, as well as substantial reserves of natural gas and petroleum. The textile, vehicle, iron and steel, pharmaceutical and electrical industries make important contributions to the economy, but India has balance-of-payment difficulties and relies upon foreign aid for development. Privatization of some state enterprises began in the early 1990s. Over one third of the population is below the official poverty line.

RECENT HISTORY British institutions, the railways and the English language – all imposed upon India by a modernizing imperial power – fostered the growth of an Indian sense of identity beyond the divisions of caste and language. However, ultimately the divisions of religion proved stronger. The Indian National Congress – the forerunner of the Congress Party – was first convened in 1885, and the Muslim League first met in 1906. Political and nationalist demands grew after British troops fired without warning on a nationalist protest meeting – the Amritsar Massacre (1919). The India Acts (1919 and 1935) granted limited autonomy and created an Indian federation, but the pace of reform did not satisfy Indian expectations. In 1920 Congress – led by Mohandas (Mahatma) Karamchand Gandhi (1869–1948) – began a campaign of non-violence and non-cooperation with the British authorities. However relations between Hindus and Muslims steadily deteriorated, and by 1940 the Muslim League was demanding a separate sovereign state.

By 1945, war-weary Britain had accepted the inevitability of Indian independence. However, religious discord forced the partition of the subcontinent in 1947 into predominantly Hindu India – under Jawaharlal (Pandit) Nehru (1889–1964) of the Congress Party – and Muslim Pakistan (including what is now Bangladesh) – under Mohammed Ali Jinnah (1876–1948) of the Muslim League. Over 70 million Hindus and Muslims became refugees and crossed the new boundaries, and thousands were killed in communal violence. The frontiers remained disputed. India and Pakistan fought border wars in 1947–49, 1965 (over Kashmir) and again in 1971 – when Bangladesh gained independence from Pakistan with Indian assistance. Kashmir is still divided along a cease-fire line. There were also border clashes with China in 1962.

Under Nehru (PM 1947–64) India became one of the leaders of the nonaligned movement of Third World states. Under the premiership (1966–77 and 1980–84) of his daughter Indira Gandhi (1917–84) India continued to assert itself as the dominant regional power. Although India remained the world's largest democracy – despite Mrs Gandhi's brief imposition of emergency rule (1975–77) – local separatism and communal unrest have threatened unity. The Sikhs have conducted an often violent campaign for an independent homeland – Khalistan – in the Punjab. In 1984 Mrs Gandhi ordered the storming of the Golden Temple of Amritsar, a Sikh holy place that extremists had turned into an arsenal. In the same year Mrs Gandhi was assassinated by her Sikh bodyguard and was succeeded as PM by her son Rajiv Gandhi (PM 1984–89), who was assassinated in the 1991 election campaign. Tension and violence between Hindus and Muslims has increased since a campaign (1990) to build a Hindu temple on the site of a mosque in the holy city of Ayodhya. The destruction of the mosque by Hindu fundamentalists (1992) led to widespread disorders.

INDONESIA

Official name: Republik Indonesia (Republic of Indonesia).

Member of: UN, OPEC, ASEAN.

Area: 1 919 443 km² (741 101 sq mi) – including East Timor which has an area of 14 874 km² (5743 sq mi).

Population: 179 322 000 (1990 census) – including East Timor which had a population of 748 000.

Capital and major cities: Jakarta 7 829 000, Surabaya 2 345 000, Medan 2 110 000, Bandung 1 613 000, Semarang 1 206 000, Palembang 874 000, Ujung Pandang (Makassar) 841 000 (all including suburbs; 1985 est).

Languages: Bahasa Indonesia (official), Javanese (34%), Madurese (6%), Sundanese (14%) and about 25 other main languages.

Religions: Sunni Islam (80%), Roman Catholic (3%), other Christians (7%), Hindu (2%).

GOVERNMENT Every five years elections are held by universal adult suffrage for 400 members of the House of Representatives; the remaining 100 members are chosen by the President. The People's Consultative Assembly – which consists of the members of the House plus 500 representatives of provincial governments, occupational and special interests – meets once every five years to oversee broad principles of state policy and to elect the President, who appoints a Cabinet. The principal political parties are (government alliance) Golkar, the (Islamic) United Development Group, and the (Christian and nationalist) Indonesian Democratic Party.

President: Gen. T.N.I. Suharto.

GEOGRAPHY Indonesia consists of nearly 3700 islands, of which about 3000 are inhabited. The southern chain of mountainous, volcanic islands comprises Sumatra, Java with Madura, Bali, and the Lesser Sunda Islands (including Lombok, Flores and Timor). Java and its smaller neighbour Madura are fertile and densely populated, containing nearly two thirds of Indonesia's people. The northern chain comprises Kalimantan (the Indonesian sector of Borneo), the irregular mountainous island of Sulawesi (Celebes), the Moluccas group, and Irian Jaya (the western half of New Guinea). Over two thirds of the country is covered by tropical rain forests. *Principal rivers:* Kapuas, Digul, Barito. *Highest point:* Ngga Pulu (Carstensz Pyramid) 5030 m (16 503 ft) (on Irian Jaya).

ECONOMY Indonesia has great mineral wealth – petroleum, natural gas, tin, nickel, coal, bauxite and copper – but is relatively poor because of its great population. Over 50% of Indonesians are subsistence farmers with rice being the major crop, but both estate and peasant farmers produce important quantities of rubber, tea, coffee, tobacco and spices for export. Industry is largely concerned with processing mineral and agricultural products. Indonesia achieved high economic growth rates throughout the 1980s and early 1990s.

RECENT HISTORY The Netherlands retained control of the East Indies from the 17th century until 1942 when Japanese invaders were welcomed by most Indonesians as liberators from colonial rule. Upon Japan's surrender in 1945, Achmed Sukarno (1901–70) – the founder of the nationalist party in 1927 – declared the Dutch East Indies to be the independent republic of Indonesia. Under international pressure, the Dutch accepted Indonesian independence (1949) after four years of intermittent but brutal fighting. Sukarno's rule became increasingly authoritarian and the country sank into economic chaos. In 1962 he seized Netherlands New Guinea, which was formally annexed as Irian Jaya in 1969, although a separatist movement persists. Between 1963 and 1966 Sukarno tried to destabilize the newly-created Federation of Malaysia by armed incursions into north Borneo.

General T.N.I. Suharto's suppression of a Communist uprising in 1965–66 enabled him to reverse Sukarno's anti-Americanism and eventually to displace him with both student and army support. Around 80 000 members of the Communist Party were killed in this period. The annexation of Portuguese East Timor by Indonesia in 1976 is unrecognized by the international community, and guerrilla action by local nationalists continues. International protests followed the killing of unarmed Timorese demonstrators by Indonesian troops in 1991. An ambitious programme of resettlement has been attempted to relieve overcrowded Java, but the Javanese settlers have been resented in the outlying, underdeveloped islands.

IRAN

Official name: Jomhori-e-Islami-e-Irân (Islamic Republic of Iran). Until 1935 Iran was known as Persia.

Member of: UN, OPEC.

Area: 1 648 000 km² (636 296 sq mi).

Population: 57 050 000 (1991 est).

Capital and major cities: Tehran 6 022 000, Mashad 1 464 000, Isfahan 987 000, Tabriz 971 000, Shiraz 848 000, Ahvaz 580 000, Bakhtaran 561 000, Qom 543 000 (all including suburbs; 1986 census).

Languages: Farsi or Persian (official; 45%), Azeri (26%), Kurdish, Luri, Baluchi.

Religion: Shia Islam (official; 98%).

GOVERNMENT A Council of Experts – 83 Shiite clerics – is elected by universal adult suffrage to appoint the Wali Faqih (religious leader), who exercises supreme authority over the executive, legislature, judiciary and military. There is no fixed term for the Wali Faqih, whose role may be taken by a joint leadership of three or five persons. The 270-member Islamic Consultative Assembly (Majlis) and the President are directly elected for four years. The President appoints a Cabinet which is responsible to the Majlis. Iran is effectively a non-party state although the Liberation Movement of Iran is allowed to operate.

Supreme Religious Leader (Wali Faqih): Ayatollah Mohammad Khamenei.

President: Hojatolislam Rafsanjani.

GEOGRAPHY Apart from restricted lowlands along the Gulf, the Caspian Sea and the Iraqi border, Iran is a high plateau, surrounded by mountains. The Elburz Mountains lie in the north; the Zagros Mountains form a barrier running parallel to the Gulf. In the east, lower areas of the plateau are covered by salt deserts. *Principal rivers:* Kàrùn, Safid, Atrak, Karkheh. *Highest point:* Demavend 5604 m (18 386 ft).

ECONOMY Petroleum is Iran's main foreign-currency earner. The principal industries are petrochemicals, carpetweaving, textiles, vehicles and cement, but the war with Iraq and Iran's international isolation severely interrupted trade in the 1980s. Iran has, however, recently actively encouraged renewed links with the West. Over a quarter of the labour force is involved in agriculture, mainly producing cereals (wheat, maize and barley) and keeping livestock, but lack of water, land ownership problems and manpower shortages have restricted yields.

RECENT HISTORY In 1921 an Iranian Cossack officer, Reza Khan Pahlavi (1877–1944), took power. Deposing the Qajar dynasty in 1925, he became Shah (emperor) himself as Reza I and modernized and secularized Iran. However, because of his pro-German sentiments, he was forced to abdicate by Britain and the USSR (1941) and was replaced by his son Mohammed Reza (1919–80). The radical nationalist prime minister Muhammad Mussadiq briefly toppled the monarchy (1953). On regaining his throne, the Shah tightened his grip through oppression and sought popularity through land reform and rapid development with US backing. However, the policy of Westernization offended the clergy, and a combination of students, the bourgeoisie and religious leaders eventually combined against him, overthrowing the monarchy in 1979 and replacing it with a fundamentalist Islamic Republic inspired by the Ayatollah Ruhollah Khomeini (1900–89). The Western-educated classes fled Iran as the clergy tightened control. Radical anti-Western students seized the US embassy and held 66 American hostages (1979–81). In 1980 Iraq invaded Iran, beginning the bitter First Gulf War, which lasted until 1988 and resulted in great losses of manpower for Iran. Following the death of Khomeini in 1989, economic necessity brought about a less militant phase of the Islamic revolution. The new president, Rafsanjani, emphasized pragmatic rather than radical policies and attempted to heal the diplomatic rift with Western powers. Iraq returned occupied Iranian territory following the invasion of Kuwait (1990). After the collapse of the USSR (1991), Iran began to look for closer ties with the Islamic former Soviet republics of Central Asia.

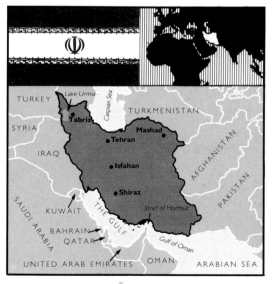

IRAQ

Official name: Al-Jumhuriya al-'Iraqiya (The Republic of Iraq).

Member of: UN, Arab League, OPEC.

Area: 441 839 km² (170 595 sq mi).

Population: 17 754 000 (1990 est).

Capital and major cities: Baghdad 5 348 000 (including suburbs; 1988 est), Basrah 617 000, Mosul (Al Mawsil) 571 000, Irbil 334 000, as-Sulaymaniyah 279 000, An Najaf 243 000 (1985 est).

Languages: Arabic (official; 80%), Kurdish (19%).

Religions: Sunni Islam (41%), Shia Islam (51%), with a small Christian minority.

GOVERNMENT The 250-member National Assembly is elected for a four-year term by universal adult suffrage. The non-elected Revolutionary Command Council appoints the President, who – in turn – appoints the Council of Ministers. The only effective legal party is the Arab Ba'ath Socialist Party, which is part of the National Progressive Front coalition.

President: Saddam Hussein.

Prime Minister: Muhammad Hamza al-Zubaydi.

GEOGRAPHY The basins of the Rivers Tigris and Euphrates contain most of the arable land and the population. Desert in the southwest occupies nearly one half of Iraq. *Principal rivers:* Tigris (Dijlah), Euphrates (al Furat). *Highest point:* Rawanduz 3658 m (12 001 ft).

ECONOMY Agriculture involves one third of the labour force. Irrigated land in the Tigris and Euphrates basins produces cereals, fruit and vegetables for domestic consumption, and dates for export. Iraq traditionally depends upon its substantial reserves of petroleum, but exports were halted by international sanctions (1990) and the Second Gulf War (1991). The Iraqi economy was badly damaged during the First Gulf War against Iran, and devastated by the Second Gulf War.

RECENT HISTORY In World War I the British occupied the area (formerly a part of the Turkish Ottoman Empire), but Iraqi nationalists were disappointed when Iraq became a British mandate with virtual colonial status (1920). In 1921 the Amir Faisal ibn Husain became King and in 1932 Iraq became fully independent. Following a military coup that brought pro-German officers to power in 1941, the British occupied Iraq until 1945. The royal family and the premier were murdered in the 'Free Officers' coup in 1958. Differences in the leadership led to a further coup in 1963 and a reign of terror against the left. In 1968 Ba'athist (pan-Arab nationalist) officers carried out another coup. Embittered by the Arabs' humiliation in the 1967 war and by US support for the Israelis, the regime turned to the Soviets.

In 1980 President Saddam Hussein attacked a weakened Iran, responding to Iran's threat to export Islamic revolution. What had been intended as a quick victory became the costly First Gulf War (1980–88), resulting in many casualties and the virtual bankruptcy of the country. In an attempt to restore Iraq's economic fortunes, Saddam Hussein invaded oil-rich Kuwait (1990). UN sanctions against Iraq were imposed. Forces from the USA, the UK and over 20 other countries (including Egypt and Syria) were dispatched to the Gulf. Following Saddam Hussein's failure to respond to repeated UN demands to withdraw from Kuwait, the Second Gulf War began (January 1991). Coalition forces routed the Iraqi army which sustained heavy casualties. Iraq accepted all the UN resolutions regarding Kuwait and agreed to a ceasefire after a campaign that lasted only 100 hours. During March and April Saddam Hussein suppressed revolts by Shiites in the south and Kurds in the north. International efforts were made to feed and protect over 1 000 000 Shiite and Kurdish refugees who had fled. Despite being forced to accept UN inspection of Iraq's chemical and biological weapons and the country's nuclear capacity, Saddam continued to defy UN demands concerning disarmament and recognition of the Kuwaiti border.

IRELAND

Official name: Poblacht na h'Éireann (Republic of Ireland).

Member of: UN, EC, CSCE, Council of Europe, OECD, WEU (associate).

Area: 70 282 km² (27 136 sq mi).

Population: 3 523 000 (1991 census).

Capital and major cities: Dublin 921 000 (city 478 000), Cork 174 000 (city 127 000), Limerick 77 000 (city 52 000), Dún Laoghaire (part of the Dublin agglomeration) 55 000, Galway 51 000, Waterford 41 000 (1986 census).

Languages: Irish (official; minority), English (universal).

Religion: Roman Catholic (95%).

GOVERNMENT The Seanad (Senate) comprises 60 members – 11 nominated by the Taoiseach (Prime

Minister), six elected by the universities and 43 indirectly elected for a five-year term to represent vocational and special interests. The Dáil (House) comprises 166 members elected for five years by universal adult suffrage under a system of proportional representation. The President is directly elected for a seven-year term. The Taoiseach and a Cabinet of Ministers are appointed by the President upon the nomination of the Dáil, to whom they are responsible. The main political parties include the (centre-right) Fianna Fáil (Soldiers of Destiny), (centre-right) Fine Gael (United Ireland Party), (left-wing) Labour Party, (centre-right) Progressive Democrats and the Worker's Party.

President: Mary Robinson.
Prime Minister: Albert Reynolds.

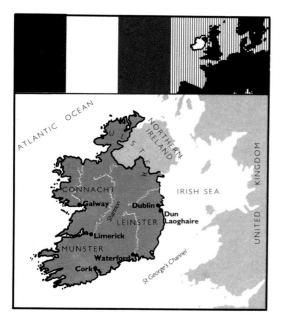

GEOGRAPHY Central Ireland is a lowland crossed by slight ridges and broad valleys, bogs and large lakes, including Loughs Derg and Ree. Except on the east coast north of Dublin, the lowland is surrounded by coastal hills and mountains including the Wicklow Mountains (south of Dublin), the Comeragh Mountains (Co. Waterford) and the Ox Mountains and the hills of Connemara and Donegal in the west. The highest uplands are the Macgillicuddy's Reeks in the southwest. The rugged Atlantic Coast is highly indented. *Principal rivers:* Shannon, Suir, Boyne, Barrow, Erne. *Highest point:* Carrauntuohill 1041 m (3414 ft).

ECONOMY Manufactured goods – in particular machinery, metals and engineering, electronics and chemical products – now account for over 80% of Ireland's exports. Agriculture – which was the tradi-

tional mainstay of the economy – concentrates upon the production of livestock, meat and dairy products. Food processing and brewing are major industries. Natural resources include lead-zinc, offshore petroleum and natural gas, and hydroelectric power sites. Ireland suffers high rates of unemployment and emigration.

RECENT HISTORY Throughout the 19th century Ireland campaigned for reform and later independence from the British Parliament. In the 1880s Charles Stewart Parnell (1846–91) led a sizeable bloc of Irish MPs to secure Irish Home Rule (i.e. self-government). Home Rule Bills were introduced in 1883 and 1893, but after their rejection by Parliament, more revolutionary nationalist groups gained support in Ireland. Fearing Catholic domination, Protestant Unionists in Ulster strongly opposed the Third Home Rule Bill in 1912. Nationalists declared an independent Irish state in the Dublin Easter Rising of 1916, which was put down by the British. After World War I, Irish nationalist MPs formed a provisional government in Dublin led by Eamon de Valera (later PM and President; 1882–1975). Except in the northeast, British administration in Ireland crumbled and most of the Irish police resigned to be replaced by British officers. Fighting broke out between nationalists and British troops and police, and by 1919 Ireland had collapsed into violence. The British response in 1920 was to offer Ireland two Parliaments – one in Protestant Ulster, another in the Catholic south. Partition was initially rejected by the south, but by the Anglo-Irish Treaty (1921) dominion status was granted, although six (mainly Protestant) counties in Ulster – Northern Ireland – opted to remain British. The Irish Free State was proclaimed in 1922 but de Valera and the Republicans refused to accept it. Civil war broke out between the provisional government – led by Arthur Griffith and Michael Collins – and the Republicans. Although fighting ended in 1923, de Valera's campaign for a republic continued and in 1937 the Irish Free State became the Republic of Eire. The country remained neutral in World War II and left the Commonwealth – as the Republic of Ireland – in 1949. Relations between south and north – and between the Republic and the UK – have often been tense during the 'troubles' in Northern Ireland (1968–). However, the Anglo-Irish Agreement (1985) provided for the participation of the Republic in political, legal and security matters in Northern Ireland. Irish political life has been characterized by the alternation of the two main parties – Fine Gael and Fianna Fáil – in government.

ISRAEL

Official name: Medinat Israel (The State of Israel).
Member of: UN.
Area: 21 946 km² (8473 sq mi), including East Jerusalem but excluding Golan, Gaza and the West Bank.
Population: 4 821 000 (1991 est) – including East Jerusalem but excluding Golan, Gaza and the West Bank.

Capital and major cities: Jerusalem (not recognized internationally as capital) 525 000, Tel-Aviv 1 157 000 (city 339 000), Haifa 395 000 (city 246 000), Netanya 132 000, Beersheba (Be'er Sheva) 122 000. Holon 157 000, Petach-Tikva 144 000, Bat-Yam 141 000, and Rishon LeZiyyon 140 000 are part of the Tel Aviv agglomeration (1990 est).

Languages: Hebrew (official; 85%), Arabic (15%).

Religions: Judaism (official; 85%), Sunni Islam (13%), various Christian denominations.

GOVERNMENT The 120-member Knesset (Assembly) is elected by proportional representation for four years by universal adult suffrage. A Prime Minister and Cabinet take office after receiving a vote of confidence from the Knesset. The President is elected for a five-year term by the Knesset. Over ten political parties are represented in the Knesset – the largest are the (right wing) Likud Party and the (centre-left) Labour Alignment.

President: Chaim Herzog.

Prime Minister: Yitzhak Rabin.

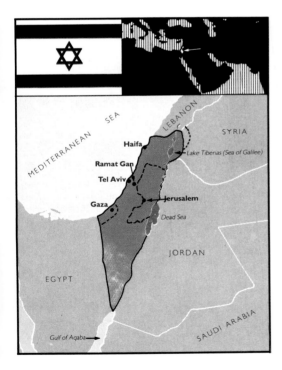

GEOGRAPHY Israel – within the boundaries established by the 1949 cease-fire line – consists of a fertile thin coastal plain beside the Mediterranean, parts of the arid mountains of Judaea in the centre, the Negev Desert in the south, and part of the Jordan Valley in the northeast. *Principal rivers:* Jordan (Yarden), Qishon. *Highest point:* Har Meron (Mt Atzmon) 1208 m (3963 ft).

ECONOMY Severe economic problems stem, in part, from Israel's large defence budget and political circumstances, which prevent trade with neighbouring countries. Israel is a major producer and exporter of citrus fruit. Much land is irrigated and over 75% of Israel's arable land is farmed by collectives (kibbutzim) and cooperatives. Mineral resources are few, but processing imported diamonds is a major source of foreign currency. Tourism – to biblical sites – is important.

RECENT HISTORY The area was captured from the Turks by British forces in 1917–18. The Zionists had hoped to establish a Jewish state, and this hope was intensified following the Balfour Declaration by the British foreign secretary in favour of a homeland (1917). However, Palestine came under British administration and it was not until 1948–9 – after the murder of some 6 million Jews in concentration camps by the Nazis – that an explicitly Jewish state emerged. The establishment of a Jewish state met with hostility from Israel's neighbours and indigenous Palestinians (many of whom left the country), leading to a series of Arab-Israeli wars. In 1956, while the UK and France were in conflict with Egypt over the Suez Canal, Israel attacked Gaza – from which the Palestinians had raided Israel – and overran Sinai, but withdrew following UN condemnation. After an uneasy peace, the UN emergency force between Israel and Egypt was expelled in 1967. Egypt imposed a sea blockade on Israel, which responded by invading Sinai. In six days, an Arab coalition of Egypt, Jordan and Syria was defeated, and Israel occupied Sinai, Gaza, the West Bank and the Golan Heights. In 1973, Egypt attacked Israel across the Suez Canal, but a ceasefire was arranged within three weeks. In 1979 Israel and Egypt signed a peace treaty; Egypt recognized Israel's right to exist and Israel withdrew from Sinai in stages.

In 1982 Israeli forces invaded Lebanon, intent on destroying bases of the PLO (Palestinian Liberation Organization), and became involved in the complex civil war there. Eventually Israeli forces withdrew in 1985. In 1987 the intifada (Palestinian uprising) against continued Israeli rule in Gaza and the West Bank began. The harsh reaction of Israeli security forces attracted international condemnation. The intifada continued sporadically and was given extra impetus by the large-scale influx of Soviet Jews into Israel (from 1990) and the encouragement given to the Palestinians by President Saddam Hussein of Iraq. Israeli politics in the 1980s and early 1990s were characterized by political instability owing to the system of proportional representation and the large number of very small parties. In the 1990s Israel has come under increased international pressure to achieve a Middle East settlement.

Information concerning the occupied territories – the Golan Heights, Gaza and the West Bank – can be found in the section on Other Territories, following this chapter.

ITALY

Official name: Italia (Italy) or Repubblica Italiana (Republic of Italy).

Member of: UN, EC, NATO, WEU, G7, Council of Europe, OECD, CSCE.

Area: 301 277 km^2 (116 324 sq mi).

Population: 57 590 000 (1991 census).

Capital and major cities: Rome (Roma) 3 000 000 (city 2 804 000), Milan (Milano) 3 700 000 (city 1 449 000), Naples (Napoli) 2 900 000 (city 1 204 000), Turin (Torino) 1 003 000, Palermo 731 000, Genoa (Genova) 707 000, Bologna 417 000, Florence (Firenze) 413 000, Catania 366 000, Bari 355 000, Venice (Venezia) 321 000, Messina 275 000, Verona 259 000, Taranto 244 000, Trieste 231 000, Padua (Padova) 218 000, Cagliari 212 000, Brescia 197 000, Reggio di Calabria 179 000, Modena 178 000, Parma 174 000, Livorno 171 000, Prato 167 000, Foggia 160 000, Salerno 151 000, Perugia 151 000 (1990 est).

Languages: Italian (official), with small minorities speaking German, French and Albanian.

Religion: Roman Catholic (over 90%).

GOVERNMENT The two houses of Parliament are elected for a five-year term under a system of proportional representation. The Senate has 315 members elected by citizens aged 25 and over to represent the regions, plus two former Presidents and five life senators chosen by the President. The Chamber of Deputies has 630 members elected by citizens aged 18 and over. The President is elected for a seven-year term by an electoral college consisting of Parliament and 58 regional representatives. The President appoints a Prime Minister – who commands a majority in Parliament – and a Council of Ministers (Cabinet) who are responsible to Parliament. The main political parties include the (conservative) Christian Democrat Party, the Democratic Party of the Left (formerly the Communist Party), the PSI (Socialist Party), the (separatist) Northern League (including the Lombard League), the (Sourthern-based anti-mafia) La Rete, the RPI (Republican Party), the Radical Party, the Liberal Party, the Social Democratic Party, and the (right-wing) MSI-DN. The 20 regions of Italy have their own regional governments.

President: Oscar Luigi Scalfaro.
Prime Minister: Giuliano Amato.

REGIONS *Abruzzi Area*: 10 794 km^2 (4168 sq mi). *Population*: 1 272 000 (1990 est). *Capital*: L'Aquila; Pescara shares some of the functions of capital with L'Aquila.

Basilicata *Area*: 9992 km^2 (3858 sq mi). *Population*: 625 000 (1990 est). *Capital*: Potenza.

Calabria *Area*: 15 080 km^2 (5822 sq mi). *Population*: 2 154 000 (1990 est). *Capital*: Catanzaro.

Campania *Area*: 13 595 km^2 (5249 sq mi). *Population*: 5 854 000 (1990 est). *Capital*: Naples (Napoli).

Emilia Romagna *Area*: 22 123 km^2 (8542 sq mi). *Population*: 3 929 000 (1990 est). *Capital*: Bologna.

Friuli-Venezia Giulia *Area*: 7846 km^2 (3029 sq mi). *Population*: 1 201 000 (1990 est). *Capital*: Trieste.

Lazio *Area*: 17 203 km^2 (6642 sq mi). *Population*: 5 191 000 (1990 est). *Capital*: Rome (Roma).

Liguria *Area*: 5413 km^2 (2090 sq mi). *Population*: 1 719 000 (1990 est). *Capital*: Genoa (Genova).

Lombardy (Lombardia) *Area*: 23 834 km^2 (9202 sq mi). *Population*: 8 939 000 (1990 est). *Capital*: Milan (Milano).

Marche *Area*: 9692 km^2 (3742 sq mi). *Population*: 1 436 000 (1990 est). *Capital*: Ancona.

Molise *Area*: 4438 km^2 (1714 sq mi). *Population*: 337 000 (1990 est). *Capital*: Campobasso.

Piedmont (Piemonte) *Area*: 25 399 km^2 (9807 sq mi). *Population*: 4 356 000 (1990 est). *Capital*: Turin (Torino).

Puglia *Area*: 19 347 km^2 (7470 sq mi). *Population*: 4 082 000 (1990 est). *Capital*: Bari.

Sardinia (Sardegna) *Area*: 24 090 km^2 (9301 sq mi). *Population*: 1 664 000 (1990 est). *Capital*: Cagliari.

Sicily (Sicilia) *Area*: 25 708 km^2 (9926 sq mi). *Population*: 5 197 000 (1990 est). *Capital*: Palermo.

Trentino-Alto Adige *Area*: 13 613 km^2 (5256 sq mi). *Population*: 891 000 (1990 est). *Capitals*: Trento and Bolzano (Bozen).

Tuscany (Toscana) *Area*: 22 992 km^2 (8877 sq mi). *Population*: 3 563 000 (1990 est). *Capital*: Florence (Firenze).

Umbria *Area*: 8456 km^2 (3265 sq mi). *Population*: 823 000 (1990 est). *Capital*: Perugia.

Valle d'Aosta *Area*: 3262 km^2 (1259 sq mi). *Population*: 116 000 (1990 est). *Capital*: Aosta.

Veneto *Area*: 18 368 km² (7092 sq mi). *Population*: 4 398 000 (1990 est). *Capital*: Venice (Venezia).

GEOGRAPHY The Alps form a natural boundary between Italy and its western and northern neighbours. A string of lakes – where the mountains meet the foothills – include Lakes Maggiore, Lugano and Como. The fertile Po Valley – the great lowland of northern Italy – lies between the Alpine foothills in the north, the foothills of the Apennine Mountains in the south, the Alps in the west and the Adriatic Sea in the east. The narrow ridge of the Ligurian Alps joins the Maritime Alps to the Apennines, which form a backbone down the entire length of the Italian peninsula. Coastal lowlands are few and relatively restricted but include the Arno Basin in Tuscany, the Tiber Basin around Rome, the Campania lowlands around Naples, and plains beside the Gulf of Taranto and in Puglia (the 'heel' of Italy). The two major islands of Italy – Sardinia and Sicily – are both largely mountainous. Much of Italy is geologically unstable and liable to earthquakes. The country has four active volcanoes, including Etna on Sicily and Vesuvius near Naples. *Principal rivers:* Po, Tiber (Tevere), Arno, Volturno, Garigliano. *Highest point:* a point just below the summit of Monte Bianco (Mont Blanc) 4760 m (15 616 ft).

ECONOMY Northern Italy, with its easy access to the rest of Europe, is the main centre of Italian industry. The south, in contrast, remains mainly agricultural, producing grapes, sugar beet, wheat, maize, tomatoes and soya beans. Most farms are small – and many farmers in the south are resistant to change – thus incomes in southern Italy (the 'Mezzogiorno') are on average substantially lower than in the north. Agriculture in the north is more mechanized and major crops include wheat, maize, rice, grapes (for the important wine industry), fruit and fodder crops for dairy herds. Industrialization in the south is being actively promoted. The industries of the north are well-developed and include electrical and electronic goods, motor vehicles and bicycles, textiles, clothing, leather goods, cement, glass, china and ceramics. The north is also an important financial and banking area, and Milan is the commercial capital of Italy. Apart from Alpine rivers that have been harnessed for hydroelectric power, Italy has few natural resources. Tourism and money sent back by Italians living abroad are important sources of foreign currency. Recession and a crippling public deficit have added to Italy's growing economic problems.

RECENT HISTORY Italy entered World War I on the Allied side in the expectation of territorial gains from Austria. However, Italy won far less territory than anticipated in the peace treaties after the war, when fear of Communist revolution led to an upsurge of Fascism. The Fascist Benito Mussolini (1883–1945) became Prime Minister in 1922 with a programme of extensive domestic modernization and an aggressive foreign policy. In 1936 Italy allied with Germany in the Rome-Berlin Axis, and declared war on Britain and France in 1940. When Italy was invaded by Allied troops in 1943, Mussolini was dismissed by the king and Italy joined the Allies. In 1946 a republic was proclaimed. Communist influence increased, both at local and national level – in 1976, for example, the Communists controlled the local administration in Rome, Naples, Florence and Bologna. However, the dominance of the (conservative) Christian Democrat Party has kept the Communists out of the succeeding coalitions that have ruled Italy. Particularly in the 1970s, terrorist movements – of both the left and the right – have been active, kidnapping and assassinating senior political and industrial figures, including the former PM Aldo Moro in 1978. Considerable attempts have been made to effect a true unification of the country by encouraging the economic development of the south. However, the political structure of Italy remains unstable and coalitions have often been short-lived – between 1945 and 1991 49 governments came to and fell from power. In the 1990s, public disillusion with state institutions grew and Italy was weakened by corruption, the activities of the Mafia and the growth of regional separatism in the North.

IVORY COAST
see COTE D'IVOIRE

JAMAICA

Member of: UN, Commonwealth, CARICOM, OAS.

Area: 10 991 km² (4244 sq mi).

Population: 2 420 000 (1991 est).

Capital and major cities: Kingston 662 000 (1990 est), Spanish Town 89 000, Montego Bay 70 000 (1985 est).

Language: English.

Religions: Church of God (17%), Anglican (10%), Baptist, Roman Catholic.

GOVERNMENT The 60-member House of Representatives (the lower house of Parliament) is elected for five years by universal adult suffrage. The 21-member Senate is appointed on the advice of the Prime Minister and the Leader of the Opposition. The Governor General – the representative of the British Queen as sovereign of Jamaica – appoints a Prime Minister who commands a majority in the House. The PM, in turn, appoints a Cabinet of Ministers who are responsible to the House. The main political parties are the (radical) People's National Party and the (centre) Jamaican Labour Party.

Prime Minister: P.J. Patterson.

GEOGRAPHY Coastal lowlands surround the interior limestone plateaux (the 'Cockpit Country') and mountains. *Principal river:* Black River. *Highest point:* Blue Mountain Peak 2256 m (7402 ft).

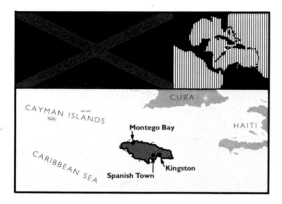

CAYMAN ISLANDS

CUBA

Montego Bay

HAITI

CARIBBEAN SEA

Spanish Town   Kingston

ECONOMY Agriculture is the mainstay of the economy, with sugar cane and bananas as the main crops. Jamaica is one of the world's leading exporters of bauxite. Tourism is a major foreign-currency earner.

RECENT HISTORY In the 1930s, severe social and economic problems led to rioting and the birth of political awareness. Since independence from Britain in 1962, power has alternated between the radical People's National Party – led by Michael Manley – and the more conservative Jamaican Labour Party – whose leaders have included Sir Alexander Bustamente and Edward Seaga.

JAPAN

Official name: Nippon or Nihon ('The Land of the Rising Sun').

Member of: UN, G7, OECD.

Area: 377 815 km² (145 874 sq mi).

Population: 123 612 000 (1990 census).

Capital and major cities: Tokyo 18 200 000 (city 11 855 000), Osaka 8 500 000 (city 2 624 000), Yokohama (part of the Tokyo agglomeration) 3 220 000, Nagoya 2 155 000, Sapporo 1 672 000, Kobe (part of the Osaka agglomeration) 1 477 000, Kyoto 1 461 000, Fukuoka 1 237 000, Kawasaki (part of the Tokyo agglomeration) 1 174 000, Hiroshima 1 086 000, Kitakyushu 1 026 000, Sendai 889 000, Chiba (part of the Tokyo agglomeration) 816 000, Sakai (part of the Osaka agglomeration) 803 000 (1990 est).

Language: Japanese.

Religions: Shintoism (86%) overlaps with Buddhism (74%), various Christian denominations (1%).

GOVERNMENT The head of state is the Emperor who has no executive power. The 252-member House of Councillors – the upper house of the Diet (Parliament) – is elected for six years by universal adult suffrage. One half of the councillors retire every three years. A system of proportional representation is used to elect 100 of the councillors. The 512-member House of Representatives is elected for four years, also by universal adult suffrage. The Diet chooses a Prime Minister who commands a majority in the lower house. The PM in turn appoints a Cabinet of Ministers who are responsible to the Diet. The main political parties are the Liberal Democratic Party, the Socialist Party, Komeito (Clean Government Party), the Communist Party, the Democratic Socialist Party, and the Social Democratic Federation.

Emperor: HIM the Heisei Emperor – known outside Japan as Emperor Akihito (who succeeded upon the death of his father, 7 January 1989).

Prime Minister: Kiichi Miyazawa.

GEOGRAPHY Japan consists of over 3900 islands, of which Hokkaido in the north occupies 22% of the total land area, and Shikoku and Kyushu in the south respectively occupy 5% and 11% of the area. The central island of Honshu occupies 61% of the total land area and contains 80% of the population. To the south of the four main islands, the Ryukyu Islands – including Okinawa – stretch almost to Taiwan. Nearly three quarters of Japan is mountainous. Coastal plains – where the population is concentrated – are limited. The principal lowlands are Kanto (around Tokyo), Nobi (around Nagoya) and the Sendai Plain in the north of Honshu. There are also over 60 active volcanoes in Japan and the country is prone to severe earthquakes. *Principal rivers:* Tone, Ishikarai, Shinano, Kitakami. *Highest point:* Fujiyama (Mount Fuji) 3776 m (12 388 ft).

ECONOMY Despite the generally crowded living conditions in the cities, the Japanese enjoy a high standard of living. The country has the second largest industrial economy in the world, despite having very few natural resources. Japanese industry is heavily dependent on imported raw materials – about 90% of the country's energy requirements come from abroad and petroleum is the single largest import. There is, therefore, considerable interest in offshore petroleum exploration, particularly in the Korean Straits. Japan's economic success is based on manufacturing industry, which – with construction – employs nearly one third of the labour force. Japan is the world's leading manufacturer of motor vehicles, and one of the major producers of ships, steel, synthetic fibres, chemicals, cement, electrical goods and electronic equipment. Rapid advances in Japanese research and technology have helped the expanding export-led economy. The banking and financial sectors have prospered in line with the manufacturing sector, and Tokyo is one of the world's principal stock exchanges and commercial centres. Agriculture is labour intensive. Although Japan is self-sufficient in rice, agriculture is not a priority and 30% of its food requirements – particularly cereals – have to be imported. The traditional Japanese diet is sea-based and the fishing industry is a large one, both for export and for domestic consumption.

RECENT HISTORY At the beginning of the 20th century Japan was rapidly industrializing and on the brink of becoming a world power. By the time of the death of the Meiji Emperor in 1912, the Japanese had established an empire. Japan had defeated China (1894–95) – taking Port Arthur and Taiwan – and startled Europe by beating Russia (1904–5) by land and at sea. Korea was annexed in 1910. Allied with Britain from 1902, Japan entered World War I against Germany in 1914, in part to gain acceptance as an imperial world power. However, Japan gained little except some of the German island territories in the Pacific and became disillusioned that the country did not seem to be treated as an equal by the Great Powers. The rise of militarism and collapse of world trade in the 1930s led to the rise of totalitarianism and a phase of aggressive Japanese expansion. In 1931 the Japanese army seized Chinese Manchuria, and in 1937 mounted an all-out attack on China itself, occupying large areas. Japan became allied to Nazi Germany and in 1941 Japanese aircraft struck Pearl Harbor in Hawaii, bringing the USA into World War II. An initial rapid Japanese military expansion across SE Asia and the Pacific was halted, and the war ended for Japan in disastrous defeat and the horrors of atomic warfare. Emperor Hirohito (reigned 1926–89) surrendered in September 1945. Shintoism – which had come to be identified with aggressive nationalism – ceased to be the state religion, and in 1946 the emperor renounced his divinity. The Allied occupation (1945–52) both democratized politics and began an astonishing economic recovery based on an aggressive export policy.

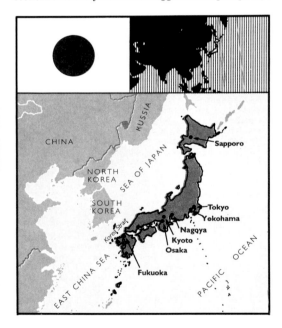

The economy was jolted by major rises in petroleum prices in 1973 and 1979, but Japan nevertheless maintained its advance to become a technological front-runner. By 1988 Japan surpassed the USA as the world's largest aid-donor. The Japanese political world is domi-

nated by the Liberal Democrats, who have held office since 1955 despite a number of financial scandals.

JORDAN

Official name: Al-Mamlaka al-Urduniya al-Hashemiyah (The Hashemite Kingdom of Jordan).

Member of: UN, Arab League.

Area: 89 206 km² (34 443 sq mi) – East Bank only (Jordan cut all legal and administrative ties with the Israeli-occupied West Bank in July 1988).

Population: 3 285 000 (1991 est).

Capital and major cities: Amman 1 160 000, Zarqa 318 000, Irbid 168 000, Salt 134 000 (1986 est).

Language: Arabic (official).

Religion: Sunni Islam (over 80%).

GOVERNMENT Jordan is a constitutional monarchy. The King appoints the 30 members of the Senate – the upper house of the National Assembly – and names a Prime Minister and Cabinet. The senators serve an eight-year term, with one half of their number retiring every four years. The 80 members of the House of Representatives are elected every four years by universal adult suffrage. The principal political party is the Muslim Brotherhood.

King: HM King Hussein I (succeeded upon the deposition of his father, on grounds of illness, 11 August 1952).

Prime Minister: Sharif Zeid bin-Shaker.

GEOGRAPHY The steep escarpment of the East Bank Uplands borders the Jordan Valley and the Dead Sea. Deserts cover over 80% of the country. *Principal* *river:* Jordan (Urdun). *Highest point:* Jabal Ramm 1754 m (5755 ft).

ECONOMY   Apart from potash – the principal export – Jordan has few resources. Arable land accounts for only about 5% of the total area. Foreign aid and money sent back by Jordanians working abroad are major sources of foreign currency.

RECENT HISTORY   In World War I the British aided an Arab revolt against (Turkish) Ottoman rule. The League of Nations awarded the area east of the River Jordan – Transjordan – to Britain as part of Palestine (1920), but in 1923 Transjordan became a separate emirate. In 1946 the country gained complete independence as the Kingdom of Jordan with Amir Abdullah (1880–1951) as its sovereign. The Jordanian army fought with distinction in the 1948 Arab-Israeli War, and occupied the West Bank territories which were formally incorporated into Jordan in April 1950. In 1951 Abdullah was assassinated. His grandson King Hussein (reigned 1952–) was initially threatened by radicals encouraged by Egypt's President Nasser. In the 1967 Arab-Israeli War, Jordan lost the West Bank, including Arab Jerusalem, to the Israelis. In the 1970s the power of the Palestinian guerrillas in Jordan challenged the very existence of the Jordanian state. After a short but bloody civil war in September 1979 the Palestinian leadership fled abroad. King Hussein renounced all responsibility for the West Bank in 1988. The Palestinians – who form the majority of the Jordanian population – supported Iraq in the Gulf Crisis of 1990–91, although King Hussein adopted a position of neutrality.

KAZAKHSTAN

Official name: Kazakhstan.
Member of: UN, CIS, CSCE.
Area: 2 717 300 km² (1 049 200 sq mi).
Population: 16 793 000 (1991 est).
Capital and major cities: Alma-Ata 1 151 000, Karaganda 615 000, Chimkent 389 000, Pavlodar 331 000, Semipalatinsk 330 000 (1989 census).
Languages: Kazakh (40%), Russian (38%), German (6%), Ukrainian (5%).
Religions: Sunni Islam majority, Russian Orthodox minority.

GOVERNMENT   A 510-member legislature and a President are elected for four years by universal adult suffrage. A new constitution is to be drafted. The main political parties are the (former Communist) Socialist Party and the (coalition) Popular Congress of Kazakhstan.
President: Nursultan Nazarbayev.
Prime Minister: Sergei Tereshchenko.

GEOGRAPHY   Kazakhstan comprises a vast expanse of low tablelands (steppes) in the middle of Central Asia.

In the W, plains descend below sea level beside the Caspian Sea. Uplands include ranges of hills in the N and mountain chains, including the Tien Shan, in the S and E. Kazakhstan has several salt lakes, including the Aral Sea, which is shrinking because of excessive extraction of irrigation water from its tributaries. Deserts include the Kyzylkum in the S, the Kara Kum in the centre, and the Barsuki in the N. *Principal river:* Syrdarya 3019 km (1876 mi). *Highest point:* Khan Tengri 6398 m (20 991 ft).

ECONOMY   Kazakhstan is a major supplier of food and raw materials for industry to other former Soviet republics, particularly Russia. The transition to a market economy has hardly begun. Agriculture employs almost one half of the labour force. Large collective farms on the steppes in the N contributed one third of the cereal crop of the former USSR. Other major farming interests include sheep, fodder crops, fruit, vegetables and rice. Kazakhstan is rich in natural resources including coal, tin, copper, lead, zinc, gold, chromite, oil and nickel. Industry is represented by iron and steel (in the Karaganda coalfield), pharmaceuticals, food processing and cement.

RECENT HISTORY   During the Tsarist period there was large-scale Russian peasant settlement on the steppes, but Russian rule was resented and there was a major Kazakh revolt during World War I. After the Russian revolution, Kazakh nationalists formed a local government and demanded autonomy (1917). The Soviet Red Army invaded in 1920 and established an Autonomous Soviet Republic. Kazakhstan did not become a full Union Republic within the USSR until 1936. Widespread immigration from other parts of the USSR became a flood in 1954–6 when the 'Virgin Lands' of N Kazakhstan were opened up for farming. By the time Kazakhstan declared independence – following the abortive coup by Communist hardliners in Moscow (September 1991) – the Kazakhs formed a minority within their own republic. When the USSR was dissolved (December 1991), Kazakhstan was internationally recognized as an independent republic. The vast new Kazakh state – in theory, a nuclear power because of former Soviet nuclear weapons on its territory – occupies a pivotal position within Central Asia.

KENYA

Official name: Jamhuri ya Kenya (Republic of Kenya).

Member of: UN, OAU, Commonwealth.

Area: 580 367 km² (224 081 sq mi).

Population: 25 905 000 (1991 est.).

Capital and major cities: Nairobi 1 505 000 (including suburbs, 1990 est), Mombasa 426 000, Kisumu 167 000, Nakuru 102 000 (1985 est.).

Languages: Swahili (official), English, Kikuyu (21%), Luhya (14%), Luo (11%), Kamba (11%).

Religions: Roman Catholic (27%), Independent African Churches (27%), various Protestant Churches (19%), animist (19%), Sunni Islam (6%)

GOVERNMENT The President and 188 members of the 202-member National Assembly are elected by universal adult suffrage every five years. The remaining 14 Assembly members, the Vice President and the Cabinet of Ministers are appointed by the President. The main political parties include (the former monopoly) KANU (Kenya African National Union), the Forum for the Restoration of Democracy (FORD-Kenya), FORD-Asili and the Democratic Party.

President: Daniel arap Moi.

GEOGRAPHY The steep-sided Rift Valley divides the highlands that run from north to south through central Kenya. Plateaux extend in the west to Lake Victoria and in the east to coastal lowlands. *Principal rivers:* Tana, Umba, Athi, Mathioya. *Highest point:* Mount Kenya 5199 m (17 058 ft).

ECONOMY Over 75% of the labour force is involved in agriculture. The main crops include wheat and maize for domestic consumption, and tea, coffee, sisal, sugar cane and cotton for export. Large numbers of beef cattle are reared, and Kenya is one of the few states in black Africa to have a major dairy industry. Tourism is an important source of foreign currency.

RECENT HISTORY The British East African Protectorate became the colony of Kenya in 1920. White settlement in the highlands was bitterly resented by the Africans – particularly the Kikuyu – whose land was taken. Racial discrimination and attacks on African customs also created discontent. Black protest movements emerged in the 1920s, and after World War II these had developed into nationalism. From the 1920s, black protest was led by Jomo Kenyatta (c. 1893–1978), who in 1947 became the first president of the Kenya African Union. When the violent Mau Mau rising – which involved mainly Kikuyu people – broke out (1952–56), Kenyatta was held responsible and was imprisoned on doubtful evidence (1953–61). After the British had crushed the Mau Mau revolt in a bloody campaign, they negotiated with Kenyatta and the other African nationalists. Independence, under Kenyatta's KANU party, followed in 1963. His moderate leadership and pro-capitalist policies earned him British support and the gratitude of the remaining whites. His policies were continued by his successor, Daniel arap Moi, but considerable restrictions on political activity followed an attempted military coup in 1982. Multi-party elections were held in 1993.

KIRIBATI

Official name: Republic of Kiribati.

Member of: Commonwealth, South Pacific Forum.

Area: 717 km² (277 sq mi).

Population: 73 000 (1991 est).

Capital: Bairiki (on Tarawa) 25 000 (1990 census).

Languages: English (official), I-Kiribati.

Religions: Roman Catholic (over 50%), Kiribati Protestant (Congregational; over 40%).

GOVERNMENT The President and 39 members of the Assembly are elected by universal adult suffrage every four years. An additional member for Banaba is appointed to the Assembly, whose members nominate three or four of their number as presidential candidates. The President appoints a Cabinet of Ministers, which is responsible to the Assembly. All the members of the Assembly are independents, although a political party has been formed in opposition.

President: Teateo Teannaki.

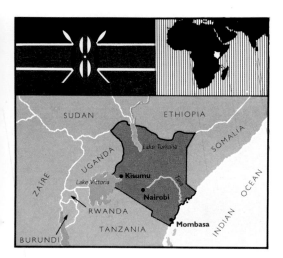

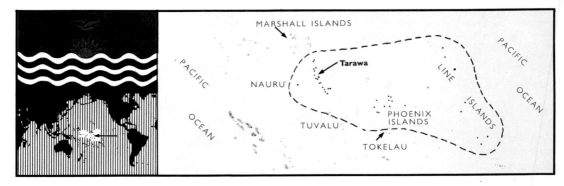

GEOGRAPHY With the exception of the island of Banaba – which is composed of phosphate rock – Kiribati comprises three groups of small coral atolls. There are no significant rivers. *Highest point:* 81 m (265 ft) on Banaba.

ECONOMY Most islanders are involved in subsistence farming and fishing. The only significant export is copra.

RECENT HISTORY The Gilbert Islands – which became British in 1892 – were occupied by Japan (1942–43). British nuclear weapons were tested on Christmas Island (1957–64). In 1979 the islands gained independence as Kiribati (pronounced Kiri-Bass).

KOREA, DEMOCRATIC PEOPLE'S REPUBLIC OF

Official name: Chosun Minchu-chui Inmin Konghwa-guk (Democratic People's Republic of Korea). Popularly known as North Korea.
Member of: UN.
Area: 120 538 km² (46 540 sq mi).
Population: 21 815 000 (1991 est).
Capital and major cities: Pyongyang 2 640 000, Hamhung 775 000, Chongjin 755 000, Chinnamp'o 690 000, Sinuiju 500 000 (1986 est).
Language: Korean.
Religions: Daoism and Confucianism (14%), Chondism (14%), Buddhism (2%).

GOVERNMENT The Party Congress of the (Communist) Korean Worker's Party elects a Central Committee, which in turn elects a Politburo, the seat of effective power. Citizens aged 17 and over vote in unopposed elections every four years for the 615-member Supreme People's Assembly. The Assembly elects the President, Prime Minister and Central People's Committee, which nominates Ministers.
President: Kim Il-Sung.
Prime Minister: Yon Hyong Muk.

GEOGRAPHY Over three quarters of the country consists of mountains. *Principal rivers:* Imjin, Ch'ongch'ŏn, Yalu. *Highest point:* Paek-tu 2744 m (9003 ft).

ECONOMY Over 30% of the labour force work on cooperative farms, mainly growing rice. Natural resources include coal, zinc, magnetite, iron ore and lead. Great emphasis has been placed on industrial development, notably the metallurgical, machine-building, chemical and cement industries. The end of barter deals with the former USSR (1990–91) brought a sharp economic decline.

RECENT HISTORY Korea – a Japanese possession from 1910 to 1945 – was divided into zones of occupation in 1945. The USSR established a Communist republic in their zone north of the 38th parallel (1948). North Korea launched a surprise attack on the South in June 1950, hoping to achieve reunification by force. The Korean War devastated the peninsula. At the ceasefire in 1953 the frontier was re-established close to the 38th parallel. North Korea has the world's first Communist dynasty, whose personality cult has surpassed even that of Stalin.

President Kim Il-Sung (1912–) and his son and anticipated successor, Kim Jong-Il, have rejected political reforms. Since the collapse of Communism in the former USSR and Eastern Europe, North Korea has become increasingly isolated.

KOREA, REPUBLIC OF

Official name: Daehan-Minkuk (Republic of Korea). Popularly known as South Korea.

Member of: UN.

Area: 99 143 km² (38 279 sq mi).

Population: 43 520 000 (1990 census).

Capital and major cities: Seoul (Soul) 10 726 000, Pusan 3 825 000, Taegu 2 248 000, Inchon 1 682 000, Kwangju 1 206 000, Taejon 1 062 000, Ulsan 683 000, Sowon 645 000 (1990 census).

Language: Korean (official).

Religions: Buddhist (24%), various Protestant Churches (16%), Roman Catholic (5%).

GOVERNMENT The 299-member National Assembly is elected by universal adult suffrage every four years – 237 members are directly elected to represent constituencies; the remaining 62 members are chosen under a system of proportional representation. The President – who appoints a State Council (Cabinet) and a Prime Minister – is directly elected for a single five-year term. The main political parties include the Democratic Liberal Party, the Democratic Party, and the Party for National Unification.

President: Kim Young Sam.

Prime Minister: Soont Jong Hyan.

GEOGRAPHY Apart from restricted coastal lowlands and the densely-populated river basins, most of the country is mountainous. *Principal rivers:* Han, Kum, Naktong, Somjin, Yongsan. *Highest point:* Halla-san 1950 m (6398 ft) on Cheju Island.

ECONOMY About 20% of the labour force is involved in agriculture. The principal crops are rice, wheat and barley. A flourishing manufacturing sector is dominated by a small number of large family conglomerates. The important textile industry was the original manufacturing base, but South Korea is now the world's leading producer of ships and footwear, and a major producer of electronic equipment, electrical goods, steel, petrochemicals, motor vehicles (Hyundai) and toys. Banking and finance are expanding. The country experienced high economic growth rates throughout the 1980s and early 1990s.

RECENT HISTORY The Yi dynasty (1392–1910) gave Korea a long period of cultural continuity, but in 1910 Korea was annexed by the Japanese, who instituted a harsh colonial rule. After World War II, the peninsula was divided into Soviet and US zones of occupation. In 1948 the Republic of Korea was established in the American (southern) zone. The surprise invasion of the South by the Communist North precipitated the Korean War (1950–53). The war cost a million lives and ended in stalemate with the division of Korea confirmed. Closely allied to the USA, an astonishing economic transformation took place in South Korea. However, the country has experienced long periods of authoritarian rule including the presidencies of Syngman Rhee and Park Chung-Hee, but the election of ex-General Roh Tae Woo – amid political unrest in 1987 – introduced a more open regime. Much prestige was gained through the successful Seoul Olympic Games, and trading and diplomatic contacts have been established with the USSR and all the former Communist countries of Eastern Europe. This has left North Korea increasingly isolated. In 1990 North and South Korea tentatively began talks at prime ministerial level.

KUWAIT

Official name: Daulat al-Kuwait (State of Kuwait).

Member of: UN, Arab League, OPEC, GCC.

Area: 17 818 km² (6880 sq mi).

Population: 1 100 000 (1992 est).

Capital: Kuwait City 750 000 (including agglomeration; 1992 unofficial est).

Language: Arabic (official).

Religions: Sunni Islam (official; about 70%), Shia Islam (30%).

GOVERNMENT Kuwait is a monarchy ruled by an Amir, who is chosen from and by the adult male members of the ruling dynasty. The Amir appoints a Prime Minister and a Council of Ministers. A 50-member National Assembly is elected for four years by literate adult male Kuwaiti nationals whose families fulfil stringent residence qualifications. There are no political parties.

Amir: HH Shaikh Jabir III bin Ahmad as-Sabah (succeeded upon the death of his cousin, 31 December 1977).
Prime Minister: HH Shaikh Saad al-Abdullah as-Sabah, Crown Prince of Kuwait.

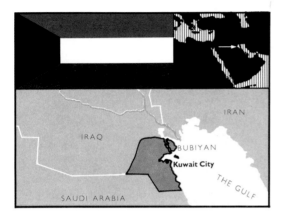

GEOGRAPHY Most of the country is desert, relatively flat and low lying. There are no permanent rivers. *Highest point:* 289 m (951 ft) at Ash Shaqaya.

ECONOMY The Kuwaiti economy was devastated by the Iraqi invasion and Gulf War (1991), but reconstruction followed rapidly. Large reserves of petroleum and natural gas are the mainstay of Kuwait's economy. Owing to lack of water, little agriculture is possible.

RECENT HISTORY From 1899 to 1961 Kuwait was a British-protected state. Oil was discovered in 1938 and was produced commercially from 1946. Iraq attempted to take over Kuwait in 1961, but the dispatch of British troops to the Gulf discouraged an Iraqi invasion. In August 1990 – despite having recognized the emirate's sovereignty in 1963 – Iraq invaded and annexed Kuwait. Iraq refused to withdraw despite repeated UN demands and in January 1991 the war to remove Iraqi forces from Kuwait – the Second Gulf War – began. In February, coalition forces entered the emirate to liberate Kuwait from Iraqi rule. The emirate was freed within 100 hours in a campaign during which the Iraqi forces were routed. The country was found to have been devastated by the occupying Iraqi forces. Following the liberation of Kuwait, pressure for constitutional reform grew, and the constitution, which had been suspended in 1968, was restored in 1992. Large numbers of Palestinians – who were perceived to have favoured Iraq – were expelled from Kuwait in 1992.

KYRGYZSTAN

Official name: Kyrgyzstan. Formerly known as Kirghizia.
Member of: UN, CIS, CSCE.
Area: 198 500 km^2 (76 600 sq mi).
Population: 4 422 000 (1991 est).
Capital and major cities: Bishkek (formerly Frunze) 626 000, Osh 213 000, Przhevalsk 56 000 (1989 census).
Languages: Kyrgyz (53%), Russian (21%), Uzbek (13%), Ukrainian (3%).
Religions: Sunni Islam majority, Russian Orthodox.

GOVERNMENT A 250-member legislature and a President are elected for four years by universal adult suffrage. A new constitution is to be drafted. The main political parties are the Kyrgyzstan Democratic Movement, the Kyrgyz Democratic Wing, and National Unity.
President and Prime Minister: Askar Akayev

GEOGRAPHY Most of Kyrgyzstan lies within the Tien Shan mountains, rising at Pik Pobedy to 7439 m (24 406 ft). Restricted lowlands – including the Chu valley and part of the Fergana valley – contain most of the population.

ECONOMIC ACTIVITY Agriculture is dominated by large collectivized farms that specialize in growing fodder crops for sheep and goats, and cotton under irrigation. Natural resources include coal, lead, zinc and considerable hydroelectric-power potential. Food processing and light industry are expanding but the economy remains centrally planned.

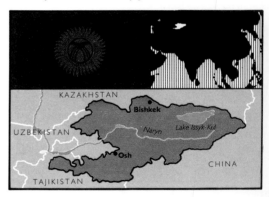

RECENT HISTORY The Kyrgyz – a Turkic people – are thought to have migrated to the region in the 12th century. Although nominally subject to Uzbek khans, the nomadic Kyrgyz retained their independence until after 1850 when the area was annexed by Russia. Opposition to the Russians – who were given most of the best land – found expression in a major revolt in 1916 and continuing guerrilla activity after the Russian Revolution. A Kirghiz Soviet Republic was founded in 1926 and became a full Union Republic within the USSR in 1936. After the abortive coup by Communist hardliners (September 1991), Kirghizia declared independence and – under its new name, Kyrgyzstan – received international recognition when the Soviet Union was dissolved (December 1991).

LAOS

Official name: Saathiaranagroat Prachhathippatay Prachhachhon Lao (The Lao People's Democratic Republic).
Member of: UN.
Area: 236 800 km² (91 400 sq mi).
Population: 4 290 000 (1991 est).
Capital: Vientiane (Viengchane) 377 000, Savannakhet 97 000, Luang Prabang (Louangphrabang) 68 000, Pakse 47 000, (1985 est).
Language: Lao (official).
Religion: Buddhism (57%), traditional local religions (over 30%).

GOVERNMENT Effective power is exercised by the Central Committee of the (Communist) Lao People's Revolutionary Party. Pending the implementation of a new constitution, representatives of directly elected local authorities have met as the National Congress to appoint the President, the Prime Minister and the Council of Ministers. There is constitutional provision for a 79-member Supreme People's Assembly to be elected for five years by universal adult suffrage.

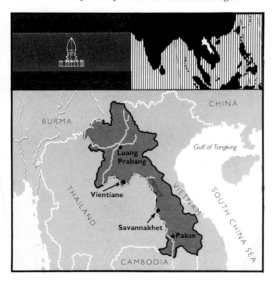

President: Kaysone Phomvihan.
Prime Minister: Khamtai Siphandon.

GEOGRAPHY Except for the Plain of Jars in the north and the Mekong Valley and low plateaux in the south, Laos is largely mountainous. *Principal river:* Mekong. *Highest point:* Phou Bia 2820 m (9252 ft).

ECONOMY War, floods and drought have retarded the development of Laos, one of the poorest countries in the world. The majority of Laotians work on collective farms, mainly growing rice. Since 1990, the Laotian government has attempted to encourage Western investment.

RECENT HISTORY A French protectorate was established in 1893. Japanese occupation in World War II led to a declaration of independence, which the French finally accepted in 1954. However, the kingdom was wracked by civil war, with royalist forces fighting the Communist Pathet Lao. The Viet Cong used Laos as a supply route in the Vietnam War, and US withdrawal from Vietnam allowed the Pathet Lao to take over Laos (1975). Since 1990, the government has begun to introduce reforms, but there is no suggestion that a multiparty system will be tolerated.

LATVIA

Official name: Latvija (Latvia).
Member of: UN, CSCE.
Area: 64 589 km² (24 938 sq mi).
Population: 2 686 000 (1991 est).
Capital and major cities: Riga 917 000, Daugavpils 128 000, Liepaja 115 000, Jelgava 75 000 (1990 est).
Languages: Lettish (over 52%), Russian (33%).
Religions: Lutheran (22%), Roman Catholic (7%), small Russian Orthodox minority.

GOVERNMENT A President – who appoints a Prime Minister and a Cabinet – and a 100-member Assembly are elected by universal adult suffrage for three years. The main political parties are the Popular Front of Latvia, (LTF), the Latvian National Independence Movement (LNNK), the Social Democratic Workers' Party (LSDSP) and the Green Party (LZP).
President: Anatolijs Gorbunovs.
Prime Minister: Ivars Godmanis.

GEOGRAPHY Latvia comprises an undulating plain, lower in the W (Courland) than in the E (Livonia). *Principal river:* Daugava. *Highest point:* Osveyskoye 311 m (1020 ft).

ECONOMY Engineering dominates a heavily industrialized economy. Latvia has relied on Russian trade and faces severe difficulties as it begins to introduce a free market. Agriculture specializes in dairying and meat production.

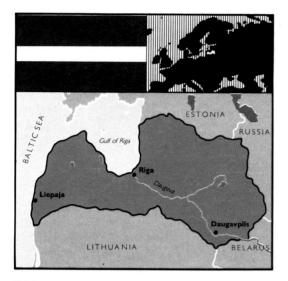

GOVERNMENT The constitution was amended in 1990 to provide for the election by universal adult suffrage of a 108-member National Assembly (comprising 54 deputies elected by Muslims and 54 deputies elected by Christians). The Assembly elects a (Maronite) President, who appoints a (Sunni Muslim) Prime Minister, who, in turn, appoints a Council of Ministers (six Christians and five Muslims). The main political parties include (Islamic fundamentalist) Hizbollah (Party of God), the (Maronite) Phalangist Party, the (pro-Syrian) Amal Party and the (mainly Druze) Progressive Socialist Party.
President: Elias Hrawi.
Prime Minister: Rafik al-Hariri.

GEOGRAPHY A narrow coastal plain is separated from the fertile Beka'a Valley by the mountains of Lebanon. To the east are the Anti-Lebanese range and Hermon Mountains. *Principal river:* Nahr al-Litāni. *Highest point:* Qurnat as-Sawdā 3088 m (10 131 ft).

ECONOMY Reconstruction of an economy devastated by civil war began in 1991. The principal agricultural crops are citrus fruit (grown mainly for export), wheat, barley and olives. The illegal cultivation of opium poppies is economically important. The textile and chemical industries and the financial sector are important.

RECENT HISTORY After World War I France received Syria as a League of Nations mandate, and created a separate Lebanese territory to protect Christian interests. The constitution under which Lebanon became independent in 1943 enshrined power-sharing between Christians and Muslims. The relative toleration between the various religious groups in

RECENT HISTORY Under Russian rule since the 18th century, Latvian national consciousness grew throughout the 19th century. Following the Communist takeover in Russia (1917), Latvian nationalists declared independence (1918). A democratic system lasted until 1936 when General Ulmanis established a dictatorship. The Non-Aggression Pact (1939) between Hitler and Stalin assigned Latvia to the USSR, which invaded and annexed the republic (1940). After occupation by Nazi Germany (1941–44), Soviet rule was reimposed. Large-scale Russian settlement replaced over 200 000 Latvians who were killed or deported to Siberia. In 1988, reforms in the USSR allowed Latvian nationalists to operate openly. Nationalists won a majority in Latvia's parliament and seceded following the failed coup by Communist hardliners in Moscow (1991). The USSR recognized Latvia's independence in September 1991. Tension remains over the large Russian minority in Latvia.

LEBANON

Official name: Al-Lubnan (The Lebanon).
Member of: UN, Arab League.
Area: 10 452 km² (4036 sq mi).
Population: 2 745 000 (1991 est).
Capital and major cities: Beirut (Bayrūt) 1 100 000, Tripoli (Tarabulus) 240 000, Zahleh 200 000, Sidon (Saida) 100 000 (all including suburbs; 1990 est).
Languages: Arabic (official).
Religions: Shia Islam (31%), Sunni Islam (27%), Maronite Christian (22%), other Christian Churches (Armenian, Greek Orthodox, Syrian; 16%), Druze.

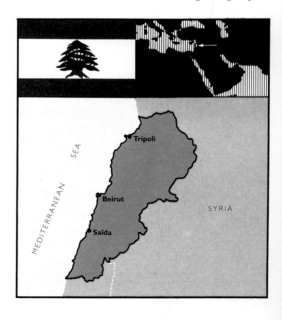

Lebanon began to break down in the late 1950s when Muslim numerical superiority failed to be matched by corresponding constitutional changes. Radical Muslim supporters of the union of Syria and Egypt in 1958 clashed with the pro-Western party of Camille Chamoun (President 1952–58). Civil war ensued, and US marines landed in Beirut to restore order. The 1967 Arab-Israeli war and the exile of the Palestinian leadership to Beirut (1970–71) destabilized Lebanon. Civil war broke out in 1975, with subsequent Syrian and Israeli interventions. The war continued, plunging the country into ungovernable chaos, with Maronites, various Sunni and Shia Lebanese groups (including Iranian-backed fundamentalists), Syrian troops, Druze militia and UN peace-keeping forces all occupying zones of the fragmented country. In 1990, the Christian militia was crushed by the Syrians and the Lebanese government was able to reassert its authority over the whole of Beirut. However, Israeli-sponsored forces continue to occupy the south. A new constitution (1990) – which enshrines Muslim-Christian equality in government – and the continuing presence of Syrian troops have allowed a reconstruction of the Lebanese state.

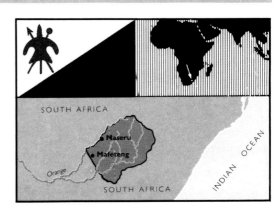

RECENT HISTORY The kingdom escaped incorporation into South Africa by becoming a British protectorate (known as Basutoland) in 1868. Although independence was achieved in 1966, the land-locked state remained dependent on South Africa. Chief Jonathan (Prime Minister 1966–86) – who curbed the monarchy's powers and attempted to limit South African influence – was deposed in a military coup. In 1990, the Military Council exiled King Moshoeshoe II and placed his son on the throne.

LESOTHO

Official name: The Kingdom of Lesotho.
Member of: UN, Commonwealth, OAU, SADCC.
Area: 30 355 km² (11 720 sq mi).
Population: 1 806 000 (1991 est).
Capital: Maseru 110 000, Maputsoe 20 000 (1988 est).
Languages: Sesotho and English (official).
Religions: Roman Catholic (44%), various Protestant Churches (mainly Lesotho Evangelical and Anglican; 49%).

GOVERNMENT Since a military coup in 1986, Lesotho has been ruled by a six-man Military Council and a Council of Ministers. A new constitution is to be introduced and multi-party elections are scheduled for 1993 or 1994. Political parties include the Marematlou Freedom Party, the Basotho National Party, the Basotho Congress Party and the United Democratic Party.
King: HM King Letsie III (succeeded upon the exile and deposition of his father, 12 November 1990).
Head of government (Chair of the Military Council): Maj.-Gen. Elias Phisoana Ramaema.

GEOGRAPHY Most of Lesotho is mountainous. *Principal rivers:* Orange, Caledon. *Highest point:* Thabana Ntlenyana 3482 m (11 425 ft).

ECONOMY Livestock – cattle, sheep and goats (for mohair) – are the mainstay of the economy. Natural resources include diamonds and abundant water, which is exported to South Africa.

LIBERIA

Official name: The Republic of Liberia.
Member of: UN, OAU, ECOWAS.
Area: 111 369 km² (43 000 sq mi).
Population: 2 607 000 (1990 est); in 1992 there were up to 700 000 Liberian refugees in neighbouring countries.
Capital: Monrovia 465 000, Buchanan 25 000 (1987 est).
Language: English (official).

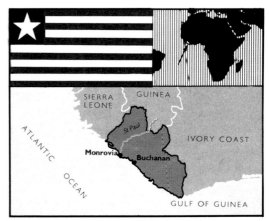

Religions: Animist (50%), Sunni Islam (26%), various Christian Churches (mainly Methodist, Baptist and Episcopalian; 24%).

GOVERNMENT The constitution provides for a President, Vice President, 26-member Senate and 64-member House of Representatives to be elected for six years by universal adult suffrage. The President appoints a Cabinet of Ministers. The Liberian political system broke down in 1990 owing to civil war.
Head of state: (acting president): Amos Sawyer.

GEOGRAPHY A low swampy coastal belt borders a higher zone of tropical forest. *Principal rivers:* St Paul, St John, Cess. *Highest point:* Mount Nimba 1380 m (4540 ft).

ECONOMY Over 70% of the labour force is involved in agriculture, producing cassava and rice as subsistence crops, and rubber, coffee and cocoa for export. Liberia is a major exporter of iron ore, but the economy has been shattered by civil war.

RECENT HISTORY Black Americans settled Liberia in the 19th century, dominated the local Africans and extended their control inland. From 1878 to 1980 power was held by presidents from the True Whig Party, including William Tubman (President 1944–71). His successor, William Tolbert, was assassinated during a military coup led by Samuel Doe, the first Liberian of local ancestry to rule. Doe was overthrown in a coup in 1990. Troops from several West African countries were dispatched by ECOWAS to restore order but civil war, initially involving two rebel forces, has continued despite a ceasefire in 1991.

LIBYA

Official name: Daulat Libiya al-'Arabiya al-Ishtrakiya al-Jumhuriya (The Great Socialist People's Libyan Arab Jamahiriya).
Member of: UN, Arab League, OPEC.
Area: 1 759 540 km² (679 363 sq mi).
Population: 4 325 000 (1991 est).
Capital and major cities: Tripoli (Tarabulus) 991 000, Benghazi (Banghazi) 485 000, Misurata (Misratah) 178 000 (1989 est). In 1988 government functions were decentralized to Sirte (Surt) and Al Jofrah as well as Tripoli and Benghazi.
Language: Arabic (official).
Religion: Sunni Islam (over 97%).

GOVERNMENT Over 1110 delegates from directly elected local Basic People's Congresses, trade unions, 'popular committees' and professional organizations meet as the Great People's Congress, which chooses a Revolutionary Leader – head of state – and the General People's Committee (which is equivalent to a Council of Ministers). The appointed General Secretariat assists the Congress. There are effectively no political parties.
Head of state: Moamar al Gaddafi.
Head of government (Secretary-General of the General People's Committee): Abdal Raziq al-Sawsa.

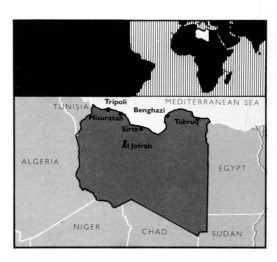

GEOGRAPHY The Sahara Desert covers most of Libya. In the northwest – Tripolitania – coastal oases and a low plain form the country's main agricultural region. In the northeast (Cyrenaica) a coastal plain and mountain ranges support Mediterranean vegetation. *Principal river:* Wādi al-Fārigh. *Highest point:* Pico Bette 2286 m (7500 ft).

ECONOMY Libya is one of the world's largest producers of petroleum. Liquefied gas is also exported. Coastal oases produce wheat, barley, nuts, dates and grapes.

RECENT HISTORY In 1911 the Italians took Libya, which had been under Ottoman (Turkish) rule. The British Eighth Army defeated the Italians in the Libyan Desert (1942), and after World War II the country was divided between British and French administrations. Libya gained independence in 1951 under King Idris, formerly Amir of Cyrenaica. Although oil revenues made Libya prosperous, the pro-Western monarchy became increasingly unpopular. In 1969 Col. Moamar al Gaddafi (1942–) took power in a coup. Gaddafi nationalized the oil industry, but his various attempts to federate with other Arab countries proved abortive. In the 1970s he began a cultural revolution, dismantled formal government, collectivized economic activity, limited personal wealth and suppressed opposition. Libya's alleged support of international terrorism provoked US air raids on Tripoli and Benghazi in 1986, since when Gaddafi has kept a lower international profile. However, alleged Libyan involvement in the bombing of a US airliner led to the imposition of UN sanctions in 1992.

LIECHTENSTEIN

Official name: Fürstentum Liechtenstein (The Principality of Liechtenstein).
Member of: UN, Council of Europe, CSCE, EFTA.
Area: 160 km² (62 sq mi).
Population: 29 000 (1991 est).
Capital and major town: Vaduz 4800, Schaan 4900 (1990 est).
Language: German (official).
Religion: Roman Catholic (87%), Lutheran (8%).

GOVERNMENT The country is a constitutional monarchy ruled by a Prince. The 25-member Landstag (Parliament) is elected under a system of proportional representation by universal adult suffrage for four years. The Landstag elects a 5-member National Committee (Cabinet) including a Prime Minister, who is then appointed by the Prince. The main political parties are the VU (Fatherland Union), the FBP (Progressive Citizens' Party) and the (Green) Free List.
Prince: HSH Prince Hans Adam II (succeeded upon the death of his father, 13 November 1989).
Prime Minister: Markus Buechel.

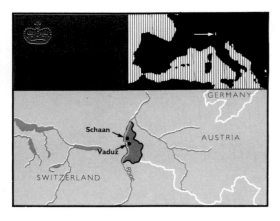

GEOGRAPHY The Alps stand in the east of the principality. The west comprises the floodplain of the River Rhine. *Principal rivers:* Rhine (Rhein), Samina. *Highest point:* Grauspitze 2599 m (8326 ft).

ECONOMY Liechtenstein has one of the highest standards of living in the world. Tourism, banking and manufacturing (precision goods) are all important.

RECENT HISTORY Liechtenstein was the only German principality not to join the German Empire in 1871. Since 1924 the country has enjoyed a customs and monetary union with Switzerland. Since 1989 the country has taken a more active role internationally, for instance, joining EFTA and the UN.

LITHUANIA

Official name: Lietuva (Lithuania).
Member of: UN, CSCE.
Area: 65 200 km² (25 174 sq mi).
Population: 3 739 000 (1991 est).
Capital and major cities: Vilnius 593 000, Kaunas 430 000, Klaipeda 206 000, Siauliai 148 000, Panevezys 129 000 (1990 est).
Languages: Lithuanian (80%), Russian (9%), Polish (7%), Belarussian (2%).
Religions: Roman Catholic (80%), Lutheran minority.

GOVERNMENT The 141-member Parliament and a President are elected by universal adult suffrage for five years. The President appoints a Prime Minister, who, in turn, appoints a Cabinet of Ministers. The principal political parties include the (former Communist) Democratic Labour Party, the (nationalist) Sajudis Movement, the Christian Democratic Party, the Social Democratic Party and the Green Party.
President: Mykolas Brazauskas.
Prime Minister: to be appointed.

GEOGRAPHY Lithuania comprises a low-lying plain dotted with lakes and crossed by ridges of glacial moraine that are covered with pine forests. A 100 km (60 mi) sandspit separates a large lagoon from the Baltic Sea. *Principal rivers:* Nemunas (Neman), Vilnya. *Highest point:* Juozapine 294 m (964 ft).

ECONOMY One fifth of the labour force is engaged in agriculture, principally cattle rearing and dairying. Much of the country is heavily forested. The engi-

neering, timber, cement and food-processing industries are important. Lithuania – whose economy is weaker than that of the other two Baltic republics – faces an uncertain future as it dismantles state control and breaks away from the former Soviet trade system.

RECENT HISTORY Lithuanians rose against Russian rule in 1830–31 and 1863. German forces invaded in 1915 and encouraged the establishment of a Lithuanian state. After World War I, the new republic faced invasions by the Red Army from the E and the Polish army from the W (1919–20). Internationally recognized boundaries were not established until 1923. The dictatorship of Augustinas Voldemaras (1926–29) was followed by that of Antonas Smetona (1929–40). The Non-Aggression Pact (1939) between Hitler and Stalin assigned Lithuania to the USSR, which invaded and annexed the republic (1940). Lithuania was occupied by Nazi Germany (1941–44). When Soviet rule was reimposed (1945), large-scale Russian settlement replaced over 250 000 Lithuanians who had been killed or deported to Siberia. In 1988, reforms in the USSR allowed Lithuanian nationalists to operate openly. Sajudis – the nationalist movement – won a majority in the republic's parliament, but their declaration of independence (1990) brought a crackdown by Soviet forces in Lithuania. Following the failed coup by Communist hardliners in Moscow (August 1991), the USSR recognized Lithuania's independence. Following the economic collapse of Lithuania (1992–93), Sajudis lost elections to the former Communists.

LUXEMBOURG

Official name: Grand-Duché de Luxembourg (Grand Duchy of Luxembourg).

Member of: UN, EC, NATO, WEU, CSCE, OECD, Council of Europe.

Area: 2586 km² (999 sq mi).

Population: 385 000 (1991 census).

Capital: Luxembourg 117 000 (city 78 000), Esch-sur-Alzette 24 000, Differdange 16 000, Dudelange 15 000, Pétange 12 000, Sanem 12 000 (1991 census).

Languages: Letzeburgish (national), French and German (both official).

Religions: Roman Catholic (95%).

GOVERNMENT Luxembourg is a constitutional monarchy with a Grand Duke or Duchess as sovereign. The 60-member Chamber of Deputies is elected under a system of proportional representation by universal adult suffrage for five years. A Council of Ministers and a President of the Council (Premier) – commanding a majority in the Chamber – are appointed by the sovereign. The main political parties are the (centre-right) Social Christian Party, the Socialist Party, the (liberal) Democratic Party, Green Alternative and Green Ecologists.

Grand Duke: HRH Grand Duke Jean I (succeeded upon

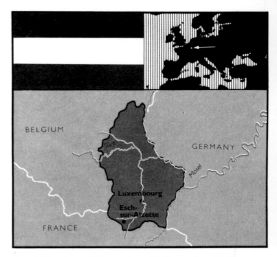

the abdication of his mother, 12 November 1964).
Prime Minister: Jacques Santer.

GEOGRAPHY The Oesling is a wooded plateau in the north. The Gutland in the south is a lowland region of valleys and ridges. *Principal rivers:* Moselle, Sûre, Our, Alzette. *Highest point:* Huldange 550 m (1833 ft).

ECONOMY The iron and steel industry – originally based on local ore – is important. Luxembourg has become a major banking centre. The north grows potatoes and fodder crops; the south produces wheat and fruit, including grapes.

RECENT HISTORY From 1815 to 1890, Dutch kings were also sovereigns of Luxembourg, but in 1890 Luxembourg was inherited by a junior branch of the House of Orange. Occupied by the Germans during both World Wars, Luxembourg concluded an economic union with Belgium in 1922 and has enthusiastically supported European unity.

MADAGASCAR

Official name: Repoblika Demokratika n'i Madagaskar (The Democratic Republic of Madagascar).

Member of: UN, OAU.

Area: 587 041 km² (226 658 sq mi).

Population: 11 197 000 (1990 est.).

Capital and major cities: Antananarivo (Tananarive) 802 000, Toamasina 145 000, Fianarantsoa 125 000, Mahajanga 122 000 (1990 est.).

Languages: Malagasy and French (official).

Religions: Animist (47%), Roman Catholic (26%), Protestant Church of Jesus Christ in Madagascar (22%).

GOVERNMENT The President is elected by universal adult suffrage for a seven-year term. He and the Supreme Revolutionary Council together appoint a Prime Minister and a Council of Ministers. The 137-member National Assembly is directly elected for five years. The main political parties are the (former monopoly) AREMA (Advanced Guard of the Malagasy Revolution), the Movement for Proletarian Power (MFM), the (centrist) VONJY (the Popular Spirit of National Unity) and the (radical) National Movement for the Independence of Madagascar.
President: Admiral Didier Ratsiraka.
Prime Minister: Guy Razanamasy.

GEOGRAPHY Massifs form a spine running from north to south through the island. To the east is a narrow coastal plain; to the west are fertile plains. *Principal rivers:* Ikopa, Mania, Mangoky. *Highest point:* Maromokotro Tsaratanana Massif 2885 m (9465 ft).

ECONOMY Three quarters of the labour force are involved in agriculture. The main crops are coffee and vanilla for export, and rice and cassava for domestic consumption. The island is an important producer of chromite. Drought and fluctuations in the prices of primary products have added to Madagascar's severe economic problems.

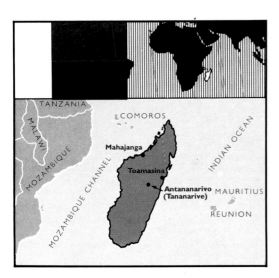

RECENT HISTORY Madagascar was annexed by France in 1896, although resistance continued until 1904. Strong nationalist feeling found expression in a major rising (1947–48) that was only suppressed with heavy loss of life. Independence was finally achieved in 1960, but the pro-Western rule of President Philibert Tsirana became increasingly unpopular. Since a military coup in 1972, Madagascar has had left-wing governments, but political and economic liberalization began in 1990.

MALAWI

Official name: The Republic of Malawi.
Member of: UN, Commonwealth, OAU, SADCC.
Area: 118 484 km² (45 747 sq mi).
Population: 9 152 000 (1991 est).
Capital and major cities: Lilongwe 220 000, Blantyre 403 000, Mzuzu 115 000 (1987 census).
Languages: English (official), Chichewa (over 50%; official).
Religions: Animist (67%), Roman Catholic (17%), Sunni Islam (6%), Presbyterian (6%).

GOVERNMENT Under the constitution the President is directly elected, but in 1971 Dr Hastings Kamuzu Banda was declared President for life. Elections are held by universal adult suffrage every five years for 112 members of the National Assembly. The President appoints additional members as well as a Cabinet of Ministers. The Malawi Congress Party is the only legal party, but a referendum on the restoration of multi-party politics is scheduled.
President: Dr Hastings Kamuzu Banda.

GEOGRAPHY Plateaux cover the north and centre. The Rift Valley contains Lake Malawi and the Shire Valley. The Shire Highlands lie on the Mozambique border. *Principal river:* Shire. *Highest point:* Mount Sapitawa 3002 m (9849 ft).

ECONOMY Agriculture is the mainstay of the economy, providing most of Malawi's exports. Tobacco, maize, tea and sugar cane are the main crops.

RECENT HISTORY A British protectorate, later called Nyasaland, was declared in 1891. In 1915 the Rev.

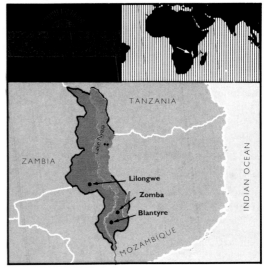

John Chilembwe led a violent rising in the fertile south where Africans had lost much land to white settlers. Dr Hastings Kamuzu Banda (c. 1902–) led the country's opposition to the resented union with the white-dominated Central African Federation (1953–63). Since independence as Malawi in 1964, Banda has provided strong rule and – despite criticism – maintained close relations with South Africa. In 1992–93, pressure for political reforms grew.

MALAYSIA

Official name: Persekutuan Tanah Melaysiu (The Federation of Malaysia).

Member of: UN, Commonwealth, ASEAN.

Area: 329 758 km² (127 320 sq mi).

Population: 17 556 000 (1991 census).

Capital and major cities: Kuala Lumpur 1 233 000 (including suburbs; 1991 census), Ipoh 390 000, George Town 325 000, Johor Baharu 325 000, Petaling Jaya 270 000, Kelang (Klang) 250 000, Kuala Trengganu (Kuala Terengganu) 235 000, Kota Baharu 220 000, Taiping 190 000, Seremban 175 000, Kuantan 170 000, Kota Kinabalu 140 000 (1990 est).

Languages: Bahasa Malaysia (Malay; official; over 58%), English, Chinese (32%), Tamil.

Religions: Sunni Islam (official; over 55%), with Buddhist, Daoist and various Christian minorities.

GOVERNMENT The Yang di-Pertuan Agong (the King of Malaysia) holds office for five years. He is elected – from their own number – by the hereditary sultans who reign in 9 of the 13 states. The 70-member Senate (upper house) comprises 40 members appointed by the King and two members elected by each of the state and territorial assemblies for a three-year term. The 180-member House of Representatives is elected by universal adult suffrage for five years. The King appoints a Prime Minister and a Cabinet commanding a majority in the House, to which they are responsible. The main political parties include the National Front (a coalition of parties including UMNO – the United Malays National Organization), the (democratic social-ist) Democratic Action Party, the Sabah United Party (PBS), the (coalition) Muslim Unity Movement (APU; including the Spirit of '46 Party). Each state has its own parliament and government.

King of Malaysia: HM Azlan Shah (ibni Sultan Yusof Izzudin), Raja of Perak, Yang di-Pertuan Agong, inaugurated 26 April 1989.

Prime Minister: Mohamad Mahathir.

STATES AND TERRITORIES **Johore (Johor)** (sul-tanate) *Area:* 18 985 km² (7330 sq mi). *Population:* 2 107 000 (1991 census). *Capital:* Johor Baharu.

Kedah (sultanate) *Area:* 9425 km² (3639 sq mi). *Population:* 1 413 000 (1991 census). *Capital:* Alor Star (Alur Setar).

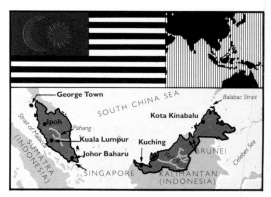

Kelantan (sultanate) *Area:* 14 931 km² (5765 sq mi). *Population:* 1 220 000 (1991 census). *Capital:* Kota Baharu.

Malacca *Area:* 1650 km² (637 sq mi). *Population:* 584 000 (1991 census). *Capital:* Malacca.

Negeri Sembilan (sultanate) *Area:* 6643 km² (2565 sq mi). *Population:* 724 000 (1991 census). *Capital:* Ser-emban.

Pahang (sultanate) *Area:* 35 965 km² (13 886 sq mi). *Population:* 1 055 000 (1991 census). *Capital:* Kuantan.

Penang (Pinang) *Area:* 1033 km² (399 sq mi). *Population:* 1 142 000 (1991 census). *Capital:* George Town.

Perak (sultanate) *Area:* 21 005 km² (8110 sq mi). *Population:* 2 222 000 (1991 census). *Capital:* Ipoh.

Perlis (sultanate) *Area:* 795 km² (307 sq mi). *Population:* 188 000 (1991 census). *Capital:* Kangar.

Sabah *Area:* 80 429 km² (29 353 sq mi). *Population:* 1 470 000 (1991 census). *Capital:* Kota Kinabalu.

Sarawak *Area:* 121 449 km² (48 250 sq mi). *Population:* 1 669 000 (1991 census). *Capital:* Kuching.

Selangor (sultanate) *Area:* 7962 km² (3074 sq mi). *Population:* 1 978 000 (1991 census). *Capital:* Shah Alam.

Trengganu (Terengganu) (sultanate) *Area:* 12 955 km² (5002 sq mi). *Population:* 752 000 (1991 census). *Capital:* Kuala Trengganu (Kuala Terengganu).

Federal Territory *Area:* 243 km² (94 sq mi). *Population:* 1 233 000 (1991 census). *Capital:* Kuala Lumpur.

Labuan *Area:* 91 km² (35 sq mi). *Population:* 26 000 (1990 census). *Capital:* Victoria.

GEOGRAPHY Western (peninsular) Malaysia con-sists of mountain ranges – including the Trengganu Highlands and Cameron Highlands – running north to south and bordered by densely populated coastal low-lands. Tropical rainforest covers the hills and moun-tains of Eastern Malaysia – Sabah and Sarawak, the northern part of the island of Borneo. *Principal rivers:* Pahang, Kelantan. *Highest point:* Kinabalu (in Sabah) 4101 m (13 455 ft).

ECONOMY Rubber, petroleum and tin are the tradi-tional mainstays of the Malaysian economy, but all three suffered drops in price on the world market in the 1980s. Pepper, cocoa and timber are also important. Over one quarter of the labour force is involved in agriculture, mainly growing rice as a subsistence crop. Manufacturing industry is now the largest exporter; major industries include rubber, tin, timber, textiles, machinery and cement. The government has greatly encouraged industrialization, investment and a more active role for the ethnic Malay population in industry, which – along with commerce and finance – has been largely the preserve of Chinese Malaysians. Malaysia has experienced high economic growth rates since the early 1980s. A growing tourist industry is being very actively promoted.

RECENT HISTORY   Before the Japanese occupation in World War II, the area comprised the British Straits Settlements – Malacca, Penang and Singapore, the nine British-protected Malay sultanates, the colony of British North Borneo (now Sabah) and the separate state of Sarawak, which was ruled by the 'White Rajas' of the Brooke family. Sarawak was ceded to the British Crown in 1946. A Federation of Malaya – the peninsula – was established in 1948, but was threatened by Communist insurgency until 1960. Malaya became independent in 1957 with a constitution protecting the interests of the Malays, who were fearful of the energy and acumen of the Chinese. Sabah, Sarawak and Singapore joined the Federation – renamed Malaysia – in 1963. Singapore left in 1965, but the unity of the Federation was maintained, with British armed support, in the face of an Indonesian 'confrontation' in Borneo (1965–66). Tension between Chinese and Malays led to riots and the suspension of parliamentary government (1969–71), but scarcely hindered the rapid development of a resource-rich economy. During the 1980s and early 1990s, the growth of Islamic fundamentalism led to a defensive re-assertion of Islamic values and practices among the Muslim Malay ruling elite.

THE MALDIVES

Official name: Dhivehi Jumhuriya (Republic of Maldives).

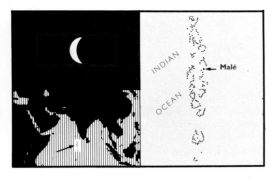

Member of: UN, Commonwealth, SAARC.
Area: 298 km² (115 sq mi).
Population: 213 000 (1990 census).
Capital: Malé 55 000 (1990 census).
Languages: Dhivehi (Maldivian; official).
Religion: Sunni Islam (official).

GOVERNMENT   The Majilis (Assembly) consists of 8 members appointed by the President, and 40 elected by universal adult suffrage for five years. The President – who is directly elected for five years – appoints a Cabinet. There are no political parties.
President: Abdul Maumoon Gayoom.

GEOGRAPHY   The country is a chain of over 1190 small low-lying coral islands, of which 203 are inhabited. There are no significant rivers. *Highest point:* 3 m (10 ft).

ECONOMY   The growing tourist industry has displaced fishing as the mainstay of the economy. However, one quarter of Maldivians subsist on fish and coconuts.

RECENT HISTORY   From 1887 until independence in 1965 the Maldives were a British protectorate, but the ad-Din sultanate, established in the 14th century, was only abolished in 1968.

MALI

Official name: La République du Mali (The Republic of Mali).
Member of: UN, OAU, ECOWAS.
Area: 1 240 192 km² (478 841 sq mi).
Population: 8 299 000 (1991 est).
Capital: Bamako 650 000, Ségou 89 000, Mopti 74 000 (1987 census).
Languages: French (official), Bambara (60%), Soninké, Fulani.
Religions: Sunni Islam (90%), animist (9%).

GOVERNMENT   The constitution provides for the election by universal adult suffrage of 116 deputies of a 129-member National Assembly (to serve for three years) and a President (to serve for six years). The remaining 13 members of the Assembly are elected by Malians living abroad. The President appoints a Premier and a Cabinet. The main political parties are the Alliance for Democracy in Mali (ADEMA), the Union for Democracy and Development (UDD) and the Sudanese Union (US-RDA).
President: Alpha Oumar Konari.
Prime Minister: Younoussi Touré.

GEOGRAPHY   Mali comprises low-lying plains but rises in the Adrar des Iforas range in the northeast. The south is savannah; the Sahara Desert is in the north. *Principal rivers:* Niger, Sénégal, Falémé. *Highest point:* Hombori Tondo 1155 m (3789 ft).

ECONOMY Drought in the 1970s and 1980s devastated Mali's livestock herds. Only one fifth of Mali can be cultivated, producing mainly rice, millet and cassava for domestic use, and cotton for export.

RECENT HISTORY Conquered by France (1880–95), Mali became the territory of French Sudan. Mali became independent in 1960. A radical socialist government was toppled in 1968 by the military regime of General Moussa Traore, whose government faced severe economic problems. A single-party system operated from 1979 to 1992 when multi-party politics were restored.

MALTA

Official name: Repubblika Ta'Malta (Republic of Malta).

Member of: UN, Commonwealth, CSCE, Council of Europe.

Area: 316 km² (122 sq mi).

Population: 357 000 (1991 est).

Capital and principal towns: Valletta 204 000 (city 9200). Birkirkara 21 000, Qormi 19 000, Hamrun 14 000 and Sliema 14 000 are part of the Valletta agglomeration (1991 est).

Languages: Maltese and English (official).

Religions: Roman Catholic (official; 98%).

GOVERNMENT The 65-member House of Representatives is elected by universal adult suffrage under a system of proportional representation for five years. The President – who is elected for five years by the House – appoints a Prime Minister and a Cabinet who command a majority in the House. The main political parties are the (conservative) National Party, the Malta Labour Party and the Democratic Alternative.

President: Vincent Tabone.

Prime Minister: Eddie Fenech Adami.

GEOGRAPHY The three inhabited islands of Malta, Gozo and Comino consist of low limestone plateaux with little surface water. There are no significant rivers. *Highest point:* an unnamed point, 249 m (816 ft).

ECONOMY The main industries are footwear and clothing, food processing and ship repairing. Tourism is the main foreign-currency earner. Malta is virtually self-sufficient in agricultural products.

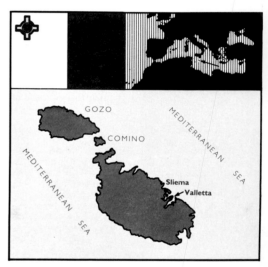

RECENT HISTORY As a British colony (from 1814), Malta became a vital naval base, and the island received the George Cross for its valour in World War II. Malta gained independence in 1964. Maltese political life has been polarized between the National Party and the Maltese Labour Party. Dom Mintoff – Labour PM (1971–84) – developed close links with Communist and Arab states, notably Libya.

MARSHALL ISLANDS

Official name: The Republic of the Marshall Islands.

Member of: UN, South Pacific Forum.

Area: 181 km² (70 sq mi).

Population: 49 000 (1991 est).

Capital: Dalap-Uliga-Darrit (on Majuro) 20 000 (1990 est).

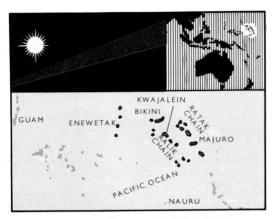

Languages: Marshallese and English (official).
Religions: Various Protestant Churches (over 50%), Roman Catholic minority.

GOVERNMENT The 33-member Nitijela (Parliament), the 12-member Senate and the President are elected by universal adult suffrage for four years. The traditional Council of Chiefs is a consultative body. There are, in effect, no political parties in government, although an opposition group has been formed.
President: Amata Kabua.

GEOGRAPHY The Marshall Islands comprise two chains of small coral atolls and islands, with over 1150 islands in total. There are no significant rivers. *Highest point*: unnamed, 6 m (20 ft).

ECONOMY The islands have practically no resources and depend upon subsistence agriculture, tourism and US grants.

RECENT HISTORY The Marshall Islands were under Spanish (1875–85), German (1885–1914), and Japanese administration (1914–45) before becoming part of the US Pacific Islands Trust Territory. They became internally self-governing in 1979. In 1986 US administration in the islands was formally terminated and the Marshall Islands became a sovereign republic, able to conduct its own foreign affairs, although under a Compact of Free Association the USA retains complete responsibility for the republic's defence and security until 2001. The UN did not recognize this new status of the Marshall Islands until December 1990, when the trusteeship was finally dissolved.

MAURITANIA

Official name: Jumhuriyat Muritaniya al-Islamiya (Islamic Republic of Mauritania).

Member of: UN, OAU, Arab League, ECOWAS.
Area: 1 030 700 km² (397 950 sq mi).
Population: 2 053 000 (1991 est).
Capital: Nouakchott 600 000 (city 393 000), Nouadhibou (Port Etienne) 59 000, Kaédi 31 000, (1988 census).
Languages: Arabic (official; 81%); French.
Religion: Sunni Islam (official; 99%).

GOVERNMENT A President and a 77-member National Assembly are elected by universal adult suffrage for six years. A Senate (upper house) is indirectly elected. The President appoints a Prime Minister and a Council of Ministers. The main political parties are the (former monopoly) Democratic and Social Republican Party, the Mauritanian Party for Renewal and the Rally for Democracy and National Unity.
President: Col. Maaouiya Ould Taya.

GEOGRAPHY Isolated peaks rise above the plateaux of the Sahara Desert that cover most of Mauritania. *Principal river:* Sénégal. *Highest point:* Kediet Ijill 915 m (3050 ft).

ECONOMY Persistent drought has devastated the nomads' herds of cattle and sheep. Fish from the Atlantic and iron ore are virtually the only exports.

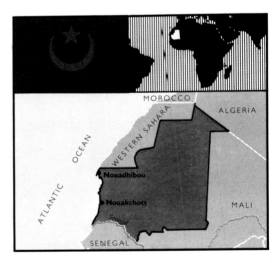

RECENT HISTORY France added the inland Arab emirates to its coastal possessions in 1903. Mauritania became independent in 1960. When Spain withdrew from the Western Sahara in 1976, Morocco and Mauritania divided the territory between them, but Mauritania could not defeat the Polisario guerrillas fighting for West Saharan independence and gave up its claim (1979). Tension between the dominant Arab north and Black African south led to violence in 1989. The country was ruled by military governments after 1976 and became a one-party state in 1979. Multi-party elections were held in 1992.

MAURITIUS

Official name Republic of Mauritius.

Member of: OAU, Commonwealth.

Area: 2040 km² (788 sq mi).

Population: 1 087 000 (1991 est).

Capital: Port Louis 142 000, Beau Bassin-Rose Hill 94 000, Curepipe 67 000, Quatre Bornes 66 000, (1990 est).

Languages: English (official), Creole (French; nearly 30%), Hindi (over 20%), Bhojpuri.

Religions: Hindu (51%), Roman Catholic (25%), Sunni Islam (17%), with Protestant minorities.

GOVERNMENT Elections are held by universal adult suffrage every five years for 62 members of the Assembly; up to 8 additional members may be appointed. The President – who is elected by the Assembly – appoints a Prime Minister who commands a majority in the Assembly. The PM, in turn, appoints a Cabinet responsible to the Assembly. The main political parties are the Mouvement Socialiste Militant, the Labour Party, the Parti Mauricien Social Democrate, the Mouvement Militant Mauricien and the Mouvement Travailliste Démocrate.

President: Cassam Uteem.

Prime Minister: Aneerood Jugnauth.

GEOGRAPHY The central plateau of Mauritius is surrounded by mountains. Other islands in the group include Rodrigues and the Agalega Islands. There are no significant rivers. *Highest point:* Piton de la Rivière Noire 826 m (2711 ft).

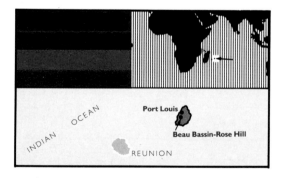

ECONOMY The export of sugar cane dominates the economy. Diversification is being encouraged, and light industry – in particular clothing – and tourism are of increasing importance.

RECENT HISTORY Britain gained the colony from France in 1814. Black slaves were imported, followed in the 19th century by Indian labourers whose descendants are the majority community. Independence was gained in 1968.

MEXICO

Official name: Estados Unidos Mexicanos (United Mexican States).

Member of: UN, OAS, ALADI, NAFTA.

Area: 1 958 201 km² (756 066 sq mi).

Population: 83 151 000 (1991 est).

Capital and major cities: Mexico City 19 480 000 (city 8 237 000; Greater Mexico City 13 636 000), Guadalajara 3 187 000 (city 2 847 000), Monterrey 2 859 000 (city 2 522 000), Puebla 1 707 000 (city 1 055 000), Nezahualcóyotl (part of the Mexico City agglomeration) 1 260 000, León 1 081 000 (city 872 000), Ciudad Juárez 798 000, Tijuana 743 000, Mexicali 602 000 (all including suburbs; 1990 census).

Languages: Spanish (92%; official), various Indian languages.

Religion: Roman Catholic (91%).

GOVERNMENT The 64-member Senate and the President – who may serve only once – are elected by universal adult suffrage for six years. The 500-member Chamber of Deputies is directly elected for three years – 200 of the members are elected under a system of proportional representation; the remaining 300 represent single-member constituencies. The President appoints a Cabinet. The principal political parties are the PRI (Institutional Revolutionary Party), the PAN (National Action Party), the PRD (Democratic Revolutionary Party), the (Marxist) Cardenista Front of National Reconstruction (PFCRN) and the Authentic Party of the Mexican Revolution (PARM). Each of the 31 states has its own Chamber of Deputies.

President: Carlos Salinas de Gortari.

STATES AND TERRITORIES Aguascalientes *Area:* 5471 km² (2112 sq mi). *Population:* 720 000 (1990 census). *Capital:* Aguascalientes.

Baja California *Area:* 69 921 km² (26 996 sq mi). *Population:* 1 658 000 (1990 census). *Capital:* Mexicali.

Baja California Sur *Area:* 73 475 km² (28 369 sq mi). *Population:* 317 000 (1990 census). *Capital:* La Paz.

Campeche *Area:* 50 812 km² (19 619 sq mi). *Population:* 529 000 (1990 census). *Capital:* Campeche.

Chiapas *Area:* 74 211 km² (28 653 sq mi). *Population:* 3 204 000 (1990 census). *Capital:* Tuxtla Gutiérrez.

Chihuahua *Area:* 244 938 km² (94 571 sq mi). *Population:* 2 440 000 (1990 census). *Capital:* Ciudad Juárez.

Coahuila *Area:* 149 982 km² (57 908 sq mi). *Population:* 1 971 000 (1990 census). *Capital:* Saltillo.

Colima *Area:* 5191 km² (2004 sq mi). *Population:* 425 000 (1990 census). *Capital:* Colima.

Durango *Area:* 123 181 km² (47 560 sq mi). *Population:* 1 352 000 (1990 census). *Capital:* (Victoria de) Durango.

Guanajuato *Area:* 30 491 km² (11 773 sq mi). *Population:* 3 980 000 (1990 census). *Capital:* Guanajuato.

Guerrero *Area*: 64 281 km² (24 819 sq mi). *Population*: 2 622 000 (1990 census). *Capital*: Chilpancingo.

Hidalgo *Area*: 20 813 km² (8036 sq mi). *Population*: 1 881 000 (1990 census). *Capital*: Pachuca de Soto.

Jalisco *Area*: 80 836 km² (31 211 sq mi). *Population*: 5 279 000 (1990 census). *Capital*: Guadalajara.

México *Area*: 21 355 km² (8245 sq mi). *Population*: 9 816 000 (1990 census). *Capital*: Toluca de Lerdo.

Michoacán *Area*: 59 928 km² (23 138 sq mi). *Population*: 3 534 000 (1990 census). *Capital*: Morelia.

Morelos *Area*: 4950 km² (1911 sq mi). *Population*: 1 195 000 (1990 census). *Capital*: Cuernavaca.

Nayarit *Area*: 26 979 km² (10 417 sq mi). *Population*: 816 000 (1990 census). *Capital*: Tepic.

Nuevo León *Area*: 64 924 km² (25 067 sq mi). *Population*: 3 086 000 (1990 census). *Capital*: Monterrey.

Oaxaca *Area*: 93 952 km² (36 275 sq mi). *Population*: 3 022 000 (1990 census). *Capital*: Oaxaca.

Puebla *Area*: 33 902 km² (11 493 sq mi). *Population*: 4 118 000 (1990 census). *Capital*: Puebla.

Querétaro *Area*: 11 449 km² (4420 sq mi). *Population*: 1 044 000 (1990 census). *Capital*: Querétaro.

Quintana Roo *Area*: 50 212 km² (19 387 sq mi). *Population*: 494 000 (1990 census). *Capital*: Chetumal.

San Luis Potosí *Area*: 63 068 km² (24 351 sq mi). *Population*: 2 002 000 (1990 census). *Capital*: San Luis Potosí.

Sinaloa *Area*: 58 328 km² (22 520 sq mi). *Population*: 2 211 000 (1990 census). *Capital*: Culiacán Rosales.

Sonora *Area*: 182 052 km² (70 290 sq mi). *Population*: 1 822 000 (1990 census). *Capital*: Hermosillo.

Tabasco *Area*: 25 267 km² (9756 sq mi). *Population*: 1 501 000 (1990 census). *Capital*: Villahermosa.

Tamaulipas *Area*: 79 304 km² (30 619 sq mi). *Population*: 2 244 000 (1990 census). *Capital*: Ciudad Victoria.

Tlaxcala *Area*: 4016 km² (1551 sq mi). *Population*: 764 000 (1990 census). *Capital*: Apizaco.

Veracruz *Area*: 71 699 km² (27 683 sq mi). *Population*: 6 215 000 (1990 census). *Capital*: Jalapa Enrique.

Yucatán *Area*: 38 402 km² (14 827 sq mi). *Population*: 1 364 000 (1990 census). *Capital*: Mérida.

Zacatecas *Area*: 73 252 km² (28 283 sq mi). *Population*: 1 278 000 (1990 census). *Capital*: Zacatecas.

Federal District *Area*: 1479 km² (570 sq mi). *Population*: 8 237 000 (1990 census). *Capital*: Mexico City.

GEOGRAPHY Between the Sierra Madre Oriental mountains in the east and the Sierra Madre Occidental in the west is a large high central plateau with several volcanoes. The coastal plains are generally narrow in the west, but wider in the east. The Yucatán Peninsula in the southeast is a broad limestone lowland; Baja California in the northwest is a long narrow mountainous peninsula. Mexico is prone to earthquakes. *Principal rivers:* Río Bravo de Norte (Rio Grande), Balsas, Grijalva, Pánuco. *Highest point:* Volcán Citlaltepetl (Pico de Orizaba) 5610 m (18 405 ft).

ECONOMY Over one fifth of the labour force is involved in agriculture and many Mexicans are still subsistence farmers growing maize, wheat, kidney beans and rice. Coffee, cotton, fruit and vegetables are the most important export crops. Mexico is the world's leading producer of silver. The exploitation of large reserves of natural gas and petroleum enabled the country's spectacular economic development in the 1970s and 1980s. An expanding industrial base includes important petrochemical, textile, motor-vehicle and food-processing industries. In the early 1990s major US companies were encouraged by a combination of government policy, the new NAFTA trade agreement and low labour costs to set up factories in Mexico. The result has been a spectacular growth in the Mexican economy which is now the 11th largest in the world. Economic problems remain, and high unemployment has stimulated immigration – often illegal – to the US.

RECENT HISTORY The long and authoritarian rule of General Porfirio Díaz (President 1876–80 and 1888–1910) brought peace and economic growth, but wealth was concentrated into a few hands. Revolution against the power of the landowners erupted in 1910. The reformist policies of President Francisco Madero (1873–1913) were supported by the outlaw Pancho Villa (1877–1923), but revolutionary violence continued, and in 1916–17 a US expeditionary force was sent against Villa. From 1924 the revolution became anticlerical and the Church was persecuted. Order was restored when the Institutional Revolutionary Party came to power in 1929. In the 1930s the large estates were divided and much of the economy was nationalized. Political opposition has been tolerated, although the ruling party is virtually guaranteed perpetual power. In 1989, the first non-PRI state governor was elected, but opposition claims of electoral fraud have continued. A more liberal economic and political climate has emerged since 1990.

MICRONESIA

Official name: The Federated States of Micronesia.
Member of: UN, South Pacific Forum.
Area: 702 km² (271 sq mi).
Population: 111 000 (1991 est).
Capital and largest towns: Palikir (on Pohnpei) 2 000, Wenn (formerly Moen) 10 400, Tol 6700, Kolonia (the former capital) 6300 (1990 est).
Languages: English, Trukese, Ponapean, Yapese, Kosraean.
Religions: Various Protestant Churches (mainly Assembly of God, Jehovah's Witnesses and Seventh-Day Adventists), Roman Catholic minority.

GOVERNMENT The President (who serves for four years) and the 14-member National Congress are elected by universal adult suffrage. The Congress comprises one senator elected by each of the four states for four years, and ten senators representing constituencies elected for two years. There are no national political parties. Each state has its own government and parliament.
President: Bailey Olter.

STATES Chuuk (formerly Truk) *Area*: 116 km² (45 sq mi). *Population*: 53 700 (1990 est). *Capital*: Wenn (formerly Moen).
Kosrae *Area*: 109 km² (42 sq mi). *Population*: 7 200 (1990 est). *Capital*: Kosrae.
Pohnpei (formerly Ponape) *Area*: 373 km² (144 sq mi). *Population*: 33 100 (1990 est). *Capital*: Kolonia.
Yap *Area*: 101 km² (39 sq mi). *Population*: 13 900 (1990 est). *Capital*: Colonia.

GEOGRAPHY The Micronesian islands comprise over 600 islands in two main groups. The majority of the islands are low coral atolls, but Kosrae and Pohnpei are mountainous. There are no significant rivers. *Highest point*: Mt Totolom 791 m (2595 ft).

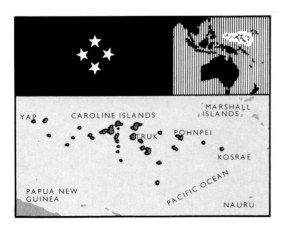

ECONOMY Apart from phosphate, the islands have practically no resources and depend upon subsistence agriculture, fishing, US grants and (increasingly) tourism.

RECENT HISTORY Previously known as the Caroline Islands, the islands were under Spanish (1874–99), German (1899–1914), and Japanese administration (1914–45) before becoming part of the US Pacific Islands Trust Territory. They became internally self-governing in 1979. In 1986 US administration in the islands was formally terminated and the Federated States became a sovereign republic, able to conduct its own foreign affairs, although under a Compact of Free Association the USA retains complete responsibility for the republic's defence and security until 2001. The UN did not recognize this new status of the Federated States until December 1990, when the trusteeship was finally dissolved.

MOLDOVA

Official name: Republica Moldoveneasca (Republic of Moldova). Formerly known as Moldavia.
Member of: UN, CIS, CSCE.
Area: 33 700 km² (13 000 sq mi).
Population: 4 367 000 (1991 est).
Capital and major cities: Chisinau (formerly Kishinev) 720 000, Tiraspol 182 000, Beltsy 159 000, Bendery 130 000 (1989 census).
Languages: Romanian (64%), Ukrainian (14%), Russian (13%), Gagauz (4%).
Religions: Romanian Orthodox majority.

GOVERNMENT A 380-member legislature and a President are elected for four years by universal adult suffrage. The President appoints a Prime Minister and a Council of Ministers. A new constitution is to be drafted. The main political party is the (coalition) National Alliance. There are several ethnic political groups.
President Mircea Snegur.
Prime Minister Andrei Sangheli.

GEOGRAPHY Moldova comprises a hilly plain between the River Prut and the Dnestr valley. *Principal rivers:* Dnestr, Prut. *Highest point:* Balaneshty 430 m (1409 ft).

ECONOMY Large collective farms produce fruit (particularly grapes for wine), vegetables, wheat, maize, tobacco and sunflower seed. Food processing and machine building are the main industries. Little progress has been made to privatize agriculture and industry.

RECENT HISTORY Known as Bessarabia, the area was ruled by Kievan Rus' (10th–12th centuries) and the Tatars (13th–14th centuries) before becoming part of the Romanian principality of Moldavia – within the (Turkish) Ottoman Empire – in the 15th century. Bessarabia

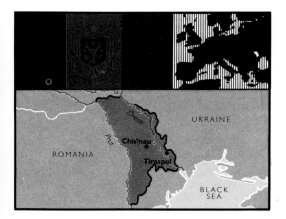

was intermittently occupied by Russia in the 18th century before being ceded to the Russians in 1812. Briefly restored to Moldavia (1856–78), Bessarabia remained Russian until World War I. An autonomous Bessarabian republic was proclaimed in 1917, but was suppressed by a Russian Bolshevik invasion (1918). The Russians were removed by Romanian forces and Bessarabia was declared, in turn, an independent Moldavian republic and a part of the kingdom of Romania (1918). When Romania entered World War II as a German ally, the USSR reoccupied Bessarabia, which was reorganized as the Moldavian Soviet Republic in 1944. Following the abortive coup by Communist hardliners in Moscow (September 1991), Moldavia declared independence. As Moldova, the republic received international recognition when the Soviet Union was dissolved (December 1991). Civil war broke out in 1992 when Russian and Ukrainian minorities – fearing an eventual reunion of Moldova with Romania – proclaimed the republic of Trans-Dnestr and attempted to secede. The intervention of CIS forces brought an uneasy peace.

MONACO

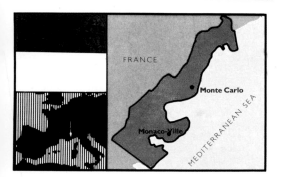

Official name: Principauté de Monaco (Principality of Monaco).
Member of: CSCE, UN (observer).
Area: 2.21 km² (0.85 sq mi).
Population: 29 900 (1990 est).
Capital and major cities: Monaco 1200, Monte-Carlo 13 200 (1990 est).
Languages: French (official), Monegasque.
Religion: Roman Catholic (90%).

GOVERNMENT Monaco is a constitutional monarchy. Legislative power is jointly held by the Prince and the 18-member National Council, which is elected by universal adult suffrage for five years. Executive power is held by the Prince, who appoints a four-member Council of Government headed by the Minister of State, a French civil servant chosen by the sovereign. There are no formal political parties, but political groupings include the (majority) National and Democratic Union and the (Marxist) Democratic Union Movement.
Prince: HSH Prince Rainier III (succeeded upon the death of his grandfather, 9 May 1949).
Minister of State: Jacques Dupont.

GEOGRAPHY Monaco consists of a rocky peninsula and a narrow stretch of coast. Since 1958 the area of the principality has increased by one fifth through reclamation of land from the sea. *Principal river:* Vésubie. *Highest point:* on Chemin de Révoirés 162 m (533 ft).

ECONOMY Monaco depends upon real estate, banking, insurance, light industry and tourism.

RECENT HISTORY The greater part of the principality was lost – and eventually annexed by France – in 1848. Since 1861 Monaco has been under French protection. Prince Rainier III granted a liberal constitution in 1962.

MONGOLIA

Official name: Mongol Uls (Mongolian Republic).
Member of: UN.
Area: 1 565 000 km² (604 250 sq mi).
Population: 2 156 000 (1992 est).
Capital and major cities: Ulan Bator (Ulaan Baatar) 575 000, Darhan 90 000, Erdenet 58 000 (1991 est).
Languages: Khalkh Mongolian (official; 78%), Kazakh (6%).
Religions: Religion was suppressed from 1924 to 1990; there has been a recent revival of Buddhism, the traditional religion.

GOVERNMENT Under the 1992 constitution, a 76-member Great Hural and a President are elected by universal adult suffrage for four years. The President appoints a Prime Minister and a Council of Ministers. The main political parties are the Mongolian People's

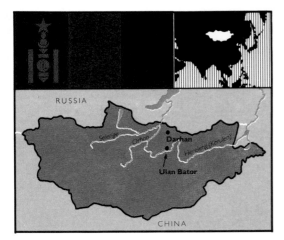

Revolutionary (Communist) Party and the Mongolian Democratic Party.

President: Punsalmaagiyn Ochirbat.
Prime Minister: Dashin Byambasuren.

GEOGRAPHY Mongolia comprises mountains in the north, a series of basins in the centre, and the Gobi Desert and Altai Mountains in the south. *Principal rivers:* Selenga, Orhon, Hereleng. *Highest point:* Mönh Hayrhan Uul 4362 m (14 311 ft).

ECONOMY Mongolia depends on collectivized animal herding (cattle, sheep, goats and camels). Cereals (including fodder crops) are grown on a large scale on state farms. The industrial sector is dominated by food processing, hides and wool. Copper is a major export.

RECENT HISTORY In 1921, Outer Mongolia broke away from China with Soviet assistance, and in 1924 the Mongolian People's Republic was established. Pro-democracy demonstrations early in 1990 led to a liberalization of the regime. The first multi-party elections were held in July 1990 when the Communists were returned to power.

MOROCCO

Official name: Al-Mamlaka al-Maghribiya (The Kingdom of Morocco).
Member of: UN, Arab League.
Area: 458 730 km² (177 115 sq mi) excluding the disputed Western Sahara; 710 850 km² (274 461 sq mi) including the Western Sahara.
Population: 25 208 000 (1990 est) excluding the Western Sahara, which had an estimated 185 000 inhabitants in 1987.

Capital and major cities: Rabat 1 472 000 (includes Salé), Casablanca (Dar el Beida) 3 210 000, Marrakech 1 517 000, Fez (Fès) 1 012 000, Oujda 962 000, Kénitra 905 000, Tetouan (with Larache) 856 000, Safi 845 000 (all including suburbs; 1990 est).
Languages: Arabic (official; 75%), Berber, French.
Religion: Sunni Islam (official; 98%), Roman Catholic (2%).

GOVERNMENT Morocco is a constitutional monarchy. The 306-member Chamber of Representatives consists of 206 members elected by universal adult suffrage for six years and 100 members chosen by an electoral college representing municipal authorities and professional bodies. The King appoints a Prime Minister and Cabinet. The main political parties include the Union Constitutionnelle, the Rassemblement National des Indépendents, the Mouvement Populaire, Istiqlal, the Union Socialiste des Forces Populaires, and the Parti National Démocrate.
King: HM King Hassan II (succeeded upon the death of his father, 26 February 1961).
Prime Minister: Mohammed Karim Lamrami.

GEOGRAPHY Over one third of Morocco is mountainous. The principal uplands are the Grand, Middle and Anti Atlas Mountains in the west and north and a plateau in the east. Much of the country – including the disputed Western Sahara territory – is desert. *Principal rivers:* Oued Dra, Oued Moulouya, Sebov. *Highest point:* Jebel Toubkal 4165 m (13 665 ft).

ECONOMY Over 40% of the labour force are involved in agriculture, producing mainly citrus fruits, grapes (for wine) and vegetables for export, and wheat and barley for domestic consumption. Morocco is the world's leading exporter of phosphates. Other resources include iron ore, lead and zinc. Since independence many important industries and services have come into state ownership. Tourism is growing.

RECENT HISTORY Under the Treaty of Fez in 1912 France established a protectorate over Morocco, although Spain retained some coastal enclaves. The 1925 Rif rebellion stirred nationalist feelings, but independence was not gained until 1956. King Hassan II (reigned 1961–) has survived left-wing challenges through strong rule and vigorous nationalism – as in his 1975 'Green March' of unarmed peasants into the then-Spanish (Western) Sahara. Morocco continues to hold the Western Sahara despite international pressure and the activities of the Algerian-backed Polisario guerrillas fighting for the territory's independence. A ceasefire was agreed in 1991. Discussions concerning a UN-sponsored referendum in the disputed territory are continuing.

For information on the disputed Western Sahara, see Other Territories, following this chapter.

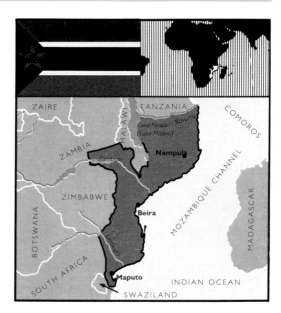

MOZAMBIQUE

Official name: A República de Moçambique (Republic of Mozambique).

Member of: UN, OAU, SADCC.

Area: 799 380 km² (308 641 sq mi).

Population: 15 656 000 (1990 est).

Capital and main cities: Maputo 1 070 000, Beira 292 000, Nampula 197 000 (1989 est).

Languages: Portuguese (official), Makua-Lomwe (52%), Malawi (12%).

Religions: Animist (60%), Sunni Islam (16%), Roman Catholic (15%).

GOVERNMENT A new constitution provides for a 250-member Assembly of the Republic and a President to be elected by universal adult suffrage for five years. The President – who appoints a Council of Ministers and a Prime Minister – is elected by the Assembly. The main legal parties are the (former monopoly) Frelimo and the National Mozambican Union.

President: Joaquim Alberto Chissano.

Prime Minister: Mario da Graca Machungo.

GEOGRAPHY The Zambezi River separates high plateaux in northern Mozambique from lowlands in the south. *Principal rivers:* Limpopo, Zambezi, Shire. *Highest point:* Mount Bingo 2436 m (7992 ft).

ECONOMY Over 80% of the labour force is involved in farming, mainly growing cassava and maize as subsistence crops. Fishing is a major employer – prawns and shrimps make up nearly one half of Mozambique's exports. The economy has been devastated by civil war and drought, and Mozambique is usually stated to be the poorest country in the world (in terms of GDP per head).

RECENT HISTORY By the end of the 19th century Portugal had control of the whole of the country. Forced labour and minimal development helped to fuel nationalist feelings, and in 1964 the Frelimo movement launched a guerrilla war against Portuguese rule. Independence was achieved in 1975, and a Marxist-Leninist state was established. The pressures of poverty and the destabilization of the country by South Africa – through support for the Renamo guerrilla movement – led to renewed ties with the West, and Marxism was abandoned by Frelimo in 1989. During the 1990s, the country has faced severe famine. A ceasefire – and a UN presence in Mozambique – were agreed in 1992.

MYANMAR (BURMA)

Official name: Myanmar Naingngandaw (The Union of Myanmar). The name Burma was officially dropped in May 1989.

Member of: UN.

Area: 676 552 km² (261 218 sq mi).

Population: 42 561 000 (1991 est).

Capital and major cities: Rangoon (Yangon) 2 513 000, Mandalay 533 000, Moulmein 220 000, Pegu (Bago) 151 000, Bassein (Pathein) 144 000, Taunggyi 108 000 (1983 census).

Languages: Burmese (official; 80%), Karen, Mon, Shan, Kachin.

Religion: Buddhist (68%).

GOVERNMENT Power is held by a 19-member State Law-and-Order Restoration Council whose Chairman is head of state. There is constitutional provision for a 489-member Assembly which is empowered to elect a

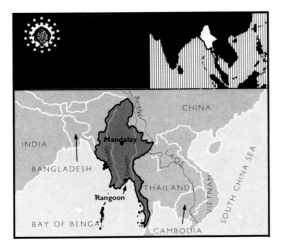

Council of Ministers and a Council of State, whose Chairman will be head of state. Multi-party elections were held in May 1990 but the military State Law-and-Order Restoration Council refused to transfer power to the majority National League for Democracy. The other main political party is the (military-backed) National Unity Party.

President and Head of Government: Gen. Than Shwe.

GEOGRAPHY   The north and west of Burma are mountainous. In the east is the Shan Plateau along the Thai border. Central and south Burma consists of tropical lowlands. *Principal rivers*: Irrawaddy, Sittang, Mekong. *Highest point*: Hkakado Razi 5881 m (19 296 ft).

ECONOMY   Burma is rich in agriculture, timber and minerals, but because of poor communications, lack of development and serious rebellions by a number of ethnic minorities, the country has been unable to realize its potential. Subsistence farming involves the majority of the labour force.

RECENT HISTORY   Separated from British India in 1937, Burma became a battleground for British and Japanese forces in World War II. In 1948, Burma left the Commonwealth as an independent republic, keeping outside contacts to a minimum, particularly following the coup of General Ne Win in 1962. Continuing armed attempts to gain autonomy by non-Burman minorities strengthened the army's role. Karen and Mon separatists created embryo states on the Thai border, while Shan separatists in the north controlled much of the opium-producing 'Golden Triangle'. In 1988–89, demonstrations for democracy appeared to threaten military rule, but were repressed. The military retained power following multi-party elections in 1990, and detained or restricted the principal members of the National League for Democracy, including the party leader, Aung San Suu Kyi. The military successfully increased their activities against separatists in the 1990s.

NAMIBIA

Official name: The Republic of Namibia or Republiek van Namibie.

Member of: UN, Commonwealth, SADCC, OAU.

Area: 823 168 km² (317 827 sq mi).

Population: 1 334 000 (1991 est).

Capital and major cities: Windhoek 115 000, Swakopmund 16 000 (1988 est).

Languages: Afrikaans and English (official), German, local languages.

Religions: Lutheran (30%), Roman Catholic (20%), other Christian Churches (30%).

GOVERNMENT   A 72-member Assembly is elected by universal adult suffrage under a system of proportional representation every five years. The President – who appoints the Prime Minister – is also directly elected for a term of five years and can nominate up to six non-voting members of the National Assembly. The main political parties include the (left wing) SWAPO (South West African People's Organization), the (centre) Democratic Turnhalle Alliance, the (coalition) United Democratic Front and Action Christian National.

President: Sam Nujoma.

Prime Minister: Hage Geingob.

GEOGRAPHY   The coastal Namib Desert stretches up to 160 km (100 mi) inland. Beyond the Central Plateau,

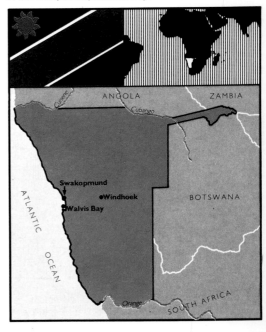

the Kalahari Desert occupies the eastern part of the country. *Principal river:* Orange. *Highest point:* Brandberg 2579 m (8461 ft).

ECONOMY Over one third of the labour force is involved in agriculture, mainly raising cattle and sheep. The economy depends upon exports of diamonds and uranium, and is closely tied to South Africa.

RECENT HISTORY South Africa conquered the German protectorate of South West Africa during World War I, and (after 1919) administered it under a League of Nations mandate. In 1966, the UN cancelled the mandate, but South Africa – which had refused to grant the territory independence – ignored the ruling. The main nationalist movement, SWAPO, began guerrilla warfare to free Namibia, the name adopted by the UN for the country. South Africa unsuccessfully attempted to exclude SWAPO's influence. After a cease-fire agreement in 1989, UN-supervised elections were held in November 1989 for a constituent assembly. Independence – under the presidency of SWAPO leader Sam Nujoma – was achieved in March 1990.

NAURU

Official name: The Republic of Nauru.
Member of: Commonwealth (special member), South Pacific Forum.
Area: 21 km² (8 sq mi).
Population: 9400 (1990 est).
Capital: No official capital, Yaren – which is the largest settlement – is capital *de facto*. Domaneab is the other main settlement.
Languages: Nauruan (official), English.
Religions: Nauruan Protestant Church (majority), Roman Catholic (minority).

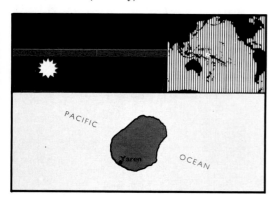

GOVERNMENT The 18-member Parliament is elected by universal adult suffrage for three years. Parliament elects the President, who in turn appoints a

Cabinet of Ministers. There is only one formal political party, the (opposition) Democratic Party of Nauru.
President: Bernard Dowiyogo.

GEOGRAPHY Nauru is a low-lying coral atoll. There are no rivers. *Highest point:* 68 m (225 ft) on the central plateau.

ECONOMY Nauru depends almost entirely upon the export of phosphate rock, stocks of which are expected to run out by 1995. Shipping and air services and 'tax haven' facilities are planned to provide revenue when the phosphate is exhausted.

RECENT HISTORY Germany annexed Nauru in 1888. Australia captured Nauru in 1914 and administered it – except for a period of Japanese occupation (1942–45) – until independence was granted in 1968.

NEPAL

Official name: Nepal Adhirajya (Kingdom of Nepal).
Member of: UN, SAARC.
Area: 147 181 km² (56 827 sq mi).
Population: 19 379 000 (1991 est).
Capital: Kathmandu 420 000 (city 235 000), Biratnagar 120 000, Lalitpur 100 000 (1987 est).
Languages: Nepali (official; 53%), Bihari (19%), Maithir (12%).
Religions: Hindu (official; 90%), Buddhist (5%), Sunni Islam (3%).

GOVERNMENT Nepal is a constitutional monarchy. Since 1990, Nepal has had a two-chamber Parliament. The Lower House consists of 205 members elected for five years by universal adult suffrage. The Upper House consists of 60 appointed and indirectly elected members, including six members appointed by the King. The main political parties are the Nepali Congress Party and the Communist Party-United Leninist Party Alliance.
King: HM King Birendra (succeeded upon the death of his father, 31 January 1972).
Prime Minister: Girija Prasad Koirala.

GEOGRAPHY In the south are densely populated subtropical lowlands. A hilly central belt is divided by fertile valleys. The Himalaya dominate the north. *Principal rivers:* Karnali, Naryani, Kosi. *Highest point:* Mount Everest 8863 m (29 078 ft).

ECONOMY Nepal is one of the least developed countries in the world, with most of the labour force involved in subsistence farming, mainly growing rice, beans and maize. Forestry is important, but increased farming has led to serious deforestation.

RECENT HISTORY From 1846 to 1950 the Rana family held sway as hereditary chief ministers of a powerless monarchy. Their isolationist policy preserved Nepal's independence at the expense of its development.

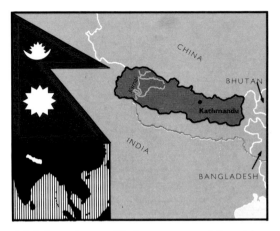

A brief experiment with democracy was followed by a re-assertion of royal autocracy (1960) by King Mahendra (reigned 1952–72). Mass unrest and violent pro-democracy demonstrations in 1990 forced King Birendra to concede a democratic constitution.

THE NETHERLANDS

Official name: Koninkrijk der Nederlanden (The Kingdom of the Netherlands).

Member of: UN, EC, NATO, CSCE, WEU, Council of Europe, OECD.

Area: 41 785 km² (16 140 sq mi).

Population: 15 065 000 (1991 est).

Capital and major cities: Amsterdam – capital in name only – 1 062 000 (city 702 000), The Hague ('s Graven-hage) – capital *de facto*; the seat of government and administration – 690 000 (city 444 000), Rotterdam 1 051 000 (city 582 000), Utrecht 535 000 (city 231 000), Eindhoven 386 000 (city 193 000), Arnhem 303 000 (city 132 000), Heerlen-Kerkrade 268 000 (Heerlen city 94 000), Enschede 252 000 (city 146 000), Nijmegen 244 000 (city 146 000), Tilburg 232 000 (city 159 000), Haarlem 214 000 (city 149 000), Groningen 208 000 (city 169 000), Dordrecht 208 000 (city 110 000), 's Hertogenbosch 198 000 (city 89 000), Leiden 189 000 (city 112 000), Geleen-Sittard 182 000 (Sittard town 43 000), Maastricht 163 000 (city 117 000), Breda 161 000 (city 125 000) (1991 est).

Language: Dutch (official).

Religions: Roman Catholic (under 30%), Netherlands Reformed Church (17%), Reformed Churches (Calvinistic; 8%).

GOVERNMENT The Netherlands is a constitutional monarchy. The 75-member First Chamber of the States-General is elected for a six-year term by the 12 provincial councils – with one half of the members retiring every three years. The 150-member Second Chamber is elected for a four-year term by universal adult suffrage under a system of proportional representation. The monarch appoints a Prime Minister who commands a majority in the States-General. The PM, in turn, appoints a Council of Ministers (Cabinet) who are responsible to the States-General. The main political parties include the (conservative) CDA (Christian Democratic Appeal Party), PvdA (the Labour Party), the (liberal) VVD (People's Party for Freedom and Democracy), D66 (Democracy 66), the (Calvinist) SGP (Political Reformed Party), and the PPR (Political Party of Reformed Democrats).

Queen: HM Queen Beatrix (succeeded on the abdication of her mother, 30 April 1980).

Prime Minister: Ruud Lubbers.

GEOGRAPHY Over one quarter of the Netherlands – one of the world's most densely populated countries – lies below sea level. A network of canals and canalized rivers cross the west of the country where sand dunes and man-made dykes protect low-lying areas and polders (land reclaimed from the sea). The coast has been straightened by sea walls protecting Zeeland in the southwest and enclosing a freshwater lake, the IJssel-meer, in the north. The east comprises low sandy plains. *Principal rivers:* Rhine (Rijn) – dividing into branches including the Lek, Waal and Oude Rijn, Maas (Meuse). *Highest point:* Vaalserberg 321 m (1053 ft).

ECONOMY Despite having few natural resources – except natural gas – the Netherlands has a high standard of living. Agriculture and horticulture are highly mechanized with a concentration on dairying and glasshouse crops, particularly flowers. Food processing is a major industry, and the country is a leading exporter of cheese. Manufacturing includes chemical, machinery, petroleum refining, metallurgical and electrical engineering industries. Raw materials are imported through Rotterdam, which is the largest port in the world and serves much of Western Europe. Banking and finance are well developed.

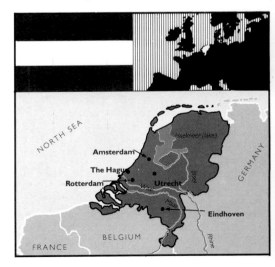

RECENT HISTORY The Dutch were neutral in World War I, but suffered occupation by the Germans 1940 to 1945. Following a bitter colonial war, the Dutch accepted that they could not reassert control over Indonesia after World War II. The Netherlands has shown enthusiasm for European unity, and, with the other Low Countries, founded Benelux, the core of the EC. Dutch politics has been characterized by a large number of small parties, some of a confessional nature, and a system of proportional representation has prevented any of these parties attaining a parliamentary majority. The formation of a new coalition government after each general election has been difficult and time-consuming.

DUTCH EXTERNAL TERRITORIES

Aruba *Area*: 193 km² (75 sq mi). *Population*: 66 000 (1991 est). *Capital*: Oranjestad 20 000 (1986 est).

Netherlands Antilles *Area*: 800 km² (309 sq mi). *Population*: 191 000 (1990 est). *Capital*: Willemstad (on Curaçao) 125 000 (including suburbs; 1985 est).

NEW ZEALAND

Official name: Dominion of New Zealand.

Member of: UN, Commonwealth, ANZUS, South Pacific Forum, OECD.

Area: 269 057 km² (103 883 sq mi).

Population: 3 435 000 (1991 census).

Capital and major cities: Wellington 325 000 (city 150 000), Auckland 885 000 (city 316 000), Christchurch 307 000 (city 293 000), Manukau 227 000 and North Shore 151 000 are part of the Auckland agglomeration, Hamilton 149 000 (city 101 000), Napier with Hastings 110 000 (Napier city 52 000), Dunedin 109 000, Palmerston North 71 000, Tauranga 71 000, Rotorua 54 000, Invercargill 52 000, New Plymouth 49 000, Nelson 47 000, Whangarei 44 000, Wanganui 41 000 (all including suburbs; 1991 census).

Languages: English (official), Maori.

Religions: Anglican (24%), Presbyterian (18%), Roman Catholic (15%), Methodist (5%).

GOVERNMENT The 97-member House of Representatives is elected by universal adult suffrage for three years to represent single-member constituencies, four of which have a Maori electorate and representative. The Governor General – the representative of the British Queen as sovereign of New Zealand – appoints a Prime Minister who commands a majority in the House. The PM, in turn, appoints a Cabinet, which is responsible to the House. The main political parties are the Labour Party, the (conservative) National Party and the New Labour Party. Tokelau is an autonomous island territory.

Prime Minister: Jim Bolger.

AUTONOMOUS TERRITORY Tokelau *Area*: 13 km² (5 sq mi). *Population*: 1700 (1986 census). *Capital*:

there is no capital; each atoll has its own administrative centre.

GEOGRAPHY On South Island, the Southern Alps run from north to south, and in the southwest reach the sea in the deeply indented coast of Fjordland. The Canterbury Plains lie to the east of the mountains. North Island is mainly hilly with isolated mountains, including volcanoes – two of which are active. Lowlands on North Island are largely restricted to coastal areas and the Waikato Valley. *Principal rivers:* Waikato, Clutha, Waihou, Rangitaiki, Mokau, Wanganui, Manawatu. *Highest point:* Mount Cook 3754 m (12 315 ft).

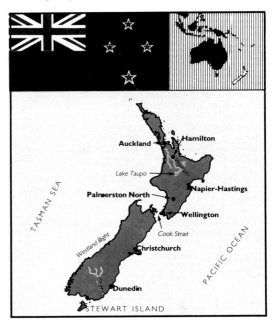

ECONOMY The majority of New Zealand's export earnings come from agriculture, in particular meat, wool and dairy products. Forestry is expanding and supports an important pulp and paper industry. Apart from coal, lignite, natural gas and gold, the country has few natural resources, although its considerable hydroelectric-power potential has been exploited to produce plentiful cheap electricity – an important basis of New Zealand's manufacturing industry. Natural gas – from the Kapuni Field on North Island and the Maui Field off the Taranaki coast – is converted to liquid fuel. Despite having only a small domestic market and being remote from the world's major industrial powers, New Zealand has a high standard of living.

RECENT HISTORY In the last quarter of the 19th century, the discovery of gold and the introduction of refrigerated ships to export meat and dairy products greatly stimulated colonization and the economy. By 1911 migrants from Britain had boosted the country's population to one million. Subsequent immigration has remained overwhelmingly British, although there are sizeable communities of Samoans, Cook Islanders, Yugoslavs and Dutch. Liberal governments (1891–1912) pioneered many reforms and social measures, including votes for women (1893) and the world's first old-age pensions (1898). Dominion status was granted in 1907, although the country did not formally acknowledge its independent status until 1947. In World War I, New Zealand fought as a British ally in Europe, achieving distinction in the disastrous Allied expedition to the Gallipoli peninsula during the campaign against Turkey (1915). When Japan entered World War II in 1941, New Zealand's more immediate security was threatened. The major role played by the USA in the Pacific War led to New Zealand's postwar alliance with Australia and America in the ANZUS pact, and the country sent troops to support the Americans in Vietnam. The entry of Britain into the EC in 1973 restricted the access of New Zealand's agricultural products to what had been their principal market. Since then New Zealand has been forced to seek new markets, particularly in the Far and Middle East. Under Labour governments (1972–75 and 1984–90), the country adopted an independent foreign and defence policy. A ban on vessels powered by nuclear energy or carrying nuclear weapons in New Zealand's waters placed a question mark over the country's role as a full ANZUS member.

NEW ZEALAND'S DEPENDENT TERRITORIES
Ross Dependency See Other Territories, following this chapter.

NEW ZEALAND'S ASSOCIATED TERRITORIES
Cook Islands *Area*: 234 km² (90 sq mi). *Population*: 19 000 (1991 est). *Capital*: Avarua 5000 (1985 est).
Niue *Area*: 259 km² (100 sq mi). *Population*: 2300 (1989 census). *Capital*: Alofi 1000 (1989 est).

NICARAGUA

Official name: República de Nicaragua (Republic of Nicaragua).
Member of: UN, OAS, CACM.
Area: 120 254 km² (46 430 sq mi).
Population: 4 000 000 (1991 est).
Capital and main cities: Managua 979 000 (city 682 000), León 101 000, Granada 89 000 (1988 est).
Languages: Spanish (official), Amerindian languages (4%).
Religion: Roman Catholic (90%).
GOVERNMENT The 92-member National Assembly is elected by proportional representation for six years by universal adult suffrage. The President – who appoints a Cabinet – is also directly elected for a six-year term. the main political parties include the (left-wing) FSLN

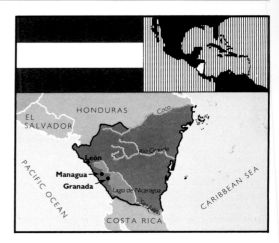

(Sandinista National Liberation Front) and the (14-party coalition) UNO (National Opposition Union).
President: Violetta Chamorro.

GEOGRAPHY A fertile plain on the Pacific coast contains the majority of the population. Mountain ranges rise in the centre of the country. Tropical jungle covers the Atlantic coastal plain. *Principal rivers:* Coco, Rio Grande, San Juan, Escondido. *Highest point:* Pico Mogotón 2107 m (6913 ft).

ECONOMY A largely agricultural economy was damaged in the 1980s by guerrilla warfare, a US trade embargo and hurricanes. Privatization and strict austerity programmes have been implemented. Coffee, cotton and sugar cane are the main export crops.

RECENT HISTORY Early in the 20th century, the political situation in Nicaragua deteriorated, provoking American intervention – US marines were based in Nicaragua from 1912 to 1925, and again from 1927 until 1933. General Anastasio Somoza became president in 1937. Employing dictatorial methods, members of the Somoza family, or their supporters, remained in power until overthrown by a popular uprising led by the Sandinista guerrilla army in 1979. Accusing the Sandinistas of introducing Communism, the USA imposed a trade embargo on Nicaragua, making it increasingly dependent on Cuba and the USSR. Right-wing Contra guerrillas, financed by the USA, fought the Sandinistas from bases in Honduras. A ceasefire between the Contras and Sandinistas was agreed in 1989. In free presidential elections in February 1990, the Sandinista incumbent Daniel Ortega was defeated by Violetta Chamorro of the opposition coalition.

NIGER

Official name: La République du Niger (The Republic of Niger).

Member of: UN, OAU, ECOWAS.
Area: 1 267 000 km² (489 191 sq mi).
Population: 8 024 000 (1991 est).
Capital and main cities: Niamey 398 000, Zinder 121 000, Maradi 113 000 (1988 census).
Languages: French (official), Hausa (85%).
Religion: Sunni Islam (85%).

GOVERNMENT A provisional High Council of the Republic exercises executive and legislative powers pending multi-party elections for a constituent assembly.
President: Brig. Gen. Ali Saibou.
Prime Minister: Amadou Cheiffou.

GEOGRAPHY Most of Niger lies in the Sahara Desert; the south and the Niger Valley are savannah. The central Aïr Mountains rise to just over 2000 m (6562 ft). *Principal rivers:* Niger, Dillia. *Highest point:* Mont Gréboun 2022 m (6634 ft).

ECONOMY Livestock herds and harvests of subsistence crops – millet, sorghum, cassava and rice – have been reduced by desertification. Uranium is mined.

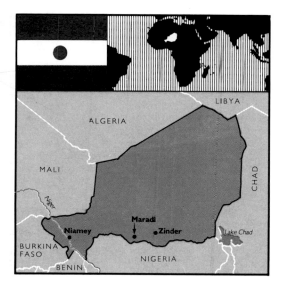

RECENT HISTORY The French territory of Niger was proclaimed in 1901, but much of the country was not brought under French control until 1920. Independence was achieved in 1960 under President Hamani Diori. After the economy was wracked by a prolonged drought, Diori was overthrown in a military coup (1974). In 1989, civilian rule was restored although the military head of state retained power. A multi-party system was restored in 1992 and free elections for a constituent assembly are scheduled for 1993.

NIGERIA

Official name: The Federal Republic of Nigeria.
Member of: UN, OAU, Commonwealth, OPEC, ECOWAS.
Area: 923 768 km² (356 669 sq mi).
Population: 88 514 000 (1991 census) – previous World Bank and UN estimates of Nigeria's population are 20 000 000 higher than the figure recorded in the 1991 census.
Capital and major cities: Abuja (new federal capital), 379 000, Lagos 5 686 000 (city 1 340 000), Ibadan 1 263 000, Ogbomosho 644 000, Kano 595 000, Ilorin 420 000, Oshogbo 400 000 (1991 census).
Languages: English (official), with over 150 local languages, of which Hausa, Yoruba and Ibo are the most widely spoken.
Religions: Sunni Islam (48%), various Protestant Churches (Anglican, Methodist, Lutheran, Baptist and Presbyterian; 17%), Roman Catholic (17%).

GOVERNMENT Since 1983 Nigeria has been ruled by the Armed Forces Ruling Council whose President is head of state and of government. Elections by universal adult suffrage are scheduled in 1993 for the 30 state administrations, a 450-member Federal Assembly and a President to serve a six-year term. Two political parties – the Social Democratic Party and the National Republican Convention – were legalized in 1989.
President: Gen. Ibrahim Babangida.

STATES AND TERRITORIES In 1991 the number of states was increased to from 21 to 30 by redrawing the boundaries of most of the existing states. As the exact limits of these new states have not been delineated, the area of these units cannot be given.

Abia *Population:* 2 298 000 (1991 census). *Capital:* Umuahia.
Adamawa *Population:* 2 124 000 (1991 census). *Capital:* Yola.
Akwa Ibom *Population:* 2 360 000 (1991 census). *Capital:* Uyo.
Anambra *Population:* 2 768 000 (1991 census). *Capital:* Akwa.
Bauchi *Population:* 4 294 000 (1991 census). *Capital:* Bauchi.
Benue *Population:* 2 780 000 (1991 census). *Capital:* Makurdi.
Borno *Population:* 2 597 000 (1991 census). *Capital:* Maiduguri.
Cross River *Population:* 1 866 000 (1991 census). *Capital:* Calabar.
Delta *Population:* 2 570 000 (1991 census). *Capital:* Asaba.
Edo *Population:* 2 160 000 (1991 census). *Capital:* Benin City.

Enugu *Population*: 3 161 000 (1991 census). *Capital*: Enugu.

Imo *Population*: 2 486 000 (1991 census). *Capital*: Owerri.

Jigawa *Population*: 2 830 000 (1991 census). *Capital*: Dutse.

Kaduna *Population*: 3 969 000 (1991 census). *Capital*: Kaduna.

Kano *Population*: 5 632 000 (1991 census). *Capital*: Kano.

Katsina *Population*: 3 878 000 (1991 census). *Capital*: Katsina.

Kebbi *Population*: 2 062 000 (1991 census). *Capital*: Birnin Kebbi.

Kogi *Population*: 1 566 000 (1991 census). *Capital*: Ilorin.

Kwara *Population*: 2 099 000 (1991 census). *Capital*: Lokoja.

Lagos *Population*: 5 686 000 (1991 census). *Capital*: Ikeja.

Niger *Population*: 2 482 000 (1991 census). *Capital*: Minna.

Ogun *Population*: 2 339 000 (1991 census). *Capital*: Abeokuta.

Ondo *Population*: 3 884 000 (1991 census). *Capital*: Akure.

Osun *Population*: 2 203 000 (1991 census). *Capital*: Oshogbo.

Oyo *Population*: 3 489 000 (1991 census). *Capital*: Ibadan.

Plateau *Population*: 3 284 000 (1991 census). *Capital*: Jos.

Rivers *Population*: 3 984 000 (1991 census). *Capital*: Port Harcourt.

Sokoto *Population*: 4 392 000 (1991 census). *Capital*: Sokoto.

Taraba *Population*: 1 481 000 (1991 census). *Capital*: Jalingo.

Yobe *Population*: 1 411 000 (1991 census). *Capital*: Damaturu.

Federal Capital Territory *Population*: 379 000 (1991 census). *Capital*: Abuja.

GEOGRAPHY Inland from the swampy forest and tropical jungles of the coastal plains, Nigeria comprises a series of plateaux covered – for the most part – by open woodland or savannah. The far north is semi-desert. Isolated ranges of hills rise above the plateaux, the highest of which are the central Jos Plateau and the Biu Plateau in the northeast. *Principal rivers*: Niger, Benue, Cross River, Yobe, Osse. *Highest point*: Vogel Peak (Dimlany) 2042 m (6700 ft).

ECONOMY Nigeria is the major economic power in West Africa. The country depends upon revenue from petroleum exports, but a combination of falling petroleum prices and OPEC quotas has resulted in major economic problems, although it has also encouraged diversification. Natural gas is to be exported in liquid form to Europe. Major industries include petrochemicals, textiles and food processing. Over 50% of the

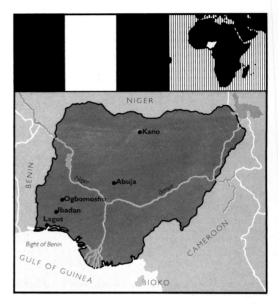

labour force is involved in agriculture, mainly producing maize, sorghum, cassava, yams and rice as subsistence crops. Cocoa is an important export.

RECENT HISTORY In 1914 the coast and the interior of Nigeria were united to form Britain's largest African colony. An unwieldy federal structure introduced in 1954 was unable to contain regional rivalries after independence (1960). In 1966, the first Prime Minister, Sir Abubakar Tafawa Balewa (1912–66), and other prominent politicians were assassinated in a military coup. After a counter-coup brought General Yakubu Gowon to power, a bitter civil war took place (1967–70) when the Eastern Region – the homeland of the Ibo – attempted to secede as Biafra. Although the East was quickly re-integrated after Biafra's defeat, Nigeria remained politically unstable. The number of states was gradually increased from 3 to 21 in an attempt to prevent any one region becoming dominant. A military coup overthrew Gowon in 1975, and an attempt at civilian rule (1979–83) also ended in a coup. Another coup brought Gen. Ibrahim Babangida to power in 1985. The reintroduction of civilian rule is planned before the end of 1993.

NORWAY

Official name: Kongeriket Norge (Kingdom of Norway).

Member of: UN, EFTA, NATO, CSCE, Council of Europe, OECD.

Area: 323 878 km² (125 050 sq mi) including the Arctic

island territories of Svalbard (formerly known as Spitsbergen) and Jan Mayen.

Population: 4 259 000 (1991 est.).

Capital and major cities: Oslo 462 000, Bergen 213 000, Trondheim 138 000, Stavanger 98 000, Kristiansand 66 000, Drammen 52 000, Tromso 51 000 (1991 est.).

Languages: Two official forms of Norwegian – Bokmaal (80%), Nynorsk (or Landsmaal; 20%); Lappish.

Religion: Lutheran (official; nearly 90%).

GOVERNMENT Norway is a constitutional monarchy. The 165-member Parliament (Storting) is elected under a system of proportional representation by universal adult suffrage for a four-year term. In order to legislate, the Storting divides itself into two houses – the Lagting (containing one quarter of the members) and the Odelsting (containing the remaining three quarters of the members). The King appoints a Prime Minister who commands a majority in the Storting. The PM, in turn, appoints a Council of Ministers who are responsible to the Storting. The main political parties include the Labour Party, the Conservative Party, the Christian Democratic Party, the Centre Party, the Socialist Left Party, the Progress Party, and the Liberal Party.

King: HM King Harald V (succeeded upon the death of his father, 17 January 1991).

Prime Minister: Gro Harlem Brundtland.

GEOGRAPHY Norway's coastline is characterized by fjords, a series of long, deep, narrow inlets formed by glacial action. The greater part of Norway comprises highlands of hard rock. The principal lowlands are along the Skagerrak coast and around Oslofjord and Trondheimsfjord. Svalbard (Spitsbergen) is a bleak archipelago in the Arctic. *Principal rivers*: Glomma (Glama), Lågen, Tanaelv. *Highest point*: Galdhøpiggen 2469 m (8098 ft).

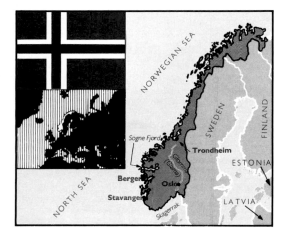

ECONOMY Norway enjoys a high standard of living. Only a small proportion of the land can be cultivated, and agriculture – which is heavily subsidized – is chiefly concerned with dairying and fodder crops. Timber is a major export of Norway, over one half of which is forested. The fishing industry is an important foreign-currency earner, and fish farming – which has been encouraged by government development schemes – is taking the place of whaling and deep-sea fishing. Manufacturing – which has traditionally been concerned with processing fish, timber and iron ore – is now dominated by petrochemicals and allied industries, based upon large reserves of petroleum and natural gas in Norway's sector of the North Sea. Petroleum and natural gas supply over one third of the country's export earnings. The development of industries such as electrical engineering has been helped by cheap hydroelectric power.

RECENT HISTORY Norway came under the rule of the kings of Sweden after the Napoleonic Wars, although a separate Norwegian Parliament was allowed a considerable degree of independence. Growing nationalism in Norway placed great strains upon the union with Sweden, and in 1905 – following a vote by the Norwegians to repeal the union – King Oscar II of Sweden gave up his claims to the Norwegian crown to allow a peaceful separation of the two countries. After a Swedish prince declined the Norwegian throne, Prince Carl of Denmark was confirmed as King of Norway – as Haakon VII – by a plebiscite. Norway was neutral in World War I, and declared neutrality in World War II, but was occupied by German forces (1940) who set up a puppet government under Vidkun Quisling. After the war, Norway joined NATO and agreed in 1972 to enter the EC, but a national referendum rejected membership. In 1992, a Norwegian reapplication for EC membership became a serious option.

NORWEGIAN EXTERNAL TERRITORIES
Norwegian Antarctic Territories (Bouvet Island, Peter I Island, Queen Maud Land): see Other Territories, following this chapter.

OMAN

Official name: Sultanat 'Uman (Sultanate of Oman).

Member of: UN, Arab League, GCC.

Area: 300 000 km^2 (120 000 sq mi).

Population: 1 502 000 (1990 est.).

Capital: Muscat 380 000 (city 85 000), Sohar 92 000 (1990 est.).

Languages: Arabic (official), Baluchi.

Religions: Ibadi Islam (75%), Sunni Islam (25%).

GOVERNMENT Oman is an absolute monarchy in which the Sultan – who rules by decree – is advised by an appointed Cabinet. The Sultan appoints the 52 members of the State Consultative Council. In 1990 it was announced that an elected consultative assembly would be established. There are no political parties.

Sultan: HM Qaboos bin Said (succeeded upon the deposition of his father, 23 July 1970).

GEOGRAPHY A barren range of hills rises sharply behind a narrow coastal plain. Desert extends inland into the Rub' al Khali ('The Empty Quarter'). A small detached portion of Oman lies north of the United Arab Emirates. There are no significant rivers. *Highest point*: Jabal ash Sham 3170 m (10 400 ft).

ECONOMY Oman depends almost entirely upon exports of petroleum and natural gas. Owing to aridity, less than 1% of Oman is cultivated.

RECENT HISTORY A British presence was established in the 19th century and Oman did not regain complete independence until 1951. Sultan Qaboos – who came to power in a palace coup in 1970 – has modernized and developed Oman. In the 1970s South Yemen supported left-wing separatist guerrillas in the southern province of Dhofar, but the revolt was suppressed with military assistance from the UK.

PAKISTAN

Official name: Islami Jamhuria-e-Pakistan (Islamic Republic of Pakistan).

Member of: UN, Commonwealth, SAARC.

Area: 803 943 km² (310 403 sq mi) or 888 102 km² (333 897 sq mi) including the Pakistani-held areas of Kashmir (known as Azad Kashmir) and the disputed Northern Areas (Gilgit, Baltistan and Diamir).

Population: 126 406 000 (1991 est; including the Pakistani-held areas of Kashmir – Azad Kashmir – and the disputed Northern Areas – Gilgit, Baltistan and Diamir).

Capital and major cities: Islamabad 266 000, Karachi 6 771 000, Lahore 3 850 000, Faisalabad 1 435 000, Rawal-pindi 1 100 000, Hyderabad 1 041 000, Multan 999 000, Gujranwala 912 000, Peshawar 770 000, Sialkot 418 000 (all including suburbs; 1992 est).

Languages: Urdu (national; 20%), Punjabi (60%), Sindhi (12%), English, Pushto, Baluchi.

Religions: Sunni Islam (official; 92%), Shia Islam (5%), with small Ismaili Muslim and Ahmadi minorities.

GOVERNMENT The 87-member Senate (the upper house of the Federal Legislature) comprises 19 senators elected for six years by each of the four provinces, plus 8 senators elected from the federally administered Tribal Areas and 3 senators chosen to represent the federal capital. The 237-member National Assembly comprises 207 members elected by universal adult suffrage for five years, 20 seats reserved for women, and 10 members representing non-Islamic minorities. The President – who is chosen by the Federal Legislature – appoints a Prime Minister who commands a majority in the National Assembly. The PM, in turn, appoints a Cabinet of Ministers, responsible to the Assembly. The President has the power to dismiss the current government and dissolve the national and provincial assemblies. The main political parties include the PPP (Pakistan People's Party) and the (coalition) Islamic Democratic Alliance. The four provinces, Azad Kashmir and the Northern Areas have their own legislatures.

President: Ghulam Ishaq Khan.

Prime Minister: Nawaz Sharif.

PROVINCES, TERRITORIES AND DISPUTED TERRITORIES Baluchistan *Area*: 347 188 km² (134 050 sq mi). *Population*: 5 670 000 (1990 est). *Capital*: Quetta.

North-West Frontier *Area*: 74 522 km² (28 773 sq mi). *Population*: 14 340 000 (1990 est). *Capital*: Peshawar.

Punjab *Area*: 205 345 km² (79 284 sq mi). *Population*: 62 060 000 (1990 est). *Capital*: Lahore.

Sind *Area*: 140 913 km² (54 407 sq mi). *Population*: 24 980 000 (1990 est). *Capital*: Karachi.

Federal Capital Territory *Area*: 907 km² (350 sq mi). *Population*: 266 000 (1991 est). *Capital*: Islamabad.

Azad Kashmir (that part of the state of Jammu and Kashmir occupied by Pakistan) *Area*: 11 639 km² (4494 sq mi). *Population*: 2 580 000 (1990 est). *Capital*: Muzaffarabad.

Northern Areas (Baltistan, Diamir and Gilgit) (administered by Pakistan but disputed by India) *Area*: (combined total) 72 520 km² (28 000 sq mi). *Population*: (combined total) 730 000 (1990 est). *Capitals*: Skardu (of Baltistan), Chilas (of Diamir) and Gilgit (of Gilgit).

GEOGRAPHY The Indus Valley divides Pakistan into a highland region in the west and a lowland region in the east. In Baluchistan – in the south – the highlands consist of ridges of hills and low mountains running northeast to southwest. In the north – in the North-West Frontier Province and the disputed territories – the mountain chains rise to over 7000 m (21 300 ft) and include the Karakoram, and parts of the Himalaya and Hindu Kush. The valley of the Indus and its tributaries form a major agricultural region and contain the majority of Pakistan's population. A continuation of the Indian Thar Desert occupies the east. *Principal rivers:* Indus, Sutlej, Chenab, Ravi, Jhelum. *Highest point:* K2 (Mount Godwin Austen) 8607 m (28 238 ft).

ECONOMY One half of the labour force is involved in subsistence farming, with wheat and rice as the main crops. Cotton is the main foreign-currency earner. The government is encouraging irrigation schemes, but over one half of the cultivated land is subject to either waterlogging or salinity. Although there is a wide range of mineral reserves – including coal, gold, graphite, copper and manganese – these resources have not been extensively developed. Manufacturing is dominated by food processing, textiles and consumer goods. Unemployment and underemployment are major problems, and the country relies heavily upon foreign aid and money sent back by Pakistanis working abroad.

RECENT HISTORY Pakistan as a nation was born in August 1947 when British India was partitioned as a result of demands by the Muslim League for an Islamic state in which Hindus would not be in a majority. Large numbers of Muslims moved to the new state and up to 1 000 000 people died in the bloodshed that accompanied partition. Pakistan had two 'wings' – West Pakistan (the present country) and East Pakistan (now Bangladesh) – separated by 1600 km (1000 mi) of Indian territory. A number of areas were disputed with India. Kashmir – the principal bone of contention – was effectively partitioned between the two nations, and in 1947–49 and 1965 tension over Kashmir led to war between India and Pakistan. The problem of Kashmir remains unsolved, with fighting continuing intermittently along parts of the cease-fire line.

The Muslim League leader Muhammad Ali Jinnah (1876–1949) was the first Governor General, but Jinnah, who was regarded as 'father of the nation', died soon after independence. Pakistan – which became a republic in 1956 – suffered political instability and periods of military rule, including the administrations of General Muhammad Ayub Khan (from 1958 to 1969) and General Muhammad Yahya Khan (from 1969 to 1971). Although East Pakistan contained the majority of the population, from the beginning West Pakistan held political and military dominance. In elections in 1970, Shaikh Mujibur Rahman's Awami League won an overwhelming majority in East Pakistan, while the Pakistan People's Party (PPP) won most of the seats in West Pakistan. Mujibur Rahman seemed less interested in leading a new Pakistani government than in winning autonomy for the East. In March 1971, after abortive negotiations, the Pakistani army was sent from the West to East Pakistan, which promptly declared its independence as Bangladesh. Civil war broke out and India supported the new state, forcing the Pakistani army to surrender by the end of the year.

The leader of the PPP, Zulfiqar Ali Bhutto (PM 1972–77), was deposed in a military coup led by the Army Chief of Staff, Muhammad Zia al-Haq. Bhutto was imprisoned (1977) for allegedly ordering the murder of the father of a former political opponent, sentenced to death (1978) and, despite international protests, hanged (1979). In 1985 Zia lifted martial law and began to return Pakistan to civilian life. In 1988 Zia was killed in a plane crash. In scheduled elections a few months later the PPP – led by Bhutto's daughter Benazir Bhutto – became the largest party, and Benazir Bhutto became the first woman prime minister of an Islamic state. In August 1990, she was accused of nepotism and corruption by the president and dismissed. The following elections were won by the Islamic Democratic Alliance.

PANAMA

Official name: La República de Panamá (The Republic of Panama).

Member of: UN, OAS.

Area: 77 082 km² (29 762 sq mi) including the former Canal Zone.

Population: 2 329 000 (1990 census).

Capital: Panama City 828 000 (city 585 000), San Miguelito (part of the Panama City agglomeration) 243 000, Colón 141 000, David 103 000 (1990 census).

Languages: Spanish (official).

Religions: Roman Catholic (85%), various Evangelical Protestant Churches (5%), Sunni Islam (5%).

GOVERNMENT The constitution provides for the election by compulsory universal adult suffrage of a 67-member Legislative Assembly, a President and two Vice Presidents for five years. The President appoints a

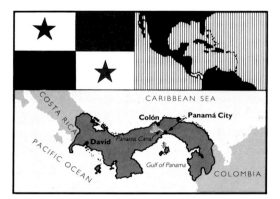

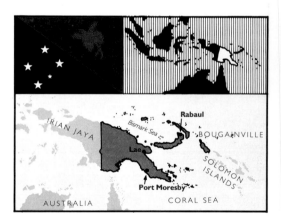

Population: 3 790 000 (1990 census).

Capital and main cities: Port Moresby 193 000 (city 174 000), Lae 81 000, Madang 27 000, Wewak 23 000 (1990 census).

Languages: English (official), Pidgin English, Motu, and over 700 other local languages.

Religions: Roman Catholic (33%), various Protestant Churches (over 60%).

GOVERNMENT A 109-member Parliament is elected for five years by universal adult suffrage. The Governor General – the representative of the British Queen as sovereign of Papua New Guinea – appoints a Prime Minister who commands a majority in Parliament. The PM, in turn, appoints a Cabinet, which is responsible to Parliament. The main political parties are the People's Democratic Movement, the Pangu Party, the National Party, and the United Party.

Prime Minister: Wiwa Koriwi.

GEOGRAPHY Broad swampy plains surround New Guinea's mountainous interior. *Principal rivers:* Fly (with Strickland), Sepik. *Highest point:* Mount Wilhelm 4509 m (14 493 ft).

ECONOMY Over 80% of the labour force is involved in agriculture – mainly subsistence farming – although agricultural exports include palm oil, copra and cocoa. The mainstay of the economy is minerals, including large reserves of copper, gold, silver and petroleum.

Cabinet of Ministers. The main political parties include the Authentic Liberal Party, the Christian Democratic Party and the Nationalist Republican Liberation Movement (who cooperated in the 1989 elections as the Democratic Alliance), the Authentic Panamenista Party, and the (coalition) Colina.

President: Guillermo Endara.

GEOGRAPHY Panama is a heavily forested mountainous isthmus joining Central America to South America. *Principal rivers:* Tuira (with Chucunaque), Bayano, Santa Maria. *Highest point:* Chiriqui 3475 m (11 467 ft).

ECONOMY Income from the Panama Canal is a major foreign-currency earner. Panama has a higher standard of living than its neighbours, although the political crisis of 1989 damaged the economy. Major exports include bananas, shrimps and mahogany.

RECENT HISTORY In the 1880s a French attempt to construct a canal from the Atlantic to the Pacific through Panama – then part of Colombia – proved unsuccessful. After Colombia rejected US proposals for completing the canal, Panama seceded from Colombia and became independent (1903), sponsored by the USA. The canal eventually opened in 1914. The USA was given land extending 8 km (5 mi) on either side of the canal – the Canal Zone – complete control of which will be handed to Panama in 2000. From 1983 to 1989 effective power was in the hands of General Manuel Noriega, who was deposed by a US invasion and taken to stand trial in the USA, where he was found guilty of criminal activities.

PAPUA NEW GUINEA

Official name: The Independent State of Papua New Guinea.

Member of: UN, Commonwealth, South Pacific Forum.

Area: 462 840 km² (178 704 sq mi).

RECENT HISTORY Papua, a British protectorate, was transferred to Australia in 1906. German New Guinea – the northeast – was occupied by Australian forces in 1914. From 1942 to 1945 Japanese forces occupied New Guinea and part of Papua. In 1949 Australia united the administration of the territories, which achieved independence as Papua New Guinea in 1975. Bougainville island – a major source of copper – attempted to secede (1990–92). Fighting on the island ended in 1992 and peace talks began.

PARAGUAY

Official name: La República del Paraguay (The Republic of Paraguay).

Member of: UN, OAS, ALADI.

Area: 406 752 km² (157 048 sq mi).

Population: 4 397 000 (1991 est.).

Capital and major cities: Asunción 732 000 (city 608 000), San Lorenzo (part of the Asunción agglomeration) 124 000, Ciudad del Este 110 000, Concepción 63 000, Encarnación 44 000 (1990 est.).

Languages: Spanish (official; 7%), Guaraní (40%), bilingual Guaraní-Spanish (48%).

Religion: Roman Catholic (official; 97%).

GOVERNMENT A 198-member Constituent Assembly was elected by universal adult suffrage in 1992 to draft a new constitution. The President currently serving was elected by universal adult suffrage for a five-year term. The main political parties are the Colorado Party and the Authentic Liberal Party.

President: Gen. Andres Rodriguez Pedotti.

GEOGRAPHY The country west of the Paraguay River – the Chaco – is a flat semiarid plain. The region east of the river is a partly forested undulating plateau. *Principal rivers*: Paraguay, Paraná, Pilcomayo. *Highest point*: Cerro Tatug 700 m (2297 ft).

ECONOMY Agriculture – the main economic activity – is dominated by cattle ranching, cotton and soyabeans. Cheap hydroelectric power has greatly stimulated industry.

RECENT HISTORY For most of the 19th and 20th centuries, Paraguay has suffered dictators. The Chaco Wars with Bolivia (1929–35) further weakened Paraguay. General Alfredo Stroessner gained power in 1954, ruling with increasing disregard for human rights until his overthrow in a military coup in 1989. Free elections for a constituent assembly were held in 1992.

PERU

Official name: República del Perú (Republic of Peru).

Member of: UN, OAS, ALADI, Andean Pact.

Area: 1 285 216 km² (496 225 sq mi).

Population: 22 881 000 (1991 est.).

Capital and major cities: Lima 6 405 000 (city 5 494 000), Arequipa 612 000, Callao (part of the Lima agglomeration) 515 000, Trujillo 513 000, Chiclayo 410 000, Piura 310 000 (1990 est.).

Languages: Spanish (68%), Quechua (27%), Aymara (3%) – all official.

Religion: Roman Catholic (official; 91%).

GOVERNMENT The President and the National Congress – comprising a 60-member Senate and a 180-member Chamber of Deputies – are elected by universal adult suffrage for five years. The President appoints a Council of Ministers headed by a Prime Minister. The main political parties include the (left-wing) APRA (American Popular Revolutionary Alliance), the (centre-right) Democratic Front, the IU (Izquierda Unida – Unified Left), the (liberal) Acción Popular, and Cambio 90.

President: Alberto Fujimori.

Prime Minister: to be announced.

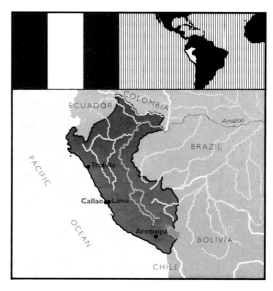

GEOGRAPHY The coastal plain is narrow and arid. The Andes – which are prone to earthquakes – run in three high parallel ridges from north to south. Nearly two thirds of Peru is tropical forest (the Selva) in the Amazon Basin. *Principal rivers:* Amazon, Ucayali, Napo, Marañón. *Highest point:* Huascarán 6768 m (22 205 ft).

ECONOMY About one third of the labour force is involved in agriculture. Subsistence farming dominates in the interior; crops for export are more important near the coast. Major crops include coffee, sugar cane, cotton and potatoes, as well as coca for cocaine. Sheep, llamas, vicuñas and alpacas are kept for wool. Rich natural resources include silver, copper, coal, gold, iron ore, petroleum and phosphates. The fishing industry – once the world's largest – has declined since 1971. A combination of natural disasters, a very high birth rate, guerrilla warfare and the declining value of exports have severely damaged the economy.

RECENT HISTORY Although Peru was governed by civilian constitutional governments at the beginning of the 20th century, instability and military coups have been common. A successful war against Ecuador (1941) added Amazonian territory. From 1968 a reformist military government instituted a programme of land reform, attempting to benefit workers and the Indians, but faced with mounting economic problems the military swung to the right in 1975. Since 1980 elections have been held regularly, but owing to the economic crisis and the growth of an extreme left-wing guerrilla movement – the Sendero Luminoso ('Shining Path') – Peru's democracy remained under threat. In 1992, the president effected a coup, suspending the constitution and detaining opposition leaders. Subsequent elections were boycotted by the principal opposition parties.

THE PHILIPPINES

Official name: Repúblika ñg Pilipinas (Republic of the Philippines).

Member of: UN, ASEAN.

Area: 300 000 km² (115 831 sq mi).

Population: 62 354 000 (1991 est).

Capital and major cities: Manila 7 832 000 (city 1 599 000), Quezon City (part of the Manila agglomeration) 1 667 000; Davao City 850 000, Caloocan City (part of the Manila agglomeration) 761 000, Cebu City 610 000, Zamboango City 442 000, Pasay City (part of the Manila agglomeration) 367 000, Bacolod City 364 000 (1990 census).

Languages: Pilipino (based on Tagalog; national 55%), Tagalog (over 20%), Cebuano (24%), Ilocano (11%), English, Spanish, with many local languages.

Religions: Roman Catholic (84%), Aglipayan Church (4%), Sunni Islam (5%).

GOVERNMENT The President and the 24-member Senate – the upper House of Congress – are elected by universal adult suffrage for six years. The House of Representatives – the lower House of Congress – comprises 200 directly elected members and no more than 50 members appointed by the President from minority groups. The President appoints a Cabinet. The main political parties include the Liberal Party, PDP-Laban (Pilipino Democratic Party–People's Power Movement), the Labor Party, and the Grand Alliance for Democracy.

President: Fidel Ramos.

GEOGRAPHY Some 2770 of the Philippines' 7000 islands are named. The two largest islands, Luzon and Mindanao, make up over two thirds of the country's area. Most of the archipelago is mountainous with restricted coastal plains, although Luzon has a large, densely populated central plain. Earthquakes are common. *Principal rivers:* Cagayan, Pampanga, Abra, Agusan, Magat, Laoang, Agno. *Highest point:* Mount Apo 2954 m (9692 ft).

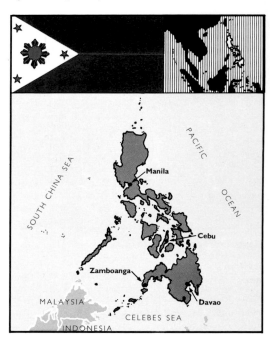

ECONOMY Almost one half of the labour force is involved in agriculture. Rice and maize are the principal subsistence crops, while coconuts, sugar cane, pineapples and bananas are grown for export. The timber industry is important, but deforestation is a problem as land is cleared for cultivation. Major industries include textiles, food processing, chemicals and electrical engineering. Mineral resources include copper (a major export), gold, petroleum and nickel. Money sent back by Filipinos working abroad is an important source of foreign currency.

RECENT HISTORY Spain ceded the islands to the USA after its defeat in the Spanish-American War (1898). However, American rule had to be imposed by force and resistance continued until 1906. In 1935 the nationalist leader Manuel Quezon became president of the semi-independent 'Commonwealth' of the Philippines. The surprise Japanese invasion of 1941 traumatized the islands' American and Filipino defenders. Japan set up a puppet 'Philippine Republic', but, after the American recapture of the archipelago, a fully independent Republic of the Philippines was established in 1946. Between 1953 and 1957 the charismatic President Ramon Magsaysay crushed and conciliated Communist-dominated Hukbalahap guerrillas, but his death ended a programme of land reforms. Coming to power in 1965, Ferdinand Marcos (1917–89) inaugurated flamboyant development projects, but his administration presided over corruption on an unprecedented scale. Marcos used the continuing guerrilla activity as a justification for his increasingly repressive rule. When he attempted to rig the result of presidential elections in 1986, Marcos was overthrown in a popular revolution in favour of Corazon Aquino. Her government faced several attempted military coups. Insurgency by groups including the (Islamic) Moro National Liberation Front and the (Communist) New People's Army remains a problem.

POLAND

Official name: Polska Rzecpospolita (Republic of Poland).

Member of: UN, CSCE, Council of Europe.

Area: 312 683 km² (120 727 sq mi).

Population: 38 273 000 (1991 est).

Capital and major cities: Warsaw (Warszawa) 1 656 000, Lódź 848 000, Kraków 751 000, Wroclaw 643 000, Poznań 590 000, Gdańsk 465 000, Szczecin 413 000, Bydgoszcz 382 000, Katowice 367 000, Lublin 351 000 (1990 est).

Language: Polish.

Religion: Roman Catholic (93%), Polish Orthodox (2%).

GOVERNMENT The 100-member Senate – the upper house – and the 460-member Sejm – the lower house – are elected for four years by universal adult suffrage. (Only 161 of the members of the Sejm were elected on a multi-party basis in 1989. The remaining 299 seats in the Sejm were reserved for candidates representing the Communists and two allied parties.) The President – who is directly elected – appoints a Prime Minister who commands a majority in the Sejm. The PM, in turn, appoints a Council of Ministers. The main political parties are the Democratic Union, the Alliance of the Democratic Left, Catholic Action, the Peasant Party, the Confederation for an Independent Poland, the Alliance of the Centre, the Congress of Liberals, Rural Solidarity and Trade Union Solidarity.

President: Lech Walesa.
Prime Minister: Hannah Suchocka.

GEOGRAPHY Most of Poland consists of lowlands. In the north are the Baltic lowlands and the Pomeranian and Mazurian lake districts. Central Poland is a region of plains. In the south are the hills of Little Poland and the Tatra Mountains, part of the Carpathian chain. *Principal rivers:* Vistula (Wisa), Oder (Odra), Narew. *Highest point:* Rysy 2499 m (8199 ft).

ECONOMY Polish agriculture remains predominantly small-scale and privately owned. Over one quarter of the labour force is still involved in agriculture, growing potatoes, wheat, barley, sugar beet and a range of fodder crops. The industrial sector is large-scale and, until the switch to a free-market economy began in 1990, centrally planned. Poland has major deposits of coal, as well as reserves of natural gas, copper and silver. Engineering, food processing, and the chemical, metallurgical and paper industries are important, but the economic situation has steadily deteriorated since the 1960s. To add to inflation and a rampant black market, Poland has crippling foreign debts. Privatization has been accelerated since 1991 but living standards have decreased.

RECENT HISTORY In the 19th century the greater part of Poland was within Imperial Russia, the remainder ruled by Austria and Prussia. After World War I, Poland was restored to statehood (1919), but the country was unstable. Marshal Józef Pilsudski (1867–1935) staged a coup in 1926, and became a virtual dictator. During the 1930s relations with Hitler's Germany – which made territorial claims on parts of Poland – became strained. An alliance with Britain was not enough to deter Hitler from attacking Poland, and thus precipitating World War II (1939). Poland was partitioned once again, this time between Nazi Germany and the USSR. Occupied Poland lost one sixth of its population, including almost all the Jews, and casualties were high after the ill-fated Warsaw Rising (1944). Poland was liberated by the Red Army (1945), and a Communist state was established. The new Poland lost almost one half its territory in the east to the USSR, but was compensated in the north and west at the expense of Germany.

A political crisis in 1956 led to the emergence of a Communist leader who enjoyed a measure of popular support, Wladyslaw Gomulka. In 1980, following the downfall of Gomulka's successor, Edward Gierek, a period of unrest led to the birth of the independent trade union Solidarity (Solidarnośc), led by Lech Walesa (1943–). Martial law was declared by General Wojciech Jaruzelski in 1981 in an attempt to restore Communist authority. Solidarity was banned and its leaders were detained, but public unrest and economic difficulties continued. In 1989 Solidarity was legalized and agreement was reached on political reform. Solidarity won free elections to the new Senate, and with the support of former allies of the Communists won enough seats to gain a majority in the Sejm, and Tadeusz Mazowiecki of Solidarity became PM. Disagreements concerning the speed at which market reforms were advancing and personality clashes during the presidential election split Solidarity. Walesa became president in 1990. Since multi-party elections in 1991, several short-lived coalition governments have held office.

PORTUGAL

Official name: A República Portuguesa (The Portuguese Republic).
Member of: UN, EC, NATO, Council of Europe, CSCE, WEU, OECD.
Area: 92 072 km² (33 549 sq mi) including Madeira and the Azores.
Population: 10 421 000 (1991 est).
Capital and major cities: Lisbon (Lisboa) 2 131 000 (city 950 000), Oporto (Porto) 1 695 000 (city 450 000), Amadora (part of the Lisbon agglomeration) 100 000, Setúbal 80 000, Coímbra 75 000, Braga 67 000, Vila Nova de Gaia (part of the Oporto agglomeration) 65 000, Barreiro (part of the Lisbon agglomeration) 55 000, Funchal 47 000 (all including suburbs; 1990 est).
Language: Portuguese (official).
Religion: Roman Catholic (nearly 90%).

GOVERNMENT An executive President is elected for a five-year term by universal adult suffrage. The 250-member Assembly is directly elected for four years. The President appoints a Prime Minister who commands a majority in the Assembly. The PM, in turn, appoints a Council of Ministers (Cabinet), responsible to the Assembly. The main political parties include PSD (the Social Democratic Party), PS (the Socialist Party), the (centre-left) Democratic Party and the Communist Alli-

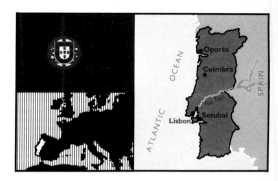

ance. Madeira and the Azores have their own autonomous governments.
President: Mario Alberto Soares.
Prime Minister: Annibal Cavaco Silva.

PORTUGUESE AUTONOMOUS REGIONS
Azores (Açores) *Area*: 2247 km² (868 sq mi). *Population*: 253 000 (1991 est). *Capital*: Ponta Delgada 22 000 (1981).
Madeira (includes Porto Santo) *Area*: 794 km² (306 sq mi). *Population*: 273 000 (1991 est). *Capital*: Funchal 47 000 (1990 est).

GEOGRAPHY Behind a coastal plain, Portugal north of the River Tagus is a highland region, at the centre of which is the country's principal mountain range, the Serra da Estrela. A wide plateau in the northeast is a continuation of the Spanish Meseta. Portugal south of the Tagus is mainly an undulating lowland. The Atlantic islands of Madeira and the Azores are respectively nearly 1000 km (620 mi) and 1200 km (745 mi) southwest of the mainland. *Principal rivers:* Tagus (Rio Tejo), Douro, Guadiana. *Highest point:* Pico 2315 m (7713 ft) in the Azores. Malhao de Estrela, at 1993 m (6537 ft), is the highest point on the mainland.

ECONOMY Agriculture involves about 20% of the labour force, but lacks investment following land reforms in the 1970s, since when production has fallen. The principal crops include wheat and maize, as well as grapes (for wines such as port and Madeira), tomatoes, potatoes and cork trees. The country lacks natural resources. Manufacturing industry includes textiles and clothing (major exports), footwear, food processing, cork products, and, increasingly, electrical appliances and petrochemicals. Tourism and money sent back by Portuguese working abroad are major foreign-currency earners. Despite recent impressive economic development – following severe disruption during and immediately after the 1974 revolution – Portugal remains Western Europe's poorest country.

RECENT HISTORY Portugal experienced political instability for much of the 19th century. The monarchy was violently overthrown in 1910, but the Portuguese republic proved unstable and the military took power in 1926. From 1932 to 1968, under the dictatorship of Premier Antonio Salazar (1889–1970), stability was achieved but at great cost. Portugal became a one-party state, and expensive colonial wars dragged on as Portugal attempted to check independence movements in Angola and Mozambique. In 1974 there was a left-wing military coup whose leaders granted independence to the African colonies (1974–75), and initially attempted to impose a Marxist system on the country. However, elections in 1976 decisively rejected the far left. Civilian rule was restored as Portugal effected a transition from dictatorship to democracy, and simultaneously – through the loss of empire and membership of the EC (from 1986) – became more closely integrated with the rest of Europe.

PORTUGUESE OVERSEAS TERRITORY Macau
Area: 17 km² (6.5 sq mi). *Population*: 402 000 (1991 census). *Capital*: Macau 402 000.

QATAR

Official name: Dawlat Qatar (State of Qatar).
Member of: UN, Arab League, OPEC, GCC.
Area: 11 437 km² (4416 sq mi).
Population: 456 000 (1991 est).
Capital: Doha 272 000 (city 217 000), ar-Rayyani 42 000 and al-Wakrah 13 000 are part of the Doha agglomeration, Umm Sa'id 6000 (1986 est).
Language: Arabic.
Religion: Wahhabi Sunni Islam (official; 98%).

GOVERNMENT Qatar is an absolute monarchy. The Amir – who is head of state and of government – appoints a Council of Ministers. There are neither formal political institutions nor parties.
Amir and head of government: HH Shaikh Khalifa bin Hamad Al-Thani (succeeded upon the deposition of his cousin, 22 February 1972).

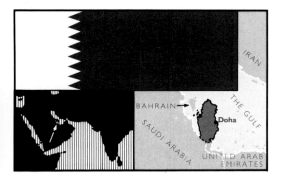

GEOGRAPHY Qatar is a low barren peninsula projecting into the Gulf. There are no rivers. *Highest point:* 73 m (240 ft) in the Dukhan Heights.

ECONOMY Qatar's high standard of living is due almost entirely to the export of petroleum and natural gas. The steel and cement industries have been developed in an attempt to diversify.

RECENT HISTORY Qatar was part of the Ottoman Empire from 1872 until 1914. Its ruler signed protection treaties with Britain in 1916 and 1934, and did not regain complete independence until 1971. Qatar joined the coalition forces against Saddam Hussein's Iraq in the Second Gulf War (1991).

ROMANIA

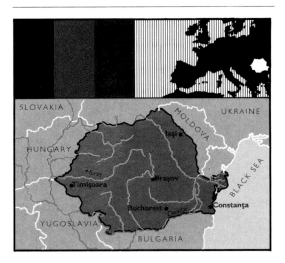

Official name: Rômania.
Member of: UN, CSCE, Council of Europe (guest).
Area: 237 500 km² (91 699 sq mi).
Population: 22 749 000 (1992 census).
Capital and major cities: Bucharest (Bucuresti) 2 325 000, Brasov 352 000, Iasi 334 000, Timisoara 325 000, Cluj-Napoca 319 000, Constanta 313 000, Galati 305 000, Craiova 298 000, Ploiesti 249 000 (1990 est).
Languages: Romanian (official; 89%), Hungarian (10%), German (1%).
Religions: Orthodox (70%), Uniat (Greek Catholic) Church (3%), Roman Catholic (5%), Calvinist (2%).

GOVERNMENT The President, directly elected by universal adult suffrage for a 30-month term, may hold office for a maximum of two terms. A 396-seat National Assembly and 119-seat Senate also serve 30-month terms of office, and are elected on a modified system of proportional representation. The main political parties include the National Salvation Front, the Magyar Democratic Union of Romania, the National Liberal

Party, the Greens, and the National Peasants' Party.

President: Ion Iliescu.

Prime Minister: Theodore Stolojan.

GEOGRAPHY The Carpathian Mountains run through the north, east and centre of Romania. To the west of the Carpathians is the tableland of Transylvania and the Banat lowland. In the south the Danube Plain ends in a delta on the Black Sea. *Principal rivers*: Danube (Dunäria), Mures, Prut. *Highest point*: Moldoveanu 2544 m (8346 ft).

ECONOMY State-owned industry – which employs nearly 40% of the labour force – includes mining, metallurgy, mechanical engineering and chemicals. Natural resources include petroleum and natural gas. Considerable forests support a timber and furniture industry. Major crops include maize, sugar beet, wheat, potatoes and grapes for wine, but agriculture has been neglected, and – because of exports – food supplies have fallen short of the country's needs. Economic mismanagement under Ceausescu decreased already low living standards.

RECENT HISTORY Romania won territory with substantial Romanian populations from the former Russian and Austro-Hungarian Empires at the end of World War I. 'Greater Romania' was beset with deep social and ethnic divisions, which found expression in the rise of the Fascist Iron Guard in the 1930s. King Carol II suppressed the Guard and substituted his own dictatorship, but he was forced by Germany to cede lands back to Hungary (1940), while the USSR retook the present Moldavian Soviet Republic. Carol fled and Romania – under Marshal Ion Antonescu – joined the Axis powers (1941), fighting the USSR to regain lost territories. King Michael dismissed Antonescu and declared war on Germany as the Red Army invaded (1944), and a Soviet-dominated government was installed (1945). The monarchy was abolished in 1947. From 1952, under Gheorghe Gheorghiu-Dej (1901–65) and then under Nicolae Ceausescu (1918–89), Romania distanced itself from Soviet foreign policy while maintaining strict Communist orthodoxy at home. Ceausescu – and his wife Elena – impoverished Romania by their harsh, corrupt and nepotistic rule. When the secret police – the Securitate – put down demonstrations in Timisoara (1989), a national revolt (backed by the army) broke out. A National Salvation Front (NSF) was formed (22 December 1989) and a military tribunal executed Nicolae and Elena Ceausescu on charges of genocide and corruption (25 December 1989). The Communist Party was dissolved and much of Ceausescu's oppressive social and economic legislation was annulled. However, opposition groups expressed doubts concerning the NSF's commitment to democracy and were unable to gain access to the media. In May 1990, Ion Iliescu was elected president, and the National Salvation Front, of which he was leader, was confirmed in power by a huge majority. An international team of monitors judged Romania's first post-war multi-party elections to be 'flawed' but not fraudulent. The NSF has been returned to power in subsequent elections.

RUSSIA

Official name: Rossiyskaya Federativnaya Respublika (Republic of the Russian Federation) or Rossiya (Russia).

Member of: UN, CIS, CSCE.

Area: 17 075 400 km^2 (6 592 800 sq mi).

Population: 148 543 000 (1991 est).

Capital and major cities: Moscow (Moskva) 8 967 000, St Petersburg (Sankt-Peterburg; formerly Leningrad) 5 020 000, Nizhny Novgorod (formerly Gorky) 1 438 000, Novosibirsk 1 436 000, Yekaterinburg (formerly Sverdlovsk) 1 367 000, Samara (formerly Kuybyshev) 1 257 000, Omsk 1 148 000, Chelyabinsk 1 143 000, Kazan 1 094 000, Perm 1 091 000, Ufa 1 083 000, Rostov 1 020 000, Volgograd 999 000, Krasnoyarsk 912 000, Saratov 905 000 (1989 est).

Languages: Russian (83%), Tatar (4%), Ukrainian (3%), Chuvash (1%), plus more than 100 other languages.

Religions: Orthodox (27%), with Sunni Muslim, Jewish, Baptist and other minorities.

GOVERNMENT Constitutional reform is expected in 1993. Under the proposed constitution, Russia will have a parliament of two houses elected for four years by universal adult suffrage – a lower house, comprising 300 representatives of constituencies elected on a system of proportional representation, and a smaller upper house, comprising delegates from each province, region and autonomous republic. An executive President – who will appoint a Council of Ministers – will also be directly elected for five years. Under the terms of a new Russian Federal Treaty (1992), varying degrees of self-government are exercised by the 22 autonomous republics and autonomous regions. (Tatarstan and Chechenya have not signed the treaty). The principal political groupings include (pro-Yeltsin) Democratic Russia, (hardline) Civic Union and the (conservative) People's Party of Free Russia.

President: Boris Yeltsin.

Prime Minister: Viktor Chernomyrdin.

REPUBLICS **Adygei** *Area*: 7600 km^2 (2934 sq mi). *Population*: 436 000 (1990 est). *Capital*: Maikop.

Bashkiria *Area*: 143 600 km^2 (55 430 sq mi). *Population*: 3 964 000 (1990 est). *Capital*: Ufa.

Buryatia *Area*: 351 500 km^2 (135 630 sq mi). *Population*: 1 049 000 (1990 est). *Capital*: Ulan-Ude.

Chechenya *Area*: 10 300 km^2 (5000 sq mi). *Population*: 700 000 (1990 est). *Capital*: Grozny.

Chuvashia *Area*: 18 300 km^2 (7064 sq mi). *Population*: 1 340 000 (1990 est). *Capital*: Cheboksary.

Dagestan *Area*: 50 300 km^2 (19 416 sq mi). *Population*: 1 823 000 (1990 est). *Capital*: Makhachkala.

Gorno-Altai *Area*: 92 600 km^2 (35 740 sq mi). *Population*: 194 000 (1990 est). *Capital*: Gorno-Altaisk.

Ingushetia *Area*: 9000 km² (3500 sq mi). *Population*: 500 000 (1990 est). *Capital*: Nazran.

Jewish Republic (Yevreysk Respublik) *Area*: 36 000 km² (13 895 sq mi). *Population*: 218 000 (1990 est). *Capital*: Birobijan (Birobidzhan).

Karbardino-Balkaria *Area*: 12 500 km² (4825 sq mi). *Population*: 768 000 (1990 est). *Capital*: Nalchik.

Kalmykia *Area*: 75 900 km² (29 300 sq mi). *Population*: 325 000 (1990 est). *Capital*: Elista.

Karachevo-Cherkess *Area*: 14 100 km² (5442 sq mi). *Population*: 422 000 (1990 est). *Capital*: Cherkessk.

Karelia *Area*: 172 400 km² (83 730 sq mi). *Population*: 796 000 (1990 est). *Capital*: Petrozavodsk.

Khakassia *Area*: 61 900 km² (23 900 sq mi). *Population*: 550 000 (1990 est). *Capital*: Abakan.

Komi Republic *Area*: 415 900 km² (160 540 sq mi). *Population*: 1 265 000 (1990 est). *Capital*: Syktyvkar.

Mari Republic *Area*: 23 200 km² (8955 sq mi). *Population*: 754 000 (1990 est). *Capital*: Yoshkar-Ola.

Mordovia *Area*: 26 200 km² (10 110 sq mi). *Population*: 964 000 (1990 est). *Capital*: Saransk.

North Ossetia *Area*: 8000 km² (3088 sq mi). *Population*: 638 000 (1990 est). *Capital*: Vladikavkaz.

Tatarstan *Area*: 68 000 km² (26 650 sq mi). *Population*: 3 658 000 (1990 est). *Capital*: Kazan.

Tuva *Area*: 170 500 km² (65 810 sq mi). *Population*: 314 000 (1990 est). *Capital*: Kyzyl.

Udmurtia *Area*: 42 100 km² (16 250 sq mi). *Population*: 1 619 000 (1990 est). *Capital*: Izhevsk.

Yakutia *Area*: 3 103 200 km² (1 197 760 sq mi). *Population*: 1 099 000 (1990 est). *Capital*: Yakutsk.

GEOGRAPHY Russia is the largest country in the world and covers over 10% of the total land area of the globe. Most of the land between the Baltic and the Ural Mountains is covered by the North European Plain, S of which the relatively low-lying Central Russian Uplands stretch from the Ukrainian border to N of Moscow. To the E of the Urals is the vast West Siberian Lowland, the greater part of which is occupied by the basin of the River Ob and its tributaries. The Central Siberian Plateau – between the Rivers Yenisey and Lena – rises to around 1700 m (5500 ft). Beyond the Lena are the mountains of E Siberia, including the Chersky Mountains and the Kamchatka Peninsula. Much of the S of Siberia is mountainous. The Yablonovy and Stanovoy Mountains rise inland from the Amur Basin, which drains to the Pacific coast. The Altai Mountains lie S of Lake Baikal and along the border with Mongolia. Between the Black and Caspian Seas are the high Caucasus Mountains on the Georgian border. The Kaliningrad enclave between Poland and Lithuania on the Baltic is a detached part of Russia. *Principal rivers:* Yenisey, Lena, Ob, Amur, Volga, Angara, Irtysh, Dvina, Pechora, Kama. *Highest point:* Elbrus (on the Georgian border) 5642 m (18 510 ft).

ECONOMY Russia is one of the largest producers of coal, iron ore, steel, petroleum and cement. However, its economy is in crisis. The economic reforms (1985–91) of Mikhail Gorbachov introduced decentralization to a centrally-planned economy. Since 1991, reform has been accelerated through the introduction of free market prices and the encouragement of private enterprise. However, lack of motivation in the labour force affects all sectors of the economy and poor distribution has resulted in shortages of many basic goods. Inflation is rampant, reaching 2200% in 1992. Manufacturing in-

volves one third of the labour force and includes the steel, chemical, textile and heavy machinery industries. The production of consumer goods is not highly developed. Agriculture is large-scale and organized either into state-owned farms or collective farms, although the right to own and farm land privately has been introduced. Despite mechanization and the world's largest fertilizer industry, Russia cannot produce enough grain for its needs, in part because of poor harvests, and poor storage and transport facilities. Imports from Ukraine and Kazakhstan have assumed added importance. Major Russian crops include wheat, barley, oats, potatoes, sugar beet and fruit.Natural resources include the world's largest reserves of coal, nearly one third of the world's natural gas reserves, one third of the world's forests, major deposits of manganese, gold, potash, bauxite, nickel, lead, zinc and copper, as well as plentiful sites for hydroelectric power installations. Machinery, petroleum and petroleum products are Russia's major exports and the republic is self sufficient in energy. Russia has a large trade surplus with the other former Soviet republics.

RECENT HISTORY Following the revolution of February 1917 – largely brought about by the catastrophic conduct of World War I – Tsar Nicholas II abdicated and a provisional government was established. On 7 November 1917 the Bolsheviks (Communists) – led by Vladymir Ilich Lenin (1870–1924) – overthrew the provisional government in a bloodless coup. Russia withdrew from the war, ceded Poland to Germany and Austria, and recognized the independence of Estonia, Finland, Georgia, Latvia, Lithuania and the Ukraine. Other parts of the former empire soon declared independence, including Armenia, Azerbaijan and Central Asia. A civil war between the Bolsheviks and the White Russians (led by former Tsarists) lasted until 1922. The Communists gradually reconquered most of the former Russian empire and in December 1922 formed the Union of Soviet Socialist Republics. The economy was reorganized under central control, but shortages and famine were soon experienced. After Lenin's death (1924), a power struggle took place between the supporters of Joseph Stalin (1879–1953) and Leon Trotsky (1879–1940). Stalin expelled Trotsky's supporters from the Communist Party and exiled him. The rapid industrialization of the country began. In 1929–30 Stalin liquidated the kulaks (richer peasants). Severe repression continued until his death – opponents were subjected to 'show trials' and summary execution, and millions died as a result of starvation or political execution.

In World War II – in which up to 20 million Soviet citizens may have died – the USSR at first concluded a pact with Hitler (1939), and invaded Poland, Finland, Romania and the Baltic states, annexing considerable territory. However, in 1941 the Germans invaded the USSR, precipitating the Soviet Union's entry into the war on the Allied side. In victory the Soviet Union was confirmed as a world power, controlling a cordon of satellite states in Eastern Europe and challenging the West in the Cold War. However, the economy stagnated and the country was drained by the burdens of an impoverished and overstretched empire. Leonid Brezhnev (leader 1964–82) reversed the brief thaw that had been experienced under Nikita Khruschev (leader 1956–64), and far-reaching reform had to await the policies of Mikhail Gorbachov (1931–) after 1985. Faced with severe economic reforms, Gorbachov attempted to introduce reconstruction (*perestroika*) and greater openness (*glasnost*) by implementing social, economic and industrial reforms. The state of the economy also influenced the desire to reduce military spending by reaching agreements on arms reduction with the West. Dissent was tolerated, a major reform of the constitution led to more open elections, and the Communist Party gave up its leading role. Many hardliners in the Communist Party were defeated by reformers (many of them non-Communists) in elections in 1989. The abandonment of the Brezhnev Doctrine – the right of the USSR to intervene in the affairs of Warsaw Pact countries (as it had done militarily in Hungary in 1956 and Czechoslovakia in 1968) – prompted rapid change in Eastern Europe, where one after another the satellite states renounced Communism and began to implement multiparty rule. From 1989 there were increased nationalistic stirrings within the USSR, particularly in the Baltic republics and the Caucasus.

In August 1991, an attempt by a group of Communist hardliners to depose Gorbachov was defeated by the resistance of Russian President Boris Yeltsin (1931–) and by the refusal of the army to take action against unarmed civilian protestors. The opposition of Yeltsin and the Russian parliament to the coup greatly enhanced the status and powers of Russia and the 14 other Union Republics. Fourteen of the 15 republics declared independence and the secession of the three Baltic republics was recognized internationally. The remaining republics began to renegotiate their relationship. Gorbachov suspended the Communist Party and – with Yeltsin – initiated far-reaching political and economic reforms. However, it was too late to save the Soviet Union, whose fate was sealed by the refusal of Ukraine, the second most important of the republics, to participate in the new looser Union proposed by Gorbachov. By the end of 1991 the initiative had passed from Gorbachov to Yeltsin, who was instrumental in establishing the Commonwealth of Independent States (CIS), a military and economic grouping of sovereign states that included the majority of the former Union republics. After Gorbachov resigned and the Soviet Union was dissolved (December 1991), Russia took over the international responsibilities of the USSR, including its seat on the UN Security Council. Externally, Russia faces disputes concerning the future of CIS forces and potential territorial claims on other former Soviet republics. Internally, Russia faces a severe economic crisis as the command economy is replaced by a market economy. These changes have been impeded by the activities of former Communist hardliners in the Congress of People's Deputies, who have also held up constitutional reform.

RWANDA

Official name: La République Rwandaise (French) or Republika y'u Rwanda (Kinyarwanda) (Republic of Rwanda).

Member of: UN, OAU.

Area: 26 338 km² (10 169 sq mi).

Population: 7 491 000 (1991 est).

Capital and main cities: Kigali 300 000, Butare 35 000 (1990 est).

Languages: French and Kinyarwanda (both official).

Religions: Roman Catholic (63%), animist (21%), Sunni Islam (8%), various Protestant Churches (8%).

GOVERNMENT The President (who appoints a Council of Ministers) and the 70-member National Development Council are elected for five years by compulsory universal adult suffrage. The Mouvement Révolutionnaire National pour le Développement (the former monopoly political party) is the main political movement.

President: Maj. Gen. Juvenal Habyarimana.

GEOGRAPHY Rwanda is a mountainous country. Most of the western boundary is formed by Lake Kivu. *Principal river:* Luvironza. *Highest point:* Mont Karisimbi 4507 m (14 787 ft).

ECONOMY Rwanda's economy is dominated by subsistence farming. Coffee and tin are the main exports. There are major (largely unexploited) reserves of natural gas under Lake Kivu.

RECENT HISTORY Rwanda, a former German possession, was taken over by Belgium after World War I. The monarchy – of the dominant minority Tutsi people – was overthrown by the majority Hutu population shortly before independence in 1962. Tribal violence followed an unsuccessful Tutsi attempt to regain power in 1963, and strife between the Hutu and Tutsi has continued intermittently. In 1990–91 an army of Tutsi refugees invaded Rwanda, occupying much of the north.

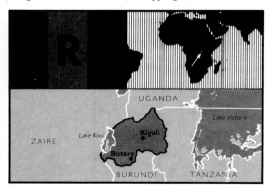

In 1991, in an attempt to solve the problem, Rwanda's neighbours agreed to grant citizenship to Tutsi refugees. The government has conceded the principle of multi-party elections.

SAINT CHRISTOPHER AND NEVIS

Official name: The Federation of Saint Christopher and Nevis. St Christopher is popularly known as St Kitts.

Member of: UN, Commonwealth, CARICOM, OAS.

Area: 262 km² (101 sq mi).

Population: 43 000 (1991 est).

Capital: Basseterre 18 500, Charlestown 1700 (1986 est).

Language: English (official).

Religion: Anglican (36%), Methodist (32%), Roman Catholic (11%).

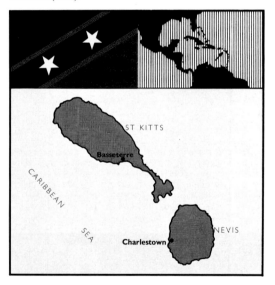

GOVERNMENT The National Assembly consists of 11 members elected by universal adult suffrage for five years and 3 or 4 appointed members. The Governor General – the representative of the British Queen as sovereign of St Kitts – appoints a Prime Minister who commands a majority in the Assembly. The PM appoints a Cabinet responsible to the Assembly. The main political parties are the People's Action Movement, the Labour Party, the Nevis Reformation Party and the Concerned Citizens Movement. Nevis has its own legislature.

Prime Minister: Kennedy Simmonds.

AUTONOMOUS ISLAND **Nevis** *Area*: 93 km² (36 sq mi). *Population*: 9600 (1986 est). *Capital*: Charlestown.

GEOGRAPHY St Kitts and Nevis are two well-watered mountainous islands, set 3 km (2 mi) apart. There are no significant rivers. *Highest point*: Nevis Peak 985 m (3232 ft).

ECONOMY The economy is based on agriculture (mainly sugar cane) and tourism.

RECENT HISTORY St Kitts was united with Nevis and the more distant small island of Anguilla in a single British colony, which gained internal self-government in 1967. When Anguilla – a reluctant partner – proclaimed independence in 1967, the British intervened, eventually restoring Anguilla to colonial rule while St Kitts-Nevis progressed to independence in 1983.

SAINT LUCIA

Member of: UN, Commonwealth, CARICOM, OAS.
Area: 616 km² (238 sq mi).
Population: 151 000 (1990 census).
Capital and main towns: Castries 57 000, Vieux Fort 23 000 (1990 census).
Languages: English (official), French patois (over 50%).
Religion: Roman Catholic (over 80%).

GOVERNMENT The 11-member Senate is appointed. The 17-member House of Assembly is elected by universal adult suffrage for five years. The Governor General – as representative of the British Queen as sovereign of St Lucia – appoints a Prime Minister who commands a majority in the House. The PM, in turn, appoints a Cabinet which is responsible to the House. The main political parties are the United Workers' Party, the Labour Party, and the Progressive Labour Party.
Prime Minister: John Compton.

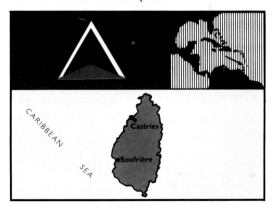

GEOGRAPHY St Lucia is a forested mountainous island. There are no significant rivers. *Highest point:* Mount Gimie 959 m (3145 ft).

ECONOMY The economy depends on agriculture, with bananas and coconuts as the main crops. Tourism is increasingly important.

RECENT HISTORY The British colony of St Lucia achieved internal self-government in 1967 and independence in 1979.

SAINT VINCENT AND THE GRENADINES

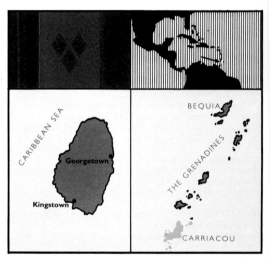

Member of: UN, OAS, CARICOM, Commonwealth.
Area: 389 km² (150 sq mi).
Population: 108 000 (1991 census).
Capital: Kingstown 34 000 (city 19 000; 1989 est).
Language: English (official).
Religions: Anglican (42%), Methodist (21%), Roman Catholic (12%).

GOVERNMENT The single-chamber House of Assembly consists of 6 nominated senators and 15 representatives elected for five years by universal adult suffrage. The Governor General – who is the representative of the British Queen as sovereign of St Vincent – appoints a Prime Minister who commands a majority of the representatives. The PM in turn appoints a Cabinet responsible to the House. The main political parties are the New Democratic Party, and the Labour Party.
Prime Minister: David Jack.

GEOGRAPHY St Vincent is a mountainous wooded

island. The Grenadines – which include Bequia and Mustique – are a chain of small islands to the south of St Vincent. There are no significant rivers. *Highest point: Mount Soufrière, an active volcano, 1234 m (4048 ft).*

ECONOMY Bananas and arrowroot are the main crops of a largely agricultural economy.

RECENT HISTORY The British colony of St Vincent gained internal self-government in 1969 and independence in 1979.

SAN MARINO

Official name: Serenissima Repubblica di San Marino (Most Serene Republic of San Marino).
Member of: UN, CSCE, Council of Europe.
Area: 61 km² (23 sq mi).
Population: 23 700 (1991 est).
Capital and main towns: San Marino 9000 (city 4200), Seravalle 7300, Borgo Maggiore (part of the San Marino city built-up area) 4200 (1991 est).
Language: Italian.
Religion: Roman Catholic (official; 95%).

GOVERNMENT The 60-member Great and General Council is elected by universal adult suffrage for five years. The Council elects two of its members to be Captains-Regent, who jointly hold office as heads of state and of government for six months. The Captains-Regent preside over a 10-member Congress of State – the equivalent of a Cabinet – which is elected by the Council for five years. The main political parties are the (conservative) Christian Democratic Party, the Socialist Party, and the Communist Party.

GEOGRAPHY The country is dominated by the triple limestone peaks of Monte Titano, the highest point at 739 m (2424 ft). There are no significant rivers.

ECONOMY Manufacturing and tourism – in particular visitors on excursions – are the mainstays of the economy.

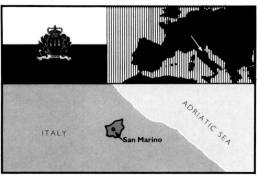

RECENT HISTORY San Marino's independence was recognized by the new Kingdom of Italy (1862). In 1957 a bloodless 'revolution' replaced the Communist-Socialist administration that had been in power since 1945.

SÃO TOMÉ E PRÍNCIPE

Official name: A República Democrática de São Tomé e Príncipe (The Democratic Republic of São Tomé and Príncipe).
Area: 964 km² (372 sq mi).
Member of: UN, OAU.
Population: 123 000 (1991 est).
Capital: São Tomé 35 000 (1989 est).
Language: Portuguese (official); Fang (90%).
Religion: Roman Catholic (50%).

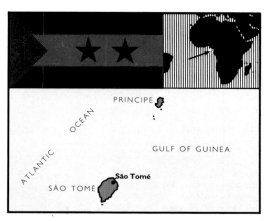

GOVERNMENT The 55-member National People's Assembly is elected by universal adult suffrage for five years. Political parties include the (left-wing former monopoly) MLSTP and the (moderate) PCD (Democratic Convergence Party). The President – who appoints a Prime Minister and Council of Ministers – is also directly elected.
President: Miguel Trovoada.
Prime Minister: Norberto Jose Costa Alegre.

GEOGRAPHY The republic consists of two mountainous islands about 144 km (90 mi) apart. There are no significant rivers. *Highest point:* Pico Gago Coutinho (Pico de São Tomé) 2024 m (6640 ft).

ECONOMY Cocoa is the mainstay of a largely agricultural economy. Most of the land is nationalized.

HISTORY Early in the 20th century, the islands' plantations were notorious for forced labour. Independence from Portugal was gained in 1975 as a one-party socialist state. Economic difficulties have since led the country to lessen its dependence on the USSR, and in 1990 the MLSTP abandoned Marxism. The opposition PCD won multi-party elections in January 1991.

SAUDI ARABIA

Official name: Al-Mamlaka al-'Arabiya as-Sa'udiya (The Kingdom of Saudi Arabia).

Member of: UN, Arab League, OPEC, GCC.

Area: 2 240 000 km² (864 869 sq mi).

Population: 14 691 000 (1991 est).

Capital and major cities: Riyadh (Ar Riyad) – the royal capital – 2 000 000, Jeddah (Jiddah) – the administrative capital – 1 400 000, Mecca (Makkah) 620 000, Medina (Al-Madinah) 500 000, Ta'if 205 000, Buraidah 185 000, Abha 155 000 (all including suburbs; 1986 est).

Language: Arabic (official).

Religion: Islam (official) – Sunni (92%; mainly Wahhabi), Shia 8%.

GOVERNMENT Saudi Arabia is an absolute monarchy with neither formal political institutions nor parties. The King appoints a Council of Ministers. In 1991 it was announced that an 80-member consultative body would be appointed.

King: HM King Fahd ibn Abdul Aziz Al Saud (succeeded upon the death of his brother, 13 May 1982).

GEOGRAPHY Over 95% of the country is desert, including the Rub 'al-Khali ('The Empty Quarter') – the largest expanse of sand in the world. The Arabian plateau ends in the west in a steep escarpment overlooking a coastal plain beside the Red Sea. There are no permanent streams. *Highest point:* Jebel Razikh 3658 m (12 002 ft).

ECONOMY Saudi Arabia's spectacular development and present prosperity are based almost entirely upon exploiting vast reserves of petroleum and natural gas. Industries include petroleum refining, petrochemicals and fertilizers. The country has developed major banking and commercial interests. Less than 1% of the land can be cultivated.

RECENT HISTORY In the 20th century the Wahhabis – a Sunni Islamic sect – united most of Arabia under Ibn Saud (1882–1953). In 1902 Ibn Saud took Riyadh and in 1906 defeated his rivals to control central Arabia (Nejd). Between 1912 and 1927 he added the east, the southwest (Asir) and Hejaz (the area around Mecca). In 1932 these lands became the kingdom of Saudi Arabia. Although the country has been pro-Western, after the 1973 Arab-Israeli War, Saudi Arabia put pressure on the USA to encourage Israel to withdraw from the occupied territories by cutting oil production. Saudi Arabia has not escaped problems caused by religious fundamentalism and the rivalry between Sunni and Shia Islam. In 1980 Saudi Arabia found itself bound to support Iraq in its war with Shiite Iran. Influenced by the Iranian revolution and the First Gulf War, Saudi Arabia formed the defensive Gulf Cooperation Council (GCC) with its neighbouring emirates. Saudi Arabia was threatened by Iraq following the invasion of Kuwait (1990), and played a major role in the coalition against Saddam Hussein in the Second Gulf War (1991).

SENEGAL

Official name: La République du Sénégal (The Republic of Senegal).

Member of: UN, OAU, ECOWAS.

Area: 196 722 km² (75 954 sq mi).

Population: 7 517 000 (1991 est).

Capital: Dakar 1 490 000, Thiès 185 000, St Louis 161 000, Kaolack 152 000, Ziguinchar 124 000, (1988 census).

Languages: French (official), Wolof (36%), Serer (19%), Fulani (13%).

Religions: Sunni Islam (94%), Roman Catholic.

GOVERNMENT Every five years the President and the 120-member National Assembly are elected by universal adult suffrage. One half of the deputies are elected by a system of proportional representation on a national basis; the remainder represent single-member constituencies. The President appoints and leads a Cabinet. Since 1983 there has been no Prime Minister.

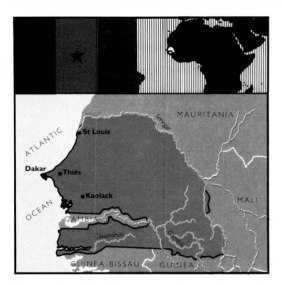

The number of political parties is constitutionally limited to three – the PS (Parti Socialiste), the (liberal) PDS, and the (Marxist) PAI.

President: Abdou Diouf.
Prime Minister: Habib Thiam.

GEOGRAPHY Senegal is mostly low-lying and covered by savannah. The Fouta Djalon mountains are in the south. *Principal rivers*: Sénégal, Gambia, Casamance. *Highest point*: Mont Gounou 1515 m (4970 ft).

ECONOMY Over three quarters of the labour force is involved in agriculture, growing groundnuts and cotton as cash crops, and rice, maize, millet and sorghum as subsistence crops. The manufacturing sector is one of the largest in West Africa, but unemployment is high.

RECENT HISTORY A national political awareness developed early in the 20th century, and contributed substantially to the nationalist awakening throughout French Africa. After independence in 1960, under the poet Léopold Sedar Senghor (1906–), Senegal maintained close relations with France, and received substantial aid. Attempted federations with Mali (1959–60) and Gambia (1981–89) were unsuccessful. Senghor retired in 1980, having re-introduced party politics.

SEYCHELLES

Official name: The Republic of Seychelles.
Member of: UN, OAU, Commonwealth.
Area: 454 km² (173 sq mi).
Population: 68 000 (1991 est).
Capital: Victoria 24 000 (1987 est).
Languages: Creole (95%), English and French – all official.
Religion: Roman Catholic (92%), Anglican (6%).

GOVERNMENT The President – who appoints a Council of Ministers – is elected for five years by universal adult suffrage. The National Assembly comprises 23 directly elected members and 2 members appointed by the President. The Seychelles People's Progressive Front is the major political party.
President: France Albert René.

GEOGRAPHY The Seychelles consist of 40 mountainous granitic islands and just over 50 smaller coral islands. There are no significant rivers. *Highest point:* Morne Seychellois 906 m (2972 ft) on the island of Mahé.

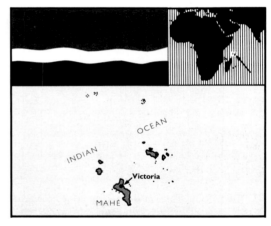

ECONOMY The economy depends heavily on tourism, which employs about one third of the labour force.

RECENT HISTORY The islands gained independence from Britain in 1976. The Prime Minister – France Albert René – led a coup against President James Mancham in 1977, and established a one-party socialist state seeking nonalignment. Attempts to overthrow René, including one involving South African mercenaries (1981), were unsuccessful. Multi-party elections were held in 1992.

SIERRA LEONE

Official name: The Republic of Sierra Leone.
Member of: UN, OAU, ECOWAS, Commonwealth.
Area: 71 740 km² (27 699 sq mi).
Population: 4 260 000 (1991 est).
Capital and main cities: Freetown 550 000 (city

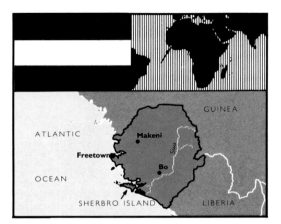

470 000), Koidu (part of the Freetown agglomeration) 80 000, Bo 26 000 (1985 census).

Languages: English (official), Krio (Creole), Mende (34%), Temne (31%).

Religions: Animist (52%), Sunni Islam (39%), Anglican (6%).

GOVERNMENT There is constitutional provision for a President – who appoints a Cabinet – to be elected for seven years by universal adult suffrage, and for a 124-member House of Representatives to be elected for five years. Power is currently exercised by a military council, but a return to multi-party rule has been agreed.

Head of State: (Chairman of the National Provisional Ruling Council) Capt. Valentine Strasser.

GEOGRAPHY The savannah interior comprises plateaux and mountain ranges. The swampy coastal plain is forested. *Principal rivers*: Siwa, Jong, Rokel. *Highest point*: Bintimani Peak 1948 m (6390 ft).

ECONOMY Subsistence farming – mainly rice – involves the majority of the labour force. Rutile, bauxite and cocoa are major exports. The decline of diamond mining has added to economic problems.

RECENT HISTORY The interior was added to the British colony of Freetown – formerly a settlement for former slaves – in 1896. Independence was gained in 1961. A disputed election led to army intervention (1967), and Dr Siaka Stevens – who came to power in a coup in 1968 – introduced a one-party state. An army junta seized power in 1992.

SINGAPORE

Official name: Hsing-chia p'o Kung-ho Kuo (Chinese) or Republik Singapura (Malay) or Republic of Singapore.

Member of: UN, ASEAN, Commonwealth.
Area: 623 km² (240 sq mi).
Population: 2 705 000 (1990 census).
Capital: Singapore 2 705 000 (1990 census).
Languages: Chinese (77%), Malay (14%), Tamil (5%), English – all official.
Religions: Buddhist and Daoist (54%), Sunni Islam (15%), various Christian Churches (13%), Hindu (4%).

GOVERNMENT The 81 members of Parliament are elected from single- and multi-member constituencies by universal adult suffrage for five years. There is constitutional provision for a small number of 'non-constituency' seats for non-elected members of the opposition. The President – who is elected by Parliament for four years – appoints a Prime Minister who commands a parliamentary majority. The PM, in turn, appoints a Cabinet which is responsible to Parliament. The constitution is to be revised to create an executive presidency in 1993. The main political party is the People's Action Party; other parties include the Singapore Democratic Party and the Workers' Party.

President: Wee Kim Wee.
Prime Minister: Goh Chok Tong.

GEOGRAPHY Singapore is a low-lying island – with 56 islets – joined to the Malay peninsula by causeway. *Principal river:* Sungei Seletar. *Highest point:* Bukit Timah 177 m (581 ft).

ECONOMY Singapore relies on imports for its flourishing manufacturing industries and entrepôt trade. Finance and tourism are important. Singapore has the second highest standard of living in Asia, after Japan.

RECENT HISTORY Singapore was part of the British Straits Settlements. Occupied by the Japanese (1942–45), it achieved self-government (1959), and joined (1963) and left (1965) the Federation of Malaysia. Since independence it has become wealthy under the strong rule of Prime Minister Lee Kuan Yew (1923– ; PM 1965–91).

SLOVAKIA

Official name: Republika Slovenská (Slovak Republic).
Member of: UN, CSCE.
Area: 49 025 km² (18 929 sq mi).
Population: 5 269 000 (1991 census).
Capital and major cities: Bratislava 442 000, Kosice 235 000, Nitra 212 000, Zilina 183 000 (all including suburbs; 1991 census).
Languages: Slovak (87%), Hungarian (12%).
Religions: Roman Catholic (60%), Evangelical Churches (6%).

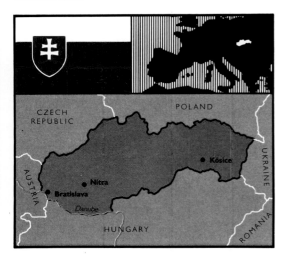

GOVERNMENT The 150-member Assembly is elected by universal adult suffrage for five years. The Assembly elects a President who appoints a Prime Minister and a Council of Ministers, responisble to the Assembly. The main political parties are the (socialist) Movement for a Democratic Slovakia, the (centre) Christian Democratic Movement, the (former Communist) Party of the Democratic Left and the Slovak National Party.
President: Michal Kovac.
Prime Minister: Vladimir Meciar.

GEOGRAPHY Slovakia mainly comprises mountain ranges including the Tatra Mountains on the Polish border. The only significant lowlands are in the South adjoining the River Danube. *Principal rivers:* Danube, Vah, Hron. *Highest Point:* Gerlachovka 2655 m (8737 ft).

ECONOMY Slovakia has a mainly agricultural economy into which heavy industry – particularly steel and chemicals – was introduced when the country was part of Communist Czechoslovakia. Wheat, maize, potatoes, barley and sheep are important. Varied natural resources include iron ore and brown coal. Slovakia has slowed the privatization of its uncompetitive out-ofdate factories.

RECENT HISTORY On the collapse of the Habsburg Empire (1918), the Slovaks joined the Czechs to form Czechoslovakia. When Hitler's Germany dismembered Czechoslovakia in 1938, Slovakia became an Axis puppet state. A popular revolt against German rule (the Slovak Uprising) took place in 1944. Following liberation (1945) Czechoslovakia was re-established. After the Communist takeover in 1948, heavy industry was introduced into rural Slovakia. In 1968, moves by Party Secretary Alexander Dubček (a Slovak) to introduce political reforms met with Soviet disapproval, and invasion by Czechoslovakia's Warsaw Pact allies. The conservative wing of the Communist party regained control until 1989, when student demonstrations developed into a peaceful revolution. The Communist Party renounced its leading role. A new government, in which Communists were in a minority, was appointed. In 1990 free multi-party elections were held, Soviet troops were withdrawn and the foundations of a market economy were laid, but the pace of economic reform brought distress to Slovakia, whose old-fashioned industries were ill-equipped to face competition. Increased Slovak separatism led to the division of the country in 1993. Independent Slovakia faces possible tension concerning the large Hungarian minority.

SLOVENIA

Official name: Republika Slovenija (The Republic of Slovenia).
Area: 20 251 km² (7819 sq mi).
Population: 1 963 000 (1991 census).
Capital and major cities: Ljubljana 338 000 (city 286 000), Maribor 186 000 (city 105 000) (1991 census).
Languages: Slovene (91%), Serbo-Croat (5%).
Religions: Roman Catholic (over 90%).

GOVERNMENT The 240-member Assembly and a President – who appoints a Prime Minister and Cabinet – are directly elected by universal adult suffrage for four years. A new constitution is under consideration. The main political parties include the (coalition) Democratic United Opposition (DEMOS) and the (former Communist) Party of Democratic Renewal.
President: Milan Kucan.
Prime Minister: Janez Drnovesk.

GEOGRAPHY Most of Slovenia comprises mountains including the Karawanken Alps and Julian Alps. In the E, hill country adjoins the Drava valley; in the W, Slovenia has a very short Adriatic coastline. *Principal rivers:* Drava, Sava, Mura. *Highest point:* Triglav 2864 m (9396 ft).

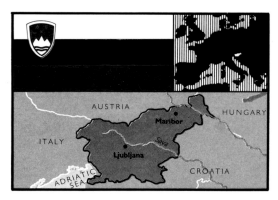

ECONOMY With a standard of living approaching that of West European countries, Slovenia was the most industrialized and economically developed part of Yugoslavia. Industries include iron and steel, textiles and coal mining. Agriculture specializes in livestock and fodder crops.

RECENT HISTORY When the Habsburg Empire collapsed (1918), the Slovenes joined the Serbs, Croats and Montenegrins in the new state that was renamed Yugoslavia in 1929. When Yugoslavia became a Communist federal state in 1945, the Slovene lands were reorganized as the republic of Slovenia. After the death of Yugoslav President Tito (1980), the federation faltered in nationalist crises. Slovenia, the wealthiest part of Yugoslavia, edged towards democracy. In free elections in 1990, nationalists gained a majority in the Slovene Assembly, which declared independence in 1991. Following reverses in a short campaign, Yugoslav federal forces were withdrawn from Slovenia, whose independence was recognized internationally in 1992.

SOLOMON ISLANDS

Member of: UN, Commonwealth, South Pacific Forum.
Area: 27 556 km² (10 639 sq mi).
Population: 328 000 (1991 est).
Capital and main cities: Honiara 35 300, Gizo 4000 (1990 est).
Languages: English (official), Pidgin English, over 85 local (mainly Melanesian) languages (85%).
Religions: Anglican (34%), Roman Catholic (19%), other Christian Churches.

GOVERNMENT The 38-member National Parliament – which is elected by universal adult suffrage for four years – elects a Prime Minister who appoints a Cabinet. A Governor General is the representative of the British Queen as sovereign of the islands. The main political parties are the Solomon Islands United Party and the People's Alliance Party. It is expected that a

federal republican system will be introduced during the 1990s.
Prime Minister: Solomon Mamaloni.

GEOGRAPHY The mountainous volcanic Solomons comprise six main islands and several hundred small islands. There are no significant rivers. *Highest point*: Mount Makarakomburu 2447 m (8028 ft).

ECONOMY One third of the labour force is involved in subsistence farming, although copra, cocoa and coconuts are exported. Lumbering is the main industry.

RECENT HISTORY Britain established a protectorate in 1893. Occupied by the Japanese (1942–45), the Solomons were the scene of fierce fighting, including a major battle for Guadalcanal. Independence was gained in 1978.

SOMALIA

Official name: Jamhuuriyadda Dimuqraadiga Soomaaliya (Somali Democratic Republic).
Member of: UN, Arab League, OAU.
Area: 637 657 km² (246 201 sq mi).
Population: 7 691 000 (1991 est).
Capital: Mogadishu 1 000 000, Hargeisa 400 000, Baidoa 300 000, Burao 300 000 (1986 est).
Languages: Somali (national), Arabic (official).
Religion: Sunni Islam (official).

GOVERNMENT The constitution provides for an Assembly comprising 171 members – 165 elected by universal adult suffrage for five years and 6 appointed by the President, who is elected by direct universal suffrage for a seven-year term. Since 1991 there has been no effective government.

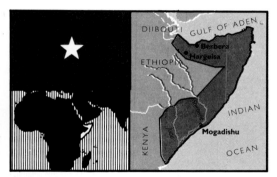

GEOGRAPHY Somalia occupies the 'Horn of Africa'. Low-lying plains cover most of the south, while semi-arid mountains rise in the north. *Principal rivers:* Juba, Shebelle. *Highest point:* Surud Ad 2408 m (7900 ft).

ECONOMY Nearly two thirds of the labour force are nomadic herdsmen or subsistence farmers. Bananas are grown for export in the south, but much of the country suffers from drought. As a result of civil war since 1991, much of the economic infrastructure of the country has been destroyed and famine is widespread.

RECENT HISTORY In 1886 Britain established a protectorate in the north, while the Italians took the south. In World War II the Italians briefly occupied British Somaliland. In 1960 the British and Italian territories united as independent Somalia. In 1969 the president was assassinated and the army, under Muhammad Siad Barre, seized control. Barre's socialist Islamic Somalia became allied to the USSR. In 1977 Somali guerrillas, with Somali military support, drove Ethiopia from the largely Somali-inhabited Ogaden. Somalia's Soviet alliance was ended when the USSR supported Ethiopia to regain the Ogaden. In 1991 rebels overran the capital and deposed Barre, but rival groups seized districts in the north and south. The infrastructure of Somalia collapsed in bitter civil war. In 1992, a US-led UN force intervened to relieve famine victims.

SOUTH AFRICA

Official name: Republic of South Africa or Republiek van Suid-Afrika.

Member of: UN.

Area: 2 347 661 km² (906 437 sq mi) including Walvis Bay – 1124 km² (434 sq mi) – and the 'independent' homelands – 1 125 500 km² (434 558 sq mi).

Population: 33 140 000 (1991 est) including Walvis Bay – 21 000 (1981) – and the 'independent' homelands – 5 954 000 (1985 est).

Capital and major cities: Pretoria (administrative capital) 823 000 (city 443 000), Cape Town (Kaapstadt) (legislative capital) 1 912 000 (city 777 000), Bloem-

fontein (judicial capital) 233 000 (city 104 000), Johannesburg 4 000 000 (city proper 632 000; Greater Johannesburg 1 762 000), Durban 982 000 (city 634 000), Soweto (part of the Johannesburg agglomeration) 915 000, Port Elizabeth 652 000 (city 273 000), Sasolburg 540 000 and Vereeniging 540 000 are part of the Johannesburg agglomeration, East London 194 000 (city 85 000) (all including suburbs; 1985 census).

Languages: Afrikaans and English (both official), Xhosa (21%), Zulu (16%), Sesotho.

Religions: Dutch Reformed Church, independent African Churches, with Anglican, Methodist, Roman Catholic, Hindu and Sunni Islam minorities.

GOVERNMENT A new power-sharing transitional government, including a collective presidency, and a multi-racial constituent assembly are under discussion. Currently, Parliament consists of three chambers elected for five years – the House of Assembly elected by adult white suffrage, the House of Representatives elected by coloured (mixed race) voters, and the House of Delegates elected by Indian voters. The State President – who appoints a Cabinet – is chosen by an electoral college in which members of the (white) House of Assembly form a majority. Blacks have no parliamentary vote, but elect the Legislative Assemblies of the ten homelands. Four homelands – Bophuthatswana, Ciskei, Transkei and Venda – have been granted 'independence' by South Africa, but this status is unrecognized internationally. The main political parties are the (mainly Xhosa) African National Congress, the (mainly Zulu) Inkatha movement, white and mixed-race (the mainly white conservative) National Party, the (white and mixed race centre) Democratic Party, and the (white right-wing) Conservative Party.

President: Frederik Willem De Klerk.

PROVINCES AND HOMELANDS Cape (Kaap) (includes Walvis Bay) *Area:* 641 379 km² (247 638 sq mi). *Population:* 5 041 000 (1985 census). *Capital:* Cape Town (Kaapstadt).

Natal *Area:* 55 281 km² (21 344 sq mi). *Population:* 2 145 000 (1985 census). *Capital:* Pietermaritzburg.

Orange Free State (Oranje Vrystaat) *Area:* 127 338 km² (49 166 sq mi). *Population:* 1 777 000 (1985 census). *Capital:* Bloemfontein.

Transvaal *Area:* 227 034 km² (87 658 sq mi). *Population:* 7 532 000 (1985 census). *Capital:* Pretoria.

Bophuthatswana* *Area:* 43 999 km² (16 988 sq mi). *Population:* 3 200 000 (1989 est). *Capital:* Mmabatho.

Ciskei* *Area:* 8495 km² (3280 sq mi). *Population:* 2 000 000 (1987 est). *Capital:* Bisho.

Gazankulu *Area:* 6565 km² (2535 sq mi). *Population:* 497 000 (1985 census). *Capital:* Giyani.

KaNgwane *Area:* 3823 km² (1476 sq mi). *Population:* 393 000 (1985 census). *Capital:* Louieville.

KwaNdebele *Area:* 3244 km² (1253 sq mi). *Population:* 236 000 (1985 census). *Capital:* Siyabuswa.

Kwazulu *Area:* 36 074 km² (13 928 sq mi). *Population:* 3 747 000 (1985 census). *Capital:* Ulundi.

Lebowa *Area*: 21 833 km² (8430 sq mi). *Population*: 1 836 000 (1985 census). *Capital*: Lebowakgomo.

Qwaqwa *Area*: 655 km² (253 sq mi). *Population*: 182 000 (1985 census). *Capital*: Phuthadithaba.

Transkei* *Area*: 41 002 km² (15 831 sq mi). *Population*: 2 876 000 (1985 est). *Capital*: Umtata.

Venda* *Area*: 6677 km² (2578 sq mi). *Population*: 460 000 (1985 census). *Capital*: Thohoyandou.

* 'independent' homelands.

GEOGRAPHY The Great Escarpment rises behind a discontinuous coastal plain and includes the Drakensberg Mountains. A vast plateau occupies the interior, undulating in the west and rising to over 2400 m (about 8000 ft) in the east. Much of the west is semi-desert, while the east is predominantly savannah grassland (veld). Walvis Bay is an enclave on the Namibian coast. *Principal rivers:* Orange (Oranje), Limpopo, Vaal. *Highest point:* Injasuti 3408 m (11 182 ft).

ECONOMY The country is the world's leading exporter of gold – which normally forms about 40% of South African exports – and a major producer of uranium, diamonds, chromite, antimony, platinum and coal (which meets three quarters of the country's energy needs). Industry includes chemicals, food processing, textiles, motor vehicles and electrical engineering. Agriculture supplies one third of South Africa's exports, including fruit, wine, wool and maize. The highest standard of living in Africa is very unevenly distributed between whites and non-whites. The withdrawal of some foreign investors has increased the drive towards self-sufficiency.

RECENT HISTORY Although the Boers (or Afrikaners) – of Dutch and French ancestry – lost the Boer War (1899–1902) against the British, they were politically dominant when the Union of South Africa was formed (1910). The creation of the African National

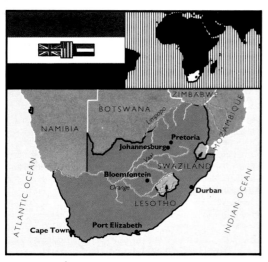

Congress (ANÇ) in 1912 was a protest against white supremacy, and by the 1920s black industrial protest was widespread. South Africa entered World War I as a British ally, taking German South West Africa (Namibia) after a short campaign; after the war, the territory came under South African administration. Despite strong Afrikaner opposition, South Africa – under General Jan Christiaan Smuts (1870–1950; PM 1919–24 and 1939–48) – joined the Allied cause in World War II. After the Afrikaner National Party came to power (1948), racial segregation was increased by the policy of apartheid ('separate development'), which deprived blacks of civil rights, segregated facilities and areas of residence by race, and confined black political rights to restricted homelands ('Bantustans'). Black opposition was crushed following a massacre of demonstrators at Sharpeville, and the ANC was banned (1960) by the government of Hendrik Verwoerd (1901–66; PM from 1958 to 1966, when he was assassinated). International pressure against apartheid increased. In 1961 South Africa left the Commonwealth, the majority of whose members continue to press for economic sanctions against South Africa. In 1966 the UN cancelled South Africa's trusteeship of South West Africa (Namibia), but South Africa continued to block the territory's progress to independence.

Black opposition revived in the 1970s and 1980s and found expression in strikes, the Soweto uprising of 1976, sabotage and the rise of the black consciousness movement. South African troops intervened in the Angolan civil war against the Marxist-Leninist government (1981) and were active in Namibia against SWAPO black nationalist guerrillas. P.W. Botha (1916– ; PM 1978–1984 and president 1984–89) granted political rights to the coloured and Indian communities, and implemented minor reforms for blacks. However, in 1986 – in the face of continuing unrest – Botha introduced a state of emergency, under which the press was strictly censored, the meetings of many organizations were banned and the number of political detainees rose sharply. His successor F.W. de Klerk released some ANC prisoners, and agreed to UN-supervised elections in Namibia leading to independence for that territory. In 1990 de Klerk lifted the ban on the ANC and released its imprisoned leader Nelson Mandela (1918–). In 1990–91, negotiations between the government and black leaders led to the dismantling of the legal structures of apartheid. Fighting between ANC and Inkatha supporters in black townships has caused concern, but negotiations concerning a new multi-racial power-sharing constitution continued intermittently.

SPAIN

Official name: Reino de España (Kingdom of Spain).

Member of: UN, NATO, EC, WEU, CSCE, Council of Europe, OECD.

Area: 504 782 km² (194 897 sq mi) including the Canary Islands, Ceuta and Melilla.

Population: 39 952 000 (1991 census) including the Canary Islands, Ceuta and Melilla.

Capital and major cities: Madrid 4 846 000 (city 3 121 000), Barcelona 3 400 000 (city 1 707 000), Valencia 777 000, Seville (Sevilla) 754 000 (city 684 000), Zaragoza 614 000, Málaga 525 000, Bilbao 477 000 (city 372 000), Las Palmas de Gran Canaria 348 000, Valladolid 345 000, Murcia 329 000, Córdoba 309 000, Palma de Mallorca 309 000, Granada 287 000, Vigo 277 000, Alicante 271 000, L'Hospitalet (part of the Barcelona agglomeration) 269 000, Gijón 260 000, La Coruña 251 000, Cádiz 240 000 (city 157 000), Vitoria 209 000, Badalona (part of the Barcelona agglomeration) 206 000, Oviedo 203 000, Santander 194 000, Móstoles (part of the Madrid agglomeration) 193 000, Santa Cruz de Tenerife 192 000, Pamplona 191 000, Salamanca 186 000, Sabadell (part of the Barcelona agglomeration) 184 000, Jérez de la Frontera 184 000, Elche 181 000, Donostia-San Sebastián 174 000, Leganés (part of the Madrid agglomeration) 173 000, Cartagena 172 000, Burgos 169 000 (all including suburbs; 1991 census).

Languages: Spanish or Castilian (official; as a first language over 70%), Catalan (as a first language over 20%), Basque (3%), Galician (4%).

Religion: Roman Catholic (98%), Sunni Islam (1%).

GOVERNMENT Spain is a constitutional monarchy. The Cortes (Parliament) comprises a Senate (Upper House) and a Chamber of Deputies (Lower House). The Senate consists of 208 senators – 4 from each province, 5 from the Balearic Islands, 6 from the Canary Islands and 2 each from Ceuta and Melilla – elected by universal adult suffrage for four years, plus 49 senators indirectly elected by the autonomous communities. The Congress of Deputies has 350 members directly elected for four years under a system of proportional representation. The King appoints a Prime Minister (President of the Council) who commands a majority in the Cortes. The PM, in turn, appoints a Council of Ministers (Cabinet) responsible to the Chamber of Deputies. The main political parties include the PSOE (Socialist Workers' Party), the (conservative) AP (Popular Alliance), the (left-wing coalition) Izquierda Unida (United Left, which includes the Communist Party), the (centre) CDS (Democratic and Social Centre), the (Catalan) Convergencia i Unio, and the (Basque) Herri Batasuna. Each of the 17 regions has its own legislature.

King: HM King Juan Carlos I (succeeded upon the restoration of the monarchy, 22 November 1975).

Prime Minister: Felipe Gonzalez Marquez.

AUTONOMOUS COMMUNITIES Andalusia (Andalucia) *Area*: 87 268 km^2 (33 694 sq mi). *Population*: 6 860 000 (1991 census). *Capital*: Seville (Sevilla).

Aragón *Area*: 47 669 km^2 (18 405 sq mi). *Population*: 1 179 000 (1991 census). *Capital*: Zaragoza.

Asturias *Area*: 10 565 km^2 (4079 sq mi). *Population*: 1 091 000 (1991 census). *Capital*: Oviedo.

Balearic Islands (Islas Baleares) *Area*: 5014 km^2 (1936 sq mi). *Population*: 703 000 (1991 census). *Capital*: Palma de Mallorca.

Basque Country (Euzkadi or Pais Vasco) *Area*: 7261 km^2 (2803 sq mi). *Population*: 2 093 000 (1991 census). *Capital*: Vitoria.

Canary Islands (Islas Canarias) *Area*: 7273 km^2 (2808 sq mi). *Population*: 1 456 000 (1991 census). *Equal and alternative capitals*: Las Palmas and Santa Cruz de Tenerife.

Cantabria *Area*: 5289 km^2 (2042 sq mi). *Population*: 524 000 (1991 census). *Capital*: Santander.

Castile-La Mancha (Castilla-La Mancha) *Area*: 79 226 km^2 (30 589 sq mi). *Population*: 1 650 000 (1991 census). *Capital*: Toledo.

Castile and León (Castilla y León) *Area*: 94 147 km^2 (36 350 sq mi). *Population*: 2 538 000 (1991 census). *Capital*: Valladolid.

Catalonia (Catalunya or Cataluña) *Area*: 31 930 km^2 (12 328 sq mi). *Population*: 5 960 000 (1991 census). *Capital*: Barcelona.

Extremadura *Area*: 41 602 km^2 (16 063 sq mi). *Population*: 1 050 000 (1991 census). *Capital*: Mérida.

Galicia (Galiza) *Area*: 29 434 km^2 (11 364 sq mi). *Population*: 2 710 000 (1991 census). *Capital*: Santiago de Compostela.

Madrid *Area*: 7995 km^2 (3087 sq mi). *Population*: 4 846 000 (1991 census). *Capital*: Madrid.

Murcia *Area*: 11 317 km^2 (4369 sq mi). *Population*: 1 032 000 (1991 census). *Capital*: Murcia (although the regional parliament meets at Cartagena).

Navarre (Navarra) *Area*: 10 421 km^2 (4024 sq mi). *Population*: 516 000 (1991 census). *Capital*: Pamplona.

La Rioja *Area*: 5034 km^2 (1853 sq mi). *Population*: 262 000 (1991 census). *Capital*: Logroño.

Valencia *Area*: 23 305 km^2 (8998 sq mi). *Population*: 3 831 000 (1991 census). *Capital*: Valencia.

Ceuta-Melilla (North African enclaves) *Area*: Ceuta – 19 km^2 (7 sq mi); Melilla – 14 km^2 (5.5 sq mi). *Population*: 125 000 (1991 census). *Capitals*: Ceuta and Melilla.

GEOGRAPHY In the north of Spain a mountainous region stretches from the Pyrenees – dividing Spain from France – through the Cantabrian mountains to Galicia on the Atlantic coast. Much of the country is occupied by the central plateau, the Meseta. This is around 600 m (2000 ft) high, but rises to the higher Sistema Central in Castile, and ends in the south at the Sierra Morena. The Sierra Nevada range in Andalusia in the south contains Mulhacén, mainland Spain's highest peak at 3478 m (11 411 ft). The principal lowlands include the Ebro Valley in the northeast, a coastal plain around Valencia in the east, and the valley of the Guadalquivir River in the south. The Balearic Islands in the Mediterranean comprise four main islands – Mallorca (Majorca), Menorca (Minorca), Ibiza and Formentera – with seven much smaller islands. The Canary Islands, off the coast of Morocco and the Western Sahara, comprise five large islands – Tenerife, Fuerteventura, Gran Canaria, Lanzarote and La Palma – plus two smaller islands and six islets. The cities of Ceuta and Melilla are enclaves on the north coast of Morocco. *Principal rivers:* Tagus (Tajo), Ebro, Douro (Duero), Guadiana, Guadalquivir. *Highest point:* Pico del Tiede 3716 m (12 192 ft) in the Canaries.

ECONOMY Over 15% of the labour force is involved in agriculture. The principal crops include barley, wheat, sugar beet, potatoes, citrus fruit and grapes (for wine). Pastures for livestock occupy some 20% of the land. Manufacturing developed rapidly from the 1960s, and there are now major motor-vehicle, textile, plastics, metallurgical, shipbuilding, chemical and engineering industries, as well as growing interests in telecommunications and electronics. Foreign investors have been encouraged to promote new industry, but unemployment remains high. Banking and commerce are important, and tourism is a major foreign-currency earner with around 50 000 000 foreign visitors a year, mainly staying at beach resorts on the Mediterranean, Balearic Islands and the Canaries. After the G7 countries, Spain has the largest gross national product in the world.

RECENT HISTORY When Cuba, the Philippines, Guam and Puerto Rico were lost at the end of the Spanish-American War (1989), doubts grew as to whether the constitutional monarchy of Alfonso XIII (1886–1941) was capable of delivering the dynamic leadership that Spain was thought to require. Spain remained neutral in World War I, during which social tensions increased. A growing disillusionment with parliamentary government and political parties led to a military coup in 1923 led by General Miguel Primo de Rivera (1870–1930). Primo was initially supported by Alfonso XIII, but in 1930 the King withdrew that support. However, the range of forces arrayed against the monarchy and the threat of civil war led Alfonso to abdicate (1931). The peace of the succeeding republic was short-lived. Neither of the political extremes – left nor right – was prepared to tolerate the perceived inefficiency and lack of authority of the Second Spanish Republic. In 1936, nationalist army generals rose against a newly elected republican government. Led by General Francisco Franco (1892–1975) and supported by Germany and Italy, the nationalists fought the republicans in the bitter Spanish Civil War. Franco triumphed

in 1939 to become ruler – Caudillo – of the neo-Fascist Spanish State. Political expression was restricted, and from 1942 to 1967 the Cortes (Parliament) was not directly elected. Spain remained neutral in World War II, although it was beholden to Germany. After 1945, Franco emphasized Spain's anti-Communism – a policy that brought his regime some international acceptance from the West during the Cold War.

In 1969, Franco named Alfonso XIII's grandson Juan Carlos (1938–) as his successor. The monarchy was restored on Franco's death (1975) and the King eased the transition to democracy through the establishment of a new liberal constitution in 1978. In 1981 Juan Carlos played an important role in putting down an attempted army coup. In 1982 Spain joined NATO and elected a socialist government, and since 1986 the country has been a member of the EC. Despite the granting of some regional autonomy since 1978, Spain continues to be troubled by campaigns for provincial independence – for example in Catalonia – and by the violence of the Basque separatist movement ETA.

SRI LANKA

Official name: Sri Lanka Prajatantrika Samajawadi Janarajaya (Democratic Socialist Republic of Sri Lanka). Known as Ceylon until 1970.

Member of: UN, Commonwealth, SAARC.

Area: 65 610 km^2 (25 332 sq mi).

Population: 17 219 000 (1991 est).

Capital and major cities: Colombo (current capital) 1 446 000 (city 615 000), (Sri Jayawardenepura) Kotte (legislative capital and capital designate; part of the Colombo agglomeration) 109 000, Dehiwala-Mt Lavinia 196 000 and Moratuwa 170 000 are part of the Colombo agglomeration, Jaffna 138 000 (city 129 000), Galle

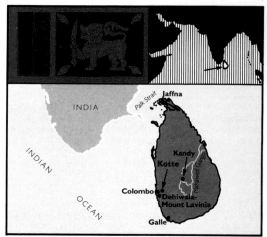

109 000 (city 84 000), Kandy 107 000 (city 104 000) (all including suburbs; 1987 est).

Languages: Sinhala (official; 72%), Tamil (official; 21%), English (official).

Religions: Buddhist (69%), Hindu (15%), with Roman Catholic and Sunni Islam minorities.

GOVERNMENT The 225-member Parliament is elected for six years under a system of proportional representation by universal adult suffrage. The President – who is also directly elected for six years – appoints a Cabinet and a Prime Minister who are responsible to Parliament. The main political parties are the UNP (United National Party), the SLFP (Sri Lanka Freedom Party), the LSSP (Lanka Sama Samaja Party), the Communist Party, and several Tamil parties. There is constitutional provision for some autonomy for the (largely Tamil) Northern and Eastern provinces.

President: Ranasinghe Premadasa.
Prime Minister: D.B. Wijetunge.

GEOGRAPHY Central Sri Lanka is occupied by highlands. Most of the rest of the island consists of forested lowlands, which in the north are flat and fertile. *Principal rivers:* Mahaweli Ganga, Kelani Ganga. *Highest point:* Pidurutalagala 2527 m (8292 ft).

ECONOMY About 50% of the labour force is involved in agriculture, growing rice for domestic consumption, and rubber, tea and coconuts for export. Major irrigation and hydroelectric installations on the Mahaweli Ganga river are being constructed. Industries include food processing, cement, textiles and petroleum refining. Tourism is increasingly important.

RECENT HISTORY Nationalist feeling against British rule grew from the beginning of the 20th century, leading to independence in 1948, and a republican constitution in 1972. The country has been bedevilled by Tamil-Sinhalese ethnic rivalry, which led to major disorders in 1958, 1961 and since 1977. In 1971 a Marxist rebellion was crushed after heavy fighting. Sri Lanka elected the world's first woman Prime Minister, Sirimavo Bandaranaike (1916– ; PM 1960–65 and 1970–77). In the 1980s separatist Tamil guerrillas fought for an independent homeland (Eelam). Fighting between rival Tamil guerrilla groups, Sinhalese extremists and government forces reduced the northeast to near civil war. An Indian 'peace-keeping' force intervened (1987), but this aggravated an already complex situation. Indian forces were completely withdrawn in 1990. The Tamil Northeast Province is scheduled to achieve autonomy under the dominant Tamil Tigers guerrillas, who registered as a political party in 1989. However, Tamil guerrilla activity continues in the northeast.

SUDAN

Official name: Al Jumhuriyat al-Sudan (The Republic of Sudan).

Member of: UN, Arab League, OAU.

Area: 2 505 813 km^2 (967 500 sq mi).

Population: 29 129 000 (1991 est).

Capital: Khartoum 1 802 000 (comprising Omdurman 526 000, Khartoum 476 000, Khartoum North 341 000), Port Sudan (Bur Sudan) 207 000, Wadi Medani 141 000, El Obeid 140 000 (1983 est).

Language: Arabic (over 50%; official).

Religions: Sunni Islam (70%), animist (22%), with various Christian Churches (8%).

GOVERNMENT Since the military coup in June 1989, the country has been ruled by the 15-member Command Council of the Revolution of National Salvation, whose chairman is head of state and of government. Political activity has been suspended, although a 300-member Transitional National Assembly was appointed. In future, the Assembly will comprise representatives from nine federal provinces, whose councils will consist of delegates from directly elected popular committees.

Head of state and government: Lt. Gen. Omar Hassan Ahmed al-Bashir.

GEOGRAPHY The Sahara Desert covers much of the north and west, but is crossed by the fertile Nile Valley. The southern plains are swampy. Highlands are confined to hill country beside the Red Sea and mountains on the Ugandan border. *Principal rivers:* Nile (Nil), Nil el Azraq (Blue Nile), Nil el Abyad (White Nile). *Highest point:* Kinyeti 3187 m (10 456 ft).

ECONOMY Almost two thirds of the labour force is involved in agriculture, growing cotton for export, and sorghum, cassava and millet for domestic consumption.

Since the early 1980s Sudan has been severely affected by drought and famine.

RECENT HISTORY From 1899 Sudan was administered jointly by Britain and Egypt. Nationalism developed strongly after World War I, but independence was only achieved in 1956. Sudan remains politically unstable, alternating between civilian and military regimes, the most recent gaining power in a coup in 1989. The civil war between the Muslim north and the animist–Christian south that began in 1955 has intensified under the current Islamic fundamentalist government. Sudan is increasingly isolated internationally owing to its backing for Iraq and Libya.

SURINAME

Official name: Republiek Suriname (Republic of Suriname).

Member of: UN, OAS.

Area: 163 265 km² (63 037 sq mi).

Population: 417 000 (1991 est).

Capital: Paramaribo 246 000 (city 68 000), Nieuw Nickerie 6000 (1988 est).

Languages: Dutch (official; 30%), Sranang Togo (Creole; 31%), Hindi (30%), Javanese (15%), Chinese, English (official), Spanish (official – designate).

Religions: Hinduism (28%), Roman Catholic (22%), Sunni Islam (20%), Moravian (15%).

GOVERNMENT A 51-member National Assembly is elected for five years by universal adult suffrage, a President and a Vice-President – who is also the Prime Minister – to be elected by the Assembly, and a Cabinet, appointed by the President. The main political parties are the New Front Coalition, the New Democratic Party and the (coalition) Democratic Alternative.

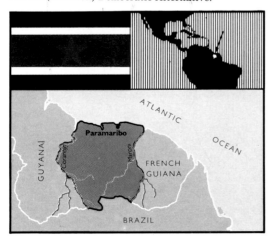

President: Ronald Venetiaan.

Prime Minister: Jules Ajodhia

GEOGRAPHY Suriname comprises a swampy coastal plain, a forested central plateau, and southern mountains. *Principal rivers*: Corantijn, Coppename, Suriname, Maroni. *Highest point*: Julianatop 1286 m (4218 ft).

ECONOMY The extraction and refining of bauxite is the mainstay of the economy. Other exports include shrimps, sugar and oranges. Economic development is hampered by political instability and emigration.

RECENT HISTORY The Dutch colony of Suriname had a mixed population, including American Indians, and the descendants of African slaves and of Javanese, Chinese and Indian plantation workers. Since independence in 1975, racial tension has contributed to instability, and there have been several coups. Constitutional rule was restored in 1991.

SWAZILAND

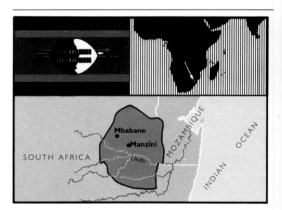

Official name: Umbuso Weswatini (The Kingdom of Swaziland).

Member of: UN, Commonwealth, OAU, SADCC.

Area: 17 363 km² (6704 sq mi).

Population: 798 000 (1991 est).

Capital and major cities: Mbabane – administrative capital – 38 000, Lobamba – legislative and royal capital – 6000, Manzini 52 000 (1986 census).

Languages: siSwati and English (both official).

Religions: Animist (majority), various Christian Churches (18%).

GOVERNMENT Swaziland is a monarchy in which the King appoints a Prime Minister and Cabinet. The King is advised by the 20-member Senate and the 50-member House of Assembly, and appoints 10 members to both. Each of the 40 traditional tribal communities elects 2 members to the Electoral College, which chooses 10 of its members to sit in the Senate and 40 in the House. No political parties are permitted.

King: HM King Mswati III (succeeded upon the resignation of his mother as Queen Regent, 25 April 1986).
Prime Minister: Obed Dlamini.

GEOGRAPHY From the mountains of the west, Swaziland descends in steps of savannah (veld) towards hill country in the east. *Principal rivers:* Usutu, Komati, Umbuluzi, Ingwavuma. *Highest point:* Emlembe 1863 m (6113 ft).

ECONOMY The majority of Swazis are subsistence farmers. Cash crops include sugar cane (the main export).

RECENT HISTORY The Swazi kingdom came under British rule in 1904. The country resisted annexation by the Boers in the 1890s and by South Africa during the colonial period. Following independence (1968), King Sobhuza II suspended the constitution in 1973 and restored much of the traditional royal authority. A bitter power struggle after his death (1982) lasted until King Mswati III was invested in 1986.

SWEDEN

Official name: Konungariket Sverige (Kingdom of Sweden).

Member of: UN, EFTA, CSCE, Council of Europe, OECD.

Area: 449 964 km^2 (173 732 sq mi).

Population: 8 586 000 (1990 census).

Capital and major cities: Stockholm 1 471 000 (city 679 000), Göteborg (Gothenburg) 720 000 (city 432 000), Malmö 466 000 (city 235 000), Uppsala 171 000 (city 168 000), Linköping 124 000, Orebro 122 000, Norrköping 121 000, Västeras 120 000, Jönköping 112 000, Helsingborg 110 000, Boras 102 000, Sundsvall 94 000, Umea 93 000, Lund (part of the Malmö agglomeration) 90 000 (all including suburbs; 1990 census).

Languages: Swedish (official), small Lappish minority.

Religion: Evangelical Lutheran Church of Sweden (over 85%), Roman Catholic (2%).

GOVERNMENT Sweden is a constitutional monarchy in which the King is ceremonial and representative head of state without any executive role. The 349-member Riksdag (Parliament) is elected for three years by universal adult suffrage under a system of proportional representation. The Speaker of the Riksdag nominates a Prime Minister who commands a parliamentary majority. The PM, in turn, appoints a Cabinet of Ministers who are responsible to the Riksdag. The main political parties are the Social Democratic Party, the (conservative) Moderate Party, the Liberal Party, the Centre Party, the Christian Democratic Party, the (right-wing) New Democracy Party and the (former Communist) Left Party.

King: HM King Carl XVI Gustaf (succeeded upon the death of his grandfather, 15 September 1973).
Prime Minister: Carl Bildt.

GEOGRAPHY The mountains of Norrland – in the north and along the border with Norway – cover two thirds of the country. Svealand – in the centre – is characterized by a large number of lakes. In the south are the low Smaland Highlands and the fertile lowland of Skane. *Principal rivers:* Ume, Torne, Angerman, Klar, Dal. *Highest point:* Kebnekaise 2123 m (6965 ft).

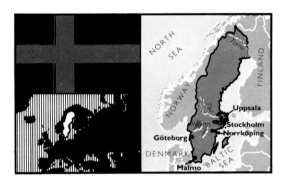

ECONOMY Sweden's high standard of living has been based upon its neutrality in the two World Wars, its cheap and plentiful hydroelectric power, and its mineral riches. The country has about 15% of the world's uranium deposits, and large reserves of iron ore that provide the basis of domestic heavy industry and important exports to Western Europe. Agriculture – like the bulk of the population – is concentrated in the south. The principal products include dairy produce, meat (including reindeer), barley, sugar beet and potatoes. Vast coniferous forests are the basis of the paper, board and furniture industries, and large exports of timber. Heavy industries include motor vehicles (Saab and Volvo), aerospace and machinery, although the shipbuilding industry – in the 1970s the world's second largest – has ceased to exist.

RECENT HISTORY The union of Norway and Sweden was dissolved in 1905 when King Oscar II (reigned 1872–1907) gave up the Norwegian throne upon Norway's vote for separation. In the 20th century neutral Sweden developed a comprehensive welfare state under social democratic governments. The country assumed a moral leadership on world issues but was jolted by the (unclaimed) assassination of PM Olof Palme (1986). In the 1990s economic necessity has obliged Sweden to dismantle aspects of the welfare system. The country has also become a candidate for EC membership.

SWITZERLAND

Official name: Schweizerische Eidgenossenschaft (German) or Confédération suisse (French) or Confederazione Svizzera (Italian) or Confederaziun Helvetica (Romansch); (Swiss Confederation).

Member of: EFTA, CSCE, OECD, Council of Europe, UN (observer).

Area: 41 293 km^2 (15 943 sq mi).

Population: 6 820 000 (1991 est).

Capital and major cities: Berne (Bern) 299 000 (city 134 000), Zürich 839 000 (city 343 000), Geneva (Genève) 389 000 (city 165 000), Basel 359 000 (city 170 000), Lausanne 263 000 (city 123 000), Lucerne (Luzern) 161 000 (city 59 000), St Gallen 126 000 (city 73 000), Winterthur 108 000 (city 86 000), Biel/Bienne 83 000 (city 53 000), Thun 78 000 (city 38 000), Lugano 69 000 (city 25 000), Neuchâtel 66 000 (city 33 000), Fribourg (Freiburg) 57 000 (city 34 000), Schaffhausen 54 000 (city 34 000), Zug 52 000 (1990 est).

Languages: German (65% as a first language), French (18% as a first language), Italian (10% as a first language), Romansch (under 1%) – all official.

Religions: Roman Catholic (48%), various Protestant Churches (44%).

GOVERNMENT Switzerland is a federal republic in which each of the 20 cantons and 6 half cantons has its own government with very considerable powers. Federal matters are entrusted to the Federal Assembly comprising the 46-member Council of States and the 200-member National Council. The Council of States is directly elected for three or four years with two members from each canton and one from each half canton. The National Council is elected for four years by universal adult suffrage under a system of proportional representation. The Federal Assembly elects a seven-member Federal Council – the equivalent of a Cabinet – for four years. The Federal Council appoints one of its members to be President for one year. All federal and cantonal constitutional amendments must be approved by a referendum. The main political parties include the (liberal) Radical Democratic Party, the Social Democratic Party, the (conservative) Christian Democratic Party, the (centre) People's Party, the Ecologists, and the Liberal Party.

President: Adolf Ogi.

CANTONS **Aargau** *Area*: 1404 km^2 (542 sq mi). *Population*: 490 000 (1990 est). *Capital*: Aarau.

Appenzell Ausser Rhoden (half canton) *Area*: 243 km^2 (94 sq mi). *Population*: 51 000 (1990 est). *Capital*: Herisau.

Appenzell Inner Rhoden (half canton) *Area*: 172 km^2 (66 sq mi). *Population*: 14 000 (1990 est). *Capital*: Appenzell.

Basel-Land (half canton) *Area*: 428 km^2 (165 sq mi). *Population*: 229 000 (1990 est). *Capital*: Liestal.

Basel-Stadt (half canton) *Area*: 37 km^2 (14 sq mi). *Population*: 190 000 (1990 est). *Capital*: Basel.

Berne (Bern) *Area*: 6049 km^2 (2336 sq mi). *Population*: 937 000 (1990 est). *Capital*: Berne (Bern).

Fribourg (Freiburg) *Area*: 1670 km^2 (645 sq mi). *Population*: 204 000 (1990 est). *Capital*: Fribourg (Freiburg).

Geneva (Genève) *Area*: 282 km^2 (109 sq mi). *Population*: 373 000 (1990 est). *Capital*: Geneva (Genève).

Glarus *Area*: 684 km^2 (264 sq mi). *Population*: 37 000 (1990 est). *Capital*: Glarus.

Graubünden (Grisons) *Area*: 7109 km^2 (2745 sq mi). *Population*: 169 000 (1990 est). *Capital*: Chur.

Jura *Area*: 838 km^2 (324 sq mi). *Population*: 65 000 (1990 est). *Capital*: Delémont.

Lucerne (Luzern) *Area*: 1494 km^2 (577 sq mi). *Population*: 315 000 (1990 est). *Capital*: Lucerne (Luzern).

Neuchâtel *Area*: 797 km^2 (308 sq mi). *Population*: 159 000 (1990 est). *Capital*: Neuchâtel.

St Gallen *Area*: 2016 km^2 (778 sq mi). *Population*: 415 000 (1990 est). *Capital*: St Gallen.

Schaffhausen *Area*: 298 km^2 (115 sq mi). *Population*: 71 000 (1990 est). *Capital*: Schaffhausen.

Schwyz *Area*: 908 km^2 (351 sq mi). *Population*: 108 000 (1990 est). *Capital*: Schwyz.

Solothurn *Area*: 791 km^2 (305 sq mi). *Population*: 224 000 (1990 est). *Capital*: Solothurn.

Thurgau *Area*: 1006 km^2 (388 sq mi). *Population*: 202 000 (1990 est). *Capital*: Frauenfeld.

Ticino *Area*: 2811 km^2 (1085 sq mi). *Population*: 283 000 (1990 est). *Capital*: Bellinzona.

Unterwalden Nidwalden (half canton) *Area*: 274 km^2 (106 sq mi). *Population*: 32 000 (1990 est). *Capital*: Stans.

Unterwalden Obwalden (half canton) *Area*: 492 km^2 (190 sq mi). *Population*: 28 000 (1990 est). *Capital*: Sarnen.

Uri *Area*: 1075 km^2 (415 sq mi). *Population*: 34 000 (1990 est). *Capital*: Altdorf.

Valais (Wallis) *Area*: 5231 km^2 (2020 sq mi). *Population*: 244 000 (1990 est). *Capital*: Sion.

Vaud *Area*: 3211 km^2 (1240 sq mi). *Population*: 572 000 (1990 est). *Capital*: Lausanne.

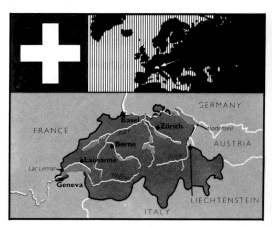

Zug *Area*: 239 km² (92 sq mi). *Population*: 84 000 (1990 est). *Capital*: Zug.

Zürich *Area*: 1729 km² (668 sq mi). *Population*: 1 145 000 (1990 est). *Capital*: Zürich.

GEOGRAPHY The parallel ridges of the Jura Mountains lie in the northwest on the French border. The south of the country is occupied by the Alps. Between the two mountain ranges is a central plateau that contains the greater part of Switzerland's population, agriculture and industry. *Principal rivers*: Rhine (Rhein), Rhône, Aare, Inn, Ticino. *Highest point*: Dufourspitze (Monte Rosa) 4634 m (15 203 ft).

ECONOMY Nearly two centuries of neutrality have allowed Switzerland to build a reputation as a secure financial centre. Zürich is one of the world's leading banking and commercial cities. The country enjoys one of the highest standards of living in the world. Industry – in part based upon cheap hydroelectric power – includes engineering (from turbines to watches), textiles, food processing (including cheese and chocolate), pharmaceuticals and chemicals. Dairying, grapes (for wine) and fodder crops are important in the agricultural sector, and there is a significant timber industry. Tourism and the international organizations based in Switzerland are major foreign-currency earners. Foreign workers – in particular Italians – help alleviate the country's labour shortage.

RECENT HISTORY Swiss neutrality – recognized internationally since 1815 – enabled Switzerland to escape involvement in the two World Wars. As a neutral country Switzerland proved the ideal base for the Red Cross (1863), the League of Nations (1920) and other world organizations, but the country avoids membership of any body it considers might compromise its neutrality – referenda in 1986 and 1992 respectively confirmed that Switzerland should not seek membership of the UN or of the EEA.

SYRIA

Official name: Al-Jumhuriya al-'Arabiya as-Suriya (The Syrian Arab Republic).

Member of: UN, Arab League.

Area: 185 180 km² (71 498 sq mi) – including the Israeli-occupied Golan Heights.

Population: 12 529 000 (1991 est).

Capital and major cities: Damascus (Dimashq) 1 361 000, Halab (formerly Aleppo) 1 308 000, Homs 464 000, Latakia 258 000, Hama 214 000 (1989 est).

Languages: Arabic (89%; official), Kurdish (6%), Armenian (3%).

Religions: Islam (official; Sunni 90%, Shia and Druze minorities), various Orthodox and Roman Catholic minorities.

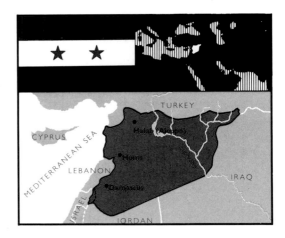

GOVERNMENT The 250-member National People's Assembly is elected by universal adult suffrage for four years. The President – who is directly elected for seven years – appoints a Prime Minister (to assist him in government) and a Council of Ministers. The National Progressive Front – including the ruling Ba'ath Arab Socialist Party, the Arab Socialist Union Party, the Syrian Arab Socialist Party, the Arab Socialist Party and the Communist Party – has a leading role.

President: Hafez al-Assad.
Prime Minister: Mahmoud Zubi.

GEOGRAPHY Behind a well-watered coastal plain, mountains run from north to south. Inland, much of the country is occupied by the Syrian Desert. *Principal river*: Euphrates (Al Furat), Asi (Orontes). *Highest point*: Jabal ash Shaik (Mount Hermon) 2814 m (9232 ft).

ECONOMY Petroleum is the main export although Syria's petroleum reserves are small by Middle Eastern standards. Agriculture involves nearly one quarter of the labour force, with cultivation concentrated in the coastal plain and irrigated land in the Euphrates Valley. Major crops include cotton, wheat and barley.

RECENT HISTORY Ottoman (Turkish) rule in Syria was ended in 1917, when a combined British-Arab army was led into Damascus by Prince Faisal ibn Husain. In 1920 independence was declared with Faisal as king, but the victors of World War I handed Syria to France (1920) as a trust territory. Independence was achieved in 1946. The pan-Arab, secular, socialist Ba'ath Party engineered Syria's unsuccessful union with Egypt (1958–61). Syria fought wars with Israel in 1948–49, 1967 and 1973, and in the 1967 Arab-Israeli War Israel captured the strategic Golan Heights from Syria. A pragmatic Ba'athist leader Hafiz al-Assad came to power in 1970, ended Syria's political instability and allied the country to the USSR. Since 1976, Syria has become increasingly involved in the Lebanon. In 1990 Syria defeated the Lebanese Christian militia of Michel Aoun and restored the authority of the Lebanese government to the whole of Beirut. Since 1989–90, economic pressures have lessened Syria's dependence upon the USSR. Syria's participation in the coalition against its old rival Iraq in 1990–91 enhanced the reputation of Syria, which had attracted criticism for its sponsorship of terrorism.

TAJIKISTAN

Official name: Respublika i Tojikiston (Republic of Tajikistan).

Member of: UN, CIS, CSCE.

Area: 143 100 km² (55 300 sq mi).

Population: 5 358 000 (1991 est).

Capital and major cities: Dushanbe 604 000, Khodzhent (formerly Leninabad) 157 000 (1989 census).

Language: Tajik (59%), Uzbek (23%), Russian (10%).

Religion: Sunni Islam majority.

GOVERNMENT   A 230-member legislature and a President are elected for four years by universal adult suffrage. A new constitution is to be drafted. The main political parties are the Communist Party, the Democratic Party and Islamic Renaissance.

Acting President: Akbar Shah Iskaudarov.

President: (in control of part of the country) Rakhmon Nabiyev.

GEOGRAPHY   The mountainous republic of Tajikistan lies within the Tien Shan range and part of the Pamirs. *Principal rivers:* Amu Darya, Pamir, Kyzylsu. *Highest point:* Mount Garmo 7495 m (24 590 ft) – which was known as Pik Kommunizma (Mount Communism) when it was the highest mountain in the USSR. The most important lowland is the Fergana valley.

ECONOMY   Cotton is the mainstay of the economy. Other agricultural interests include fruit, vegetables and raising cattle. Major natural resources include coal, natural gas, iron ore, oil, lead, zinc and hydroelectric-

power potential. Industries include textiles and carpet-making. The economy remains centrally planned and largely state-owned.

RECENT HISTORY   The area was annexed by Tsarist Russia (1860–68). After the Russian Revolution, the area was reoccupied by the Soviet Red Army (1920), but Tajik revolts simmered from 1922 to 1931. Tajikistan became a Union Republic within the USSR in 1929, declared independence after the abortive coup by Communist hardliners in Moscow (September 1991), and was internationally recognized when the Soviet Union was dissolved (December 1991). Since independence, the country has been wracked by civil war between former Communists and Islamic fundamentalists.

TANZANIA

Official name: Jamhuri ya Muungano wa Tanzania (Swahili) or The United Republic of Tanzania.

Member of: UN, Commonwealth, OAU.

Area: 945 087 km² (364 900 sq mi).

Population: 25 096 000 (1991 est).

Capital and major cities: Dodoma (legislative and de jure capital) 204 000, Dar es Salaam (administrative capital) 1 361 000, Mwanza 223 000, Tanga 188 000, Zanzibar 158 000 (1988 census).

Languages: English, Swahili (90%; 9% as a first language) – both official.

Religions: Sunni Islam (33%), animist (40%), Roman Catholic (20%).

GOVERNMENT   The President is elected by universal adult suffrage for a five-year term. The President appoints a Cabinet of Ministers and two Vice Presidents – one President of Zanzibar, the other concurrently Prime Minister. The 244-member National Assembly comprises 119 members directly elected from the mainland, 50 members directly elected from Zanzibar, plus appointed and indirectly elected members. Zanzibar has its own legislature.

President: Ali Hassan Mwinyi.

Prime Minister: John Malecela.

AUTONOMOUS STATE   Zanzibar *Area*: 1660 km² (641 sq mi). *Population*: 376 000 (1988 census). *Capital*: Zanzibar.

GEOGRAPHY   Zanzibar comprises three small islands. The mainland – formerly Tanganyika – comprises savannah plateaux divided by rift valleys and a north–south mountain chain. *Principal rivers*: Pangani (Ruvu), Rufiji, Rovuma. *Highest point*: Kilimanjaro 5894 m (19 340 ft), the highest point in Africa.

ECONOMY   Subsistence agriculture involves over 80% of the labour force. Cash crops include coffee, tea, cotton and tobacco. Mineral resources include diamonds and gold. Tanzania had a centrally planned

economy, but more pragmatic policies have been implemented since 1985–87.

RECENT HISTORY The mainland became a German colony in 1884, the British trust territory of Tanganyika in 1919 and an independent state in 1961. Shortly after the British protectorate of Zanzibar became independent in 1963, its sultan was deposed in a radical left-wing coup. In 1964 Tanganyika and Zanzibar united to form Tanzania. President Julius Nyerere's policies of self-reliance and egalitarian socialism were widely admired, but proved difficult to implement and were largely abandoned by the time he retired as President in 1985.

THAILAND

Official name: Prathet Thai (Kingdom of Thailand).
Member of: UN, ASEAN.
Area: 513 115 km² (198 115 sq mi).
Population: 57 150 000 (1991 est).
Capital and major cities: Bangkok 5 876 000, Nakhon Ratchasima (Khorat) 207 000, Songkhla 173 000, Chiang Mai 164 000 (all including suburbs; 1990 census).
Language: Thai (official).
Religions: Buddhism (95%), Sunni Islam (4%).

GOVERNMENT Thailand is a constitutional monarchy. The constitution provides for a National Assembly, which comprises a non-political Senate – whose 270 members are appointed by the (military) National Peacekeeping Council – and a 360-member House of Representatives elected by universal adult suffrage for four years. The King appoints a Prime Minister who commands a majority in the House. The

PM in turn appoints a Cabinet of Ministers responsible to the House. The main political parties include the (conservative) Samakkhi Tham, (right-wing) Chart Thai, the New Aspiration Party, the (liberal) Democrat Party, Palang Dharma (Righteous) Party, and (conservative) Social Action.
King: HM King Bhumibol Adulyadej (Rama IX) (succeeded upon the death of his brother, 9 June 1946).
Head of military junta: Gen. Sunthorn Kongsompong.
Prime Minister: Anand Panyarachun.

GEOGRAPHY Central Thailand is a densely populated fertile plain. The north is mountainous. The infertile Khorat Plateau occupies the northeast, while the mountainous Isthmus of Kra joins southern Thailand to Malaysia. *Principal rivers*: Mekong, Chao Pyha, Mae Nam Mun. *Highest point*: Doi Inthanon 2595 m (8514 ft).

ECONOMY Two thirds of the labour force is involved in agriculture, mainly growing rice – Thailand is the world's largest exporter of rice. Tin and natural gas are the main natural resources. Manufacturing – based on cheap labour – is expanding and includes textiles, clothes, electrical and electronic engineering, and food processing. Thailand achieved high economic growth rates throughout the 1980s and early 1990s. Tourism has become a major foreign-currency earner.

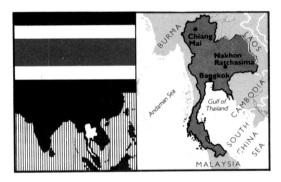

RECENT HISTORY In Southeast Asia, only Siam – as Thailand was known before 1939 – was able to resist 19th-century European colonialism. A constitutional monarchy was established by a bloodless coup (1932), whose Westernized leaders – Pibul Songgram and Pridi Phanomyang – struggled for political dominance for the next quarter of a century. During World War II Thailand was forced into an alliance with Japan. Since then Thailand has made a decisive commitment to the US political camp, which has brought major benefits in military and technical aid. Despite continuing army interventions in politics – in February 1991 the military took over the government for the 17th time in 50 years – Thailand has prospered. However, the stability of the country was compromised by the wars in Vietnam and by the continuing Cambodian conflict (until 1991). Constitutional rule was restored in 1992.

TOGO

Official name: La République Togolaise (The Togolese Republic).

Member of: UN, OAU, ECOWAS.

Area: 56 785 km² (21 925 sq mi).

Population: 3 531 000 (1990 est).

Capital: Lomé 366 000, Sokodé 48 000, Kpalimé 28 000 (1983 est).

Languages: French, Ewe (47%), Kabre (22%).

Religions: Animist (50%), Roman Catholic (26%), Sunni Islam (15%), various Protestant Churches (9%).

GOVERNMENT The President – who appoints a Council of Ministers – is elected by universal adult suffrage for seven years. The 79-member National Assembly is elected for five years. The main political parties are the (former monopoly) Rassemblement du peuple togolais, the Coalition for Democratic Opposition (COD) and the Union of the Forces for Change (UFC).

President: Gen. Gnassingbe Eyadema.

Prime Minister: Joseph Kokou Koffigoh.

GEOGRAPHY Inland from a narrow coastal plain is a series of plateaux rising in the north to the Chaine du Togo. *Principal rivers*: Moni, Oti. *Highest point*: Pic Baumann 983 m (3225 ft).

ECONOMY The majority of the labour force is involved in subsistence farming, with yams and millet as the principal crops. Phosphates are the main export.

RECENT HISTORY Colonized by Germany in 1884,

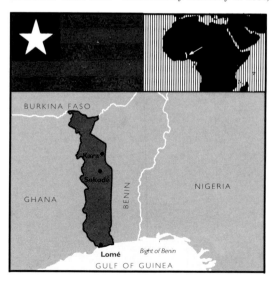

Togoland was occupied by Franco-British forces in World War I, after which the territory was divided between them. British Togoland became part of Ghana; the French section gained independence as Togo in 1960. Togo has experienced great political instability and several coups. A multi-party system was restored in 1991.

TONGA

Official name: Pule'anga Fakatu'i'o Tonga (The Kingdom of Tonga).

Member of: Commonwealth, South Pacific Forum.

Area: 748 km² (289 sq mi).

Population: 97 000 (1991 est).

Capital and major towns: Nuku'alofa 28 900, Mu'a 4000 (1986 est).

Languages: Tongan, English.

Religions: Methodist (40%; official), Roman Catholic.

GOVERNMENT Tonga is a constitutional monarchy. The King appoints a Prime Minister and other Ministers to the Privy Council, which acts as a Cabinet. The 31-member Legislative Assembly comprises the King, the Privy Council, 9 hereditary nobles (chosen by their peers) and 9 representatives of the people elected for three years by universal adult suffrage. There are no political parties.

King: HM King Taufa'ahau Tupou IV (succeeded upon the death of his mother, 15 December 1965).

Prime Minister: Baron Vaea.

GEOGRAPHY The 172 Tongan islands – 36 of which are inhabited – comprise a low limestone chain in the east and a higher volcanic chain in the west. There are no significant rivers. *Highest point*: Kao 1030 m (3380 ft).

ECONOMY Agriculture involves most Tongans, with yams, cassava and taro being grown as subsistence crops. Coconut products are the main exports.

RECENT HISTORY King George Tupou I (reigned 1845–93) reunited Tonga after civil war, preserved its independence and gave it a modern constitution. From 1900 to 1970 Tonga was a British protectorate. Since 1987 pressure for constitutional reform has increased.

TRINIDAD AND TOBAGO

Official name: Republic of Trinidad and Tobago.
Member of: UN, Commonwealth, CARICOM, OAS.
Area: 5130 km² (1981 sq mi).
Population: 1 234 000 (1990 census).
Capital: Port of Spain 51 000, San Fernando 30 000, Arima 29 000 (1990 census).
Languages: English (official), Hindi (25%).
Religions: Roman Catholic (34%), Hinduism (25%), Anglican (15%), Sunni Islam (6%).

GOVERNMENT The 31-member Senate – the Upper House of Parliament – is appointed by the President, who is elected by a joint sitting of Parliament. The 36-member House of Representatives is elected for five years by universal adult suffrage. The President appoints a Prime Minister who commands a majority in the House. The PM, in turn, appoints a Cabinet, which is responsible to the House. The main political parties include the (socialist coalition) National Alliance for Reconstruction, the (centre) People's National Movement, and the (socialist) United National Congress. Tobago has full internal self-government.

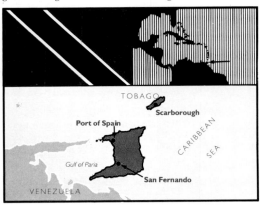

President: Noor Mohammed Hassanali.
Prime Minister: Patrick Manning.

GEOGRAPHY Trinidad is generally undulating. Tobago is more mountainous. *Principal rivers*: Caroni, Orotoire, Oropuche. *Highest point*: Cerro Aripo 940 m (3085 ft) in Trinidad.

ECONOMY Petroleum and petrochemicals are the mainstay of the economy. Trinidad also has important reserves of natural gas and asphalt. Tourism is a major foreign-currency earner.

RECENT HISTORY The islands merged as a single British colony in 1899 and gained independence in 1962 under Dr Eric Williams. His moderate policies brought economic benefits but provoked a Black Power revolt and an army mutiny in 1970. The country has been a republic since 1976. In 1990, a small group of Islamic fundamentalists held the PM and several government ministers and parliamentarians hostage during an attempted coup.

TUNISIA

Official name: Al-Jumhuriya at-Tunisiya (Republic of Tunisia).
Member of: UN, Arab League, OAU.
Area: 163 610 km² (63 170 sq mi).
Population: 8 293 000 (1991 est).
Capital and major cities: Tunis 1 395 000 (city 597 000), Nabeul (part of the Tunis agglomeration) 335 000, Sfax 232 000, Bizerta 95 000, Djerba 92 000, Gabès 92 000, Sousse 84 000 (1984 census).
Languages: Arabic (official), Berber minority.
Religion: Sunni Islam (official; 99%).

GOVERNMENT The President and the 141-member National Assembly are elected by universal adult suffrage for a five-year term. The President appoints a Cabinet, headed by a Prime Minister. The main political parties are the (socialist) RCD (Democratic Constitutional Rally), the MDS (Movement of Democratic Socialists), and independents standing for the (banned Islamic) Renaissance Party.
President: Zine el-Abidine Ben Ali.
Prime Minister: Hamed Karoui.

GEOGRAPHY The north is occupied by the Northern Tell and High Tell mountains. Wide plateaux cover central Tunisia. The Sahara Desert lies south of a zone of shallow salt lakes. *Principal river*: Medjerda. *Highest point*: Jabal ash-Shanabi 1544 m (5066 ft).

ECONOMY Phosphates and petroleum are the mainstay of the economy, normally providing over 40% of Tunisia's exports. The principal crops are wheat, barley

President – who is elected by the Assembly for seven years – appoints a Prime Minister and a Cabinet commanding a majority in the Assembly. The main political parties are the (conservative) Motherland Party, the Social Democratic Populist Party, the True Path Party, the Prosperity Party and the Democratic Left.
President: Turgut Ozal.
Prime Minister: Suleyman Demirel.

GEOGRAPHY Turkey west of the Dardenelles – 5% of the total area – is part of Europe. Asiatic Turkey consists of the central Anatolian Plateau and its basins, bordered to the north by the Pontic Mountains, to the south by the Taurus Mountains, and to the east in high ranges bordering the Caucasus. *Principal rivers:* Euphrates (Firat), Tigris (Dicle), Kizilirmak (Halys), Sakarya. *Highest point*: Büyük Ağridaği (Mount Ararat) 5185 m (17 011 ft).

ECONOMY Agriculture involves just under one half of the labour force. Major crops include wheat, rice, tobacco, and cotton. Both tobacco and cotton have given rise to important processing industries, and textiles account for one quarter of Turkey's exports. Manufacturing – in particular the chemical and steel industries – has grown rapidly. Natural resources include copper, coal and chromium. Unemployment is severe. Money sent back by the large number of Turks working in Western Europe is a major source of foreign currency. Tourism is increasingly important.

RECENT HISTORY In 1908 the Young Turks revolt attempted to stop the decline of the once-powerful Turkish Ottoman Empire, but defeat in the Balkan Wars (1912–13) virtually expelled Turkey from Europe. Alliance with Germany in World War I ended in defeat and the loss of all non-Turkish areas. The future of Turkey in Asia itself seemed in doubt when Greece took the area around Izmir and the Allies defined zones of influence. General Mustafa Kemal (1881–1938) – later known as Atatürk ('father of the Turks') – led forces of resistance in a civil war and went on to defeat Greece. Turkey's

and vegetables, as well as olives and citrus fruit for export. Tourism is a major foreign-currency earner.

RECENT HISTORY In 1881 France established a protectorate, although the bey (monarch) remained the nominal ruler. Nationalist sentiments grew in the 20th century. Tunisia was occupied by the Germans from 1942 to 1943, but French rule was restored until 1956, when independence was gained under Habib Bourguiba (1903–). In 1957 the monarchy was abolished. In the late 1980s the regime became increasingly unpopular and intolerant of opposition. Since Bourguiba was deposed by his PM (1988) – because of 'incapacity' – multi-party politics have been permitted.

TURKEY

Official name: Türkiye Cumhuriyeti (Republic of Turkey).
Member of: UN, NATO, OECD, CSCE, Council of Europe.
Area: 779 452 km² (300 948 sq mi).
Population: 58 376 000 (1991 est).
Capital and major cities: Ankara 2 560 000, Istanbul 6 620 000, Izmir 1 757 000, Adana 916 000, Bursa 835 000, Gaziantep 603 000, Konya 513 000, Mersin (Icel) 422 000, Kayseri 421 000, Eskisehir 413 000, Diyarbakir 381 000, Antalya 378 000, Samsun 304 000 (all including suburbs; 1990 census).
Languages: Turkish (official); Kurdish (20%).
Religion: Sunni Islam (67%), Shia Islam (30%), various Christian Churches (3%).

GOVERNMENT The 450-member National Assembly is elected by universal adult suffrage for five years. The

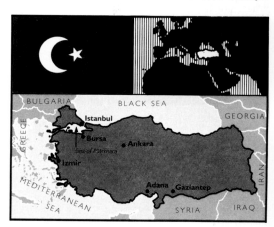

present boundaries were established in 1923 by the Treaty of Lausanne. With the abolition of the sultanate (1922) Turkey became a republic, which Atatürk transformed into a secular Westernized state. Islam was disestablished, Arabic script was replaced by the Latin alphabet, the Turkish language was revived, and women's veils were banned.

Soviet claims on Turkish territory in 1945 encouraged a pro-Western outlook, and in 1952 Turkey joined NATO. PM Adnan Menderes was overthrown by a military coup (1960) and hanged on charges of corruption and unconstitutional rule. Civilian government was restored in 1961, but a pattern of violence and ineffective government led to a further army takeover in 1980. In 1974, after President Makarios was overthrown in Cyprus by a Greek-sponsored coup, Turkey invaded the island and set up a Turkish administration in the north (1975). Differences with Greece over Cyprus have damaged the country's attempts to join the EC, as has the country's record on human rights. In 1983 civilian rule was restored. Since then Turkey has drawn as close as possible to Western Europe, although the emergence of Islamic fundamentalism in the late 1980s has raised doubts concerning Turkey's European identity. Since the dissolution of the USSR (1991), Turkey has forged economic and cultural links with the former Soviet republics of Central Asia, most of which are Turkic in language and tradition. Unrest among Turkey's ethnic Kurds – in the SE – has increased.

TURKMENISTAN

Official name: Tiurkmenostan (Turkmenistan).
Member of: UN, CIS, CSCE.
Area: 488 100 km² (188 500 sq mi).
Population: 3 714 000 (1991 est).

Capital and major cities: Ashkabad 411 000, Chardzhou 166 000 (1989 census).
Languages: Turkmen (72%), Russian (9%), Uzbek (9%), Kazakh (3%).
Religions: Sunni Islam majority.

GOVERNMENT A legislature and a President are elected by universal adult suffrage for four years. A new constitution is to be drafted. The main political parties are the (former Communist) Democratic Party, Agzybirlik, and the Party of Islamic Renaissance, The Democratic Party has a leading role.
President: Saparmuryad Niyazov.
Prime Minister: Khan Akhmedov.

GEOGRAPHY The sandy Kara-Kum Desert occupies the centre of the republic, over 90% of which is desert. The Kopet Dag mountains form the border with Iran. *Principal rivers:* Amu Darya, Murgab. *Highest point:* Firyuza 2942 m (9652 ft).

ECONOMY Turkmenistan is rich in oil and natural gas. Industries include engineering, metal processing and textiles. Collective farms grow cotton under irrigation and raise sheep, camels and horses. The economy remains largely state-owned and centrally planned.

HISTORY The Turkmens are a nomadic Turkic people who were nominally subject to Persia, or to the khans of Khiva and Bukhara (now both in Uzbekistan), before coming under Russian rule between 1869 and 1881. The Turkmens fiercely resisted the Russians and rose in revolt in 1916. An autonomous Transcaspian government was formed after the Russian Revolution (see p. 438), and the area was not brought under Soviet control until the Red Army invaded in 1919. The Turkmen territories were reorganized as the Republic of Turkmenistan in 1924 and admitted to the USSR as a full Union Republic in 1925. Independence was declared following the abortive coup by Communist hardliners in Moscow (September 1991), and the republic received international recognition when the USSR was dissolved (December 1991).

TUVALU

Member of: Commonwealth (special member), South Pacific Forum.
Area: 26 km² (10 sq mi).
Population: 9300 (1991 est).
Capital: Fongafale (on Funafuti) 2800 (1985 est).
Languages: Tuvaluan and English.
Religion: Protestant Church of Tuvalu (98%).

GOVERNMENT The 12-member Parliament – which is elected by universal adult suffrage for four years – chooses a Prime Minister who appoints other Ministers. A Governor General represents the British Queen as sovereign of Tuvalu. There are no political parties.

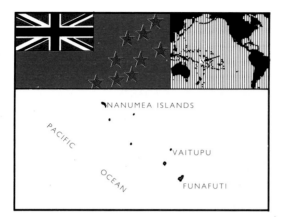

NANUMEA ISLANDS

PACIFIC

VAITUPU

OCEAN

FUNAFUTI

Prime Minister: Bikenibeu Paeniu.

GEOGRAPHY Tuvalu comprises nine small islands. There are no rivers. *Highest point*: an unnamed point, 6 m (20 ft).

ECONOMY Subsistence farming – based on coconuts, pigs and poultry – involves the majority of the population. The only export is copra from coconuts.

RECENT HISTORY Tuvalu was claimed for Britain in 1892 as the Ellice Islands, which became linked administratively with the Gilbert Islands. A referendum in 1974 showed a majority of Polynesians in the Ellice Islands in favour of separation from the Micronesians of the Gilbert Islands (Kiribati). Independence was achieved as Tuvalu in 1978.

UGANDA

Official name: The Republic of Uganda.
Member of: UN, Commonwealth, OAU.
Area: 241 139 km² (93 104 sq mi).
Population: 16 583 000 (1991 census).
Capital: Kampala 773 000, Jinja 61 000, Mbale 54 000, Masaka 49 000, Entebbe 42 000 (1991 census).
Languages: English and Swahili (both official), with local languages including Luganda.
Religions: Roman Catholic (45%), various Protestant Churches (17%), animist (32%), Sunni Islam (6%).

GOVERNMENT The commander of the National Resistance Army – which took power in 1986 – is President. He appoints a Prime Minister and other Ministers. The advisory 278-member National Resistance Council comprises 210 indirectly elected members and 68 members appointed by the President. Political activity has been suspended.

President: Yoweri Museveni.
Prime Minister: George Adyebo.

GEOGRAPHY Most of Uganda is a plateau that ends in the west at the Great Rift Valley and the Ruwenzori Mountains. Lake Victoria covers southeast Uganda. *Principal rivers*: Nile, Semliki. *Highest point*: Ngaliema 5118 m (16 763 ft).

ECONOMY Agriculture involves over three quarters of the labour force. Coffee normally accounts for 90% of Uganda's exports. Subsistence crops include plantains, cassava and sweet potatoes.

SUDAN | ETHIOPIA
Lake Mobutu Sese Seko
Lake Kyoga
ZAIRE | Mbale | KENYA
Kampala | Jinja
Entebbe
Lake Victoria
RWANDA | TANZANIA

RECENT HISTORY The British protectorate of Uganda – established in 1894 – was built around the powerful African kingdom of Buganda, whose continuing special status contributed to the disunity that has plagued the country since independence in 1962. Dr Milton Obote, who suppressed the Buganda monarchy in 1966, was overthrown in a coup by General Idi Amin in 1971. Amin earned international criticism when political and human rights were curtailed, opponents of the regime were murdered and the Asian population was expelled. The army took over in 1979, supported by Tanzanian troops. Obote was restored but was ousted in a military coup in 1985, since when instability and guerrilla action have continued.

UKRAINE

Official name: Ukraina (The Ukraine).
Member of: UN, CIS, CSCE.
Area: 603 700 km² (233 100 sq mi).
Population: 51 944 000 (1991 est).
Capital and major cities: Kiev (Kyiv) 2 587 000, Kharkov (Kharkiv) 1 611 000, Dnepropetrovsk (Dnipropetrovske) 1 179 000, Odessa 1 141 000, Donetsk (Donetske) 1 110 000, Zaporozhye (Zaporizhia) 875 000,

Lvov (Lviv) 767 000, Krivoy Rog (Kryvyi Rih) 698 000 (1989 census).
Languages: Ukrainian (73%), Russian (22%), Belarussian (2%).
Religions: Ukrainian Uniat (Roman Catholic), Ukrainian Autocephalous Orthodox, Russian Orthodox.

GOVERNMENT A 450-member legislature and a President – who appoints a Council of Ministers – are elected for four years by universal adult suffrage. A new constitution is to be drafted. The principal political parties are the former Communist Party, the People's Movement of Ukraine (Rukh), The Republican Party and the Greens.
President: Leonid Kravchuk.
Prime Minister: Leonid Kuchma.

GEOGRAPHY Most of Ukraine – after Russia, the largest country in Europe – comprises plains (steppes), interrupted by low plateaux and basins. The N includes part of the Pripet Marshes; the S is a coastal lowland beside the Black Sea and the Sea of Azov. Central Ukraine comprises the Dnepr Lowland and the Dnepr Plateau, the most extensive upland in the republic. Eastern Ukraine comprises the Don Valley and part of the Central Russian Upland. The most diverse scenery is in the west which includes an extensive lowland and the Carpathian Mountains. The Crimean Peninsula consists of parallel mountain ridges and fertile valleys.
Principal rivers: Dnepr, Don, Dnestr, Donets, Bug.
Highest point: Hoverla 2061 m (6762 ft).

ECONOMY Ukraine was known as the bread basket of the USSR. Large collectivized farms on the steppes grow cereals, fodder crops and vegetables. Potatoes and flax are important in the N; fruit farming (including grapes and market gardening) is widespread, particularly in the Crimea. Natural resources include iron ore, oil, manganese and rock salt, but the vast Donets coalfield is the principal base of Ukraine's industries.

The Ukrainian iron and steel industry is almost as large as that of Russia. Other major industries include consumer goods, heavy engineering (railway locomotives, shipbuilding, generators), food processing, and chemicals and chemical equipment. Within the USSR, Ukraine had surpluses of electricity, cereals and many industrial goods. The first steps in privatization have been taken but the economy faces serious difficulties including rampant inflation and declining industries.

RECENT HISTORY The Ukrainians in Russia took the opportunity afforded by World War I and the Russian Revolution to proclaim independence (January 1918), but a Ukrainian Soviet government was established in Kharkov. Ukraine united with Galicia when the Austro-Hungarian Empire collapsed (November 1918). The new state was invaded by Poland in pursuit of territorial claims and by the Soviet Red Army in support of the Kharkov Soviet. The Red Army prevailed and in 1922 Ukraine became one of the founding republics of the USSR, but the Lvov district of Galicia remained in Polish hands. From 1928, Soviet leader Joseph Stalin instituted purges in Ukraine and a new programme of Russification. After World War II – when Ukraine was occupied by Nazi Germany – Soviet Ukraine was enlarged by the addition of Lvov (from Poland), Bukovina (from Romania), and Ruthenia (from Czechoslovakia), and, finally, Crimea (from Russia) in 1954. Ukrainian nationalism was spurred by the perceived Soviet indifference to Ukraine at the time of the nuclear accident at Chernobyl, N of Kiev, in 1986. Ukrainian politicians responded to the restructuring of the USSR in the late 1980s by seeking increased autonomy. The decision of the republic to declare independence following the abortive coup by Communist hardliners (September 1991) hastened the demise of the USSR. Ukraine gained international recognition in December 1991 when the Soviet Union was dissolved, but tension remained between Moscow and Kiev concerning the allegiance of Soviet forces in Ukraine, and the status of Crimea and the Black Sea fleet.

UNITED ARAB EMIRATES

Official name: Al-Imarat Al'Arabiya Al-Muttahida (The United Arab Emirates).
Member of: UN, Arab League, OPEC, GCC.
Area: 77 700 km² (30 000 sq mi).
Population: 1 945 000 (1991 est).
Capital: Abu Dhabi 243 000, Dubai 266 000, Sharjah 125 000, al'Ayn 102 000 (1985 census).
Languages: Arabic (official); English (commercial).
Religion: Sunni Islam (official).

GOVERNMENT The hereditary rulers of the seven emirates – who are absolute monarchs – form the Supreme Council of Rulers, which elects one of its members as President. The Prime Minister and Council of Ministers are appointed by the President. The Supreme Council appoints a 40-member advisory Federal National Council. There are no political parties.

President: HH Shaikh Zayid bin Sultan Al Nihayyan.
Prime Minister: HH Shaikh Maktum bin Rashid Al Maktum.

EMIRATES   Abu Dhabi *Area*: 67 350 km² (26 000 sq mi). *Population*: 670 000 (1985 census). *Capital*: Abu Dhabi.

Ajman *Area*: 250 km² (100 sq mi). *Population*: 64 000 (1985 census). *Capital*: Ajman.

Dubai *Area*: 3900 km² (1510 sq mi). *Population*: 419 000 (1985 census). *Capital*: Dubai.

Fujairah *Area*: 1150 km² (440 sq mi). *Population*: 54 000 (1985 census). *Capital*: Fujairah.

Ras al-Khaimah *Area*: 1700 km² (660 sq mi). *Population*: 116 000 (1985 census). *Capital*: Ras al-Khaimah.

Sharjah *Area*: 2600 km² (1000 sq mi). *Population*: 269 000 (1985 census). *Capital*: Sharjah.

Umm al-Qaiwain *Area*: 750 km² (290 sq mi). *Population*: 29 000 (1985 census). *Capital*: Umm al-Qaiwain.

GEOGRAPHY The country is a low-lying desert except in the Jajar Mountains in the east. There are no permanent streams. *Highest point*: Al-Hajar 1189 m (3901 ft).

ECONOMY Based upon the export of offshore and onshore reserves of petroleum and natural gas, the country has one of the highest standards of living in the world. Dry docks, fertilizer factories, commercial banking interests, international airports and an entrepôt trade have been developed. Immigrants from the Indian subcontinent and Iran form the majority of the labour force. Agriculture is confined to oases and a few coastal sites irrigated by desalinated water.

RECENT HISTORY During the 19th century, the local rulers on the Gulf coast signed treaties, bringing

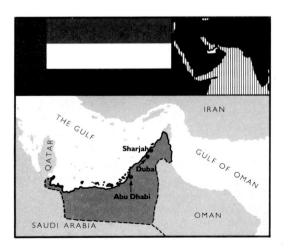

the Trucial States under British protection. In 1958 oil was discovered in Abu Dhabi. In 1968 the Trucial States, Bahrain and Qatar laid the foundations of a federation, but when the British withdrew in 1971 only six states formed the United Arab Emirates. Bahrain and Qatar gained separate independent statehood, while Ras al-Khaimah joined the federation in 1972. The UAE – as members of the GCC – joined the coalition against Saddam Hussein's Iraq (1990–91).

UNITED KINGDOM

Official name: The United Kingdom of Great Britain and Northern Ireland.

Member of: UN, EC, NATO, Commonwealth, G7, OECD, CSCE, Council of Europe.

Area: 244 103 km² (94 249 sq mi).

Population: 57 410 000 (1990 est).

Capital and major cities: London 7 797 000 (London Urban Area – Greater London 6 794 000), Birmingham 2 324 000 (West Midlands Urban Area; city 992 800), Manchester 2 310 000 (Greater Manchester Urban Area; city 446 700), Glasgow 1 650 000 (Central Clydeside Urban Area; city 689 200), Leeds-Bradford 1 547 000 (West Yorkshire Urban Area; Leeds city 712 200, Bradford city 468 800), Newcastle-upon-Tyne 762 000 (Tyneside Urban Area; city 277 800), Liverpool 659 000 (Urban Area; city 462 900), Sheffield 649 000 (Urban Area; city 525 800), Nottingham 615 000 (Urban Area; city 274 900), Bristol 530 000 (Urban Area; city 374 300), Edinburgh 523 000 (Urban Area; city 434 500), Brighton 471 000 (Brighton-Worthing Urban Area; borough 141 200), Portsmouth 453 000 (Urban Area; city 184 100), Belfast 441 000 (Urban Area; city 295 100), Leicester 407 000 (Urban Area; city 278 000), Stoke-on-Trent 371 000 (The Potteries Urban Area; city 246 700), Middlesbrough 368 000 (Teesside Urban Area; borough 141 600), Bournemouth 353 000 (Urban Area; borough 154 000), Coventry 333 000 (Coventry-Bedworth Urban Area; city 303 700), Cardiff 317 000 (Urban Area; city 287 200), Preston 316 000 (Urban Area; borough 128 500), Hull 302 000 (Kingston-upon-Hull Urban Area; city 245 300), Southampton 301 000 (Urban Area: city 197 400), Southend 291 000 (Urban Area; borough 167 300), Swansea 284 000 (Urban Area; city 186 600), Blackpool 283 000 (Urban Area; borough 139 100), Birkenhead 278 000 (Urban Area; town 99 000), Plymouth 253 000 (Urban Area; city 252 800), Rochester 244 000 (The Medway Towns Urban Area; city 149 300), Aldershot 241 000 (Urban Area; Aldershot-with-Farnborough 82 100), Luton 220 000 (Luton-Dunstable Urban Area; borough 171 400), Derby 217 000 (Urban Area; city 217 300), Reading 216 000 (Urban Area; borough 129 900), Aberdeen 216 000 (Urban Area; city 211 100), Sunderland 202 000 (Sunderland-Whitburn Urban Area; part of Sunderland city 296 100), Northampton 185 000 (Urban Area; borough 185 100), Milton Keynes 185 000 (Urban Area; borough 185 000), Norwich 181 000 (Urban Area; city

117 200) (1990 est; the population figures are for Urban Areas – that is, cities and their agglomerations – rather than for local government districts.)

Languages: English, Welsh (21% of the population of Wales, though only 1% of the population of Wales speak Welsh as their first language), Gaelic (under 1% of the population of Scotland).

Religions: Anglican (55% nominal, 4% practising), Roman Catholic (9%), Presbyterian (3%, including Church of Scotland), Methodist (2%), various other Christian Churches (4%), Sunni Islam (2%), Judaism (under 1%).

GOVERNMENT The UK is a constitutional monarchy without a written constitution. The House of Lords – the Upper (non-elected) House of Parliament – comprises over 750 hereditary peers and peeresses, over 20 Lords of Appeal (non-hereditary peers), over 370 life peers, and 2 archbishops and 24 bishops of the Church of England. The House of Commons consists of 651 members elected for five years by universal adult suffrage. The sovereign appoints a Prime Minister who commands a majority in the Commons. The main political parties include the Conservative Party, the Labour Party, the Liberal Democrats and regional parties including the Scottish National Party, the (Welsh Nationalist) Plaid Cymru, the Ulster Unionists, the Democratic Unionist Party and the (Northern Ireland) Social Democratic and Labour Party. The UK comprises four countries – England, Scotland, Wales and Northern Ireland; there is constitutional provision for devolved government for the latter.

Queen: HM Queen Elizabeth II (succeeded upon the death of her father, 6 February 1952).

Prime Minister: John Major.

COUNTRIES OF THE UNITED KINGDOM

England *Area*: 130 441 km² (50 363 sq mi). *Population*: 47 837 300 (1990 est). *Capital*: London.

Northern Ireland *Area*: 14 120 km² (5452 sq mi). *Population*: 1 589 400 (1990 est). *Capital*: Belfast.

Scotland *Area*: 78 775 km² (30 415 sq mi). *Population*: 5 102 400 (1990 est). *Capital*: Edinburgh.

Wales *Area*: 20 768 km² (8019 sq mi). *Population*: 2 881 000 (1990 est). *Capital*: Cardiff.

CROWN DEPENDENCIES The Crown Dependencies are associated with but not part of the UK.

Guernsey (includes Alderney, Sark and smaller dependencies) *Area*: 75 km² (29 sq mi) — Guernsey (island) 63.3 km² (24.5 sq mi); Alderney 7.9 km² (3.07 sq mi); Sark 5.1 km² (1.99 sq mi). *Population*: 57 000 (Guernsey island; 1989 est); Alderney 2000 (1986 est); Sark 600 (1986 est). *Capital*: St Peter Port 18 000 (1986 est). The capital of Alderney is St Anne's. There are no towns or villages on Sark, on which settlement is scattered.

Isle of Man *Area*: 572 km² (221 sq mi). *Population*: 70 000 (1991 census). *Capital*: Douglas 22 000 (1991 census).

Jersey *Area*: 116.2 km² (44.8 sq mi). *Population*: 83 000 (1989 est). *Capital*: St Helier 30 000 (1986 est).

GEOGRAPHY The UK comprises the island of Great Britain, the northeast part of Ireland plus over 4000 other islands. Lowland Britain occupies the south, east and centre of England. Clay valleys and river basins – including those of the Thames and the Trent – separate relatively low ridges of hills, including the limestone Cotswolds and Cleveland Hills, and the chalk North and South Downs and the Yorkshire and Lincolnshire Wolds. In the east, low-lying Fenland is largely reclaimed marshland. The flat landscape of East Anglia is covered by glacial soils. The northwest coastal plain of Lancashire and Cheshire is the only other major lowland in England. A peninsula in the southwest – Devon and Cornwall – contains granitic uplands, including Dartmoor and Exmoor. The limestone Pennines form a moorland backbone running through northern England. The Lake District (Cumbria) is an isolated mountainous dome rising to Scafell Pike, the highest point in England at 978 m (3210 ft).

Wales is a highland block, formed by a series of plateaux above which rise the Brecon Beacons in the south, Cader Idris and the Berwyn range in the centre, and Snowdonia in the north, where Snowdon reaches 1085 m (3560 ft).

In Scotland, the Highlands in the north and the Southern Uplands are separated by the rift valley of the Central Lowlands, where the majority of Scotland's population, agriculture and industry are to be found. The Highlands are divided by the Great Glen in which lies Loch Ness. Although Ben Nevis is the highest point, the most prominent range of the Highlands is the Cairngorm Mountains. The Southern Uplands lie below 853 m (2800 ft). Other Scottish lowlands include Buchan in the northeast, Caithness in the north, and a coastal plain around the Moray Firth. To the west of Scotland are the many islands of the Inner and Outer Hebrides, while to the north are the Orkney and Shetland Islands.

Northern Ireland includes several hilly areas, including the Sperrin Mountains in the northwest, the uplands in County Antrim, and the Mourne Mountains rising to Slieve Donard at 852 m (2796 ft). Lough Neagh – at the centre of Northern Ireland – is the UK's largest lake. *Principal rivers*: Severn, Thames (with Churn), Trent-Humber, Aire (with Ouse), (Great or Bedford) Ouse, Wye, Tay (with Tummel), Nene, Clyde. *Highest point*: Ben Nevis 1392 m (4406 ft).

ECONOMY Over one fifth of the British labour force is involved in manufacturing. The principal industries include iron and steel, motor vehicles, electronics and electrical engineering, textiles and clothing, aircraft, and consumer goods. British industry relies heavily upon imports of raw materials. The country is self-sufficient in petroleum (from the North Sea) and has important reserves of natural gas and coal – although the coal industry is declining as seams in traditional mining areas become uneconomic. As Britain is a major trading nation, London is one of the world's leading banking, financial and insurance centres, and the 'invisible earnings' from these services make an important contribution to exports. Tourism is another major foreign-currency earner. Agriculture (with forestry)

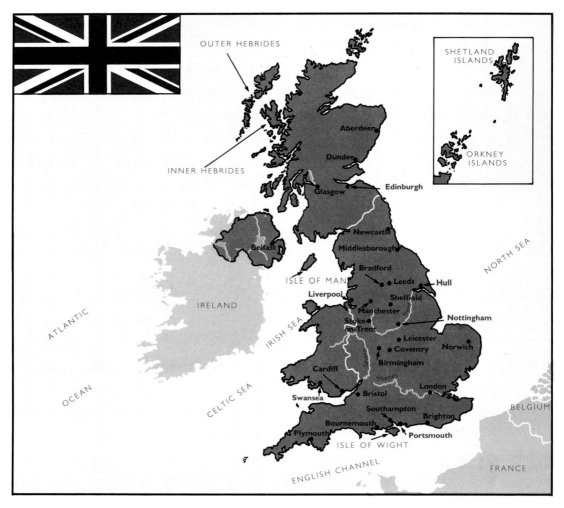

OUTER HEBRIDES

SHETLAND ISLANDS

ORKNEY ISLANDS

Aberdeen

Dundee

INNER HEBRIDES

Glasgow

Edinburgh

Newcastle

Belfast

Middlesborough

Bradford

ISLE OF MAN

Leeds

Hull

Liverpool

Sheffield

Manchester

Nottingham

Stoke-on-Trent

IRELAND

Leicester

Coventry

Norwich

Birmingham

Cardiff

London

Bristol

Swansea

Southampton

Brighton

Bournemouth

Plymouth

Portsmouth

ISLE OF WIGHT

BELGIUM

FRANCE

ATLANTIC

OCEAN

IRISH SEA

CELTIC SEA

NORTH SEA

ENGLISH CHANNEL

involves about 2% of the labour force and is principally concerned with raising sheep and cattle. Arable farming is widespread in the east, where the main crops are barley, wheat, potatoes and sugar beet. Since the 1970s the UK has not experienced the same rate of economic growth as most other West European states. Economic problems have included repeated crises of confidence in the value of the pound, credit squeezes and high (regional) rates of unemployment. Since 1980 most major nationalized industries have been privatized.

RECENT HISTORY By the end of the 19th century the economic dominance Britain had enjoyed since the industrial revolution was beginning to be challenged by the USA and, more particularly, by Germany. Rivalry with Imperial Germany was but one factor contributing to the causes of World War I. PM Herbert Asquith

(1852–1928) led a reforming Liberal Government from 1908 to 1916 but – after criticism of his conduct of the war – he was replaced by David Lloyd George (1863–1945), who as Chancellor of the Exchequer had introduced health and unemployment insurance.

The 'old dominions' – Canada, Australia, New Zealand and South Africa – emerged from the war as autonomous countries, and their independent status was confirmed by the Statute of Westminster (1931). The Easter Rising in Ireland (1916) led to the partition of the island in 1922. Only Northern Ireland – the area with a Protestant majority – stayed within the United Kingdom, but in the 1970s and 1980s bitter conflict resurfaced in the province as Roman Catholic republicans – seeking unity with the Republic of Ireland – clashed with Protestant Loyalists intent upon preserving the link with Britain. British troops were stationed in Northern Ireland to keep order and to defeat the terrorist violence of the IRA.

In World War II Britain – led by PM Sir Winston Churchill (1874–1965), who had strenuously opposed appeasement in the 1930s – played a major role in the defeat of the Axis powers, and from 1940 to 1941 the UK stood alone against an apparently invincible Germany. Following the war, the Labour government of Clement Attlee (1883–1967) established the 'welfare state'. At the same time, the British Empire began its transformation into a Commonwealth of some 50 independent states, starting with the independence of India in 1947. By the late 1980s decolonization was practically complete and Britain was no longer a world power, although a British nuclear deterrent was retained. By the 1970s the United Kingdom was involved in restructuring its domestic economy and, consequently, its welfare state – from 1979 to 1990 under the Conservative premiership of Margaret Thatcher (1925–). The country has also joined (1973) and has attempted to come to terms with the European Community. Under John Major (1943–) – Prime Minister since 1990 – the UK participated in the coalition against Iraq in the Second Gulf War (1991).

UK DEPENDENCIES

Anguilla *Area*: 96 km² (37 sq mi) – Anguilla 91 km² (35 sq mi); Sombrero 5 km² (2 sq mi). *Population*: 6900 (all on Anguilla; 1989 est). *Capital*: The Valley 500 (1988 est).

Bermuda *Area*: 54 km² (21 sq mi). *Population*: 60 000 (1990 est). *Capital*: Hamilton 6000 (1990 est).

British Antarctic Territory see Other Territories, following this chapter.

British Indian Ocean Territory *Area*: 60 km² (23 sq mi). *Population*: no civilian population; 2900 military personnel (1991 est).

British Virgin Islands *Area*: 153 km² (59 sq mi). *Population*: 16 600 (1991 census). *Capital*: Road Town 2500 (1991 census).

Cayman Islands *Area*: 259 km² (100 sq mi). *Population*: 25 500 (1989 census). *Capital*: George Town 12 900 (1989 census).

Falkland Islands *Area*: 12 170 km² (4698 sq mi). *Population*: 2100 (1991 census). *Capital*: Port Stanley 1300 (1991 census).

Gibraltar *Area*: 6·5 km² (2·5 sq mi). *Population*: 31 000 (1990 est). *Capital*: Gibraltar 31 000 (1990 est).

Hong Kong *Area*: 1045 km² (403 sq mi). *Population*: 5 674 000 (1991 census). *Capital*: Victoria (part of the Hong Kong agglomeration) 1 251 000 (1991 census).

Montserrat *Area*: 98 km² (38 sq mi). *Population*: 12 400 (1989 est). *Capital*: Plymouth 1500 (1989 est).

Pitcairn Islands *Area*: 48 km² (18·5 sq mi). *Population*: 52 (1990 est). *Capital*: Adamstown 52 (1990 est).

St Helena and Dependencies *Area*: 419 km² (162 sq mi) – St Helena 12 km² (47 sq mi), Ascension 88 km ² (34 sq mi), Tristan da Cunha Group 209 km² (81 sq mi). *Population*: 7100 (1991 est) – St Helena 5600 (1991 est), Ascension 1100 (1991 census), Tristan da Cunha 300 (1990 census). *Capital*: Jamestown (St Helena) 1400 (1987

census); the capital of Ascension is Georgetown; the capital of Tristan da Cunha is Edinburgh.

South Georgia and South Sandwich Islands *Area*: 4091 km² (1580 sq mi). *Population*: no permanent population. *Settlement*: Grytviken.

Turks and Caicos Islands *Area*: 430 km² (166 sq mi). *Population*: 12 400 (1990 census). *Capital*: Cockburn Town (on Grand Turk) 2500 (1990 census).

UNITED STATES OF AMERICA

Member of: UN, NATO, OAS, CSCE, G7, NAFTA.

Population: 252 177 000 (1991 est).

Area: 9 372 614 km² (3 618 770 sq mi).

Capital and major cities: Washington D.C. 3 924 000 (city 598 000), New York 18 087 000 (city 7 323 000, Newark 275 000), Los Angeles 14 532 000 (city 3 485 000, Long Beach 429 000, Anaheim 266 000), Chicago 8 066 000 (city 2 784 000), San Francisco 6 253 000, (city 724 000, San Jose 782 000, Oakland 372 000), Philadelphia 5 899 000 (city 1 586 000), Detroit 4 665 000 (city 1 028 000), Boston 4 172 000 (city 574 000), Dallas 3 885 000 (city 1 007 000; Fort Worth 478 000), Houston 3 711 000 (city 1 631 000), Miami 3 193 000 (city 359 000), Atlanta 2 834 000 (city 394 000), Cleveland 2 760 000 (city 506 000), Seattle 2 559 000 (city 516 000), San Diego 2 498 000 (city 1 111 000), Minneapolis – St Paul 2 464 000 (city 368 000; St Paul 272 000), St Louis 2 444 000 (city 397 000), Baltimore 2 382 000 (city 736 000), Pittsburgh 2 243 000 (city 370 000), Phoenix 2 122 000 (city 983 000), Tampa 2 068 000 (city 280 000), Denver 1 848 000 (city 468 000), Cincinnati 1 744 000 (city 364 000), Milwaukee 1 607 000 (city 628 000), Kansas City 1 566 000 (city 435 000), Sacramento 1 481 000 (city 369 000), Portland 1 478 000 (city 437 000), Norfolk 1 396 000 (city 261 000, Columbus 1 377 000 (city 633 000), San Antonio 1 302 000 (city 936 000), Indianapolis 1 250 000 (city 742 000), New Orleans 1 239 000 (city 497 000), Buffalo 1 189 000 (city 328 000), Charlotte 1 162 000 (city 396 000), Providence 1 142 000 (city 161 000), Hartford 1 086 000 (city 140 000), Orlando 1 073 000 (city 165 000), Salt Lake City 1 072 000 (city 160 000), Rochester 1 002 000 (city 232 000), Nashville 985 000 (city 511 000), Memphis 982 000 (city 610 000), Oklahoma City 959 000 (city 445 000), Louisville 953 000 (city 269 000), Dayton 951 000 (city 182 000), Greensboro 942 000 (city 184 000), Birmingham 908 000 (city 266 000), Jacksonville 907 000 (city 673 000), Albany 874 000 (city 101 000), Richmond 866 000 (city 203 000), West Palm Beach 864 000 (city 365 000), Honolulu 836 000 (city 365 000), Austin 782 000 (city 466 000), Las Vegas 741 000 (city 258 000), Raleigh 735 000 (city 208 000), Scranton 734 000 (city 82 000), Tulsa 709 000 (city 367 000) (all including suburbs; 1990 census).

Languages: English (official), Spanish (6%, as a first language).

Religions: Roman Catholic (23%), Baptist (10%), Methodist (5%), Lutheran (3%), Judaism (2%), Orthodox (2%), Presbyterian (2%), Mormons (2%).

GOVERNMENT Congress comprises the Senate (the Upper House) and the House of Representatives (the Lower House). The Senate has 100 members – two from each state – elected by universal adult suffrage for six years, with one third of the senators retiring every two years. The 435-member House of Representatives is directly elected for a two-year term from single-member constituencies. Additional non-voting members of the House are returned by the District of Columbia, Guam, Puerto Rico, United States Virgin Islands and American Samoa. Executive federal power is vested in the President, who serves a maximum of two four-year terms. Presidential candidates submit to a series of 'state primary' elections to enable individual parties to select a preferred candidate. The President and Vice President are elected by an electoral college of delegates pledged to support individual presidential candidates – the college itself is elected by universal adult suffrage. Upon the approval of the Senate, the President appoints a Cabinet of Secretaries. Each of the 50 states has a separate constitution and legislature with wide-ranging powers. Executive power in each state is held by a Governor who is elected by direct popular vote. The main political parties are the Democratic Party and the Republican Party.

President: William Jefferson Clinton.

AMERICAN STATES Population figures for the states are 1991 estimates.

Alabama *Area:* 133 915 km² (51 705 sq mi). *Population:* 4 089 000. *Capital:* Montgomery.

Alaska *Area:* 1 530 693 km² (591 004 sq mi). *Population:* 570 000. *Capital:* Juneau 20 000.

Arizona *Area:* 295 259 km² (114 000 sq mi). *Population:* 3 750 000. *Capital:* Phoenix.

Arkansas *Area:* 137 754 km² (53 187 sq mi). *Population:* 2 372 000. *Capital:* Little Rock.

California *Area:* 411 047 km² (158 706 sq mi). *Population:* 30 380 000. *Capital:* Sacramento.

Colorado *Area:* 269 594 km² (104 091 sq mi). *Population:* 3 377 000. *Capital:* Denver.

Connecticut *Area:* 12 997 km² (5018 sq mi). *Population:* 3 291 000. *Capital:* Hartford.

Delaware *Area:* 5292 km² (2044 sq mi). *Population:* 680 000. *Capital:* Dover.

Florida *Area:* 151 939 km² (58 664 sq mi). *Population:* 13 277 000. *Capital:* Tallahassee.

Georgia *Area:* 152 576 km² (58 910 sq mi). *Population:* 6 623 000. *Capital:* Atlanta.

Hawaii *Area:* 16 760 km² (6471 sq mi). *Population:* 1 135 000. *Capital:* Honolulu.

Idaho *Area:* 216 430 km² (83 564 sq mi). *Population:* 1 039 000. *Capital:* Boise City.

Illinois *Area:* 149 885 km² (57 871 sq mi). *Population:* 11 543 000. *Capital:* Springfield.

Indiana *Area:* 94 309 km² (36 413 sq mi). *Population:* 5 610 000. *Capital:* Indianapolis.

Iowa *Area:* 145 752 km² (56 275 sq mi). *Population:* 2 795 000. *Capital:* Des Moines.

Kansas *Area:* 213 096 km² (82 277 sq mi). *Population:* 2 495 000. *Capital:* Topeka.

Kentucky *Area:* 104 659 km² (40 409 sq mi). *Population:* 3 713 000. *Capital:* Frankfort.

Louisiana *Area:* 123 677 km² (47 752 sq mi). *Population:* 4 252 000. *Capital:* Baton Rouge.

Maine *Area:* 86 156 km² (33 265 sq mi). *Population:* 1 235 000. *Capital:* Augusta.

Maryland *Area:* 27 091 km² (10 460 sq mi). *Population:* 4 860 000. *Capital:* Annapolis.

Massachusetts *Area:* 21 455 km² (8284 sq mi). *Population:* 5 996 000. *Capital:* Boston.

Michigan *Area:* 251 493 km² (97 102 sq mi). *Population:* 9 368 000. *Capital:* Lansing.

Minnesota *Area:* 224 329 km² (86 614 sq mi). *Population:* 4 432 000. *Capital:* St Paul.

Mississippi *Area:* 123 514 km² (47 689 sq mi). *Population:* 2 592 000. *Capital:* Jackson.

Missouri *Area:* 180 514 km² (69 697 sq mi). *Population:* 5 158 000. *Capital:* Jefferson City.

Montana *Area:* 380 847 km² (147 046 sq mi). *Population:* 808 000. *Capital:* Helena.

Nebraska *Area:* 200 349 km² (77 355 sq mi). *Population:* 1 593 000. *Capital:* Lincoln.

Nevada *Area:* 286 352 km² (110 561 sq mi). *Population:* 1 284 000. *Capital:* Carson City.

New Hampshire *Area:* 24 023 km² (9279 sq mi). *Population:* 1 105 000. *Capital:* Concord.

New Jersey *Area:* 20 168 km² (7787 sq mi). *Population:* 7 760 000. *Capital:* Trenton.

New Mexico *Area:* 314 924 km² (121 593 sq mi). *Population:* 1 548 000. *Capital:* Santa Fe.

New York *Area:* 136 583 km² (52 735 sq mi). *Population:* 18 058 000. *Capital:* Albany.

North Carolina *Area:* 136 412 km² (52 669 sq mi). *Population:* 6 737 000. *Capital:* Raleigh.

North Dakota *Area:* 183 117 km² (70 702 sq mi). *Population:* 635 000. *Capital:* Bismarck.

Ohio *Area:* 115 998 km² (44 787 sq mi). *Population:* 10 939 000. *Capital:* Columbus.

Olkahoma *Area:* 181 185 km² (69 956 sq mi). *Population:* 3 175 000. *Capital:* Oklahoma City.

Oregon *Area:* 251 418 km² (97 073 sq mi). *Population:* 2 922 000. *Capital:* Salem.

Pennsylvania *Area:* 119 251 km² (46 043 sq mi). *Population:* 11 961 000. *Capital:* Harrisburg.

Rhode Island *Area:* 3139 km² (1212 sq mi). *Population:* 1 004 000. *Capital:* Providence.

South Carolina *Area:* 80 582 km² (31 113 sq mi). *Population:* 3 560 000. *Capital:* Columbia.

South Dakota *Area:* 199 730 km² (77 116 sq mi). *Population:* 703 000. *Capital:* Pierre.

Tennessee *Area:* 109 152 km² (42 144 sq mi). *Population:* 4 953 000. *Capital:* Nashville.

Texas *Area:* 691 027 km² (266 807 sq mi). *Population:* 17 349 000. *Capital:* Austin.

Utah *Area:* 219 887 km² (84 899 sq mi). *Population:*

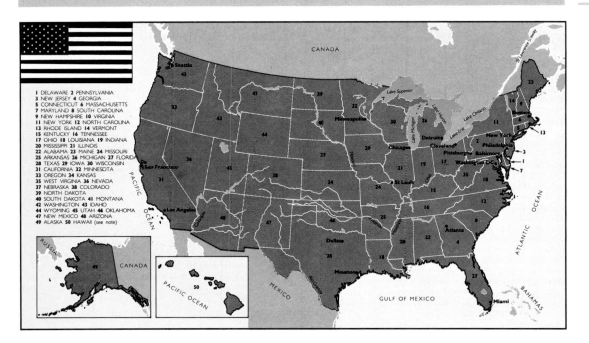

1 770 000. *Capital:* Salt Lake City.

Vermont *Area:* 24 900 km² (9614 sq mi). *Population:* 567 000. *Capital:* Montpelier.

Virginia *Area:* 105 586 km² (40 767 sq mi). *Population:* 6 286 000. *Capital:* Richmond.

Washington *Area:* 176 479 km² (68 139 sq mi). *Population:* 5 018 000. *Capital:* Olympia.

West Virginia *Area:* 62 758 km² (24 231 sq mi). *Population:* 1 801 000. *Capital:* Charleston.

Wisconsin *Area:* 171 496 km² (66 215 sq mi). *Population:* 4 955 000. *Capital:* Madison.

Wyoming *Area:* 253 324 km² (97 809 sq mi). *Population:* 460 000. *Capital:* Cheyenne.

FEDERAL DISTRICT   District of Columbia *Area:* 179 km² (69 sq mi). *Population:* 598 000. *Capital:* Washington.

GEOGRAPHY The Atlantic coastal plain stretches along the entire east coast, including the lowland peninsula of Florida, and along the coast of the Gulf of Mexico, where it reaches up to 800 km (500 mi) inland. The Blue Ridge escarpment rises sharply to the west of the plain. This is the most easterly part of the forested Appalachian Mountains, which stretch north – south for some 2400 km (1500 mi) and reach 2037 m (6684 ft) at Mount Mitchell. The largest physical region of the USA is a vast interior plain drained by the Mississippi and major tributaries, including the Missouri, Arkansas, Nebraska, Ohio and Red River. This lowland stretches from the Great Lakes in the north to the coastal plain in

the south, and from the Rocky Mountains in the west to the Appalachians in the east. The Central Lowlands – the eastern part of the lowland – comprise the Cotton Belt in the south and the Corn (maize) Belt in the north. The Great Plains – the drier western part of the lowland – begin some 480 km (300 mi) west of the Mississippi. The west of the USA is the country's highest region and includes the Rocky Mountains in the east and the Cascades, the Sierra Nevada and the Coastal Ranges in the west. The mountains continue north through Canada into Alaska. The western mountainous belt is prone to earthquakes, in particular along the line of the San Andreas Fault in California. Within the mountains are deserts – including the Mojave and the Arizona Deserts – and the large Intermontane Plateau containing the Great Basin, an area of internal drainage around the Great Salt Lake. The 20 islands of Hawaii – in the Pacific – are volcanic in origin and contain active volcanoes. The USA's natural vegetation ranges from tundra in Alaska to the tropical vegetation of Hawaii, and includes coniferous forest in the northwest, Mediterranean scrub in southern California, steppe and desert in the Intermontane Plateau, and prairie grasslands on the Great Plains. *Principal rivers:* Mississippi (with Missouri and Red Rock), Rio Grande, Yukon (with Nisutlin), Arkansas, Colorado, Ohio (with Allegheny), Red River, Columbia. *Highest point:* Mount McKinley 6194 m (20 320 ft) in Alaska.

ECONOMY The position of the USA as the world's leading economic power is threatened by Japan. The USA is self-sufficient in most products apart from petroleum, chemicals, certain metals and manufactured machinery, and newsprint. Agriculture is heavily mechanized and produces considerable surpluses for export. The main crops include maize, wheat, soyabeans, sugar cane, barley, cotton, potatoes and a wide variety of fruit (including citrus fruit in Florida and California). More than one quarter of the USA is pastureland, and cattle and sheep are important in the Great Plains. Forests cover over 30% of the country and are the basis of the world's second largest timber industry. The USA has great natural resources, including coal (mainly in the Appalachians), iron ore, petroleum and natural gas (mainly in Texas, Alaska and California), copper, bauxite, lead, silver, zinc, molybdenum, tungsten, mercury and phosphates, and major rivers that have proved suitable for hydroelectric power plants. The industrial base of the USA is diverse. Principal industries include iron and steel, motor vehicles, electrical and electronic engineering, food processing, chemicals, cement, aluminium, aerospace industries, telecommunications, textiles and clothing, and a wide range of consumer goods. Tourism is a major foreign-currency earner. Service industries involve over three quarters of the labour force. Finance, insurance and banking are important, and Wall Street (New York) is one of the world's major stock exchanges. US economic policy exerts an influence throughout the world; thus a revival of pressure for trade protectionism in the late 1980s and the early 1990s caused international concern.

RECENT HISTORY Between 1880 and 1900 the USA emerged as an industrial giant. At the same time, the population increased dramatically as immigrants flocked to the New World, in particular from Germany, Eastern Europe and Russia. Interest in world trade increased American involvement abroad. The Cuban revolt against Spanish rule led the USA into a war against Spain (1898) and brought US rule to the Philippines, Puerto Rico and Guam. American participation in World War I from 1917 hastened the Allied victory, but the idealistic principles favoured by President Woodrow Wilson (1856–1924) were compromised in the post-war settlement.

After the war the USA retreated into isolationism and protectionism in trade. The imposition of Prohibition (1919–33) increased smuggling and the activities of criminal gangs, but the 1920s were prosperous until the Depression began in 1929 with the collapse of the stock market. Federal investment and intervention brought relief through the New Deal programme of President Franklin Roosevelt (1882–1945). The Japanese attack on Pearl Harbor brought the USA into World War II (1941). American involvement in the European and Pacific theatres of war was decisive and committed the USA to a world role as a superpower in 1945. US assistance was instrumental in rebuilding Europe (through the Marshall Plan) and Japan.

From the late 1940s to the end of the 1980s, the USA confronted the Soviet Union's perceived global threat in the Cold War. As the leader of the Western alliance, the USA established bases in Europe, the Far East and the Indian and Pacific Oceans, so encircling the Soviet bloc. The USA was involved in the Korean War (1950–53)

against Chinese and North Korean forces, and in direct military intervention in Guatemala (1954), Lebanon (1958 and 1983–85), the Dominican Republic (1965), Panama (1968 and 1989) and Grenada (1983). The greatest commitment, however, was in Vietnam, where from 1964 to 1973 US forces attempted to hold back a Communist takeover of Indochina, but a growing disenchantment with the war forced an American withdrawal.

From the 1950s the civil rights movement – led by Martin Luther King (1929–68) – campaigned for full political rights for blacks and for desegregation of schools, hospitals, buses, etc. In the early 1960s President John F. Kennedy (1917–63) made racial discrimination illegal. Kennedy supported the unsuccessful invasion of Cuba by right-wing exiles (1961), successfully pressured the USSR to withdraw its missiles from Cuba (1962), and was assassinated in 1963. Growing economic problems in the 1970s led to the election of a monetarist President, Ronald Reagan (1911–   ), in 1981. The USA continued to support movements and governments perceived as being in the Western interest – for example, backing Israel in the Middle East and providing weapons to the UNITA guerrillas in Angola and the Contra guerrillas in Nicaragua. However, the increasing economic challenge from Japan, and the collapse of Soviet power in Eastern Europe in 1989, raised questions about the USA's future world role. Early in 1990 President George Bush (1924–   ) announced plans to close certain overseas bases, but later in the same year he organized the international coalition against Iraq after the invasion of Kuwait. American forces played a major role in the massive but short air and ground war (January to February 1991) that liberated Kuwait. In 1992, American forces led relief efforts in Somalia.

US DEPENDENCIES Commonwealth Territories in Association with the USA
North Mariana Islands *Area*: 471 km² (184 sq mi). *Population*: 43 300 (1990 census). *Capital*: Chalan Kanoa (on Saipan). (Saipan had a population of 17 200 in 1985.)
Puerto Rico *Area*: 9104 km² (3515 sq mi). *Population*: 3 522 000 (199o census). *Capital*: San Juan 1 836 000 (city 438 000; 1990 census).

US External Territories
American Samoa *Area*: 197 km² (76 sq mi). *Population*: 47 000 (1990 est). *Capital*: Pago Pago 3100 (1990 est).
Guam *Area*: 541 km² (209 sq mi). *Population*: 133 000 (1990 census). *Capital*: Agaña 43 000 (city 1100; 1990 est).
Palau (Belau) *Area*: 497 km² (192 sq mi). *Population*: 15 100 (1990 census). *Capital*: Koror 10 500 (1990 census).
Virgin Islands of the United States *Area*: 352 km² (136 sq mi). *Population*: 102 000 (1990 census). *Capital*: Charlotte Amalie 12 300 (1990 census).

Territory administered by US Fish and Wildlife Service
Howland, Baker and Jarvis Islands *Area:* 5 km² (2 sq mi). Uninhabited.

Territories administered by US Department of Defense

Johnston Atoll *Area*: under 1 km² (0.5 sq mi). *Population*: 330 service personnel (1990 est). No permanent population.

Kingman Reef *Area*: 0.03 km² (0.01 sq mi). Uninhabited.

Midway Islands *Area*: 5 km² (2 sq mi). *Population*: 450 service personnel (1990 est). No permanent population.

Wake Island *Area*: 8 km² (3 sq mi). *Population*: 300 service personnel (1990 est). No permanent population.

URUGUAY

Official name: La República Oriental del Uruguay (The Eastern Republic of Uruguay).

Member of: UN, OAS, ALADI, Mercosur.

Area: 176 215 km² (68 037 sq mi).

Population: 3 112 000 (1991 est.).

Capital and major cities: Montevideo 1 312 000 (including suburbs), Salto 80 000, Paysandú 76 000, Las Piedras (part of the Montevideo agglomeration) 58 000, Rivera 57 000 (1985 census).

Language: Spanish (official).

Religions: Roman Catholic (58%), various Protestant Churches.

GOVERNMENT The President and Congress – consisting of a 31-member Senate and a 99-member Chamber of Deputies – are elected for four years by universal adult suffrage. The President appoints a Council of Ministers. The main political parties are the (conservative) National Blanco Party, the (centre) Colorado Party, and the (left-wing coalition) Broad Front.

President: Luis Alberto Lacalle.

GEOGRAPHY Uruguay consists mainly of low undulating plains and plateaux. The only significant ranges of hills are in the southeast. *Principal rivers:* Río Negro, Uruguay, Yi. *Highest point:* Cerro de las Animas 500 m (1643 ft).

ECONOMY Pastureland – for sheep and beef cattle – covers about 80% of the land. Meat, wool and hides are the leading exports. Despite a lack of natural resources, Uruguay has a high standard of living. However, the country faces economic difficulties as a result of high inflation and the financial demands of a large public sector and social security system.

RECENT HISTORY From independence (1828) until 1903 Uruguay was ruled by dictators and wracked by civil war. However, prosperity from cattle and wool, and the presidencies of the reformer José Battle (1903–7 and 1911–15), turned Uruguay into a democracy and an advanced welfare state. A military dictatorship held power during the Depression. By the late 1960s severe economic problems had ushered in a period of social and political turmoil, and urban guerrillas became active. In 1973 a coup installed a military dictatorship that made Uruguay notorious for abuses of human rights. In 1985 the country returned to democratic rule.

UZBEKISTAN

Official name: Ozbekiston (Uzbekistan).

Member of: UN, CIS, CSCE.

Area: 447 400 km² (172 700 sq mi).

Population: 20 708 000 (1991 est.).

Capital and major cities: Tashkent 2 079 000, Samarkand 388 000, Namangan 291 000, Andizhan 288 000 (1989 census).

Languages: Uzbek (71%), Russian (8%), Tajiks (5%), Kazakhs (4%).

Religions: Sunni Islam majority.

GOVERNMENT A 500-member legislature and a President are elected for four years by universal adult suffrage. A new constitution is to be drafted. The main political parties are the (former Communist) People's Democratic Party, Birlik (Unity) and Erk (Freedom).

President: Islam A. Karimov.

Prime Minister: Abdulhashim Mutalov.

GEOGRAPHY Western Uzbekistan is flat and mainly desert. The mountainous E includes ridges of the Tien Shan and part of the Fergana valley. *Principal rivers:* Amu Darya, Kara Darya. *Highest point:* Bannovka 4488 m.

ECONOMY Uzbekistan is one the world's leading producers of cotton, but the extraction of irrigation from the Amu Darya and its tributaries has contributed to the gradual shrinkage of the Aral Sea. The republic has

important reserves of natural gas and major machine and heavy engineering industries. The economy is still mainly state-owned and centrally planned.

RECENT HISTORY The Uzbeks did not finally come under Russian rule until the khans of Bukhara and Khiva became vassals of the Tsar (1868–73). After the Russian Revolution, the Basmachi revolt (1918–22) resisted Soviet rule, but the khans were eventually deposed (1920) and Soviet republics established (1923–4). Uzbekistan was created in 1924 when the USSR reorganized the boundaries of Soviet Central Asia. Independence was declared after the abortive coup in Moscow by Communist hardliners (September 1991) and international recognition was achieved when the USSR was dissolved (December 1991).

VANUATU

Official name: The Republic of Vanuatu or La République de Vanuatu.

Member of: UN, Commonwealth, South Pacific Forum.

Area: 12 189 km² (4706 sq mi).

Population: 150 000 (1991 est).

Capital: Port-Vila 19 000, Luganville 7000 (1989 census).

Languages: English (official; 60%), French (official; 40%), Bislama (national; 82% as a first language), and 130 other local dialects.

Religions: Presbyterian (33%), Anglican (30%), animist (20%), Roman Catholic (17%).

GOVERNMENT The 46-member Parliament is elected for four years by universal adult suffrage. It elects a Prime Minister who appoints a Council of Ministers. The President is elected for five years by Parliament and the Presidents of Regional Councils.

The main political parties include the (socialist) Vanuaaku Pati, the Union of Moderate Parties, the National United Party, the Melanesian Progressive Party and a number of regional parties.

President: Fred Timakata.
Prime Minister: Maxim Carlot.

GEOGRAPHY Vanuatu comprises over 75 islands, some of which are mountainous and include active volcanoes. There are no significant rivers. *Highest point:* Mt Tabwebesana 1888 m (6195 ft).

ECONOMY Subsistence farming occupies the majority of the labour force. The main exports include copra, fish and cocoa. Tourism is increasingly important.

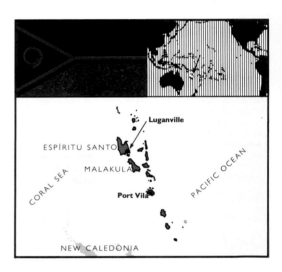

RECENT HISTORY British and French commercial interests in the 19th century resulted in joint control over the islands – then known as the New Hebrides – and the establishment of a condominium in 1906. The islands gained independence as Vanuatu in 1980, but have been troubled by attempted secession and political unrest.

VATICAN CITY

Official name: Stato della Città del Vaticano (State of the Vatican City). Also known as the Holy See.

Member of: CSCE, UN (observer).

Area: 0.44 km² (0.17 sq mi).

Population: 750 (1989 est).

Languages: Italian and Latin (both official).

Religion: The Vatican is the headquarters of the Roman Catholic Church.

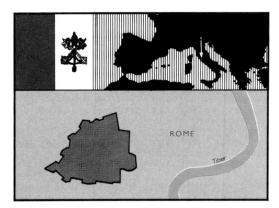

GOVERNMENT The Pope is elected Bishop of Rome and head of the Roman Catholic Church for life by the Sacred College of Cardinals. The administration of the Vatican City is in the hands of a Pontifical Commission appointed by the Pope.

Pope: HH (His Holiness) Pope John Paul II (elected 16 October 1978).

GEOGRAPHY The state consists of the Vatican City, a walled enclave on the west bank of the River Tiber in Rome, plus a number of churches in Rome (including the cathedral of St John Lateran) and the papal villa at Castelgandolfo.

RECENT HISTORY The tiny Vatican City state is all that remains of the once extensive Papal States. When the French troops protecting the Pope were withdrawn in 1870, Italian forces entered Rome, which became the capital of the new kingdom of Italy. Pope Pius IX (reigned 1846–78) protested at the loss of his temporal power and retreated into the Vatican, from which no Pope emerged until 1929, when the Lateran Treaties provided for Italian recognition of the Vatican City as an independent state. Since the 1960s the Papacy has again played an important role in international diplomacy, particularly under Popes Paul VI (reigned 1963–78) and John Paul II (1978–).

VENEZUELA

Official name: La República de Venezuela (Republic of Venezuela).

Member of: UN, OAS, ALADI, Andean Pact.

Area: 912 050 km² (352 144 sq mi).

Population: 20 226 000 (1991 est).

Capital and major cities: Caracas 3 436 000, Maracaibo 1 401 000, Valencia 1 274 000, Maracay 957 000, Barquisimeto 787 000, Ciudad Guayana 543 000 (all including suburbs; 1990 est).

Language: Spanish (official; 98%), various Amerindian languages (2%).

Religion: Roman Catholic (92%).

GOVERNMENT The President and both Houses of the National Congress are elected for five years by universal adult suffrage. The Senate – the upper House – comprises 49 elected senators, plus former Presidents and additional senators to represent minority parties. The Chamber of the Deputies has 200 directly elected members. The President appoints a Council of Ministers. The main political parties are AD (Democratic Action), COPEI (the Social Christian Party), and the (left-wing) Radical Cause Party.

President: Carlos Perez.

GEOGRAPHY Mountains in the north include the north-south Eastern Andes and the Maritime Andes, which run parallel to the Caribbean coast. Central Venezuela comprises low-lying grassland plains (the Llanos). The Guiana Highlands in the southeast include many high steep-sided plateaux. *Principal rivers:* Orinoco, Rio Meta, Coroni, Apure. *Highest point:* Pico Bolivar 5007 m (16 423 ft).

ECONOMY Petroleum and natural gas normally account for over 80% of export earnings. Consequently, the fall in petroleum prices in the early 1990s deepened the effects of the worldwide recession in Venezuela. High rates of inflation add to the economic problems. Agriculture is mainly concerned with raising beef cattle, and growing sugar cane and coffee for export; bananas, maize and rice are grown as subsistence crops.

RECENT HISTORY For most of the early 20th century Venezuela has suffered a series of military

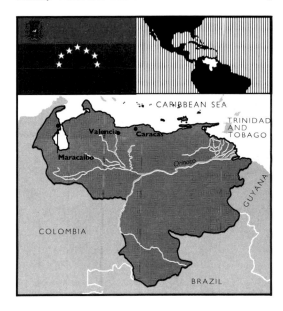

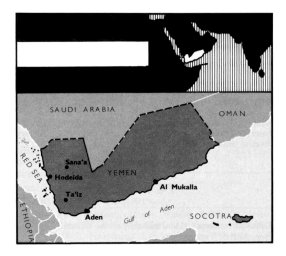

reserves are small by Middle Eastern standards. Money sent back by Yemenis working in Saudi Arabia is an important source of revenue.

RECENT HISTORY The Ottoman Turks were expelled from the north in 1911, when Imam Yahya secured (North) Yemen's independence. In the south, Britain ruled Aden and had established a protectorate over the 20 sultanates inland. Tension grew in the Aden Protectorate in 1959 when Britain created a federation of the feudal sultanates and the city of Aden. In 1963 an armed rebellion began against British rule. After much bloodshed – and a civil war between two rival liberation movements – independence was gained in 1967 as South Yemen. In (North) Yemen, a republican revolution broke out in 1962, and from 1963 until 1970 a bloody civil war was fought, with President Nasser's Egypt supporting the victorious republicans and Saudi Arabia supporting the royalists. Marxist South Yemen became an ally of the USSR and was frequently in conflict with North Yemen, although eventual union of the two Yemens was the objective of both states. The collapse of the Communist regimes in Eastern Europe and the end of considerable Soviet aid (1989–90) hastened the collapse of South Yemen's weak economy, and the two countries merged in May 1990.

YUGOSLAVIA

Official name: Federativna Republika Jugoslavija (The Federal Republic of Yugoslavia).

Member of: UN (suspended), CSCE (suspended).

Area: 102 173 km² (39 449 sq mi).

Population: 10 407 000 (1991 census).

Capital and major cities: Belgrade (Beograd) 1 555 000 (city 1 500 000), Novi Sad 260 000 (city 179 000), Nis 230 000 (city 176 000), Pristina 210 000, Subotica 155 000 (city 100 000), Podgorica 130 000 (city 118 000) (1991 census).

Languages: Serbo-Croat (including Montenegrin; 80%) Albanian (13%), Hungarian (4%).

Religions: Orthodox (over 75%), Sunni Islam (over 12%), small Roman Catholic minority.

GOVERNMENT Under the terms of a new federal constitution (April 1992), Yugoslavia consists of two equal republics – Serbia and Montenegro. A Federal Assembly and a Federal President are elected by universal adult suffrage. The President appoints a Prime Minister and a Council of Ministers. The republics have their own legislatures with considerable powers – the Serbian presidency has assumed virtual sovereign powers. The main political parties include the (former Communist) Socialist Party of Serbia, the (former Communist Montenegrin) Democratic Party of Socialists, the Alliance of Reform Forces for Montenegro, the (right-wing) Serbian Renaissance Movement, and the National Peasants' Party.

President: Dobrica Cosic.

Prime Minister: Radoje Kontic.

REPUBLICS Montenegro (Crna Gora) *Area*: 13 812 km² (5333 sq mi). *Population*: 615 000 (1991 census). *Capital*: Podgorica (formerly Titograd).

Serbia (Srbija) (includes the formerly autonomous provinces of Kosovo and Vojvodina) *Area*: 88 361 km² (34 116 sq mi). *Population*: 9 791 000 (1991 census). *Capital*: Belgrade.

GEOGRAPHY Ridges of mountains occupy the south and centre of the country. The north (Vojvodina) is occupied by plains drained by the rivers Danube and Tisa. Since the secession of Croatia, Slovenia, Bosnia and Macedonia, the Yugoslav coastline is confined to a short stretch on the Adriatic in Montenegro. *Principal rivers:* Danube, Tisa, Morava, Drina. *Highest point:* Titov Vrh 2747 m (9012 ft).

ECONOMY Agriculture involves about one quarter of the labour force. Most of the land is privately owned. Major crops include maize, wheat, sugar beet, grapes, potatoes, citrus fruit and fodder crops for sheep. Industry – which is mainly concentrated around Belgrade – includes food processing, textiles, metallurgy, motor vehicles and consumer goods. The country's economy was severely damaged by the civil wars that began in 1991, by rampant inflation – over 20 000% in 1992 – and by international sanctions imposed upon Serbia and Montegro.

RECENT HISTORY Both Serbia and Montenegro were recognized as independent in 1878. By the start of the 20th century a Croat national revival within the Habsburg Empire looked increasingly to Serbia to create a South ('Yugo') Slav state. After Serbia gained Macedonia in the Balkan Wars (1912–13), Austria grew wary of Serbian ambitions. The assassination of the Habsburg heir (1914) by a Serb student in Sarajevo provided Austria with an excuse to try to quash Serbian independence. This led directly to World War I and the subsequent dissolution of the Habsburg Empire, whose South Slav peoples united with Serbia and Montenegro in 1918 to form the country known since 1929 as Yugoslavia. Yugoslavia was run as a highly centralized 'Greater Serbia'. The country was wracked by nationalist tensions, and Croat separatists murdered King Alexander in 1934. Attacked and dismembered by Hitler in 1941, Yugoslavs fought the Nazis and each other. The Communist-led partisans of Josip Broz Tito (1892–1980) emerged victorious in 1945, and re-formed Yugoslavia on Soviet lines. Expelled by Stalin from the Soviet bloc in 1948 for failing to toe the Moscow line, the Yugoslav Communists rejected the Soviet model, and pursued policies of decentralization, workers' self-management and non-alignment.

After Tito's death in 1980, the Yugoslav experiment faltered in economic and nationalist crises. The wealthier northern republics of Slovenia and Croatia led the movement towards democracy and Western Europe, while Serbia forcefully resisted the separatist aspirations of Albanian nationalists in Kosovo province. In 1990 the Communists conceded the principle of free elections. By the end of the year, the League of Communists of Yugoslavia had ceased to exist as a national entity, and elections were won by various centre-right, nationalist and regional socialist parties in all the republics except Serbia and Montenegro, where Communist parties won. Serbia exacerbated ethnic Albanian, and (to a much lesser extent) ethnic Hungarian, nationalism by the legal removal of most of the autonomous powers of Kosovo and Vojvodina. In June 1991 Slovenia and Croatia declared independence. Following reverses in a short campaign, Yugoslav federal forces were withdrawn from Slovenia, but Serb insurgents, backed by Yugoslav federal forces, occupied one third of Croatia including Krajina and parts of Slavonia, areas with an ethnic Serb majority.

In 1992 the fierce Serbo-Croat war was halted and a UN peace-keeping force was agreed. The international community recognized the independence of Slovenia and Croatia. When Bosnia-Herzegovina received similar recognition, Bosnian Serbs, encouraged by Serbia, seized 70% of Bosnia, killing or expelling Muslims and Croats in a campaign of 'ethnic cleansing'. Serbia was widely blamed for the continuation of the conflict and – with Montenegro – was subjected to international trade and diplomatic sanctions. Together Serbia and Montenegro form the (largely unrecognized) new Yugoslav federation. International peace and humanitarian efforts to end the Bosnian war were attempted but the conflict spread back to Croatia in 1993 and tension increased in Kosovo.

Macedonia also declared sovereignty (1991). However, owing to Greek opposition to the use of the name Macedonia, it was denied international recognition although it was effectively an independent state. (For details on Macedonia, see Other Territories, following this chapter.)

ZAÏRE

Official name: La République du Zaïre (Republic of Zaïre).

Member of: UN, OAU.

Area: 2 344 885 km² (905 365 sq mi).

Population: 34 964 000 (1991 est).

Capital and major cities: Kinshasa 3 741 000, Lubumbashi 710 000, Mbuji-Mayi 524 000, Kisangani 321 000, Kananga 303 000, Kolwezi 250 000, Likasi 200 000 (1991 est).

Languages: French (official), four national languages (Kiswahili, Tshiluba, Kikongo and Lingala), with over 200 local languages.

Religions: Roman Catholic (48%), various Protestant Churches (28%), Kimbanguists (17%), animist (6%).

GOVERNMENT The 222-member National Legislative Council is elected by compulsory universal suffrage for five years. The President – who is directly elected for seven years – appoints the National Executive Council of Commissioners (Ministers). The one-party state was abolished and some 160 political groups, including the (former monopoly) Mouvement populaire de la révolution, are active. Multi-party elections have yet to be held.

President: Marshal Mobutu Sese Seko.

Prime Minister: Etienne Tshisekedi.

GEOGRAPHY Over 60% of the country comprises a basin of tropical rain forest, drained by the River Zaïre (Congo) and its tributaries. Plateaux and mountain ranges surrounding the basin include the Ruwenzori Massif in the east. *Principal rivers*: Zaïre, Lualaba, Lomami, Oubangui, Uganbi, Kasai. *Highest point*: Mont Ngaliema 5109 m (16 763 ft).

ECONOMY   Over two thirds of the labour force is involved in agriculture. Although subsistence farming predominates, coffee, tea, cocoa, rubber and palm products are exported. Minerals are the mainstay of the economy, with copper, cobalt, zinc and diamonds normally accounting for about 60% of Zaïre's exports. Zaïre suffers rampant inflation and one of the lowest standards of living in Africa.

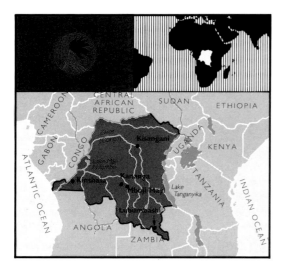

RECENT HISTORY   In 1908 international outrage at the brutal regime in the territory forced the Belgian King Leopold II to cede the Congo, his personal possession, to Belgium. As the Belgian Congo, the colony became a major exporter of minerals. The provision of social services, especially primary education, was relatively advanced, but the administration curbed African political activity. As a result, the Congo was inadequately prepared when Belgium suddenly granted independence in 1960. Within days, the army mutinied and the richest region – Katanga, under Moïse Tshombe – attempted to secede. The Congo invited the UN to intervene, but the UN force was only partly successful in overcoming continuing civil wars. Colonel Mobutu twice intervened and in 1965 made himself head of state. Pursuing 'authenticity', he renamed the country Zaïre. He gradually restored the authority of the central government and introduced a one-party state (1967). Mobutu's strong rule has attracted international criticism, but he has maintained the support of Western countries that value Zaïre as a source of strategic minerals. In 1990, popular discontent won some reforms and – following the legal abolition of the one-party state – a national conference was summoned to bring democracy to Zaïre (1991). In 1992–93 conflicts developed between the national conference and the prime minister on one side and President Mobutu on the other. Sections of the armed forces became disaffected, and law-and-order has broken down in parts of the country.

ZAMBIA

Official name: The Republic of Zambia.
Member of: UN, Commonwealth, OAU, SADCC.
Area: 752 614 km² (290 586 sq mi).
Population: 7 818 000 (1990 census).
Capital and major cities: Lusaka 870 000, Kitwe 472 000, Ndola 443 000, Kabwe 200 000, Mufulira 199 000, Chingola 195 000 (1988 est).
Languages: English (official), with local languages including Nyanja, Bemba (34%) and Tonga (16%).
Religions: Various Protestant Churches (50%), animist (25%), Roman Catholic (20%).

GOVERNMENT   The 150-member National Assembly is elected by universal adult suffrage for five years. The President – who is directly elected for five years – appoints a Cabinet. The 27-member House of Chiefs has advisory powers. The main political parties are the Movement for Multiparty Democracy (MMD) and the United National Independence Party (UNIP).

President: Frederick Chiluba.

GEOGRAPHY   Zambia comprises plateaux some 1000 to 1500 m (3300 to 5000 ft) high, above which rise the Muchinga Mountains and the Mufinga Hills. *Principal rivers:* Zambezi, Kafue, Luapula. *Highest point:* an unnamed peak in the Muchinga Mountains, 2164 m (7100 ft).

ECONOMY   Zambia's economy depends upon the mining and processing of copper, lead, zinc and cobalt. Agriculture is underdeveloped and many basic foodstuffs have to be imported. Maize, groundnuts and tobacco are the main crops.

RECENT HISTORY   The area was brought under the

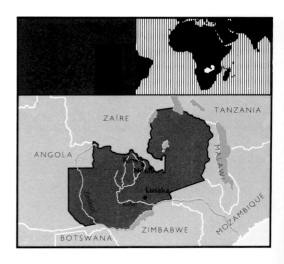

control of Cecil Rhodes' British South Africa Company in the 1890s. In 1924 Britain took over the administration of what became Northern Rhodesia from the Company. Skilled mining jobs were reserved for white immigrants, and, fearing increased discrimination, Africans unsuccessfully opposed inclusion in the Central African Federation – with Nyasaland (Malawi) and Southern Rhodesia (Zimbabwe) – in 1953. Against strong opposition from white settlers, Kenneth Kaunda (1924–) led Northern Rhodesia, renamed Zambia, to independence in 1964. A one-party state was introduced in 1972–73. Popular discontent at the lack of a democratic alternative erupted in mid-1990 and free elections were held in October 1991 when Kaunda was defeated in the first democratic change of government in English-speaking Black Africa.

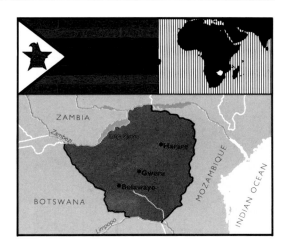

ZIMBABWE

Official name: The Republic of Zimbabwe.

Member of: UN, Commonwealth, OAU, SADCC.

Area: 390 759 km² (150 873 sq mi).

Population: 9 619 000 (1991 est).

Capital and major cities: Harare (formerly Salisbury) 863 000, Bulawayo 495 000, Chitungwiza 229 000, Gweru 79 000, Mutare (Umtali) 70 000 (1989 est).

Languages: English (official), Chishona, Sindebele.

Religions: Animist (42%), Anglican (30%) Roman Catholic (15%), Presbyterian.

GOVERNMENT The 150-member House of Assembly comprises 120 members directly elected by universal adult suffrage for six years, 12 nominated members, 10 traditional chiefs and 8 appointed provincial governors. The House elects a President for a six-year term of office. The ZANU-PF (Zimbabwe African National Union) party has a leading role, although other parties – including ZUM (Zimbabwe Unity Movement) – are permitted.

President: Robert Mugabe.

GEOGRAPHY Central Zimbabwe comprises the ridge of the Highveld, rising to between 1200 and 1500 m (about 4000 to 5000 ft). The Highveld is bounded on the southwest and northeast by the Middle Veld and the Lowveld plateaux. *Principal rivers*: Zambezi, Limpopo, Sabi. *Highest point*: Mount Inyangani 2592 m (8504 ft).

ECONOMY Agriculture involves about two thirds of the labour force. Tobacco, sugar cane, cotton, wheat and maize are exported as well as being the basis of processing industries. Natural resources include coal, gold, asbestos and nickel.

RECENT HISTORY The British South Africa Company controlled what became Southern Rhodesia from the 1890s. In 1923 Britain took over the administration and granted self-government to the white colonists who had deprived Africans of land and reduced them to a cheap labour force. Immigration from Britain and South Africa increased after World War II, but the whites remained outnumbered by the Africans by more than 20 to 1. Racial discrimination stimulated African nationalism, initially led by Joshua Nkomo (1917–). Southern Rhodesia – with Northern Rhodesia (Zambia) and Nyasaland (Malawi) – formed the Central African Federation in 1953. When the Federation was dissolved (1963), Britain refused the white Southern Rhodesian administration independence without progress to majority rule. The white government led by Ian Smith unilaterally declared independence in 1965, renaming the country Rhodesia. Internal opposition was crushed and international economic sanctions were overcome, but guerrilla wars, mounted by African nationalists during the 1970s, became increasingly effective. In 1979 Smith had to accept majority rule, but the constitution he introduced was unacceptable to the ZAPU party of Joshua Nkomo and to the ZANU party of Robert Mugabe (1928–). All parties agreed to the brief reimposition of British rule to achieve a settlement. ZANU under Mugabe took the country to independence in 1980. In 1987 ZANU and ZAPU finally agreed to unite, effectively introducing a one-party state, although proposals for an official one-party system have been shelved.

OTHER TERRITORIES

ANTARCTICA

All territorial claims south of latitude 60° S are in abeyance under the terms of the Antarctic Treaty (signed in 1959), which came into force in 1961. Territorial claims in Antarctica have been made by Argentina, Australia, Chile, France, New Zealand, Norway, and the UK. The Argentinian, Chilean and British claims overlap, while that part of the continent

between 90° W and 150° W is not claimed by any country. Neither the USA nor Russia recognize any territorial claim in Antarctica.
Area: 14 245 000 km² (5 500 000 sq mi).
Population: no permanent population, but over 40 scientific stations are maintained.

Adélie Land France claims that part of Antarctica between 136° E and 142° E, extending to the South Pole. *Area:* 432 000 km² (166 800 sq mi). Adélie Land is part of the French Southern and Antarctic Territories (Terres Australes et Antarctiques Françaises).

Argentinian Antarctic Territory Argentina claims that part of Antarctica between 74° W and 25° W, extending to the South Pole, a claim that overlaps with the British territorial claim.

Australian Antarctic Territory Australia claims that part of Antarctica between 160° E and 45° E, except for Adélie Land. *Area:* 6 120 000 km² (2 320 000 sq mi).

Bouvet Island A Norwegian Antarctic territory (54° 25 S and 3° 21 E). *Area:* 50 km² (19 sq mi). As Bouvet Island is north of 60° S, the Antarctic Treaty does not apply and Norway's claim to the island is uncontested.

British Antarctic Territory The UK claims that part of Antarctica between 20° W and 80° W, extending to the South Pole. *Area:* 1 810 000 km² (700 000 sq mi).

Chilean Antarctic Territory Chile claims that part of Antarctica between 90° W and and 53° W, extending to the South Pole, a claim that overlaps with the British and Argentinian territorial claims.

Peter I Island Norway claims the island, which is 68° 48 S and 90° 35 W. *Area:* 180 km² (69 sq mi).

Queen Maud Land Norway claims that part of Antarctica between 20° W and 45° E. *Area:* as no inland limit has been made to the Norwegian claim, no estimate of the area of the territory can be made.

Ross Dependency New Zealand claims that part of Antarctica between 160° E and 150° W, extending to the South Pole. *Area:* 450 000 km² (175 000 sq mi).

EAST TIMOR   See Indonesia

GAZA, THE WEST BANK AND GOLAN
Area: 7433 km² (2870 sq mi) – Gaza 378 km² (146 sq mi); the West Bank 5879 km² (2270 sq mi); Golan 1176 km² (454 sq mi).
Population: 1 623 000 (1990 est) – Gaza 642 000 (1990 est); West Bank 955 000 (1990 est); Golan 26 000 (1990 est).
Main cities: Gaza (Ghazzah) 175 000, Nablus (Nabulus) 106 000, Hebron (Al-Khalil) 87 000 (1989 est).
Languages: Arabic.
Religions: Sunni Islam majority, Christian and small Jewish minorities.
Government: Gaza, the West Bank and Golan are under Israeli occupation. Golan was formally annexed by Israel in 1981, an action that has not received general international recognition.
Geography: The Gaza Strip is a small lowland area, between Israel and Egypt, beside the Mediterranean. The West Bank is a mountainous arid area between the Israeli border in the west and the River Jordan and the

Dead Sea in the east. Golan is a mountainous region on the Syrian border. *Principal river* (West Bank): Jordan. *Highest point:* unnamed, south of Khan Yunis (Gaza), 110 m (361 ft); unnamed, north of Hebron (West Bank), 1013 m (3323 ft); Mt Hermon (Golan) 2814 m (9232 ft).

Economy: The overpopulated Gaza Strip has little industry and a little agriculture. Only the Jordan Valley in the West Bank can support arable farming. Both areas rely heavily upon foreign (largely Arab) aid and money sent back by Palestinians working abroad. The *intifada* (see below) has retarded recent development. Golan has been settled by Israeli farmers who have established kibbutzim.

Recent history: The Gaza Strip, formerly under Egyptian rule, and the West Bank, formerly under Jordanian administration, were occupied by Israeli forces in June 1967. At the same time, Golan – legally part of Syria – was also occupied by Israeli forces. Golan was annexed by Israel in 1981. In 1988, Jordan severed all legal ties with the West Bank. Beginning in 1988, an uprising (*intifada*) by Palestinians living in Gaza and the West Bank increased tension in these areas. On 15 November 1988, the Palestinian Liberation Organization issued a declaration of Palestinian independence in Gaza and the West Bank. This declaration has received recognition by over 30 countries.

MACEDONIA
(FORMER YUGOSLAV REPUBLIC)
Official name: Republika Makedonija (Republic of Macedonia).
Area: 25 713 km² (9928 sq mi).
Population: 2 034 000 (1991 census).
Capital and major cities: Skopje (Skoplje) 563 000, Bitola 140 000 (all including suburbs; 1991 est).
Languages: Macedonian (67%), Albanian (20%), Turkish (4%).
Religions: Macedonian Orthodox (over 60%), Sunni Islam (nearly 25%).

GOVERNMENT The 120-member Assembly and a President – who appoints a Cabinet and a Prime Minister – are directly elected for four years by universal adult suffrage. The main political parties include the (former Communist) Democratic Alliance of Macedonia, the Internal Macedonian Revolutionary Organization (IMRO), the Party of Democratic Prosperity and the Alliance of Reform Forces.
President: Kiro Gligorov.
Prime Minister: Branko Crvenkovski.

GEOGRAPHY Macedonia is a plateau about 760 m (2500 ft) high, bordered by mountains including the Sar range. The central Vardar valley is the only major lowland. *Principal rivers:* Vardar, Strumica. *Highest point:* Korab 2753 m (9032 ft).

ECONOMY Macedonia was one of the least developed regions of Yugoslavia. The republic is largely agricultural, raising sheep and cattle and growing cereals and tobacco. Steel, chemical and textile industries rely, in part, upon local resources that include iron ore, lead and zinc. The economy has been severely damaged by a Greek economic blockade.

RECENT HISTORY After centuries of rule by the (Turkish) Ottoman Empire, Macedonia was partitioned following the First Balkan War (1912). Those areas with a Greek-speaking majority were assigned to Greece and the remainder was partitioned between Bulgaria and Serbia, the latter gaining the area comprising the present republic. Bulgaria continued to claim all Macedonia and occupied the region during World War I. In 1918 Serbian Macedonia was incorporated within the new kingdom of Serbs, Croats and Slovenes, which was renamed Yugoslavia in 1929. When Yugoslavia was reorganized on Soviet lines by Marshal Tito in 1945 a separate Macedonian republic was formed within the Communist federation. After Tito's death (1980), the Yugoslav experiment faltered and local nationalist movements arose. Following the secession of Slovenia and Croatia and the outbreak of the Yugoslav civil war (1991), Macedonia declared its own sovereignty. Despite fierce opposition from Greece, which objected to the use of the name 'Macedonia' and denied the existence of a 'Macedonian' people, the republic eventually gained international recognition in 1993.

SOVEREIGN MILITARY ORDER OF MALTA
Area: 1.2 ha (3 acres), comprising the Villa del Priorato di Malta (on the Aventine Hill in Rome) and 68 via Condotti (in the same city).

Government: The Knights of Justice of this charitable, monastic Roman Catholic order live as a religious community in two buildings in Rome. They elect for life one of their number to be Prince and Grand Master, who is recognized as a sovereign by over 40 countries. The military order, which issues its own passports, has many of the trappings of a state and is frequently said to be the 'smallest country in the world'.
Head of State: HEH (His Eminent Highness) Fra' (Brother) Andrew Bartie, Prince and Grand Master (elected on 8 April 1988).

Recent history: The 'Knights of Malta' ruled Rhodes until 1523, and then Malta until expelled by Napoleon I (1798). Since the 1830s, their sovereignty has been confined to their properties in Rome.

WESTERN SAHARA
Area: 266 000 km² (102 676 sq mi).
Population: 185 000 (1987 est) – including many Moroccan settlers in El-Aaiun (Laayoune).
Capital: El-Aaiun (Laayoune) 97 000 (1982).
Language: Arabic.
Religion: Sunni Islam.

Government: Most of the Western Sahara is under Moroccan administration. In 27 February 1976 Sahrawi exiles in Algeria proclaimed the Saharan Arab Democratic Republic, which has been recognized by over 70 countries and admitted to membership of the OAU.
President: Mohammed Abdulaziz.

Geography: Western Sahara is a low flat desert region with no permanent streams.

Economy: All trade is controlled by the Moroccan government. The territory has few resources except for phosphate deposits.

Recent history: Spain, Morocco and Mauritania reached an agreement to end Spanish rule (1975) and to divide Western Sahara between Morocco and Mauritania (1976). Morocco absorbed the Mauritanian sector when Mauritania withdrew (1979). The Polisario liberation movement – which had been fighting Spanish rule since 1973 – declared the territory independent. They control the eastern part of Western Sahara and continued guerrilla activity against the Moroccans until informal UN talks between the Sahrawis (the indigenous population) and Morocco began (1988–89). Agreement for a ceasefire and a referendum on the future of the territory was reached (1991), but no date has been agreed to hold the referendum.